Exploratory Data Analysis

This book is a comprehensive guide to exploratory data analysis (EDA), providing readers with the tools, techniques, and knowledge needed to conduct effective and thorough data exploration. Throughout the seven main chapters, this book details various aspects of EDA, from data description and preprocessing to visualization, storytelling, and dashboard design. We will explore real-world datasets, uncovering hidden patterns and gaining insights along the way. This book is filled with illustrations using practical examples, Python codes, and different types of exercises designed to reinforce the concepts and processes discussed. Whether you are a student just starting out in the field of data science, a senior professional looking to improve your skills, or a curious individual interested in the power of data, this book is for you.

W0234941

AK Peters Visualization Series

Visualization plays an ever-more prominent role in the world, as we communicate about and analyze data. This series aims to capture what visualization is today in all its variety and diversity, giving voice to researchers, practitioners, designers, and enthusiasts. It encompasses books from all subfields of visualization, including visual analytics, information visualization, scientific visualization, data journalism, infographics, and their connection to adjacent areas such as text analysis, digital humanities, data art, or augmented and virtual reality.

Series Editors:
Tamara Munzner, *University of British Columbia, Vancouver, Canada*
Alberto Cairo, *University of Miami, USA*

Recent titles:

The Golden Age of Data Visualization: How Did We Get Here?
Kimbal Marriott

Data Visualization for People of All Ages
Nancy Organ

Data Visualization in Excel
Jonathan Schwabish

Building Science Graphics
Jen Christiansen

Joyful Infographics
Nigel Holmes

Making with Data
Edited by Samuel Huron, Till Nagel, Lora Oehlberg, Wesley Willett

Questions in Dataviz
By Neil Richards

Mobile Data Visualization
Edited by Bongshin Lee, Raimund Dachselt, Petra Isenberg, Eun Kyoung Choe

Data Sketches
Nadieh Bremer, Shirley Wu

Exploratory Data Analysis: Descriptive Analysis, Visualization, and Dashboard Design (with Code Snippets in Python)
Leandro Nunes de Castro

For more information about this series please visit: https://www.routledge.com/AK-Peters-Visualization-Series/book-series/CRCVIS

Exploratory Data Analysis
Descriptive Analysis, Visualization, and Dashboard Design
(with Code Snippets in Python)

Leandro Nunes de Castro

CRC Press
Taylor & Francis Group
Boca Raton London New York

CRC Press is an imprint of the
Taylor & Francis Group, an **informa** business

AN A K PETERS BOOK

Designed cover image: Leandro Nunes de Castro

First edition published 2026
by CRC Press
2385 NW Executive Center Drive, Suite 320, Boca Raton FL 33431

and by CRC Press
4 Park Square, Milton Park, Abingdon, Oxon, OX14 4RN

CRC Press is an imprint of Taylor & Francis Group, LLC

© 2026 Leandro Nunes de Castro

ISBN: 9781032944302 (hbk)
ISBN: 9781032939827 (pbk)
ISBN: 9781003570691 (ebk)

DOI: 10.1201/9781003570691

Typeset in Minion
by codeMantra

¹ The proverbs of Solomon son of David, king of Israel:

² for gaining wisdom and instruction;

for understanding words of insight;

³ for receiving instruction in prudent behavior,

doing what is right and just and fair;

⁴ for giving prudence to those who are simple,

knowledge and discretion to the young —

⁵ let the wise listen and add to their learning,

and let the discerning get guidance —

⁶ for understanding proverbs and parables,

the sayings and riddles of the wise.

⁷ The fear of the Lord is the beginning of knowledge,

but fools despise wisdom and instruction.

Proverbs 1:1-7 (NIV)

To all families, as a symbol and ultimate expression of love. To my children André and Isadora, my wife Elizabete, my parents José and Lásara, and my siblings Alessandra and Sandro, whose unwavering support and love have been my greatest blessings and inspiration.

Contents

Preface

"DATA IS THE NEW oil!" I believe many of you have already heard this expression or some variations of it, such as "data is the new currency" or "data is the new electricity". What is meant by this saying is that data has become abundant, incredibly valuable, and essential for powering various aspects of modern society, just as oil has been, and still is, a fundamental resource for powering economies. I like to say that data has become a strategic asset for people, brands, and institutions.

Virtually everything we do, everywhere we go, and every word we say is being monitored and stored by some device. It is common to talk about a certain subject with a colleague or parent and then receive a recommendation related to what you were talking about. As another example, I remember a few days after my son got his driver permit, I received an e-mail from my insurance company advising me to add him to my policy so that he could also be covered. His permit data was made available by the government to the insurance company, which contacted me to extend the policy. Another illustration of how data, including our data, is constantly being stored somewhere is when I received a historical update from Google Maps. It provided a detailed review of everywhere I had been over the past 10 years, including countries, cities, and shops. I didn't even remember having been to some of those places, but they were stored there, very likely being used to target me with something.

This overwhelming abundance of data has created a need for specialized professionals capable of extracting knowledge and developing solutions based on data. The ability to transform data into meaningful insights is not just a specialized skill, but a necessity for anyone who wishes to understand the world around them.

This textbook, dedicated to the art and science of *Exploratory Data Analysis*, is a testament to that necessity. EDA is the first step in the data analysis process, where patterns, anomalies, and relationships within the data are identified, visualized, and presented. It is the stage where data analysts get to know data, understand its characteristics, visualize it, and prepare it for further analysis or modeling.

This book is designed to be a comprehensive guide to EDA, providing readers with the tools, techniques, and knowledge needed to conduct effective and thorough data exploration. Whether you are a student just starting out in the field of data science, a senior professional looking to improve your skills, or a curious individual interested in the power of data, this book is for you.

Throughout the chapters, I will discuss various aspects of EDA, from data description and preprocessing to visualization, storytelling, and dashboard design. We will explore real-world datasets, uncovering hidden patterns and gaining insights along the way. This book is filled with illustrations using practical examples, Python code, and different types of exercises designed to reinforce the concepts and processes discussed.

It is my hope that this book will inspire you to look at data differently, to see beyond the numbers and find the stories they tell. EDA is not just a process, but a mindset, a way of thinking that encourages curiosity and skepticism, demanding that we ask questions of our data and seek out the answers.

In the end, the goal of this book, and of EDA itself, is to empower you to make better decisions and tell compelling stories with data. As you read through it, I hope you may find the inspiration and knowledge to do just that.

Happy exploring!

Leandro Nunes de Castro

Acknowledgments

WRITING A TEXTBOOK IS a very intense endeavor, and having formal courses and students supporting this development is a privilege. The writing of this volume lasted around two and a half years and during this period I had the opportunity to test its contents and proposals in two different institutions and various courses:

- Two graduate courses on *Exploratory Data Analysis* were taught at the Graduate Program of Technology at University of Campinas, Brazil, in 2023 and 2024.

- An undergraduate course on *Exploratory Data Analysis* was taught at the Department of Computing and Software Engineering at the Florida Gulf Coast University, USA, also in 2023.

- Two graduate courses on *Business Intelligence and Visualization Tools* were taught at Lutgert College of Business at the Florida Gulf Coast University, USA, in 2024 and 2025.

Although I cannot name all the students involved, I would like to thank them for helping me shape, refine, correct, and improve this book. In these five courses I had the opportunity to test the content, correct the exercises, practice case studies, and evaluate some proposed processes, mainly those introduced in Chapter 7.

A special thank you goes to John Peller, my undergraduate student at FGCU, at the time of writing, who reviewed most of the text and provided me with precious feedback for its structure, content, and grammar. On a similar token I would like to also thank my colleague Anna Koufakou and my former BI student Paul Myrin for taking the time to look at the book and provide me with some feedback. Another very special thank you goes to Jeremy Martin who reviewed all code snippets and reformatted them to meet the publisher demands.

Last, but not least, all the institutional and financial support I received from FGCU, the Dendritic AI and Data Science Institute at FGCU, the University of Campinas (Unicamp), the University of São Paulo (USP), and the São Paulo State Research Foundation (FAPESP), were crucial for the development of this project.

Thank you all so much!

Leandro Nunes de Castro
June 2025

About the Author

Leandro Nunes de Castro received his degree in Electrical Engineering from the Federal University of Goiás (1996), his Master's degree in Electrical Engineering (1998), and a Ph.D. in Computer Engineering (2001), both from Unicamp, Brazil. He also has an MBA in Strategic Business Management from the Catholic University of Santos (2008). He was a research associate at the Computing Laboratory of the University of Kent in Canterbury from June 2001 to May 2002, a Visiting Professor at the Technological University of Malaysia in September 2005, a Visiting Specialist Professor at Unicamp between March and June 2012, and a visiting researcher at the University of Salamanca between January and July 2014. He was a Professor and researcher in the Master's Program in Informatics at Unisantos from 2003 to 2008, and in the Graduate Program in Electrical Engineering and Computing at Mackenzie Presbyterian University from 2008 to 2022. His main lines of research are natural computing and machine learning, with applications in intelligent data analysis and optimization. He is the main author of the book *Artificial Immune Systems: A New Computational Intelligence Approach* (Springer-Verlag, 2002); one of the organizers of *Recent Developments in Biologically Inspired Computing* (Idea Group Publishing, 2004); author of *Fundamentals of Natural Computing: Basic Concepts, Algorithms, and Applications* (CRC Press, 2006); author of the book *Natural Computing: An Illustrated Journey* (Livraria da Física, 2010); organizer of the book *Nature-Inspired Computing Design, Development, and Application* (IGI-Global, 2012); and main author of the book *Introduction to Data Mining: Basic Concepts, Algorithms and Applications* (In Portuguese, Saraiva, 2016). He was the proponent and Editor-in-Chief of the *International Journal of Natural Computing Research* (*IJNCR*) between 2010 and 2015, published by IGI Global. His research work has been recognized globally since 2020 as among the 2% of most influential researchers worldwide, based on scientific impact indices monitored by *PLoS Biology*. He has published over 250 papers in journals and conferences. His scholarly contributions also include founding two research laboratories and serving as Research Chair and as the Chief Innovation and Entrepreneurship Officer at Mackenzie. In addition to his academic achievements, he is also a successful entrepreneur. He has participated in the founding of three Artificial Intelligence startups and invested, as an angel investor, in three others. Some of the notable startups he has been involved with include Tuilux, a company that offered intelligent recommendation services to e-commerce, and Somma.ai, a low/no code data science platform that allows the building of highly complex analytical applications without having to program. Currently, he is a Full Professor at the Florida Gulf Coast University (FGCU) in the Department of Computing & Software Engineering, United States, and the Director of Dendritic: A Human-Centered Artificial Intelligence and Data Science Institute at FGCU.

Structure of the Book

THIS BOOK WAS DESIGNED to provide a comprehensive guide to understanding and analyzing data through the lens of *Exploratory Data Analysis* (EDA). Whether you are a student, a teacher, a professional, or someone interested in the world of data, this book aims to equip you with the knowledge and skills needed to characterize and extract insights from data. This book was structured into seven chapters and three appendices to offer full coverage of the field, as summarized below.

1. **Introduction to Exploratory Data Analysis**

   This chapter lays the foundation for understanding the fundamental concepts of data science, including an explanation of the various terminologies available in the literature, the main careers, the data science workflow, and a brief history of artificial intelligence. It describes what exploratory data analysis is and its main goals, placing it in the broader context of data science. Emphasis is given to the career in data analysis, its profile, and required skills.

2. **Data Description and Preparation**

   What is data? How do we go from data to information to knowledge? How can we classify the various types of data? These are some of the topics presented in this chapter. Furthermore, this chapter covers data that can be presented in tabular form and interpreted geometrically. Another concept relevant to the description of datasets is that of a data dictionary, that is, a structure describing all variables in the dataset and some of their characteristics. This chapter also presents various datasets used throughout this book and concludes with some techniques for data preparation, such as sampling, handling missing values, and normalization.

3. **Descriptive Analysis**

   Descriptive analysis is one of the most important analytical phases in data science, generating numerical values that aim at understanding the dataset structure, its variables, and their characterization. These will be useful to summarize the data and extract valuable insights for informed decision-making. This chapter explores descriptive statistics, frequency distributions, summary measures (central tendency, variability, and measures of shape), association measures, and linear regression. Attention is also given to normal distributions, commonly used in science and engineering to represent specific phenomena and processes.

4. Principles of Data Visualization

Despite their importance, summary measures may not alone be sufficient to characterize and describe data, mainly because some data may present the same summary measures but significantly different distributions. From a visualization perspective, it is important to acknowledge that some features are quickly perceived by our eyes without the need for attention; these are called pre-attentive features. There are also principles related to how we perceive and organize information that are useful for the selection and use of visualization tools. Finally, a set of data visualization principles for graphs and tables should be considered to adequately choose and apply visualization tools. All these concepts are reviewed in this chapter before the visualization methods are introduced in the next chapter.

5. Data Visualization Methods

Visualization is one of the most effective ways to understand and extract insights from data. There is a vast array of visualization methods, and based on the type of information to be displayed, they are organized in this chapter as distributions, associations, amounts, proportions, evolution and flow, and geospatial. For each type of visualization method, emphasis is given to the purpose, the common type of data used, how to interpret the plot, and some examples of applications.

6. Special Types of Data

In addition to the standard structured data, there are some specific types of data that deserve particular attention and analysis. Time series have a temporal dimension, bringing added complexity and significance to the analysis; texts and documents have linguistic content; and trees and networks emphasize relational data in which objects are somehow connected to one another. This chapter presents descriptive analysis and visualization techniques specific to each of these data types, expanding the types of data covered by this book.

7. Data Storytelling and Dashboard Design

So far, this book has covered the main contents and technical aspects of exploratory data analysis, from descriptive analysis to visualization. Beyond all that, it is still the data analyst's job to communicate the data, its characterization, analysis, and insights obtained. This special type of communication has been named data storytelling and requires hybrid skills between data analysis and storytelling design. This chapter introduces a process to build a story around data. Then it proposes guidelines for the design of dashboards as visual interfaces to intuitively and aesthetically display the result of the data analysis workflow.

Appendix A: Python – A Quick Reference Guide

Almost all visuals presented in this book were created using Python, and all code snippets are available at the author's Github. This appendix was created as a quick reference guide for those readers interested in having some knowledge and/or reviewing the basics of Python. It starts with the syntax and evolves into data types, control structures, and functions.

Appendix B: Code Snippets for the Gestalt Principles of Chapter 4

Chapter 4 presents seven Gestalt principles of the visual organization of information in the brain: continuity, proximity, similarity, closure, symmetry, figure-ground, and common fate. Some of the code snippets to generate the illustration for these principles are longer than those used to plot most of the visuals presented in Chapters 3, 5, and 6, and all the code snippets related to the Gestalt principles were moved to this appendix, saving space in the main corpus of this book.

Appendix C: LIWC and Stanford POS Tagger Categories

LIWC and the POS Tagger are categories of words used to categorize or tag words in natural language processing applications. They can be employed in some of the processes described in Chapter 6 regarding the analysis of text and document data.

How to Use This Book and Additional Resources

THIS VOLUME WAS WRITTEN as a comprehensive introduction to exploratory data analysis, covering the most relevant and up-to-date contents in descriptive analysis, visualization principles and guidelines, visualization methods, special types of data, data storytelling, and dashboard design. It is a complete guide for Business Intelligence professionals and Data Analysts.

The text was written with a linear sequence, but there are only a few interdependencies among some chapters; more specifically, Chapters 4–6 should be studied in sequence. The study of this book depends on your learning goals, as summarized in the table below.

Learning Goal	Chapter
01: Understand EDA and the history of AI	1
02: Understand what data science is, its workflow, and data-related careers	1
03: Describe, categorize, and prepare data for analysis	2
04: Perform numeric characterization of data	3
05: Understand data distributions	3
06: Understand the limitations of descriptive analysis	4
07: Understand how the brain naturally organizes visual information and how it helps design more effective and engaging visualizations	4
08: Learn the most common and useful visualization methods for structured data	5
09: Learn how to analyze time series	6
10: Learn how to analyze texts and documents	6
11: Learn how to analyze trees and networks	6
12: Learn how to create compelling stories around data	7
13: Learn how to create intuitive and aesthetically appealing dashboards	7
14: Learn the basics of Python	Appendix A

In a standard full course on EDA, the following uses or activities are recommended:

- Start with the introductory chapters (Chapters 1 and 2) to familiarize yourself with data science concepts and terminologies.

- Work through each section sequentially, completing the exercises, quizzes, computational exercises, and case studies to reinforce your learning.

- Use this book as a reference guide when working on data analysis projects or building visualizations.

- Experiment with Python code snippets provided in this book to facilitate your understanding and application of the concepts presented.

- Visit the author's YouTube channel to access series and short courses related to this book and general AI concepts.

- Engage in discussions, research, and exploration of additional resources to deepen your understanding of exploratory data analysis.

Additional resources:

The author has made available all the code snippets presented in this book, organized by chapter, in his Github: https://github.com/lndecastro

The author also has a YouTube channel with series and courses related to AI and data science: https://www.youtube.com/@lndecastro

Notation

W HEN WRITING A TECHNICAL book, a major concern is uniformity and notation. Special care was taken to provide a concise and uniform notation to the text. The readers are invited to review this section before commencing reading this book.

- Scalars are denoted by italic lowercase Roman letters: e.g., a, b, x, y, z.

- Vectors are denoted by boldface lowercase Roman letters: e.g., $\mathbf{x}$, $\mathbf{y}$, $\mathbf{z}$.

- Matrices are denoted by boldface uppercase Roman letters: e.g., $\mathbf{X}$, $\mathbf{Y}$, $\mathbf{Z}$.

- Sets are denoted by italic uppercase Roman letters: e.g., X, Y, Z.

- n-dimensional Euclidean space: $\Re^n$.

- Matrix with n rows and m columns and real-valued entries: $\mathbf{X} \in \Re^{n \times m}$.

- Vector with n entries (always assumed to be a column vector, unless otherwise specified): $\mathbf{x} \in \Re^n$.

- The transpose of a vector or matrix is denoted by an italic uppercase letter "T": e.g., $\mathbf{x}^T$, $\mathbf{X}^T$.

- *Words* or *expressions in italics* mean that a concept is presented and defined in that part of the text.

List of Abbreviations

BI-RADS	Breast Imaging Reporting and Data System
BMI	Body Mass Index
CDO	Chief Data Officer
CSV	Comma-Separated Value
CV	Coefficient of Variation
DARPA	Defense Advanced Research Projects Agency
DB	Database
DC	Drought Code
DMC	Duff Moisture Code
DS	Data Science
DSS	Decision Support Systems
EDA	Exploratory Data Analysis
FFMC	Fine Fuel Moisture Code
GAN	Generative Adversarial Network
GDP	Gross Domestic Product
HDI	Human Development Index
IQR	Interquartile Range
ISI	Initial Spread Index
KDD	Knowledge Discovery in Databases
KDE	Kernel Density Estimate
KPI	Key Performance Indicators
KRCC	Kendall's Rank Correlation Coefficient
LIWC	Linguistic Inquiry and Word Count
LSTM	Long-Short Term Memory
ML	Machine Learning
MPG	Miles Per Gallon
NER	Named Entity Recognition
NLP	Natural Language Processing
PCC	Pearson Correlation Coefficient
PoS	Part of Speech
Q1, Q2, Q3	Quartiles
RH	Relative Humidity

SRCC   Spearman Rank Correlation Coefficient
TF-IDF Term Frequency-Inverse Document Frequency
UCI   University of California at Irvine

About the Code Snippets

In my previous books about artificial immune systems, natural computing, and data mining, I always presented pseudocodes instead of code snippets in a specific language. This has ever been a rational choice motivated by the belief that programming languages are always specific and may become obsolete, but the fundamentals of a certain area tend to remain constant for a much longer period of time.

In the present case, however, I decided to include Python code snippets in the text and make them available to the readers due to the sheer use of Python as one of the main programming languages in data-related fields. The code snippets were placed in Jupyter notebooks and organized to have a header with a brief explanation of what the code is about, followed by a list of libraries to be imported, and then the main commands and/ or functions to be run. They were placed here as images instead of text because I wanted to maintain their real structure, including indentation and colors, as these are central in Python. All functions, methods, and running outputs placed within the text are presented in Courier New font for the reader to quickly identify them.

How This Book Was Written and the Use of AI-Assisted Tools

THIS IS THE FIFTH book I have authored or co-authored. I started my career as a book writer in the year 2000 when I drafted my first book on Artificial Immune Systems (AIS), published in 2002 by Springer with the co-authorship of Jon I. Timmis (L. N. de Castro & J. I. Timmis, *Artificial Immune Systems – A New Computational Intelligence Approach*, Springer, 2002).[1] That volume was an extension of my Ph.D. thesis and contributed to the community in three ways: as the first text to bring a principled introduction to how to design AIS; as a comprehensive review of the field up to that time; and as an up-to-date guide to AIS. So, the AIS book was written based on long and deep bibliographical research, years of work, and deep knowledge in the field.

The last book I wrote is titled *Introduction to Data Mining: Basic Concepts, Algorithms, and Applications*, published in Portuguese by Saraiva in 2016 and co-authored by Daniel G. Ferrari. This one has a different style of writing, tailored as a textbook instead of a state-of-the-art volume. The development of such a text is also based on a lot of work and profound knowledge, but it requires research that emphasizes well-established knowledge and concepts within a field. There was no work of adding state-of-the-art contributions, but some personal perspectives and adjustments of what had already been addressed by other authors.

By July 2022, almost 6 years after publishing my last book, I decided to begin this *Exploratory Data Analysis* volume, mainly motivated by a new course I was introducing in the Graduate Program in Technology at the School of Technology, Unicamp, Brazil. I was also motivated by the fact that every time I looked at Data Visualization courses, I had the feeling that this discipline could be enhanced by three topics: descriptive analysis, data storytelling, and dashboard design. Altogether, they form a unique body of knowledge necessary to train data analysts, one of the most important careers related to data.

After exhaustively searching the literature for texts involving data visualization, descriptive analysis, data storytelling, dashboard design, and exploratory data analysis, I noted a gap in terms of a unique volume covering all these concepts in a cohesive and consistent manner.

---

[1] https://www.amazon.com/author/lndecastro

This, combined with my need to deepen my knowledge, sparked my desire to dive deep and begin my journey into the writing of this volume.

Now, after three years of work and dedication to this project, it has finally come to an end. But before that, I want to discuss how the process of writing this book differed from all my previous works. Approximately in the middle of 2023, that is, halfway through writing this book, I started using ChatGPT as a generative model to support my professional life, including my writings. This has changed the way I write, receive feedback, and make decisions about what, when, and how to include content in my work. Specifically for this book, I used ChatGPT, Bing Copilot, and Google Gemini as AI-assistant tools, as follows:

- *To generate, debug, and explain some of the code snippets presented.* Including the appendices, this book has approximately 90 snippets of Python code to perform virtually all the analysis tasks covered here. Some of these code snippets were created using generative models, others were debugged or optimized by them, and in some cases, I also used them to modify or quickly explain the code snippets.

- *To generate quizzes and exercises.* As a professor for over 25 years, I know that one of the most complex tasks we have is to create assignments to assess learning. This was one of the tasks for which I used the generative models to create quizzes and exercises related to this book's contents.

- *As tools to review and refine parts of the text.* For me, writing is the best way to consolidate what I am studying. I like to write technical books because they express my understanding of a subject. This was the case in my earlier works as well, and the only difference with this one is the fact that I now use some AI assistants to review and refine parts of my text.

- *As tools to help me organize specific sections of the text.* One last use I made of the AI assistants was to gather ideas about how to organize some sections of this book, as a sort of advanced search engine.

In all and every case where I used AI assistants, I carefully reviewed and edited the content to ensure its accuracy and fit within the whole volume. I do take full responsibility for all contents presented in this text, from code snippets to concepts to exercises.

## CHAPTER 1

Introduction to Exploratory Data Analysis

"Exploratory data analysis can never be the whole story, but nothing else can serve as the foundation stone – as the first step."

– John W. Tukey, Exploratory Data Analysis

Until recently, business managers made most decisions based solely on their knowledge and experience, and businesses operated using pre-defined systems and processes. The operating hours of a business service used to be the same as the working hours of its collaborators. Nowadays, however, the world is much more dynamic, and users and consumers are more impatient, connected, and demanding. This change in behavior and increased market competitiveness is forcing companies to adapt themselves.

Technological advances allowed the generation and storage of large amounts of data, not only by the companies themselves but also regarding them and their interests. This data can and must now be used to draw insights into the company and the market, support decision-making at all levels, and allow the automation of systems and processes. Data has thus become a *strategic asset* today. However, data is only the raw material that must be collected, prepared, analyzed and used for the benefit of the organization.

This use of data for the benefit of society and businesses promoted the emergence of new areas of research and development, such as *data science, data mining,* and *data analytics.* New business units and careers, such as *data scientists, machine learning engineers,* and *data analysts,* among others, also emerged. These and some related concepts will be discussed in detail later in the chapter.

Exploratory data analysis (EDA) is an important part in the journey of using data to build a *data-driven culture,* that is, a company in which data is intensively used to drive operations, decisions, and results. This journey starts with the identification of the useful data available and the definition of which data can be collected and what can be done with them. It then continues with the data preparation, analysis, analytics, model validation, and, finally, integration. Within this journey, EDA focuses on the understanding, characterization, summarization, and visualization of data.

EDA involves any data analysis method that does not include *modeling* or *inference*; that is, data are simply manipulated, summarized, and visualized (presented), with the objective of understanding their characteristics and trends and extracting indicators and visualizations (Komorowski et al., 2016). It is usually the first stage in the analytical process and may strongly influence modeling and inference. In summary, the goals of EDA are:

- To understand the distribution and structure of data.

- To summarize data characteristics.

- To extract insights and indicators from data.

- To identify relevance and/or select variables.

- To visualize potential relationships between variables.

- To identify anomalies.

- To allow the application and/or selection of learning-based methods.

This book introduces EDA across seven chapters: An Introduction to EDA; Data Description and Preparation; Descriptive Analysis; Principles of Data Visualization; Data Visualization Methods; Special Types of Data; and Data Storytelling and Dashboard Design. *Jupyter Notebooks* are provided for most of the computational methods presented, and almost all graphs in the book were generated using Python code.

This chapter places EDA in the broader context of data science by first presenting the main terminologies in the field. It then continues with a description of the principal careers in the area, a presentation of the data science workflow, and a brief history of artificial intelligence (AI). As a final reminder, it is important to stress that this book is not intended to cover data science or machine learning, but descriptive data analysis and visualization, the main topics covered in EDA. As such, it is expected to provide the first steps for a researcher or professional interested in beginning in the area.

1.1 DATA SCIENCE AND RELATED TERMINOLOGIES

The data-related fields have gained a lot of traction over the past years, and as sometimes happens with fast-growing fields, a number of different terminologies emerged describing the area and its possible branches. In this case, attention can be drawn to the terminologies *data science* (Provost & Fawcett, 2013; Cao, 2017; Kelleher & Tierney, 2018), *data analytics* (Elgendy & Elragal, 2014; Tsai et al., 2015; Mikalef et al., 2018), *Big Data* (Chong & Shi, 2015; Erl & Khattak, 2016; Song & Zhu, 2016), *data mining* (Han et al., 2011; de Castro & Ferrari, 2016), and *data analysis*. The literature on these topics is vast, and their frontiers may seem fuzzy. Thus, instead of trying to define boundaries and differentiate the terminologies, let us discuss the meaning and scope of each of them, bearing in mind that variations of their meanings are the rule in the literature, not the exception.

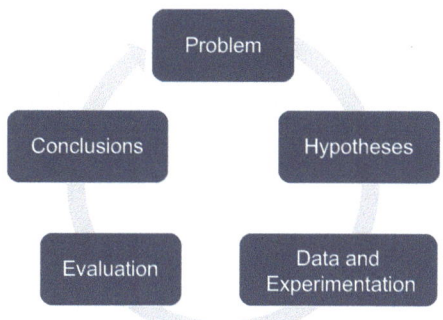

FIGURE 1.1   The scientific method iterative cycle.

1.1.1 Data Science

Data science is the combination of *data*, as the *raw material*, and *science*, more specifically the *scientific method*, as the *process*. This means that data science will take data as input and, by using the scientific method, will produce a certain output. The scientific method is a systematic process of finding answers or solutions to a given problem starting from one or more given hypotheses. It is composed of a specific set of steps (Figure 1.1):

1. Start with an observation or a problem to be solved;

2. Define questions to be answered or hypotheses to be validated;

3. Gather data and perform experiments based on the data and the hypotheses;

4. Evaluate (analyze) the results; and

5. Draw conclusions.

These steps are iterated until a satisfactory result is obtained.

The first aspect to be noted here is that, differently from the standard computing (programming) paradigm, the result of a data science process is not known in advance. Instead, it is obtained from the application of an iterative process over the available data. In a standard programming approach, by contrast, the result is known, and programming is only successful when such a result is obtained. To illustrate, a program to control the stock of goods in a warehouse must add an item if it is entering the warehouse and subtract one if it is leaving the warehouse. This is a simple and predictable task. By contrast, a program to learn to perform anomaly detection can only have its performance assessed after the model is created and tested on certain data, and it may, or may not, achieve a satisfactory result. In this case, the result will only be known after the solution is designed, implemented, and tested.

The computing application that results from a data science project can be of one of three types (Figure 1.2):

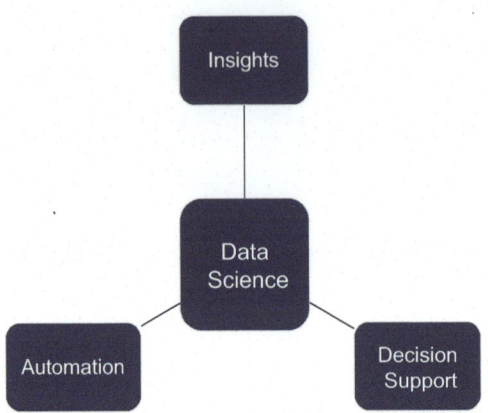

FIGURE 1.2 Main uses of data science.

1. **Insights**: sometimes all that is desired from a data science project is to extract some general knowledge that will help us understand more about the data and its structure, and this can be delivered, for instance, by building a *dashboard* with some extracted knowledge and/or *key performance indicators* (KPIs). For example, data from a cable TV provider may allow us to understand what TV shows are most watched, the peak periods of the day, the consumption pattern of users, and many other types of strategic information useful for business operations and management.

2. **Decision support system (DSS)**: in some situations, it is possible and of interest to use the available data to design tools that support decision-making processes. Examples span several areas, from health (e.g., image diagnosis) to logistics (e.g., route planning). The DSS goal is to provide tentative answers or solutions based on the available data, such that the decision maker can make a faster and more informed decision.

3. **Automation**: automating a system or process means that human intervention is no longer necessary for something to be done or a decision to be made. Thus, automation can be understood as a step further above what a DSS provides, replacing the human labor in the operation with an algorithm or machine. As an example, consider the problem of reading documents and extracting information from them. This type of task appears in several settings; for instance, a law firm that must read cases and identify the judge, the court, the defendant, etc. It is possible to automate this entity recognition process by using data science techniques.

1.1.2 Big Data

Big Data, in contrast to data science, can be understood as the area that deals with the storage, processing, and analysis of large datasets presenting some specific characteristics: velocity, variety, and volume, which, altogether, became known as the 3 Vs of Big Data. Although there are additions to the 3 Vs of Big Data to include veracity, value, variability, and even more Vs, we will limit this explanation to the standard 3 Vs. The volume refers to the large size or growing rate of the dataset, both in terms of objects and variables; velocity refers to the speed with which the data is collected, updated, and analyzed; and, finally, variety corresponds to the diversity of data sources and types (e.g., numeric, text, video, audio, etc.) in a given dataset.

Although part of the literature summarizes Big Data using the 3 Vs of data, a more complete view of the area must include the computational infrastructure necessary to store and process these data to harness their power. The storage components of Big Data require specific hardware and software capable of suitably handling data with the above-mentioned 3 Vs, because standard personal computers, at least in principle, cannot deal with Big Data. In terms of software, some are responsible for manipulating the data, while others can be used to extract insights, implement decision support systems, or automate processes.

1.1.3 Data Analytics and Data Analysis

Data analytics is a broad term encompassing the concepts, applications, and tools to develop data-driven solutions. It includes all the steps necessary to gather, prepare, and analyze the data to deliver solutions (insights, decision support, and automation). *Data analysis*, by contrast, is a more restricted concept that describes the steps used to preprocess the data (e.g., data transformation and modeling), extract basic descriptive statistics, insights, and indicators, and visualize data, with reports and dashboards as the main deliverables. Therefore, data analysis can be seen as a subset of data analytics, being responsible for part of the analytics process. To provide a clearer differentiation between data analysis and data analytics, the description presented here will assume that data analytics involves some type of *machine learning* algorithm in its process, which is not the case for data analysis. Thus, the former requires learning from data, while the latter is, in essence, a descriptive and visualization approach.

1.1.4 Data Mining and Knowledge Discovery in Databases

Data mining is a concept introduced as an allusion to the mining process of precious minerals, in which a mine is explored using appropriate tools and methods to obtain valuable materials. It is part of a broader process known as *knowledge discovery in databases*, or simply KDD, which involves the whole process, from data recovery to business analysis, data preparation, data analysis and mining, and finally solution integration.

In summary, one can say that data science is the name of the whole field, KDD corresponds to the process of using data science to achieve its goals, and data analysis, mining, and analytics are processes within KDD, as illustrated in Figure 1.3.

1.2 CAREERS IN DATA SCIENCE

When data science first saw increasing attention of the community, around 2010, the *data scientist* was considered the single career in the field. The skills needed for this position ranged from *hard* (technical skills acquired by means of training, courses, and formal education) to *soft* (behavioral and more subjective skills that influence the way one interacts with others and oneself in daily activities), as follows (Figure 1.4):

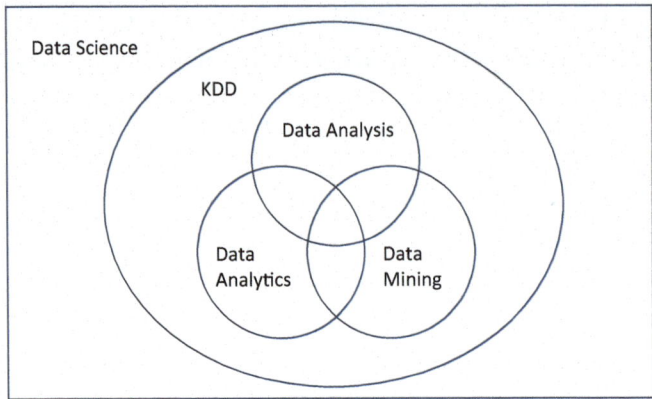

FIGURE 1.3 Relationship between the data-related areas.

- **Data scientist's desired hard skills:**

  - **Mathematics and statistics**: these skills are necessary from an analytical perspective; that is, the data scientist needs to be capable of employing mathematics and statistics in the analysis and synthesis of data-driven solutions to problems. Knowledge in machine learning, deep learning, statistical modeling, probability, graph theory, linear algebra, and mathematical programming are the main subjects required.

  - **Computing**: data science is an intrinsically computational approach, and mastering it requires knowledge in programming, databases, software engineering, high-performance computing, parallel and distributed processing, spreadsheets, dashboard design, project management, and related fields.

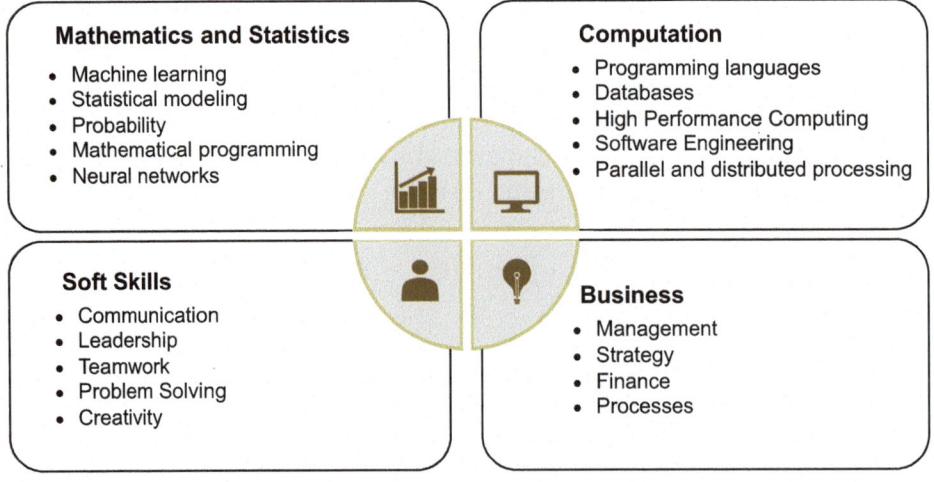

FIGURE 1.4 Some of the desired fields of knowledge and skills for a data scientist.

- **Business**: data science is about using data to extract knowledge (insights), to design DSSs, or to automate systems and processes. To achieve such goals, it is often necessary for the data scientist to have some general knowledge of business, including areas such as management, finance, operations, human resources, and other key areas of the target business. Data science is almost invariably used in developing solutions to real-world and business problems; thus, a good understanding of business is of paramount importance.

- **Data scientist's desired soft skills:**

  - **Intrapersonal**: part of your success comes from resilience, your capacity to work under pressure, stand wins and losses, and have the emotional intelligence to keep calm and carry on your duties despite your own problems and the ones that arise in the work environment.

  - **Interpersonal**: working with data will usually involve working in multidisciplinary teams and will require skills like communication, storytelling, leadership, teamwork, problem solving, creativity, conflict resolution, and others.

Even if we considered only the hard skills, it would still be very difficult to find all of them in a single person. Over the years, various specializations have emerged, and are still emerging, with the aim of more easily building and organizing data science teams around well-defined and sustainable career paths. To date, the most common careers in data science are *business analyst, data scientist, data analyst, data engineer, machine learning engineer*, and *chief data officer* (CDO). These will be described in the following sections, emphasizing their main roles, needed skills, and typical college degrees obtained by these professionals.

1.2.1 Business Analyst

The *business analyst's* main roles are:

1. Understanding the problem from a business perspective;

2. Performing the requirements analysis;

3. Preparing the use cases;

4. Understanding the analytics potential of the data available and translating them into potential business results; and

5. Structuring data-driven solutions.

Therefore, the business analyst must be capable of performing a strategic interface between business and data science, ensuring that the expected business results can be achieved.

This role will require conceptual and practical knowledge of business and market, a profound knowledge and experience of the types of analysis and solutions that can be made from the data available, communication skills and storytelling, budgeting and forecasting, and multidisciplinarity. As the business analyst is not usually required to do any programming or model validation, its most common background knowledge may be business administration, economics, engineering, and standard IT degrees, such as computer science and information systems.

1.2.2 Data Scientist

The *data scientist* is responsible for:

1. Identifying the most suitable data necessary to perform each type of analysis desired;

2. Planning, designing, developing, and applying data science algorithms to the data;

3. Analyzing the results;

4. Translating business into analytics; and

5. Making the bridge between the software and the business area.

To suitably perform these roles, he must have a profound knowledge of computing, including programming and algorithms, software engineering, complexity analysis, machine learning, deep learning, mathematical programming, statistics, neural networks, problem modeling, and all the other technical areas necessary for extracting the most out of data. The need for hard skills in math and programming makes professionals with backgrounds in mathematics, statistics, economics, physics, engineering, and IT the most common data scientists.

1.2.3 Data Analyst

The *data analyst* is responsible for:

1. Extracting the raw data from various sources;

2. Applying specific software to the data in search of actionable insights; generating visualizations and interpretations; discussing and implementing *KPIs* that can be drawn from the data; and

3. Consolidating all the results into reports and/or *dashboards*.

One of the main necessary skills is the use of data manipulation tools, including database software (e.g., SQL and MongoDB), electronic spreadsheets, and dashboards (e.g., Power BI, Tableau, and Data Studio). He also needs to effectively communicate the results with the peers, both in business and technological areas. With these roles, data analysts may come from areas such as business administration and economics, in addition to mathematics, statistics, engineering, and IT careers. It is sometimes considered an entry role for the data science career.

1.2.4 Data Engineer

The main role of a *data engineer* lies in the initial stages of the data science workflow, commonly referred to as ETL, which stands for *extract, transform,* and *load. Extraction* means accessing the data in its origin and consolidating it in a location where it can be prepared and accessed by other team members, like the data analysts and scientists. *Transformation* is another critical stage in data science, as it involves applying several methods to prepare the data so that they can be used for analytical purposes. For instance, transformation may involve selecting objects and variables, standardizing the data, treating missing values, and performing other preparation tasks. Finally, *loading* means delivering the prepared data into a *data warehouse* or *data lake* for analysis and inference.

To perform these tasks, data engineers must be versed in data management systems, data structures and algorithms, data pipelines, software engineering, and programming. The soft skills required for a data scientist, such as teamwork and communication, are equally beneficial for data engineers. As this role demands more computing skills, typical backgrounds are in technological areas, such as engineering and IT.

In summary, data engineers are responsible for:

1. Managing the ETL process;

2. Extracting and consolidating data;

3. Applying various methods to transform raw data into a usable format;

4. Building and maintaining data pipelines; and

5. Collaborating and communicating with other team members to ensure data integration and usage across the organization.

1.2.5 Machine Learning Engineer

The *machine learning engineer*, or simply *ML engineer*, is a combination of a software engineer and a data scientist who must be capable of:

1. Researching ML algorithms;

2. Designing, developing, testing, and validating machine learning systems;

3. Improving and extending ML algorithms, libraries, and frameworks;

4. Exploring and analyzing data; and

5. Developing ML solutions based on complex data.

The tasks performed by ML engineers require a strong background in mathematics, statistics, and computing, mainly software engineering. Although the difference between the ML engineer and the data scientist may seem subtle, the former is considered a more senior role responsible for developing models, while the latter is more oriented to the use and application of ML tools. Similar to data scientists, ML engineers usually have a background in mathematics, engineering, and IT.

1.2.6 Chief Data Officer

The *chief data officer*, also known as CDO, is the leading management position in the data science area. It involves:

1. Data governance for new products, services, and strategic decision-making;

2. Viewing data as strategic assets of the company;

3. Defining priorities and harnessing the power of data;

4. Managing the data teams; and

5. Building and guiding the company's data culture.

As a strategic business leader, knowledge and skills must be stronger from a management and leadership perspective. The background can range from an engineering and IT area to a business degree.

1.2.7 Skills-Based Comparison

To make an overall comparison of various data science profiles, let us consider the main skills described in the beginning of the section and select eight of them as the most relevant ones: Predictive Statistics, Descriptive Statistics, Business Analysis, Storytelling, Visualization, Software Engineering, Databases, and Programming. Let us now assume that the knowledge in each one of them can range on a scale from 0 to 100. Figure 1.5 presents the radar chart of each professional profile described with grades that fairly represent what is expected in the industry.

1.3 THE DATA SCIENCE WORKFLOW

The data science workflow is the sequence of steps necessary to conduct a data science project from planning to production. The literature also contains variations of this workflow, mainly the data mining and KDD literature (Han et al., 2011; de Castro & Ferrari, 2016; Witten et al., 2016). Figure 1.6 presents a proposal for the careers described and the process to be followed in a successful and comprehensive data science area.

The workflow starts with Step 1, the *analytical mapping* step, usually performed by the business analyst in conjunction with the CDO. The goal here is to understand the main business processes, needs, goals, and data available. With that information, the data analyst and the CDO will be capable of performing a *requirement analysis*, designing the *use cases*, identifying how the data available can be used to improve results and reduce costs and losses, and, most importantly, designing the solutions to be built. This is an essential step that will guide all the remaining workflow, from data capture to model validation.

Requirement analysis is a critical phase in the software development lifecycle where the needs and expectations of stakeholders are gathered, analyzed, and documented to understand what the software system must accomplish. This process ensures that the

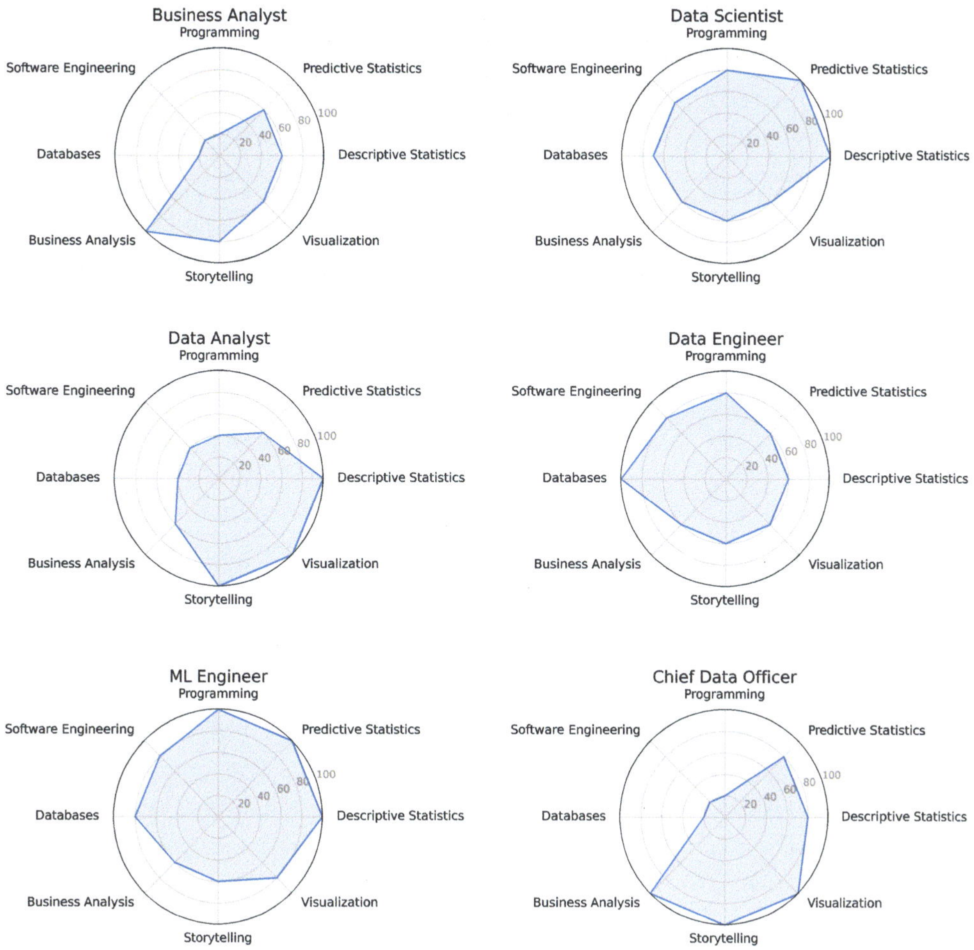

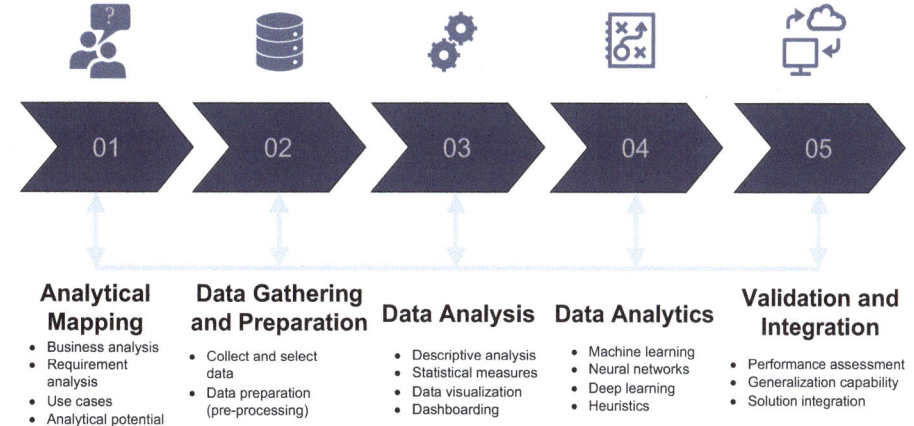

FIGURE 1.5 Radar charts for the six data science professional profiles emphasizing the relative presence of eight main hard and soft skills.

FIGURE 1.6 The data science workflow.

software solution meets the users' needs and business goals. Use cases are a technique used to describe how a user (or another system) interacts with a software system to achieve a specific goal (Sommerville, 2015).

In Step 2, data engineers are responsible for *collecting* the data necessary to implement the designed solutions and *preparing* them for the analysts and/or scientists. Specific software packages are used to manipulate data, usually producing what are known as data warehouses or data lakes. Data preparation is another process that may take a large amount of time, sometimes most of the data science work time, and involves steps such as data cleansing, integration, reduction, and transformation. The goal here is to prepare the data so that it can be suitably explored or used to design solutions to the problems at hand.

Step 3 is *data analysis*, the main subject of this book. Although the terminology data analysis may be broader in scope, *EDA* has a more restricted meaning encompassing, in essence, three tasks:

1. **Performing descriptive analyses** on the data to summarize them, discovering patterns, tendencies, anomalies, and testing hypotheses;

2. **Visualizing the data** and key indicators using graphical representations; and

3. **Creating narratives around data (data storytelling) and building dashboards**.

These tasks are the responsibility of the data analysts but are sometimes performed by the data scientists and/or machine learning engineers, who can accumulate these roles.

Step 4 is *data analytics*, which differs from data analysis in that it involves the application of learning algorithms to the data so that insights and new knowledge can be extracted, decision-support solutions can be devised, and systems or processes can be automated. Analytics will invariably result in finding novelties or designing models that allow the extrapolation of what is available in the data itself. For instance, a clustering algorithm can be used to find groups (clusters) of similar objects, while a classification algorithm allows the inference of the class of an object whose class is unknown. This step is under the umbrella of data scientists and machine learning engineers.

Step 5 involves validating a model before final delivery and is crucial to ensure that the overall project goal will be met. Model validation must consider performance (e.g., accuracy and response time), uptime, scaling, and other variables, according to the application domain. Model validation and the preparation of the final solution to be placed into production may require revisiting many of the previous steps and adding other, more specific ones, such as lifecycle management, orchestration, deployment, diagnostics, and governance. All these will involve IT and other areas, like *DevOps*, which is a combination of development and operations in the software development process, and Machine Learning Operations (*MLOps*), which defines a set of practices that simplify the management process, improve the quality, and automate the deployment of data science applications. This final step may require the involvement of all professionals described, in addition to IT members, MLOps engineers, and DevOps.

To conclude our discussion about the data science workflow, it is important to note that it does not have a unidirectional path. It is an iterative and interactive process, in the sense that one can move forward or backward at any time, from and to anywhere in the cycle, depending on the results and observations achieved.

1.4 A BRIEF HISTORY OF ARTIFICIAL INTELLIGENCE

Some pioneer contributions in the field of AI appeared back in the 1940s with works on Robotics and Artificial Neural Networks. When compared with more traditional scientific areas, however, such as Mathematics and Philosophy, whose initial evidence dates back to 3,000 BC in ancient civilizations, AI is still a young field of research.

As a field tied to computing, AI has already achieved some maturity in its few decades of existence, and, as expected, much has happened since its early days. In this direction, writing about AI history will naturally require selecting specific events to describe, because it would not be possible to talk about all that has happened so far. Therefore, this book brings some milestones of AI history that relate to EDA, helping you understand the evolution of the field, why some things happened, and where it is heading next.

1.4.1 The Early Days

The brain remains the most fascinating biological structure known. The capacity for creation and transformation of the human brain is staggering, and we are still unable to fully explain many of its basic functions, such as emotions and the emergence of ideas. The way the brain works and makes decisions was also the main inspiration for the development of AI. In the early days of the area, initiatives followed one of two paths. There were two main lines of work: one that simply tried to imitate our way of making decisions based on condition-action rules and another that sought to build computational structures inspired by the brain and other natural systems. The first line, which we call the *top-down* approach, focuses on programming our decision-making process based on how we believe it works. The second approach is the *bottom-up* one, which aims to build an AI that is capable of learning to make decisions.

Warren McCulloch and Walter Pitts (1943) proposed the first mathematical model of a biological neuron capable of carrying out elementary logical operations but sufficient to transform it into a *universal computer*, that is, a machine capable of carrying out any processing that can be expressed by a sequence of steps, known as an *algorithm*. This *universal computability* was proposed by Allan Turing a few years earlier, in his seminal work on *Universal Turing Machines* (Turing, 1936). In 1949, Donald Hebb (1949) proposed a learning rule applicable to these brain-inspired processing structures, and, in the following year, Turing (1950) published yet another relevant work on computational intelligence. In the paper entitled *Computing Machinery and Intelligence*, Turing proposed what is now known as the *Turing Test*, which proposes that for a machine to be considered intelligent, it should be capable of communicating indistinguishably from a human. The Turing test works as follows. If you place a computer in a closed room, a human in another, and an interviewer communicating with both anonymously, with the interviewer unable to differentiate between them, one can say that the computer is intelligent. Note that Turing's proposal assesses intelligence by means of the *natural language* communication capability of a machine.

In the early 1950s, Norbert Wiener (1950) coined the term *cybernetics* as the study of control and communication in animals and machines, Claude Shannon (1959) analyzed the game of Chess as a search problem, and Isaac Asimov (1950) published the famous *three laws of Robotics*:

1. A robot may not injure a human or allow a human to come to harm.

2. Robots must obey human orders, except where such orders conflict with the first law.

3. A robot must protect its own existence so long as it does not conflict with the forego-ing laws.

Although the three laws of robotics are not specifically about AI, they bring to discussion one of the most relevant themes in AI nowadays, which is ethics: What should machines be allowed to do, and how do we protect ourselves from machines turning around humans?

Of all the events that contributed to the birth of the area, the Dartmouth Summer Research Project on AI in 1956 is considered by many to be the cornerstone of the area. This school brought together several pioneer researchers, such as John McCarthy, Marvin Minsky, Nathanael Rochester, and Claude Shannon. During the years following the summer school, many people created an over-optimism, with bold promises of *General Problem Solvers* and humanoid robots. However, the lack of abundant computational resources, the absence of data, and the lack of knowledge of effective algorithms for building AI models ended up promoting the discredit of the area, which became known as the *AI winter*. During this period, resources for AI research became scarce, and the credibility of its real innovative potential was shaken.

Despite this, important advances occurred, such as the writing of the first program to play checkers by Arthur Samuel (1959), the creation of the Lisp programming language by John McCarthy (1960), and the publication of the book *Perceptrons* by Marvin Minsky and Simon Papert (1969).

The AI winter lasted until the early 1980s, when some new developments marked the field. Two volumes entitled *Parallel Distributed Processing*, organized by James McClelland and David Rumelhart (1987), concatenated many works involving mainly neural networks that allowed the area to take a great leap. Among these, we can highlight the reinterpretation of the algorithm for training multilayer perceptron networks, popularly known as the *backpropagation* algorithm, as well as algorithms for training recurrent and unsupervised networks. These volumes also brought the works that allowed the emergence of networks capable of generating distributed representations of words and recent models of *deep networks*.

Between the mid and late 1980s, AI went through a new low period, which became known as the *second AI winter*, mainly due to the decline in the use of the LISP language by the industry and the ineffectiveness of *expert systems* (top-down approaches).

In the years leading up to the turn of the millennium, there was an explosion in AI research, especially the techniques that came to be known as *Computational Intelligence*, which includes *artificial neural networks, evolutionary algorithms,* and *fuzzy systems.* At the same time, *Machine Learning* emerged, characterized by algorithms focused on learning from data. Coincidentally, these two areas started gaining traction in 1994 and 1997, respectively, with the publication of books and the creation of major technical-scientific events.

1.4.2 Recent Breakthroughs

The first two decades of the new millennium ushered in a new phase in AI, marked by significant advances and a wide penetration in the industry.

The United States *Defense Advanced Research Projects Agency* (DARPA) launched a Grand Challenge for the development of autonomous vehicles in 2004, and in 2005 a Stanford University autonomous vehicle (Thrun et al., 2007) won the challenge by driving in a desert for 131 miles. At the same time, Honda developed the humanoid robot ASIMO, capable of walking and interacting with humans, while *recommender systems* gained a lot of expression, mainly as tools for optimizing the shopping experience and personalization in e-commerce.

In the same period, we saw important evolutions that led to the consolidation of what became known as *Big Data.* Of course, the history of Big Data can be traced back to a much more remote time, but we will focus here on the events that led to the explosion of the area. In 2000, Seisint Inc. developed a distributed file-sharing framework, and in 2001, the Meta Group (now called the Gartner Group) published a report outlining challenges and opportunities for growing data as a 3D element, increasing the *volume, velocity,* and *variety* of data. This 3D element became known as the *3 Vs of Big Data.* In 2004, Google published a paper on a process called *MapReduce,* and an open-source implementation called *Hadoop* was made and had wide visibility. Big Data also gained a lot of traction with the increase in web traffic and the development of mobility, which promoted an exponential increase in the amount of semi- and unstructured data generated and stored, mainly multimedia data such as texts, images, and videos.

In these last two decades, there have also been significant advances in *deep learning,* whose initial history is intertwined with the history of neural networks. Let us take a small step back in time and highlight the proposition of the Long-Short Term Memory *recurrent networks* in 1997 by Sepp Hochreiter and Jurgen Schmidhuber (1997), who changed the history of deep learning. In 2006, Geoffrey Hinton, Osindero, and Teh (2006) published a paper proposing a fast-learning algorithm for networks called *deep belief nets.* In 2008, Andrew Ng's research group at Stanford University started using GPUs to train deep networks, increasing the processing speed of networks by orders of magnitude. In 2009, another Stanford group, this time led by researcher Fei-Fei Li (Deng et al., 2009), launched the *ImageNet database*, with 14 million labeled images for community use. In 2011, Yoshua Bengio, Antoine Bordes, and Xavier Glorot (Glorot et al., 2011) published a paper in which they showed that a specific type of activation function could solve the numerical problem caused by very low gradient values, and in 2012 *AlexNet*, an implementation of

Convolutional Networks on GPUs, promoted a leap in accuracy in the performance of deep networks applied to ImageNet data. In 2014, *Generative Adversarial Networks* emerged, proposed by Ian Goodfellow et al. (2014), and in 2016, a *deep reinforcement learning model* created by the company DeepMind won the world championship in the game AlphaGo.

In the last decade, AI algorithms and solutions have become part of many systems and products, solving complex problems in areas such as *speech recognition, robotics, medical diagnostics, natural language processing* (NLP), *logistics* and *operations research, anomaly detection* (e.g., frauds, crises, disasters, etc.), and many others. To illustrate some of these developments and public perception, we can mention that in 2011 IBM's Watson won two great championships by a wide margin in the quiz program Jeopardy! A year earlier, Microsoft had released Kinect for the XBOX 360 game console, based on machine learning technology for motion capture. Apple's Siri, Google Now, and Microsoft's Cortana have also emerged as AI solutions using advances in the field of NLP, with the aim of answering questions and providing recommendations for users.

In addition to the greater scientific rigor of AI, high data availability, and the possibility of buying storage space and processing on demand, another factor that contributed to the acceleration of the area in recent years is the fact that the Big Tech companies, such as Google, Amazon, Microsoft, Apple, Facebook, and Intel, have started to open some of their technology to the community. Frameworks, infrastructure, toolkits, platforms, libraries, etc., have been made available openly so that professionals, companies, entrepreneurs, and educational and research institutions could use and advance knowledge and technology. Keras, TensorFlow, NLTK, Spark, Scikit-learn, DAAL, Gensim, MongoDB, and Tika are just a few examples of these.

Finally, a striking aspect of the advancement of AI in the new millennium was the fact that research in the area began to focus more on conceptual and theoretical aspects, ceasing to be a mostly empirical discipline and becoming a more scientific area. The application of mathematical knowledge and formalisms, mainly linear algebra, probability and statistics, economic theories, and mathematical programming (operations research), brought greater rigor to AI. A major scientific recognition for AI came with the Turing Award for research involving deep learning for Yoshua Bengio, Geoffrey Hinton, and Yann Lecun in 2019.

1.4.3 Bridging the History of AI and Data Analysis

The evolution of AI, as presented here, reveals that data has always been a central element in the development of AI, shaping its trajectory and capabilities. In the early days, when Warren McCulloch and Walter Pitts developed the first mathematical model of a neuron, their work laid the foundation for data-driven analysis, highlighting the need to simulate how the human brain processes information. This early focus on replicating human decision-making marked an initial stage in the development of data analysis tools.

As AI progressed, the rise and fall of the AI winters brought a key lesson: without access to abundant data and efficient data processing methods, AI struggled to reach its potential. The resurgence of AI in the 1980s, fueled by the development of neural networks and algorithms capable of handling more complex datasets, was a turning point that would contribute to advances in data analysis. EDA gained relevance as it allowed researchers to understand, clean, preprocess, and visualize data before feeding it into AI models, making the data more suitable for training and improving model accuracy.

In recent years, the explosion of Big Data and deep learning has further solidified the relationship between AI and data analysis. The ability to collect, store, and analyze vast amounts of data has been instrumental in AI breakthroughs, from training autonomous vehicles to enhancing NLP capabilities. This interdependence means that AI's success today relies on robust data analysis practices, with EDA serving as a critical step in transforming raw data into valuable insights that may be used to inform AI models. Therefore, understanding the history of AI helps us appreciate how EDA has evolved as a foundational practice, enabling AI systems to make sense of complex, real-world data and leading to the intelligent solutions we see today.

1.5 EXERCISES

1.5.1 Research Topics and Questions

1. You have just been hired by a company (or decided to found a startup) that makes a social media analysis of data related to TV. The problem that you must solve is the following. Today people use social media to talk about TV and interact with actors, filmmakers, TV stations, etc. This interaction can be quantified and transformed into audience indices, and also qualified so that all stakeholders know what the consumers think about shows, actors, products, services, etc. The quantification and qualification of social media data related to TV generates what is now known as Social TV Analytics. Your mission is to design an analytical dashboard for the quantification and qualification of social TV data. In groups, discuss what you would include in this dashboard and why.

2. Discuss the underlying principles and philosophies that guide the field of data science. What are some of the ethical considerations in data science?

3. Investigate the presence of bias in data and how it can influence decision-making in various domains. Discuss the challenges of mitigating bias in algorithms and the ethical implications of biased data.

4. Examine the challenges and importance of creating AI systems that are transparent and understandable. Discuss the trade-offs between complexity and interpretability in machine learning models and their implications for trust and accountability.

5. Section 1.2 introduced the main careers in data science, emphasizing their main activities, needed knowledge, and backgrounds. Provide a description of at least one other career in data science that was not included in the text and stress the same three aspects used in the text.

6. Section 1.4 presented an overview of some milestones in the historical development of AI. In groups of students, draw a summarized timeline of what you consider the main developments in data science.

7. Data science is about extracting value from data, either by drawing insights, by building decision support tools, or by automating systems and processes. Throughout time, a vast number of data repositories have been developed, not only to share data for experimentation or competition, as provided by the UCI Machine Learning Repository and Kaggle, but also to make information available and transparent for the community, as is the case with governmental data. Provide a list of three online data repositories that could be used for data analysis and explain why these repositories were chosen.

1.5.2 Quizzes

1. What is the main role of a Business Analyst in the context of data science and AI?

   a. Develop machine learning algorithms.

   b. Extract raw data from various sources.

   c. Design data pipelines.

   d. Understand the business problem and translate it for data science.

2. Which role is responsible for identifying the most suitable data for analysis, applying data science algorithms, and translating business needs into analytics?

   a. Data Scientist.

   b. Data Analyst.

   c. Data Engineer.

   d. Machine Learning Engineer.

3. What is one of the main skills required for a Data Analyst?

   a. Software engineering and algorithms.

   b. Data manipulation using tools like SQL and dashboards.

   c. Research machine learning algorithms.

   d. Design data pipelines.

4. What does ETL stand for in the context of data engineering?

   a. Extract, Transform, Learn.

   b. Enhance, Transform, Load.

   c. Extract, Transfer, Load.

   d. Extract, Transform, Load.

5. What is the main responsibility of a Chief Data Officer (CDO)?

   a. Develop machine learning models.

   b. Extract data from various sources.

   c. Manage data teams and build a data culture.

   d. Research ML algorithms.

6. What is the purpose of the analytical mapping step in the data science workflow?

   a. Design data warehouses and data lakes.

   b. Apply learning algorithms to data.

   c. Perform exploratory data analysis.

   d. Understand business processes and data needs.

7. Which step involves collecting and preparing the data necessary for implementing designed solutions?

   a. Data analysis.

   b. Data analytics.

   c. Data preparation.

   d. Model validation.

8. What is the primary responsibility of data analysts during the data analysis phase?

   a. Build machine learning models.

   b. Design data pipelines.

   c. Perform descriptive analyses and visualization.

   d. Orchestrate model deployment.

9. What is the key distinction between data analysis and data analytics?

   a. Data analysis involves model validation, while data analytics does not.

   b. Data analysis focuses on pattern discovery, while data analytics applies learning algorithms.

   c. Data analytics involves data cleansing and integration, while data analysis does not.

   d. Data analytics requires business process understanding, while data analysis does not.

10. Why is model validation an important step in the data science workflow?

    a. It involves collecting and preparing data.

    b. It focuses on data visualization and dashboards.

    c. It ensures that project goals are met and models perform well.

    d. It prepares data for deployment in production.

11. What does the term "MLOps" refer to in the context of the data science workflow?

    a. Managing lifecycle management and orchestration.

    b. Combining development and operations in machine learning software development.

    c. Applying learning algorithms to data.

    d. Exploring data for patterns and anomalies.

12. Which statement accurately reflects the nature of the data science workflow?

    a. It follows a strict unidirectional path from planning to production.

    b. It is a linear process without room for iteration.

    c. It is interactive and can move forward or backward based on results and observations.

    d. It involves only data scientists and machine learning engineers.

## CHAPTER 2

Data Description and Preparation

"No data is clean, but most is useful"

– Dean Abbott

In essence, *data* is everything that can be used, moved, processed, or translated to carry some meaning. A number, a word, an image, a text, a graph, and a sound are all examples of data. In computational terms, anything that can be stored and/or processed is a kind of data. Data requires a context to bring it meaning, becoming what is known as *information*. The result of using information to make decisions or to extract insights from data is called *knowledge*. In summary, data is any piece of information that comes in isolation, with no context, while information is the result of adding context or meaning to data, and knowledge is what results from the use, interpretation, and processing of information.

To illustrate, consider numbers 48 and 130 (Figure 2.1). By themselves, they are simply numbers (data), and we cannot give any specific meaning to them. However, if we add the context that 48 refers to the age of a person and 130 mg/dL is this person's blood sugar level, this information allows us to conclude that this person has diabetes (knowledge acquired). Note that data is simply a collection of facts or items, while information requires context and meaning. While data is raw, information brings value and can be interpreted or used for knowledge extraction.

2.1 TABULAR AND MATHEMATICAL REPRESENTATIONS

Data can come in different formats, such as numbers, characters, texts, signals, images, videos, and sounds, among others. Although not commonly used in the literature, the singular form of data is *datum*, and we will use data and datum interchangeably in this text.

In general, all data can be divided into two parts: the *objects* (also called *instances*, *items*, *observations*, or *patterns*) and their *variables* (also called *features*, *attributes*, or *characteristics*). Each object represents a datum with its variables. For example, a mobile phone is

DOI: 10.1201/9781003570691-2

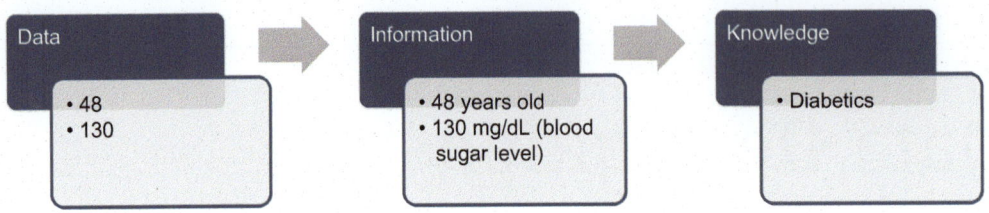

FIGURE 2.1   From data to information to knowledge.

an object, and its amount of memory, screen size, weight, type of processor, and all other descriptors are its variables or features. This pair of *objects* and *variables* can be used to describe almost all types of data, from personal files to videos.

Table 2.1 provides an example of a dataset where each row corresponds to an object and each column to a variable. This is the typical organization of a *structured dataset* and will be the standard format used in this book, although sometimes, the objects may appear in the columns and the variables in the rows. Such cases will be explicitly identified.

In mathematical terms, each variable in the dataset represents one dimension in a multidimensional space used to represent the data. Let $\mathbf{x}^i$ be an object from the dataset, N the number of objects, and m the number of variables (dimension). The dataset S can be represented as $S = \{\mathbf{x}^i\}_{i=1, \ldots, N}$, and each object $\mathbf{x}^i = [x_j^i]_{j=1, \ldots, m}$.

To illustrate the mathematical and visual representation of the objects, consider the sample of Table 2.1. In this dataset sample, there are $N=4$ objects and $m=8$ variables. As each variable represents one dimension in the space, it is possible to plot them in an 8-dimensional space. It is important to recognize that, as the first variable in this dataset is an *identifier* rather than a standard variable, it is not treated as the other variables. This is because it has a unique value that distinguishes (identifies) each object and does not contain any inherent information about the objects. Therefore, identifiers are usually not considered from an analytical perspective and are removed from the dataset while doing the analyses.

As we are unable to visualize a graph in a seven-dimensional space, Figure 2.2 shows a bidimensional graph with the four objects in Table 2.1 plotted considering only variables "Lug_boot" and "Safety" (see Table 2.2 for a description of the dataset's variables). Note that the first three objects have the same value, "small", for the "Lug_boot" variable and increasing values for the variable "Safety", and the last object has values "med" and "low" for the two variables, respectively.

TABLE 2.1   First Four Objects of the Car Evaluation Dataset Available at UCI

Car ID	Buying	Maintenance	Doors	Persons	Lug_boot	Safety	Class
1	vhigh	vhigh	2	2	Small	low	unacc
2	vhigh	vhigh	2	2	Small	med	unacc
3	vhigh	vhigh	2	2	Small	high	unacc
4	vhigh	vhigh	2	2	Med	low	unacc

Source: https://archive.ics.uci.edu/ml/datasets/car+evaluation

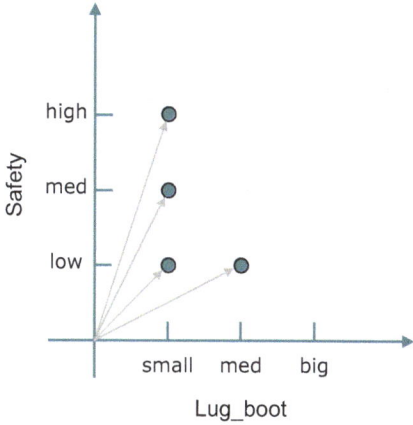

FIGURE 2.2   Graph for variables "safety" vs "lug_boot" of the four objects in Table 2.1.

Another important concept to be discussed here is the role of each variable in an analytical task. In this sense, variables can be divided into *dependent* and *independent*. In most cases, there is one single dependent variable and one or more independent variables. The independent variables are those that can be experimentally manipulated, controlled, and measured, exerting an influence on the value of the dependent variable. For example, the Body Mass Index (*BMI*) measures body fat by dividing the weight (*w*) in kilograms by the square of your height (*h*) in meters: $BMI = w/h^2$. In this case, *BMI* is the dependent variable, and the weight *w* and height *h* are the independent variables.

When the dependent variable is discrete, that is, can only assume a finite number of values, these values are called *class labels*, because they represent the specific class value of one object. Examples abound: the classification used for clothes' sizes (extra-small, small, medium, large, extra-large); classification of temperature (hot, mild, fresh, cold, etc.); classification of e-mails (spam, not spam); etc. In many exploratory data analysis problems, knowing what the dependent and independent variables are helps guiding the analysis process.

TABLE 2.2   Example of a Simple Data Dictionary for the Car Evaluation Dataset Presented in Table 2.1

Variable Name	Definition (Meaning)	Domain
Car ID	ID number of each car in the dataset	Integer number
Buying	Buying price	{v-high, high, med, low}
Maintenance	Price of the maintenance	{v-high, high, med, low}
Doors	Number of doors	{2, 3, 4, 5-more}
Persons	Number of persons accommodated	{2, 4, more}
Lug-boot	Trunk size	{small, med, big}
Safety	Level of safety	{low, med, high}
Class	Car acceptability	{unacc, acc, good, vgood}

2.2 DATA DICTIONARY

When organizing a dataset to perform any type of analysis, it is useful to build a *data dictionary*, that is, a structure describing all variables in the dataset, including their definitions and other information necessary for the analysis, such as the variables' domain. For the dataset of Table 2.1, one possible data dictionary is presented in Table 2.2.

Note that there are different ways to present a data dictionary, but the minimum includes at least the definition or meaning of each variable. This is because sometimes these meanings are not obvious, and the data analyst needs to know them to perform the analysis. Concerning the variables' domains, they are important because they allow us to instantly detect domain violations or other types of inconsistencies. In this case, it is important to note that braces (curly brackets), {}, represent *sets*, that is, a collection of distinct items or objects, while square brackets, [ ], represent *ranges* or *domains*, referring to an interval of values.

2.3 CLASSIFYING DATA

The large variety of data allows us to classify them in different forms, depending on specific characteristics, applications, and methods. For instance, data can be classified based on their structure, nature, type, time variability, dimension, and ownership, as summarized in Figure 2.3. Each of these classifications is useful in different cases and, thus, will be described in more detail in the following subsections.

2.3.1 Structure

The *structure* of the data refers to how they are organized and how they can be broken down into parts to be analyzed. Concerning the structure, data can be *structured*, *semi-structured*, or *unstructured*.

Structured data can be organized in a specific structure, such as a *table* or a *spreadsheet*. This organization usually requires a *data model*, that is, a description of the objects, their relations, and properties. The model describes how the data are going to be stored,

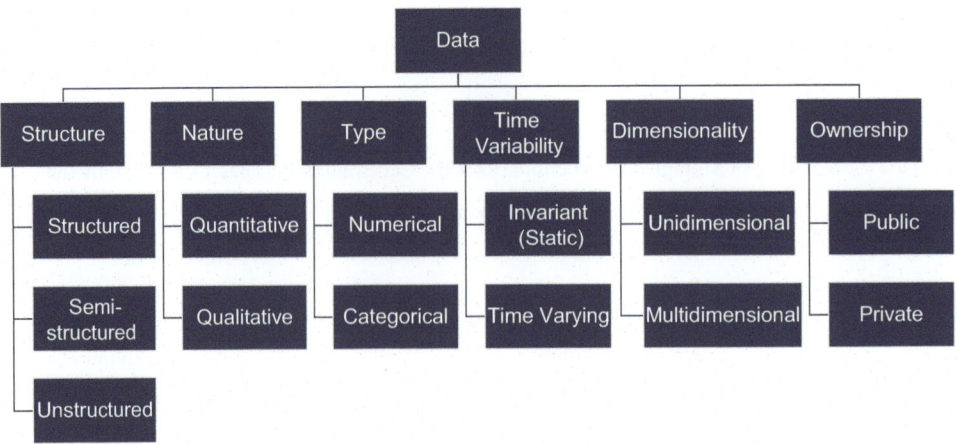

FIGURE 2.3 Different forms of data classification.

accessed, and processed, and this includes defining which fields (features) will be used, their types (e.g., numeric, nominal, etc.), and all constraints associated with the data. Their structured characteristic makes their storage, access, and analysis easier when compared with the other two types of data. As an example, one can think of a table with a description of a set of cars: for each car, there is a rate of buyer interest, a rate for maintenance level, a specification about its number of doors and passengers, its trunk size, safety, and one final result indicating its class, that is, if it is acceptable or not to be purchased (Table 2.1).

Semi-structured data has some level of organization or structure but is not in conformity with a data model or a rigid schema, such as the structured data. They often come with *metadata* (e.g., *tags* or *markers*) that provide additional information to describe the objects. In many cases, this level of structure does not allow them to be stored in standard databases, but it does allow them to incorporate different types of data into an existing database and to be indexed and queried with more flexibility. Some of the most common semi-structured data are e-mails, XML files, TCP/IP packets, and web pages. E-mails, for example, have the subject line, sender name, attached files, body text, and signature. Although each of these parts is open in terms of content, all of them are tagged in the message, allowing a clear separation of their content.

Unstructured data do not conform with a data model and do not even have metadata associated with them. Therefore, they cannot be stored in standard relational databases that require a data model, and are better managed by non-relational databases, known as NoSQL. Examples of unstructured data include videos, images, sounds (audio), texts, and geospatial data.

Table 2.3 provides a comparison of structured, semi-structured, and unstructured data based on the use of a data model and metadata, providing examples of each one of them.

2.3.2 Nature

Quantitative data relate to quantity, that is, something that can be measured or counted, and are expressed by numbers or *numerical variables* (e.g., distance, how many). *Qualitative data* or *variables*, by contrast, are those that can be represented by names, symbols, code snippets, or *categorical variables* (e.g., how good, how well, how are you feeling). Table 2.4 provides a comparison between quantitative and qualitative data concerning their nature and some of their characteristics.

As discussed previously, some numeric values can be used as an ID, a unique identification or identifier, such as the ID of an object in a database, a Social Security Number (SSN), and a driver's license number. In these cases, the numbers are considered qualitative variables, because they are unique and categorical. To illustrate, consider the car

TABLE 2.3 Comparison among Structured, Semi-structured, and Unstructured Data

	Data Model	Metadata	Examples
Structured	Yes	No	Tables, spreadsheets
Semi-structured	No	Yes	E-mail, XML files, web pages
Unstructured	No	No	Photos, images, audio, text

TABLE 2.4   Comparison between Quantitative and Qualitative Data

Quantitative	Qualitative
Numerical	Categorical
Statistical	Non-statistical
Structured	Semi- or Unstructured
Objective	Subjective
Measurable	Understandable

dataset sample presented in Table 2.1. In this dataset, all variables are considered categorical, including Doors and Persons, which represent the number of doors and the number of passengers that can be accommodated in the vehicle, respectively. Although their values are numbers, these numbers represent categories. A variable such as the 0 to 100 miles/h acceleration of a car would be considered a numeric variable.

2.3.3 Type

Knowing the type of data that you are going to deal with is a prerequisite for a successful data analysis process. In essence, there are two types of data when the emphasis is on the type of variable (Figure 2.4): *numerical* and *categorical*.

Numeric data or *numeric variables* are the ones also called quantitative data, as described before. They are expressed by means of numbers and can be mathematically determined. Numerical data can be divided into *discrete*, which are countable numerical data, such as years, age, number of votes, number of children, etc.; or *continuous*, which are uncountable, such as height, weight, grades, etc. Continuous data are expressed in the form of *ranges* or *intervals*, representing measurements. They can be further divided into *interval data* (i.e., that can be measured using a scale) and *ratio data* (i.e., having a well-defined zero point on the scale). Examples of continuous ratio data are grades in an exam, which usually span a [0, 10] or [0, 5] scale, and market share, which spans the interval [0%, 100%].

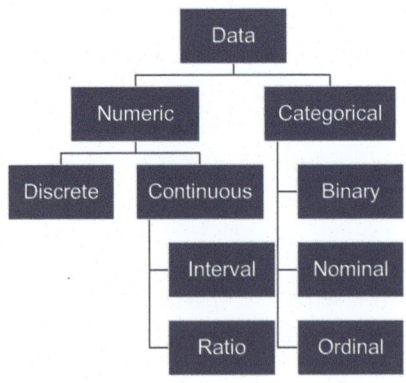

FIGURE 2.4   Types of data variables.

The *categorical data* can be stored, accessed, and identified using symbols, labels, or names associated with them. These are the qualitative data described previously and allow three subdivisions: *binary, nominal,* and *ordinal.* Binary data can only assume one of two values, such as 0 or 1, and is represented using set theory (instead of a range): {0,1}. Nominal data are those whose values have distinct symbols or labels, like marital status that could be {single, married, divorced, separated, widowed}. Finally, ordinal data are those that have a specific order of categories, such as {high, medium, low} or {very slow, slow, fast, very fast}. Note that ordinal data may not necessarily present an explicit or homogeneous notion of the distance among its values.

2.3.4 Time Variability

The *time variability* (*time scale* or *stationary nature*) of the data allows them to be characterized as *static* (*stationary*) or *dynamic* (*non-stationary*). *Static data* are fixed data in the sense that they do not change (vary) with time, while *dynamic data* are those that are periodically updated, that is, change over time.

To illustrate, consider a dataset with information about some stones. The variables associated with the stones may include their weight, dimensions, colors, etc. In principle, these values do not change with time and are, thus, static. By contrast, consider the values of stocks in the stock market. These are extremely volatile, varying constantly depending on buying and selling pressure during the stock market operating hours. Therefore, the value of a stock is a dynamic or time-varying variable.

Although there are different types of dynamics and dynamic data, the focus here is on time variability. Two types are of particular interest for data analysis: *time-series data* and *data streams.* The exploratory analysis of time-series data will be studied in more detail in Section 6.1.

Traditional static data are sometimes referred to as *batch data*, meaning that the whole dataset is stored and available for analysis (Wares et al., 2019). However, there are some data types that may appear in a sequential and continuous mode. *Data streams* can be defined as (potentially) unbounded sequences of data objects that are continuously generated (Aggarwal, 2007; Silva et al., 2013). Examples of data streams include video and audio streams, player-game interactions in a gaming platform, web logs, computer network traffic, and social media messages.

A *time series* is a collection of observations indexed by or obtained from sequential measurements taken at uniformly spaced instants of time and following a given sampling rate. The series can be *univariate* or *multivariate* when several series simultaneously span multiple dimensions within the same time range (Hamilton, 1994; Esling & Agon, 2012). Mathematically, it can be represented as $T = (t_1, t_2, ..., t_N), t_i \in \mathfrak{R}$. When plotted on a graph, a time series will always have one of the axes, usually the *x*-axis, representing time. Examples of time series include body measurements, such as heart rate and brain monitoring, stock prices, interest rates, and temperature.

Although data streams and time series both vary with time, these concepts do not mean the same thing. For instance, data streams may not be analyzed as a time series if time is not an important feature of the data. Time-series analysis, by contrast, must always have time as a crucial variable in its analysis. Therefore, a differentiating aspect of time series when compared with data streams is that the time series aims at showing how one or more variables behave (vary) with time. Data streams are any flow of data, and the time scale or interval is not of major relevance. Thus, data streams may involve time-series data or not.

To illustrate this difference, consider social media data, like the *trending topics* (TT) on X (former Twitter). Trending topics change constantly with time, and most analysts are interested in knowing what the new TTs are; however, the time scale usually neither influences the new TTs nor is relevant for the analysis. This is an example of a data stream. If one takes, for example, the price of a stock over time, it is always influenced by its previous price and other external variables. In this case, we have a time series, and the dependence on time is inescapable.

2.3.5 Dimensionality

In the standard structured data organization with objects in the rows and variables in the columns, *dimensionality* refers to the number of columns in the dataset. This is because, in the mathematical and spatial representations of the data, each variable requires one dimension in the space where the data is represented. Therefore, data with a single variable are called *univariate*, and data with two or more variables are called *multivariate*. Sometimes data with two variables are called *bivariate*, but this should not be confused with the concept of a binary variable, which is a variable that can only assume one of two potential values.

In the example of Table 2.1, the attributes "Buying", "Maintenance", "Doors", "Persons", "Lug_boot", "Safety", and "Class" are dimensions of the dataset. Note that all variables that have a unique value for each object, such as the variable "Car ID", serve as an identification variable and are usually not accounted for in the analysis. For example, a social security number, a person's name, or an ID number all represent a single object and do not add any value in the characterization of the dataset. Also, some datasets have one or more variables that are used as *labels* to identify a specific group or class of objects. In many cases, this label is analyzed separately from the other variables and is not counted as a dimension of the data.

2.3.6 Ownership

In relation to ownership, data can be classified as *private* or *public*. Private data are all that belong to and are generated by you or your enterprise. Public data, by contrast, are all those that are generated by a third party but that are of interest or relevance to you or your business.

One of the most remarkable examples of public data is online data, including social media data. For example, a well-known brand has its data generated by its sales, processes, performance, etc., but is also interested in knowing what is being said about it on social media. Thus, its operation and decisions will be guided by both its private data and the public data that is of interest.

2.4 DATASETS USED IN THE BOOK

To work and illustrate the concepts that will be presented here, several datasets from the literature were chosen. Some of them were taken from the UCI Machine Learning Repository,[1] others from Kaggle,[2] and others from Python's libraries or other open sources. This section provides a brief description of each one of them and a sample (when possible) with the first and last five objects in the dataset. The .csv files of all of them are also available at the author's GitHub.[3]

Before starting any analysis, it is important to understand what the data is about, which types of analysis can be performed with it, and what types of conclusions can be drawn from them, because these will guide the analytical process. So, before performing any calculus or computation, first, rationalize the data, make some assumptions and questions about it, and, only after all that, start the analysis.

2.4.1 Mammographic Dataset

This dataset is related to mammograms, which are X-ray images of the breast used to screen for breast cancer. The objects in the dataset are described by six variables, including the patient's age, the mass shape and margin, the breast density, and the severity of the detected abnormality. This dataset is commonly used in data science research to develop algorithms to diagnose breast cancer from mammography data.

The UCI Mammographic dataset[4] contains 961 objects with six variables representing information about the mammogram results of patients. Each object corresponds to the mammogram results of one patient, and the following variables compose the dataset (Table 2.5):

- **BI-RADS**: indicates the mammogram result assessment by a radiologist using the Breast Imaging Reporting and Data System.
  Type: categorical.
  Scale: 1–5, where 1 is "negative" and 5 is "highly suggestive of malignancy".

TABLE 2.5 Mammographic Dataset Sample: First and Last Five Objects in the Dataset

Patient	BI-RADS	Age	Shape	Margin	Density	Severity
0	5	67	Lobular	Spiculated	Low	Malignant
1	4	43	Round	Circumscribed	?	Malignant
2	5	58	Irregular	Spiculated	Low	Malignant
3	4	28	Round	Circumscribed	Low	Benign
4	5	74	Round	Spiculated	?	Malignant
...	...	...	...	...	...	...
956	4	47	Oval	Circumscribed	Low	Benign
957	4	56	Irregular	Spiculated	Low	Malignant
958	4	64	Irregular	Spiculated	Low	Benign
959	5	66	Irregular	Spiculated	Low	Malignant
960	4	62	Lobular	Obscured	Low	Benign

Question marks, "?", indicate missing values.

- **Age**: patient age in years.
  Type: integer.
  Range: 18–96.

- **Shape**: mass shape seen in the mammogram.
  Type: categorical.
  Scale: 1=round, 2=oval, 3=lobular, 4=irregular.

- **Margin**: mass margin observed in the mammogram.
  Type: categorical.
  Scale: 1=circumscribed, 2=microlobulated, 3=obscured, 4=ill-defined, 5=spiculated.

- **Density**: mass density observed in the mammogram.
  Type: categorical.
  Scale: 1=high, 2=iso, 3=low, 4=fat-containing.

- **Severity**: severity of the mammogram result.
  Type: Boolean.
  Values: 0=benign or 1=malignant.

Sample question and hypothesis about the mammographic dataset:

Question: What are the significant features associated with the likelihood of breast cancer based on the mammographic data?

Hypothesis: Dense patterns in mammograms are positively correlated with an increased risk of breast cancer.

2.4.2 Forest Fires Dataset

This dataset involves environmental observations related to forest fires in the Montesinho Natural Park in the northeastern region of Portugal. This dataset is described by 12 variables, including the location of the observation, the month and day, the temperature, relative humidity, wind speed, and rainfall on that day. This dataset is commonly used to understand the factors that contribute to forest fires and to develop models that can predict the occurrence and severity of fires based on environmental data.

The UCI Forest Fires dataset[5] contains 517 objects and 13 variables. Each object contains one measure of the following variables (Table 2.6):

- **X**: x-axis spatial coordinate within the Montesinho park map.
  Type: integer.
  Values: {1,2,3,4,5,6,7,8,9}.

- **Y**: y-axis spatial coordinate within the Montesinho park map.
  Type: integer.
  Values: {2,3,4,5,6,7,8,9}.

TABLE 2.6   Forest Fires Dataset Sample: First and Last Five Objects in the Dataset

Obj	X	Y	Month	Day	FFMC	DMC	DC	ISI	Temp	RH	Wind	Rain	Area
0	7	5	Mar	fri	86.2	26.2	94.3	5.1	8.2	51	6.7	0.0	0.00
1	7	4	Oct	tue	90.6	35.4	669.1	6.7	18.0	33	0.9	0.0	0.00
2	7	4	Oct	sat	90.6	43.7	686.9	6.7	14.6	33	1.3	0.0	0.00
3	8	6	Mar	fri	91.7	33.3	77.5	9.0	8.3	97	4.0	0.2	0.00
4	8	6	Mar	sun	89.3	51.3	102.2	9.6	11.4	99	1.8	0.0	0.00
...	...	...	...	...	...	...	...	...	...	...	...	...	...
512	4	3	Aug	sun	81.6	56.7	665.6	1.9	27.8	32	2.7	0.0	6.44
513	2	4	Aug	sun	81.6	56.7	665.6	1.9	21.9	71	5.8	0.0	54.29
514	7	4	Aug	sun	81.6	56.7	665.6	1.9	21.2	70	6.7	0.0	11.16
515	1	4	Aug	sat	94.4	146.0	614.7	11.3	25.6	42	4.0	0.0	0.00
516	6	3	Nov	tue	79.5	3.0	106.7	1.1	11.8	31	4.5	0.0	0.00

- **Month**: month of the year.
  Type: categorical.
  Values: {"jan", "feb", "mar", "apr", "may", "jun", "jul", "aug", "sep", "oct", "nov", "dec"}.

- **Day**: day of the week.
  Type: categorical.
  Values: {"mon", "tue", "wed", "thu", "fri", "sat", "sun"}.

- **FFMC**: Fine Fuel Moisture Code, which is a numeric rating of the moisture content of litter and other cured fine fuels.
  Type: continuous.
  Range: [18.7, 96.20].

- **DMC**: Duff Moisture Code, which is a numeric rating of the average moisture content of loosely compacted organic layers.
  Type: continuous.
  Range: [1.1, 291.3].

- **DC**: Drought Code, which is a numeric rating of the drying potential of deep organic layers.
  Type: continuous.
  Range: [7.9, 860.6].

- **ISI**: Initial Spread Index, which is a numeric rating of the potential spread of fire.
  Type: continuous.
  Range: [0.0, 56.10].

- **Temp**: temperature in degrees Celsius.
  Type: continuous.
  Range: [2.2, 33.30].

- **RH**: Relative Humidity in percentage.
  Type: continuous.
  Range: [15.0, 100].

- **Wind**: wind speed in km/h.
  Type: continuous.
  Range: [0.40, 9.40].

- **Rain**: outside rain in mm/m^2.
  Type: continuous.
  Range: [0.0, 6.4].

- **Area**: burned area of the forest (in ha).
  Type: continuous.
  Range: [0.00, 1090.84].

Sample question and hypothesis about the forest fires dataset:

Question: What are the key factors influencing the occurrence and spread of forest fires?

Hypothesis: Higher temperatures and lower humidity levels contribute to increased forest fire occurrences.

2.4.3 Iris Dataset of Fisher

The Iris dataset of Fisher is one of the most well-known and used datasets in the data science literature. It was generated in 1936 by R. A. Fisher to study taxonomic problems (Fisher, 1936),[6] that is, problems involving the organization and classification of organisms. In terms of structure, the Iris data is very simple; it contains 150 objects divided into three classes with 50 objects each, representing the species of Iris plants (setosa, virginica, and versicolor). It is important to acknowledge that one of the classes is linearly separable from the other two. The data has four numerical (float) attributes (sepal length, sepal width, petal length, and petal width) plus the predictive class and no missing values (Table 2.7):

TABLE 2.7   Iris Dataset Sample: First and Last Five Objects in the Dataset

Object	Sepal Length	Sepal Width	Petal Length	Petal Width	Class
0	5.1	3.5	1.4	0.2	Iris-setosa
1	4.9	3.0	1.4	0.2	Iris-setosa
2	4.7	3.2	1.3	0.2	Iris-setosa
3	4.6	3.1	1.5	0.2	Iris-setosa
4	5.0	3.6	1.4	0.2	Iris-setosa
...	...	...	...	...	...
145	6.7	3.0	5.2	2.3	Iris-virginica
146	6.3	2.5	5.0	1.9	Iris-virginica
147	6.5	3.0	5.2	2.0	Iris-virginica
148	6.2	3.4	5.4	2.3	Iris-virginica
149	5.9	3.0	5.1	1.8	Iris-virginica

- **sepal length:**
  Type: numerical (float).
  Range: [4.3, 7.9]

- **sepal width:**
  Type: numerical (float).
  Range: [2.0, 4.4]

- **petal length:**
  Type: numerical (float).
  Range: [1.0, 6.9]

- **petal width:**
  Type: numerical (float).
  Range: [0.1, 2.5]

- **class**: plant species.
  Type: categorical.
  Values: {Iris-setosa, Iris-virginica, Iris-versicolor}

Sample question and hypothesis about the Iris dataset of Fisher:

Question: Can we distinguish between different species of iris flowers based on their sepal and petal measurements?

Hypothesis: The combination of sepal length, sepal width, petal length, and petal width can be used to accurately classify iris species.

2.4.4 Auto MPG Dataset

The auto-mpg dataset consists of a slight variation of the data about cars used by R. Quinlan to predict fuel consumption in miles per gallon (mpg) (Quinlan, 1993).[7] The dataset has three categorical and five numerical (float) attributes, plus the target attribute (mpg), with a total of 398 objects (Table 2.8):

TABLE 2.8   Auto MPG Dataset Sample: First and Last Five Objects in the Dataset

Obj	mpg	Cyl	Disp	HP	Weight	Acc	MY	OG	Car name
0	18	8	307	130	3,504	12.0	70	1	Chevrolet Chevelle Malibu
1	15	8	350	165	3,693	11.5	70	1	Buick Skylark 320
2	18	8	318	150	3,436	11.0	70	1	Plymouth Satellite
3	16	8	304	150	3,433	12.0	70	1	AMC Rebel SST
4	17	8	302	140	3,449	10.5	70	1	Ford Torino
393	27	4	140	86	2,790	15.6	82	1	Ford Mustang GL
394	44	4	97	52	2,130	24.6	82	2	VW Pickup
395	32	4	135	84	2,295	11.6	82	1	Dodge Rampage
396	28	4	120	79	2,625	18.6	82	1	Ford Ranger
397	31	4	119	82	2,720	19.4	82	1	Chevy S-10

Cyl, cylinders; Disp, displacement; HP, horsepower; WG, weight; Acc, acceleration; MY, model year; OG, origin.

- **mpg**: fuel consumption in miles per gallon (mpg).
  Type: numerical (float).
  Range: [9.0, 46.6]

- **cylinders**: number of cylinders in the car's engine.
  Type: categorical.
  Values: {3,4,5,6,8}

- **displacement**: total volume of air (cubic inches) displaced by all the cylinders in the car's engine.
  Type: numerical (float).
  Range: [68, 455]

- **horsepower**: horsepower of the car's engine.
  Type: numerical (float).
  Range: [46, 230], with six missing values.

- **weight**: car's weight.
  Type: numerical (float).
  Range: [1,613, 5,140]

- **acceleration**: time, in seconds, taken to accelerate from 0 to 60 miles/hour.
  Type: numerical (float).
  Range: [8, 24.8]

- **model year**: manufacture year of the car model.
  Type: categorical.
  Values: {70 … 82}

- **origin**: country of origin of the car.
  Type: categorical.
  Values: {1 (USA), 2 (Europe), 3 (Japan)}

- **car name:**
  Type: categorical.
  Values: unique for each instance.

Sample question and hypothesis about the auto MPG data:

Question: What factors are most strongly correlated with a vehicle's fuel efficiency?

Hypothesis: Smaller and lighter cars with lower horsepower tend to have higher miles per gallon (MPG).

2.4.5 Gapminder Dataset

The Gapminder dataset available on Kaggle[8] was compiled from the Gapminder Foundation,[9] a Swedish non-profit organization that promotes sustainable global development through data analysis and visualization, containing socioeconomic indicators for 175 countries around the world, spanning from 1998 to 2018. The dataset available in Kaggle has 3,675 objects and the following variables (Table 2.9):

- **country**: country name.
  Type: categorical.
  Values: 175 unique values.

- **continent**: continent to which the country belongs.
  Type: categorical.
  Values: {Africa, Americas, Asia, Europe, Oceania}.

- **year**: year to which the data belongs.
  Type: numerical (integer).
  Values: {1998 ... 2018}.

- **life_exp**: life expectancy.
  Type: numerical (float).
  Values: [32.5, 84.8].

- **hdi_index**: human development index (HDI).
  Type: numerical (float).
  Values: [0.26, 0.96].

- **co2_consump**: CO_2 emissions in tons per person.
  Type: numerical (float).
  Values: [0.02, 67.10].

- **gdp**: Gross Domestic Product (GDP) per capita in dollars.
  Type: numerical (float).
  Values: [238, 105,000], with missing values represented by NaN.

- **services**: % of service workers.
  Type: numerical (float).
  Values: [5.59, 88.5].

Sample question and hypothesis about the Gapminder dataset:

Question: How has the relationship between life expectancy and GDP per capita evolved over time across different countries?

Hypothesis: Generally, higher GDP per capita is associated with increased life expectancy, but the strength of the relationship may vary by region.

2.4.6 Naturalearth_lowres Dataset

The naturalearth_lowres dataset, available in the GeoPandas library, is a geospatial dataset that provides a low-resolution map of the world's landmasses and coastlines. It contains data about 177 countries and includes the following variables (Table 2.10):

TABLE 2.9 Gapminder Dataset Sample Available on Kaggle: First and Last Five Objects in the Dataset

Obj	Country	Continent	Year	life_exp	hdi_index	co2_consump	gdp	Services
0	Afghanistan	Asia	1998	53.3	0.344	0.052	NaN	24.4
1	Afghanistan	Asia	1999	54.7	0.348	0.040	NaN	24.6
2	Afghanistan	Asia	2000	54.7	0.350	0.037	NaN	24.7
3	Afghanistan	Asia	2001	54.8	0.353	0.038	NaN	24.7
4	Afghanistan	Asia	2002	55.5	0.384	0.047	333	25.6
...	...	...	...	...	...	...	...	...
3670	Zimbabwe	Africa	2014	58	0.547	0.881	1,440	25.4
3671	Zimbabwe	Africa	2015	58.6	0.553	0.881	1,450	25.7
3672	Zimbabwe	Africa	2016	59.2	0.558	0.771	1,430	26.1
3673	Zimbabwe	Africa	2017	59.9	0.563	0.845	1,480	26.6
3674	Zimbabwe	Africa	2018	60.6	0.569	0.850	1,510	27.2

The NaN in the table represents missing values.

- **pop_est**: estimated population count for each country.
    Type: numerical (integer).
    Range: [0 ... 1,439,324,000]

- **continent**: continent.
    Type: categorical.
    Values: {Africa, Antarctica, Asia, Europe, North America, South America}.

- **name**: official name of the country.
    Type: categorical.
    Values: 177 unique values in this variable.

- **iso_a3**: three-letter ISO code for the country.
    Type: categorical.
    Values: 177 unique values in this variable.

- **gdp_md_est**: estimated GDP in millions of US$ for the country.
    Type: numerical (float).
    Range: [0.002, 21,439,700]

- **geometry**: shapely geometry objects that represent the polygons of each country on the map using a variety of shapes.
    Type: geometry.
    Domain: {MultiPolygon, Polygon, GeometryCollection}. This variable also includes coordinates not shown here for simplicity.

Sample question and hypothesis about the Naturalearth dataset:

Question: What are the geographic patterns of population density across countries?

Hypothesis: Regions with higher population density are more likely to be concentrated near coastlines and major urban areas.

TABLE 2.10   Naturalearth_lowres Dataset Sample Available at the GeoPandas Library: First and Last Five Objects in the Dataset

Obj	pop_est	Continent	Name	iso_a3	gdp_md_est	Geometry[a]
0	889,953	Oceania	Fiji	FJI	5,496	MULTIPOLYGON
1	58,005,463	Africa	Tanzania	TZA	63,177	POLYGON
2	603,253	Africa	W. Sahara	ESH	907	POLYGON
3	37,589,262	America	Canada	CAN	1,736,425	MULTIPOLYGON
4	328,239,523	America	USA	USA	21,433,226	MULTIPOLYGON
...	...	...	...	...	...	...
172	6,944,975	Europe	Serbia	SRB	51,475	POLYGON
173	622,137	Europe	Montenegro	MNE	5,542	POLYGON
174	1,794,248	Europe	Kosovo	−99	7,926	POLYGON
175	1,394,973	America	Trinidad and Tobago	TTO	24,269	POLYGON
176	11,062,113	Africa	S. Sudan	SSD	11,998	POLYGON

[a] The coordinates were suppressed in order not to overload the table.

2.4.7 The Daily Delhi Climate Train Dataset

The Daily Climate Time-Series Data available at Kaggle[10] was developed in 2019 as part of a Data Analytics course assignment at PES University in Bangalore (Table 2.11). The dataset for training (DailyDelhiClimateTrain.csv) provides 1,462 rows of data from 1 January 2013 to 1 January 2017 in the city of Delhi, India, with the following variables:

- **meantemp**: average temperature in Delhi at a given day.
  Type: numerical (float).
  Range: [6, 38.71].

- **humidity**: daily air humidity.
  Type: numerical (float).
  Range: [13.43, 100].

TABLE 2.11   Daily Delhi Climate Dataset Sample: Five First and Last Objects in the Dataset

Date	meantemp	humidity	wind_speed	meanpressure
01/01/2013	10.000	84.500	0.000	1,015.667
01/02/2013	7.400	92.000	2.980	1,017.800
01/03/2013	7.167	87.000	4.633	1,018.667
01/04/2013	8.667	71.333	1.233	1,017.167
01/05/2013	6.000	86.833	3.700	1,016.500
...	...	...	...	...
12/28/2016	17.217	68.043	3.548	1,015.565
12/29/2016	15.238	87.857	6.000	1,016.905
12/30/2016	14.095	89.667	6.267	1,017.905
12/31/2016	15.053	87.000	7.325	1,016.100
01/01/2017	10.000	100.000	0.000	1,016.000

- **wind_speed**: daily wind speed in Delhi.
  Type: numerical (float).
  Range: [0, 42.22].

- **meanpressure**: average pressure in Delhi at a given day.
  Type: numerical (float).
  Range: [−3.04, 7,679.33].

Sample question and hypothesis about the Daily Delhi Climate dataset:

Question: How does air quality in Delhi vary with seasonal changes?

Hypothesis: Air quality deteriorates during winter months due to factors such as temperature inversion and increased pollution.

2.4.8 IMDb Movie Reviews Dataset

The Internet Movie Database (IMDb) is a dataset containing movie reviews written by users of the IMDb website,[11] one of the most popular sources of content about movies, TVs, and celebrities. There are different versions of this dataset available, with varying numbers of reviews, and it is a popular text corpus to study and assess natural language processing tasks and solutions. The version to be used here is the one available at the Natural Language Toolkit (NLTK) in Python, with 2,000 reviews classified into two categories: positive (pos) and negative (neg). These categories refer to the sentiment of the users in relation to the movie reviewed.

The following list shows the first five documents in the "movie_reviews" dataset available at NLTK. Only the first 80 words of each review were plotted, followed by a "…" sign. Also, the category of each review was included right after the review. The list shows the texts exactly as they are retrieved from NLTK.

```
Document 1:
plot: two teen couples go to a church party, drink and then drive. they
get into an accident. one of the guys dies, but his girlfriend
continues to see him in her life, and has nightmares. what's the deal?
watch the movie and " sorta " find out . . . critique : a mind - fuck
movie for the teen generation that touches on a very cool idea , ...
Category: neg
```

```
Document 2:
the happy bastard's quick movie review damn that y2k bug. it's got
a head start in this movie starring jamie lee curtis and another
baldwin brother ( william this time ) in a story regarding a crew
of a tugboat that comes across a deserted russian tech ship that
has a strangeness to it when they kick the power back on. little
do they know the power within . . . going for the ...
Category: neg
```

Document 3:
it is movies like these that make a jaded movie viewer thankful
for the invention of the timex indiglo watch. based on the late
1960's television show by the same name, the mod squad tells the
tale of three reformed criminals under the employ of the police
to go undercover. however , things go wrong as evidence gets
stolen and they are immediately under suspicion. of course, the
ads make it seem like ...
Category: neg

Document 4:
" quest for camelot " is warner bros. ' first feature - length ,
fully - animated attempt to steal clout from disney's cartoon
empire , but the mouse has no reason to be worried. the only other
recent challenger to their throne was last fall's promising, if
flawed, 20th century fox production " anastasia , " but disney's "
hercules, " with its lively cast and colorful palate ...
Category: neg

Document 5:
synopsis : a mentally unstable man undergoing psychotherapy saves
a boy from a potentially fatal accident and then falls in love
with the boy's mother , a fledgling restauranteur. unsuccessfully
attempting to gain the woman's favor , he takes pictures of her
and kills a number of people in his way. comments : stalked is
yet another in a seemingly endless string of spurned - psychos -
getting - their - revenge type movies ...
Category: neg

Sample question and hypothesis about the IMDb Movies Review dataset:

Question: What factors contribute to the success of movies, as indicated by user reviews and ratings?

Hypothesis: Movies with higher budgets, popular actors, and positive critical reviews are more likely to receive higher user ratings.

2.4.9 Zachary's Karate Club Dataset

Wayne W. Zachary (1977)[12] used a dataset from a university-based karate club to study an information flow model in small groups. The karate club was observed over 3 years, during which the club maintained between 50 and 100 members. Each member is represented by a node in a network, and their interactions are the network connections. The resultant network contains 34 members and the links between those pairs of members who interacted with each other. At the beginning of the experiment, there was a divergence between the club president and the karate instructor over the karate class prices, and this promoted a clustering of members around each of them.

Table 2.12 shows the *adjacency matrix* of Zachary's Karate Club dataset. This is a mathematical representation of the relationships between various objects and serves to indicate which objects are connected with which other objects. It is commonly used to represent graphs (see Section 6.3.1), where each row and column corresponds to a node (object) in the graph, and the values in the table indicate if there is (1) or there is not (0) a connection between each pair of nodes.

To illustrate, Figure 2.5 shows two different network (graph) representations of Zachary's Karate Club dataset. The first one, Figure 2.5a, is a circular representation, and the second one, Figure 2.5b, has a partially random architecture. By looking at Table 2.12 and

TABLE 2.12 Adjacency Matrix of the Zachary's Karate Club Dataset

```
0 1 1 1 1 1 1 1 0 1 1 1 1 0 0 0 1 0 1 0 1 0 0 0 0 0 0 0 0 0 1 0 0
1 0 1 1 0 0 0 1 0 0 0 0 0 1 0 0 0 1 0 1 0 1 0 1 0 0 0 0 0 1 0 0 0
1 1 0 1 0 0 0 1 1 1 0 0 0 1 0 0 0 0 0 0 0 0 0 0 0 0 1 1 0 0 0 1 0
1 1 1 0 0 0 0 1 0 0 0 0 1 1 0 0 0 0 0 0 0 0 0 0 0 0 0 0 0 0 0 0 0
1 0 0 0 0 0 1 0 0 0 1 0 0 0 0 0 0 0 0 0 0 0 0 0 0 0 0 0 0 0 0 0 0
1 0 0 0 0 0 1 0 0 0 1 0 0 0 0 0 1 0 0 0 0 0 0 0 0 0 0 0 0 0 0 0 0
1 0 0 0 1 1 0 0 0 0 0 0 0 0 0 0 1 0 0 0 0 0 0 0 0 0 0 0 0 0 0 0 0
1 1 1 1 0 0 0 0 0 0 0 0 0 0 0 0 0 0 0 0 0 0 0 0 0 0 0 0 0 0 0 0 0
1 0 1 0 0 0 0 0 0 0 0 0 0 0 0 0 0 0 0 0 0 0 0 0 0 0 0 0 0 0 1 0 1 1
0 0 1 0 0 0 0 0 0 0 0 0 0 0 0 0 0 0 0 0 0 0 0 0 0 0 0 0 0 0 0 0 0 1
1 0 0 0 1 1 0 0 0 0 0 0 0 0 0 0 0 0 0 0 0 0 0 0 0 0 0 0 0 0 0 0 0
1 0 0 0 0 0 0 0 0 0 0 0 0 0 0 0 0 0 0 0 0 0 0 0 0 0 0 0 0 0 0 0 0
1 0 0 1 0 0 0 0 0 0 0 0 0 0 0 0 0 0 0 0 0 0 0 0 0 0 0 0 0 0 0 0 0
1 1 1 1 0 0 0 0 0 0 0 0 0 0 0 0 0 0 0 0 0 0 0 0 0 0 0 0 0 0 0 0 1
0 0 0 0 0 0 0 0 0 0 0 0 0 0 0 0 0 0 0 0 0 0 0 0 0 0 0 0 0 0 0 0 1 1
0 0 0 0 0 0 0 0 0 0 0 0 0 0 0 0 0 0 0 0 0 0 0 0 0 0 0 0 0 0 0 0 1 1
0 0 0 0 0 1 1 0 0 0 0 0 0 0 0 0 0 0 0 0 0 0 0 0 0 0 0 0 0 0 0 0 0
1 1 0 0 0 0 0 0 0 0 0 0 0 0 0 0 0 0 0 0 0 0 0 0 0 0 0 0 0 0 0 0 0
0 0 0 0 0 0 0 0 0 0 0 0 0 0 0 0 0 0 0 0 0 0 0 0 0 0 0 0 0 0 0 0 1 1
1 1 0 0 0 0 0 0 0 0 0 0 0 0 0 0 0 0 0 0 0 0 0 0 0 0 0 0 0 0 0 0 0 1
0 0 0 0 0 0 0 0 0 0 0 0 0 0 0 0 0 0 0 0 0 0 0 0 0 0 0 0 0 0 0 0 1 1
1 1 0 0 0 0 0 0 0 0 0 0 0 0 0 0 0 0 0 0 0 0 0 0 0 0 0 0 0 0 0 0 0
0 0 0 0 0 0 0 0 0 0 0 0 0 0 0 0 0 0 0 0 0 0 0 0 0 0 0 0 0 0 0 0 1 1
0 0 0 0 0 0 0 0 0 0 0 0 0 0 0 0 0 0 0 0 0 0 0 0 0 1 0 1 0 1 0 0 1 1
0 0 0 0 0 0 0 0 0 0 0 0 0 0 0 0 0 0 0 0 0 0 0 0 0 1 0 1 0 0 0 1 0 0
0 0 0 0 0 0 0 0 0 0 0 0 0 0 0 0 0 0 0 0 0 0 0 1 1 0 0 0 0 0 0 1 0 0
0 0 0 0 0 0 0 0 0 0 0 0 0 0 0 0 0 0 0 0 0 0 0 0 0 0 0 0 0 0 1 0 0 1
0 0 1 0 0 0 0 0 0 0 0 0 0 0 0 0 0 0 0 0 0 0 0 1 1 0 0 0 0 0 0 0 0 1
0 0 1 0 0 0 0 0 0 0 0 0 0 0 0 0 0 0 0 0 0 0 0 0 0 0 0 0 0 0 0 1 0 1
0 0 0 0 0 0 0 0 0 0 0 0 0 0 0 0 0 0 0 0 0 0 0 1 0 0 1 0 0 0 0 0 1 1
0 1 0 0 0 0 0 0 1 0 0 0 0 0 0 0 0 0 0 0 0 0 0 0 0 0 0 0 0 0 0 0 1 1
1 0 0 0 0 0 0 0 0 0 0 0 0 0 0 0 0 0 0 0 0 0 0 1 1 0 0 1 0 0 0 0 1 1
0 0 1 0 0 0 0 0 1 0 0 0 0 0 1 1 0 0 1 0 1 0 1 1 0 0 0 0 0 1 1 1 0 1
0 0 0 0 0 0 0 0 1 1 0 0 0 1 1 1 0 0 1 1 1 0 1 1 0 0 1 1 1 1 1 1 1 0
```

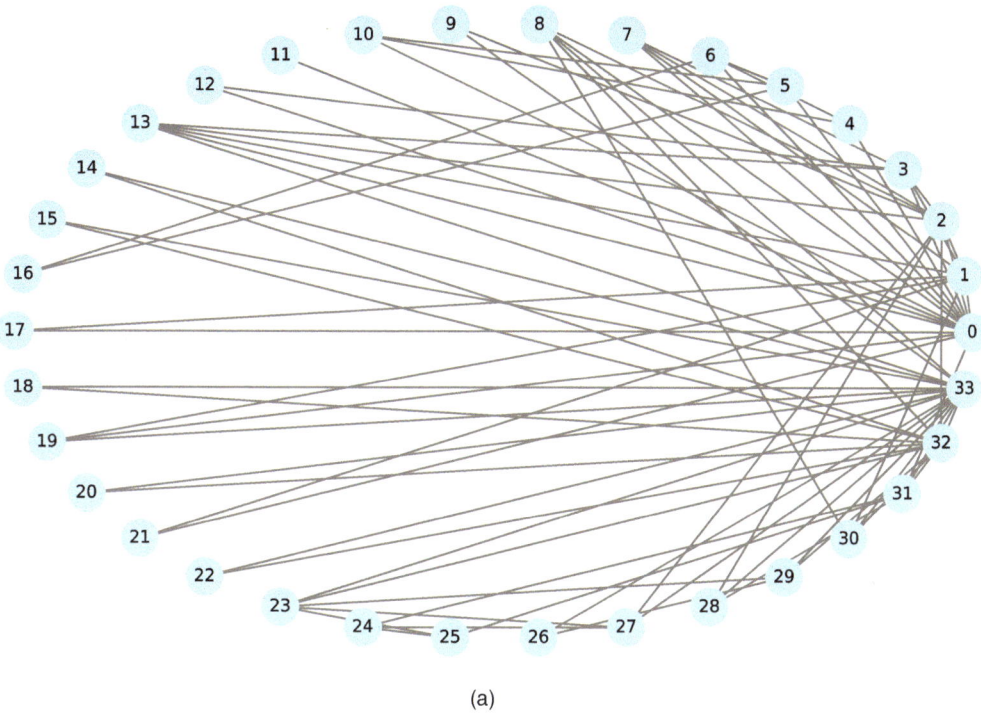

(a)

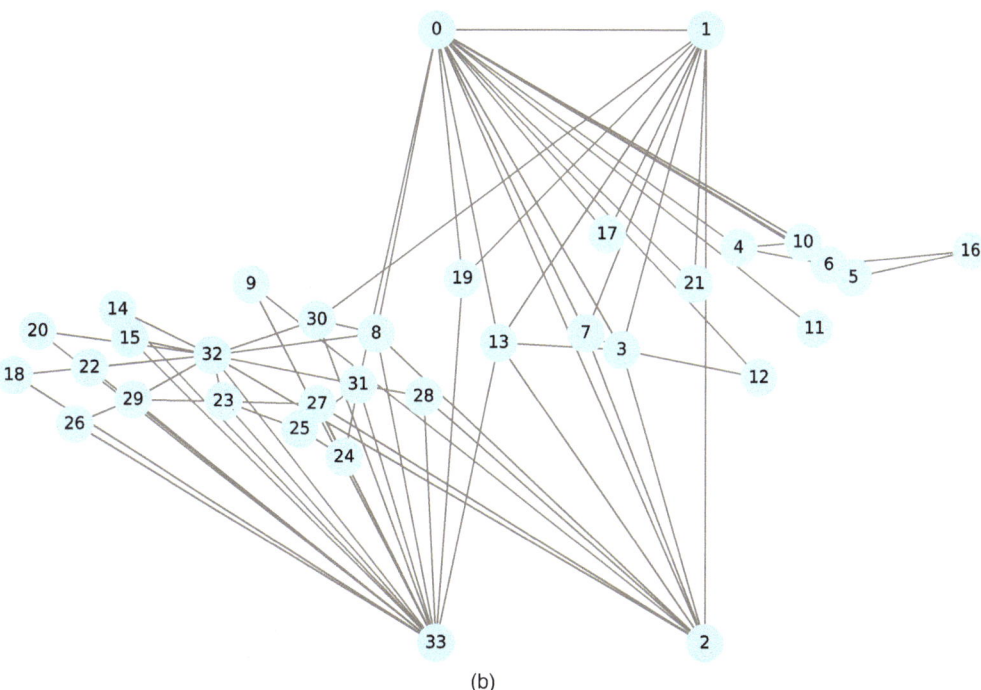

(b)

FIGURE 2.5 Network representations of the Zachary's Karate Club data. (a) Circular representation. (b) Partially random representation.

Figure 2.5b, it is possible to observe that node 0 is connected with nodes 1, 2, 3, 4, 5, 6, 7, 8, 10, 11, 12, 13, 17, 19, 21, and 31. A similar analysis can be performed for all network nodes. The exploratory analysis of this dataset will be presented in Section 6.3.

Sample question and hypothesis about the Zachary's Karate Club dataset:

Question: What social network patterns can be observed within Zachary's karate club?

Hypothesis: The network structure may reveal cliques or groups within the karate club, impacting social dynamics.

2.5 DATA PREPARATION

Raw data, that is, source or primary data that has not been prepared or processed for being used, is the one originally input in a database by operators, sensors, or any person or device. As such, it may contain several problems that make their analysis difficult and subject to errors and misinterpretations. The main problems that can be found are data overload (excessive number of objects or variables), incompleteness (missing objects, values, or variables), inconsistency (domain violations and discrepancies), and noise.

2.5.1 Sampling

In statistics, a *population* corresponds to the whole set of items (e.g., individuals, fruits, and parts) in a given context. For example, the population of a country is the total number of people living in that country. A *sample* is a subset of the population that can be obtained in many ways. For example, a sample may be *random*, meaning that the individuals in the sample were chosen by chance, or obtained through *group sampling methods*, such as selecting people older than 55 years. Sampling may serve to reduce the amount of data and the complexity of the analysis or to select a specific subset of items.

The standard sampling steps are: (i) define the sample size or the subset characteristic, (ii) choose the sampling method, and (iii) do the sampling. The simplest and most useful sampling methods are (de Castro & Ferrari, 2016):

- **Random sampling with replacement**: this method allows the repeated selection of objects from the original set of objects into the subset. It works like a *copy* method in a text editor; it is possible to create as many copies of an object as you want in the sample.

- **Random sampling without replacement**: after one object is selected from the original set to compose the sample, it is not allowed to be selected again. It works like a *cut* method in a text editor; that is, once an object is selected to compose the sample, it is moved to the sample and cannot be selected again.

- **Systematic sampling**: it involves the application of one method that will extract a specific sample from the dataset at a regular interval. For example, the objects can be ordered based on one criterion, and the first *n* objects are selected, or the odd objects are selected.

- **Group sampling**: this sampling is different from the systematic in the sense that it selects one specific group or cluster of objects, and the groups have a contextual meaning. To illustrate, a group of people may be defined by gender, age, stature, income, level of education, etc., and a group of items may be defined by size, weight, color, price, etc.

- **Stratified sampling**: when the dataset contains groups, the stratified sampling method ensures that the proportions of objects in each group are maintained after sampling. For example, assume a group of 50 women and 30 men and a stratified sampling of 10% of the people; then, five women and three men will be selected to compose the sample.

To illustrate the different sampling methods, consider the example presented in T2able 2.13

TABLE 2.13   Some Rows of the Mammographic Dataset and the Different Sampling Methods

Row #	BI-RADS	Age	Shape	Margin	Density	Severity
			(a) Illustrative Dataset			
1	5	67	Lobular	Spiculated	Low	Malignant
2	4	43	Round	Circumscribed	?	Malignant
3	5	58	Irregular	Spiculated	Low	Malignant
4	4	28	Round	Circumscribed	Low	Benign
5	5	74	Round	Spiculated	?	Malignant
6	4	47	Oval	Circumscribed	Low	Benign
7	4	56	Irregular	Spiculated	Low	Malignant
8	4	64	Irregular	Spiculated	Low	Benign
9	5	66	Irregular	Spiculated	Low	Malignant
10	4	62	Lobular	Obscured	Low	Benign
			(b) Sampling with Replacement. Note That Some Rows Were Sampled More Than Once, and the Sample Size Is 50% of the Original Data			
1	5	67	Lobular	Spiculated	Low	Malignant
4	4	28	Round	Circumscribed	Low	Benign
4	4	28	Round	Circumscribed	Low	Benign
4	4	28	Round	Circumscribed	Low	Benign
1	5	67	Lobular	Spiculated	Low	Malignant
			(c) Sampling without Replacement. Note That No Row Was Sampled More Than Once, and the Sample Size Is 50% of the Original Data			
2	4	43	Round	Circumscribed	?	Malignant
4	4	28	Round	Circumscribed	Low	Benign
5	5	74	Round	Spiculated	?	Malignant
6	4	47	Oval	Circumscribed	Low	Benign
10	4	62	Lobular	Obscured	Low	Benign

(*Continued*)

TABLE 2.13   Some Rows of the Mammographic Dataset and the Different Sampling Methods

Row #	BI-RADS	Age	Shape	Margin	Density	Severity
(d) Systematic Sampling: Odd Objects (Rows). Note That Only the Odd Rows (Objects) Were Selected, and the Sample Size Is 50% of the Original Data						
1	5	67	Lobular	Spiculated	Low	Malignant
3	5	58	Irregular	Spiculated	Low	Malignant
5	5	74	Round	Spiculated	?	Malignant
7	4	56	Irregular	Spiculated	Low	Malignant
9	5	66	Irregular	Spiculated	Low	Malignant
(e) Group Sampling: Class Severity = Benign. Note That Only the Objects of Class Benign Were Sampled						
4	4	28	Round	Circumscribed	Low	Benign
6	4	47	Oval	Circumscribed	Low	Benign
8	4	64	Irregular	Spiculated	Low	Benign
10	4	62	Lobular	Obscured	Low	Benign
(f) Stratified Sampling: 50%. Note That Half of the Objects in Each Class Were Sampled						
1	5	67	Lobular	Spiculated	Low	Malignant
3	5	58	Irregular	Spiculated	Low	Malignant
6	4	47	Oval	Circumscribed	Low	Benign
9	5	66	Irregular	Spiculated	Low	Malignant
10	4	62	Lobular	Obscured	Low	Benign

2.5.2 Missing Values

A dataset is said to be *incomplete* when there are objects, variables, or values missing. To identify a missing object, it is first necessary to acknowledge its existence. For example, when taking the attendance of the students in a class, the teacher takes note of the presence or absence of the students. In this case, an absence means that the teacher knows the student is part of the class but is not present. The same is true for variables; to identify their absence, it is necessary to know they exist. For example, earlier in this chapter, we used the BMI to explain the concepts of dependent and independent variables. In this case, if either the weight or the height is missing, it is not possible to calculate the BMI, which means that the variable weight or height is missing.

The case of missing values is different from the previous ones because a missing value is simply the lack of input in a variable of a given object, which, in principle, means an empty cell in a table. Although missing values are directly identified in a dataset, they can be represented in different ways, like using a "?" or a "NaN". Examples of datasets with missing values were presented in Table 2.5 (Mammographic dataset) and Table 2.9 (Gapminder dataset).

Missing values can be the result of lack of input, failure in a sensor, failure in a copying process, or another issue. Depending on the data, they may have a major impact on the data analysis process, significantly affecting summary measures and data visualization. Therefore, being able to identify and solve missing value problems is of primary importance in data analysis.

The insertion of a value in the place of a missing one is called *imputation* or *replacement*, and it basically consists of estimating the value that should be placed in the empty cell if it were input correctly by the standard input method. Some methods to impute or replace missing values include ignoring the object, manually inputting the missing values, using a global constant, inputting based on object similarity, and using the central tendency measures (de Castro & Ferrari, 2016).

2.5.2.1 Ignore the Object

The simplest and most common way of dealing with missing values is to remove the object with the missing value from the dataset. However, it is important to acknowledge that removing an object from a dataset implies eliminating the information available in all the other variables of that object. If you are performing a descriptive analysis of a single variable, this may not have a major impact, as a missing value may have the same meaning as a missing object in a dataset.

2.5.2.2 Manually Inputting Missing Values

This method consists of heuristically choosing one value to impute for a given variable, for example, the most frequent or most probable value. If the analysis is over a single nominal variable, then one can look at the set of values and select the most frequent one.

2.5.2.3 Global Constant Imputation

This method corresponds to replacing all missing values of a certain variable with a single constant value.

2.5.2.4 Hot-Deck Imputation

This method can only be used with datasets that have more than one variable, because it works by inputting a value in a variable based on the value of the same variable of a similar object. In this case, it is first necessary to determine which object is similar to the one with a missing value, and this is performed by taking into account the other variables of the object.

2.5.2.5 Central Tendency Measure of the Variable

This method is also a common choice in the literature and works by calculating one of the central tendency measures of a variable (e.g., mean, mode, median, etc.) and using this value to replace the missing one.

2.5.2.6 Central Tendency Measure of the Class Variable

This method is similar to the previous one but, if available, uses the class or group label of the object to calculate the central tendency measure of that specific object and then replaces the missing value.

2.5.3 Normalization

The goal of exploratory data analysis is to summarize the data, to investigate the shape and patterns of variables, and to visualize them. In all these situations, it is important to maintain the variables in their original ranges so that we can understand the real meanings of the trends and values observed. However, in EDA, there are situations, mainly when one variable has to be analyzed and compared to others, where we need to standardize the ranges of variables. One way of doing it is by *normalizing* the variables such that all of them are within the same range of values or are transformed using the same reference. This process is also called features scaling.

2.5.3.1 Min-Max Normalization

The simplest and most common normalization method changes the values of a variable, placing them in a range [*nmin*, *nmax*], where *nmin* and *nmax* are predefined values that will set the new variable range:

$$x_i' = \frac{x_i - min}{max - min}\left(nmax - nmin\right) + nmin, \tag{2.1}$$

where x_i is the *i*-th value of variable *x*, x_i' is its value after normalization, *min* is the minimal value of *x*, *max* is its maximal value, and *nmin* and *nmax* are the new minimal and maximal values, respectively.

In most cases, *nmin* is chosen to be 0, and *nmax* is chosen to be 1, meaning that the new minimum value of variable *x* will be 0, while its maximum value will be 1. By performing this type of normalization, it is possible to directly compare the distributions of variables with significantly different units of measure.

2.5.3.2 z-Score Normalization

Section 3.2.5 will present *relative position measures*, that is, measures that allow the assessment of where a given value is located in relation to other(s). The *z-score normalization*, also known as *zero mean normalization*, normalizes the values of a variable based on the variable mean (*mean*) and standard deviation (σ):

$$x_i' = \frac{x_i - mean}{\sigma}, \tag{2.2}$$

where x_i is the *i*-th value of variable *x*, and x_i' is its value after normalization.

2.6 EXERCISES

2.6.1 Research Topics and Questions

1. Discuss the ethical considerations surrounding data ownership. Who should own data, especially when it is collected from the public? What responsibilities do data owners have?

2. Explore the philosophical dimensions of sampling in data preparation. Discuss the role of sampling in shaping our perception of the whole, the potential for bias, and the philosophical implications of generalizing from a subset to the entire population.

3. Stock market data can be both time series and data streams, and the distinction lies in how the data is observed and processed. Explain when stock market data is seen as a time series and when it is seen as a data stream.

4. Prepare a data dictionary for the following datasets: Mammographic, Forest Fires, Auto MPG, Gapminder, and Naturalearth_lowres.

5. How does the nature of data preparation, including sampling, missing value han-dling, and normalization, affect the reliability and accuracy of insights derived from data analysis?

6. How do the various aspects of data description and preparation covered in this chapter contribute to the foundation of successful data analysis and decision-making processes?

7. Choose two datasets from the book (Section 2.4) and classify the data based on the aspects mentioned in the chapter: structure, nature, type, time variability, dimen-sionality, and ownership. Explain your classifications.

2.6.2 Quizzes

1. What does the term "data" encompass?

   a. Information with context.

   b. Isolated pieces of information.

   c. Processed insights.

   d. Knowledge extraction.

2. Which of the following is NOT an example of data?

   a. An image.

   b. A graph.

   c. An insight.

   d. A word.

3. What is the outcome of using information to draw conclusions or make decisions?

   a. Data.

   b. Processed data.

   c. Context.

   d. Knowledge.

4. Which type of data is organized in a specific structure like a table or a spreadsheet?

   a. Semi-structured data.

   b. Unstructured data.

   c. Text data.

   d. Structured data.

5. What is a key characteristic of structured data?

    a. It lacks any kind of organization.

    b. It is best managed by NoSQL databases.

    c. It requires a data model for organization.

    d. It is often found in e-mails and XML files.

6. Which of the following is an example of unstructured data?

    a. A spreadsheet with sales figures.

    b. A web page with embedded videos.

    c. A database table with customer names.

    d. An XML file with metadata.

7. What distinguishes quantitative data from qualitative data?

    a. Both are structured.

    b. Quantitative data is measurable, while qualitative data is not.

    c. Qualitative data is numeric, while quantitative data is categorical.

    d. Qualitative data can be processed mathematically, while quantitative data cannot.

8. How is time variability different for static data and dynamic data?

    a. Static data changes over time, while dynamic data remains constant.

    b. Static data is stored in non-relational databases, while dynamic data is stored in relational databases.

    c. Static data is fixed and unchanging, while dynamic data is updated over time.

    d. Static data has more dimensions than dynamic data.

9. What are the main problems associated with raw data that make their analysis challenging?

    a. Organization and labeling issues.

    b. Noise and inconsistencies.

    c. Lack of metadata and sampling.

    d. Excessive domain knowledge.

10. What is the purpose of sampling in data analysis?

    a. To increase the complexity of the analysis.

    b. To expand the population size.

    c. To reduce the amount of data and analysis complexity.

    d. To eliminate outliers from the dataset.

11. Which sampling method allows repeated selection of objects from the original set into the subset?

    a. Systematic sampling.

    b. Group sampling.

    c. Random sampling with replacement.

    d. Random sampling without replacement.

12. In the context of missing values, what does "imputation" refer to?

    a. Removing an object from the dataset.

    b. Reducing the dataset dimensionality.

    c. Replacing a missing value with an estimated value.

    d. Ignoring the object's contribution to analysis.

13. What is a disadvantage of using the "Ignore the Object" method for handling missing values?

    a. It is computationally intensive.

    b. It may remove valuable information.

    c. It requires expert domain knowledge.

    d. It leads to overfitting.

14. What does normalization aim to achieve in data analysis?

    a. To exchange the original data values for smaller values.

    b. To expand the dataset size.

    c. To visualize data in its original form.

    d. To standardize the ranges of variables.

15. Which normalization method places variable values in a range between a *min* and a *max* value?

    a. Min-Max normalization.

    b. *z*-Score normalization.

    c. Group sampling.

    d. Central tendency measure.

2.6.3 Computational Exercises

1. For the Gapminder dataset, use the Pandas library to identify and count missing values in variable "gdp". Implement two or more of the missing value imputation techniques discussed in the chapter and compare the resulting effects on dataset metrics.

2. Normalize all four attributes of the Iris dataset using the methods presented in the chapter and compare the normalization range of each method.

3. Choose a dataset and simulate a data preparation workflow. Apply sampling, handle missing values, and perform normalization on the dataset. Document each step and explain how it contributes to the analysis process.

NOTES

1 https://archive.ics.uci.edu/
2 https://www.kaggle.com/
3 https://github.com/lndecastro/
4 https://archive.ics.uci.edu/ml/datasets/Mammographic+Mass
5 https://archive.ics.uci.edu/ml/datasets/forest+fires
6 https://archive.ics.uci.edu/ml/datasets/iris
7 https://archive.ics.uci.edu/ml/datasets/auto+mpg
8 https://www.kaggle.com/datasets/albertovidalrod/gapminder-dataset
9 https://www.gapminder.org/
10 https://www.kaggle.com/datasets/sumanthvrao/daily-climate-time-series-data
11 https://www.imdb.com/
12 https://networkrepository.com/ucidata-zachary.php

## CHAPTER 3

Descriptive Analysis

"Without data, you're just another person with an opinion."

– W. Edwards Deming

When faced with a data set for analysis, one of the first steps involves the understanding of the data set structure, its variables, and their characterization. This information will allow you to summarize the data and extract valuable insights for informed decision-making. To illustrate, assume a data set containing bank account information such as account holder ID, address, age, marital status (single, married, divorced, etc.), level of education (primary, secondary, post-secondary, graduate, etc.), type of account (checking, savings, business, etc.), balance, income, loans, default (yes, no), place of work, and credit score.

An initial *descriptive analysis* will allow you to find the distribution, average, and variability of each variable, in addition to the relative position of clients and potential associations among variables. For instance, it is possible to know the average age, income, loans, defaults, and credit score; the most common marital status, level of education, type of account, and place of work; how all these variables are distributed and vary; and the associations among them.

Altogether, the type of analysis described above forms what is known as *descriptive data analysis*, an area imported from *descriptive statistics* (Peck et al., 2008; OpenStax, 2013; Triola, 2017) that involves a range of methods and techniques capable of summarizing, organizing, characterizing, and describing data in numerical terms. Therefore, descriptive data analysis offers insights about the data that help us monitor the status of a given system, process, or phenomenon, and it is used as a strategic tool to start the analytical process.

Descriptive data analysis differs from data analytics in the sense that it does not involve *generalizing* beyond the data available. *Generalization* is the capability of responding appropriately to unknown data, which usually requires building a model or a solution that is capable of extrapolating what it learned from a given set of data to these new, unknown data samples. For example, by training a system to detect fraud in credit card transactions,

DOI: 10.1201/9781003570691-3

it is expected to be able to detect future, novel (those that have not been used for training the system) fraudulent transactions.

The descriptive data analysis methods are divided into three main groups:

1. **Frequency distributions**: series used to organize the values of a variable in groups or classes, so that one can observe its distribution. This is a powerful tool to observe the range of a variable, its shape, center, spread, and the presence of outliers. For example, if we plot a graph with the age of all college students, we may find an approximately bell-shaped curve.

2. **Summary measures**: provide a numerical synthesis of the data, allowing the observation of central tendencies (typical values), variability (dispersion), and form (shape). Using the same example as above, the summary measures will tell us the average age of the students, their level of variability around this average, and how the data is distributed.

3. **Measures of association**: association measures are applied to two or more variables, indicating their interdependence. Although there may be unassociated variables, it is common to have positive or negative associations between variables. For example, an increase in height normally implies an increase in weight (positive association between height and weight), while the older you get, the less agile you become (negative association between age and agility).

In summary, these methods provide answers to the following questions:

1. How are the variables distributed?

2. What are the typical values of each variable?

3. What is the dispersion (variability) of each variable?

4. What is the shape of the variable's distribution?

5. What is the type and level of association among variables?

This chapter introduces descriptive data analysis as the first step of our journey into exploratory data analysis. It is important to remark that the descriptive analysis comes hand in hand with data visualization, and thus, this chapter uses some of the *dataviz* tools that will be described in detail in the next chapter.

3.1 DISTRIBUTIONS

A *frequency distribution* is a listing that specifies all possible values, categories, or intervals of a given variable and quantifies its frequency, that is, the number of times each value occurs. Frequency distributions are usually visualized using a *frequency table* or by plotting specific *charts*, depending on the variable type. For instance, the frequency distribution of continuous variables can be observed using histograms, while the frequency distribution of nominal variables is usually observed using a pie or a bar chart.

TABLE 3.1   Frequency Table and Pie Chart of Variable "Shape" in the Mammographic Dataset

Shape	Absolute Frequency	Relative Frequency (%)	Cumulative Frequency (%)	
Irregular	400	41.62	41.62	
Round	224	23.31	64.93	
Oval	211	21.96	86.89	
Lobular	95	9.89	96.77	
?	31	3.23	100.00	

To illustrate, consider the mammographic dataset presented in Table 3.1. Variable "Shape" can assume the values "Irregular", "Round", "Oval", and "Lobular", and there are also missing values represented by a question mark "?". Table 3.1 shows the frequency table of variable "Shape" with the *absolute frequency* (count), *relative frequency*, and *cumulative frequency* of each of its possible values, including the missing values, and a pie chart with its relative frequency. The relative frequency is calculated by dividing the absolute frequency by the total number of objects (samples). The cumulative frequency is obtained by iteratively adding the current frequency value with its predecessor value, and the last value is the sum of all frequencies. The cumulative frequency can be calculated from the absolute or relative frequency, and, in the latter case, it will sum up to 100%.

Code 3.1 contains a script to calculate the absolute, relative, and cumulative frequency distributions for variable "Shape" of the mammographic dataset. In this script, we used the `Series()` method in `Pandas` to generate a one-dimensional array with the data in variable "Shape". Then, we calculated the absolute, relative, and cumulative frequencies, generated a dataframe, and printed and plotted the pie chart, `pie()` from `Matplotlib`, with the relative frequency distribution of variable "Shape".

CODE 3.1   Script to generate the frequency table and plot a pie chart for variable "Shape" of the mammographic dataset.

```
# Determining the frequency distribution, frequency table and pie chart
# of variable 'Shape' in the Mammographic dataset

import pandas as pd
import matplotlib.pyplot as plt
import seaborn as sns
from ucimlrepo import fetch_ucirepo

# fetch dataset (https://archive.ics.uci.edu/dataset/161/mammographic+mass)
dmammo = fetch_ucirepo(id=161)["data"]["original"]

SShape = pd.Series(dmammo['Shape'])
ftable = SShape.value_counts(dropna=False) # Generate the frequency table
rftable = ftable / len(SShape) * 100  # Relative frequency
cftable = ftable.cumsum() / len(SShape) * 100  # Cumulative frequency
df = pd.DataFrame({
    "Frequency": ftable.to_list(),
```

```
    "Relative Frequency": rftable.to_list(),
    "Cumulative Frequency": cftable.to_list()})

placeholders = {1.0:'Round', 2.0:'Oval', 3.0:'Lobular', 4.0:'Irregular'}
ftable.index = ftable.index.map(lambda x: placeholders.get(x, '?'))

print(df)
fig, figftable = plt.subplots()

# Using a color palette with different levels of the same color
colors = sns.color_palette("Blues", len(ftable)* 3)[::-3]

# Plotting the pie chart with the new color palette
figftable.pie(
    ftable.to_list(), labels=ftable.index.to_list(),
    autopct='%1.2f%%', colors=colors)
```

By looking at all the variables in the mammographic dataset, it is possible to note that they are either nominal or discrete. The nominal variables have a well-defined set of categories that they can assume, while the numeric variables will require the definition of *ranges* to calculate the frequency distributions of objects within those ranges. To illustrate how to build the frequency table of numeric variables (quantitative data), consider the variable temperature ("temp") from the Forest Fires dataset presented in Table 2.6.

To build the frequency distribution for quantitative data, the following steps are necessary:

1. Define the desired number of *bins*, that is, the number of classes (intervals or categories) that will be used to divide the data.

2. Determine the amplitude of each class.

3. Determine the inferior limit of the distribution.

4. Determine the inferior limit of each class (the inferior limit of the previous class plus the class amplitude).

5. Determine the superior limit of each class.

6. Assign the label of each category.

In the example shown in Table 3.2, the number of bins chosen was *nbins* = 10, and the inferior limit of the distribution was chosen as 0°C minus the amplitude of the bin, which was determined by subtracting the maximum temperature from the minimum temperature and then dividing by *nbins*. After that, the inferior limit of each class is calculated by adding the class amplitude with the inferior limit of the previous class and continuing until all bins have been determined.

After the frequency table has been built, it is possible to represent the frequency distribution using a graph called a *histogram*. To build the histogram, it is just necessary to plot the frequencies (Count) on the vertical axis and the class intervals (bins) on the horizontal axis, as illustrated in Figure 3.1.

TABLE 3.2   Frequency Table for Variable "temp" of the Forest Fires
Dataset

Bins	Absolute Frequency	Relative Frequency	Cumulative Frequency (%)
(0.0, 3.33]	1	0.19	0.19
(3.33, 6.66]	20	3.87	4.06
(6.66, 9.99]	15	2.90	6.96
(9.99, 13.32]	47	9.09	16.05
(13.32, 16.65]	75	14.51	55.32
(16.65, 19.98]	128	24.76	40.81
(19.98, 23.31]	119	23.02	78.34
(23.31, 26.64]	69	13.35	91.68
(26.64, 29.97]	30	5.80	97.49
(29.97, 33.3]	13	2.51	100.00

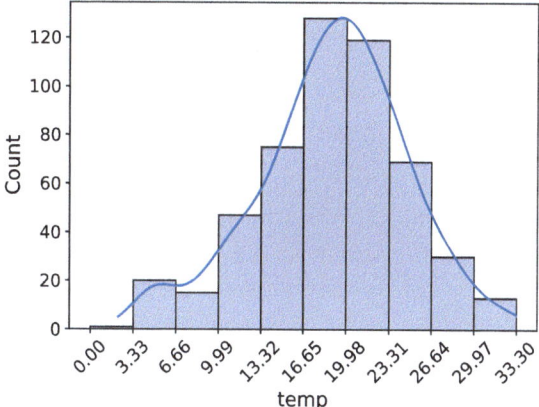

FIGURE 3.1   Histogram for the variable "temp" of the Forest Fires dataset.

Code 3.2 presents a script to calculate and print the frequency table for a numeric variable (quantitative data) using the method `Series()` in `Pandas`. The script allows setting the number of bins (*nbins*), as well as the inferior and superior limits of the histogram, and then builds and plots the dataframe with the bins and their respective frequencies.

CODE 3.2   Script to generate the frequency table and plot a histogram for variable "temp" of the Forest Fires dataset.

```
# Determining the frequency distribution, frequency table and histogram
# of continuous variables in the Forest Fires dataset

import pandas as pd
import numpy as np
import matplotlib.pyplot as plt
import seaborn as sns
from ucimlrepo import fetch_ucirepo
```

```
# fetch dataset (https://archive.ics.uci.edu/ml/datasets/forest+fires)
dforest = fetch_ucirepo(id=162)["data"]["original"]

var = "temp" # Choose the target variable
SShape = pd.Series(dforest[var])
nbins = 10; inflimit = 0; suplimit = max(SShape)
ampl = (suplimit - inflimit) / nbins

# Define the range of the variable and bin size
fbins = np.arange(0, suplimit + ampl, ampl)

# The pandas.cut function groups data into bins and counts frequency
ftable = pd.cut(SShape, fbins).value_counts()   # Absolute frequency
rftable = ftable / len(SShape) * 100   # Relative frequency
cftable = ftable.cumsum() / len(SShape) * 100   # Cumulative frequency
df = pd.DataFrame({"Bins": ftable.index.to_list(),
                   "Frequency": ftable.to_list(),
                   "Relative Frequency": rftable.to_list(),
                   "Cumulative Frequency": cftable.to_list(),})
print(df)
plt.xticks(fbins)
sns.histplot(dforest, x=var, bins=fbins, kde=True)
```

3.1.1 Shapes of Distributions

Distributions may have different *shapes*, indicating their range and the pattern of the data distribution. Histograms are particularly important for the analysis of data distributions because they allow the visualization of the overall distribution pattern, shape, center, and spread. Also, histograms allow the identification of *outliers*, that is, values or ranges that occur infrequently or that significantly differ from others.

To present and discuss the shapes of distributions, consider the Forest Fires dataset summarized in Table 2.6. Figure 3.2 displays the histogram and *density curves* for the following variables in the dataset: "month", "day", "FFMC", "DMC", "DC", "ISI", "RH", and "wind". It is usual to display the pattern of a variable with many values with a *smooth curve* called a density curve, whose role is to describe the overall pattern of a distribution. The density curves over the histograms were generated by a *kernel density estimation* that approximates the underlying *probability density function* that generated the data. A density curve associated with a quantitative variable usually has the following properties (Lane et al., 2003): (i) it is non-negative; (ii) the area under the curve is 1; and (iii) the area under the curve between two values represents the proportion of observations that fall in that range.

The script presented in Code 3.3 was used to generate the graphs in Figure 3.2. The dataset was loaded directly from the UCI repository, and the `histplot()` method from the Seaborn library was used to plot the graphs. It was chosen the automatic determination of the number of bins by `histplot()` and allowed the use of the kernel estimator, `kde`, to draw the smooth functions over the distributions.

CODE 3.3   Script to generate the plots of Figure 3.2.

```
# Plot distributions with different shapes

import matplotlib.pyplot as plt
import seaborn as sns
from ucimlrepo import fetch_ucirepo
```

```
# fetch dataset (https://archive.ics.uci.edu/ml/datasets/forest+fires)
dforest = fetch_ucirepo(id=162)["data"]["original"]

# Set up the x-labels for each Plot Distribution
x_labels = ["month", "day", "FFMC", "DMC", "DC", "ISI", "RH", "wind"]

# Set up sub-plots layout
fig, axes = plt.subplots(4, 2, figsize=(13, 18), layout="constrained")

for idx, x_label in enumerate(x_labels):
    # Flatten the axes array for easy iteration
    ax = axes.flat[idx]
    sns.histplot(dforest, x=x_label, bins="auto", kde=True, ax=ax)

# Show plot
plt.show()
```

The first description to be observed in the shape of a distribution is related to the number of peaks, also called *modes* (Peck et al., 2008). A function or histogram is known as *unimodal* if it contains a single peak, *bimodal* if it contains two peaks, and *multimodal* if it contains three or more peaks. Figure 3.2 shows that variables "FFMC", "ISI", "RH", and "wind" are unimodal, while variables "DMC" and "DC" are bimodal, and variable "month" is multimodal with peaks of varying heights in March, August-September, July, and December. Note that bimodality means that a variable has a significant number of values (Count) for two different subranges. As an example, consider the Drought Code (DC) index, which has around 85 objects (observations) for DC < 150 (in the first two bins), and then a higher concentration of values for $600 \leq DC \leq 800$.

If we look at the histogram shape for variable "temp" (Figure 3.1), it is possible to observe that it is almost perfectly *symmetric* in relation to the temperature 20°C, except for a few values of "temp" $\cong 5°C$. A symmetric unimodal histogram is the one for which a vertical line of symmetry can be drawn dividing it in the middle so that one side is the mirror of the other. The symmetric shape presented by variable "temp" is particularly important and common in data analysis; it is called a *normal distribution*. It has several important qualitative and quantitative properties that will be explored later.

In Figure 3.2, it can be observed that the variable "FFMC" is *skewed to the left*, also called *negatively skewed*, while the variables "ISI" and "RH" are *skewed to the right*, or *positively skewed*. In short, a unimodal histogram is skewed if it is not symmetric, and it is positively skewed if its upper (right-hand) tail stretches farther than its lower (left-hand) tail and is negatively skewed if its lower tail stretches farther than its upper tail. Such long-stretching tails are called *long tails* and may be indicative of *outliers*, that is, values that significantly differ from the others. For example, it can be observed the presence of outliers for FFMC < 50 and for ISI > 30. Outlier detection is also a subject topic to be explored further.

Another type of distribution that is relevant to know is the so-called *uniform distribution*, which has equally spread bins and no peaks. An approximately uniform distribution that can be found in the variables of the Forest Fires dataset is observed for the variable day. Almost every day of the week has a frequency of occurrence between 60 and 80.

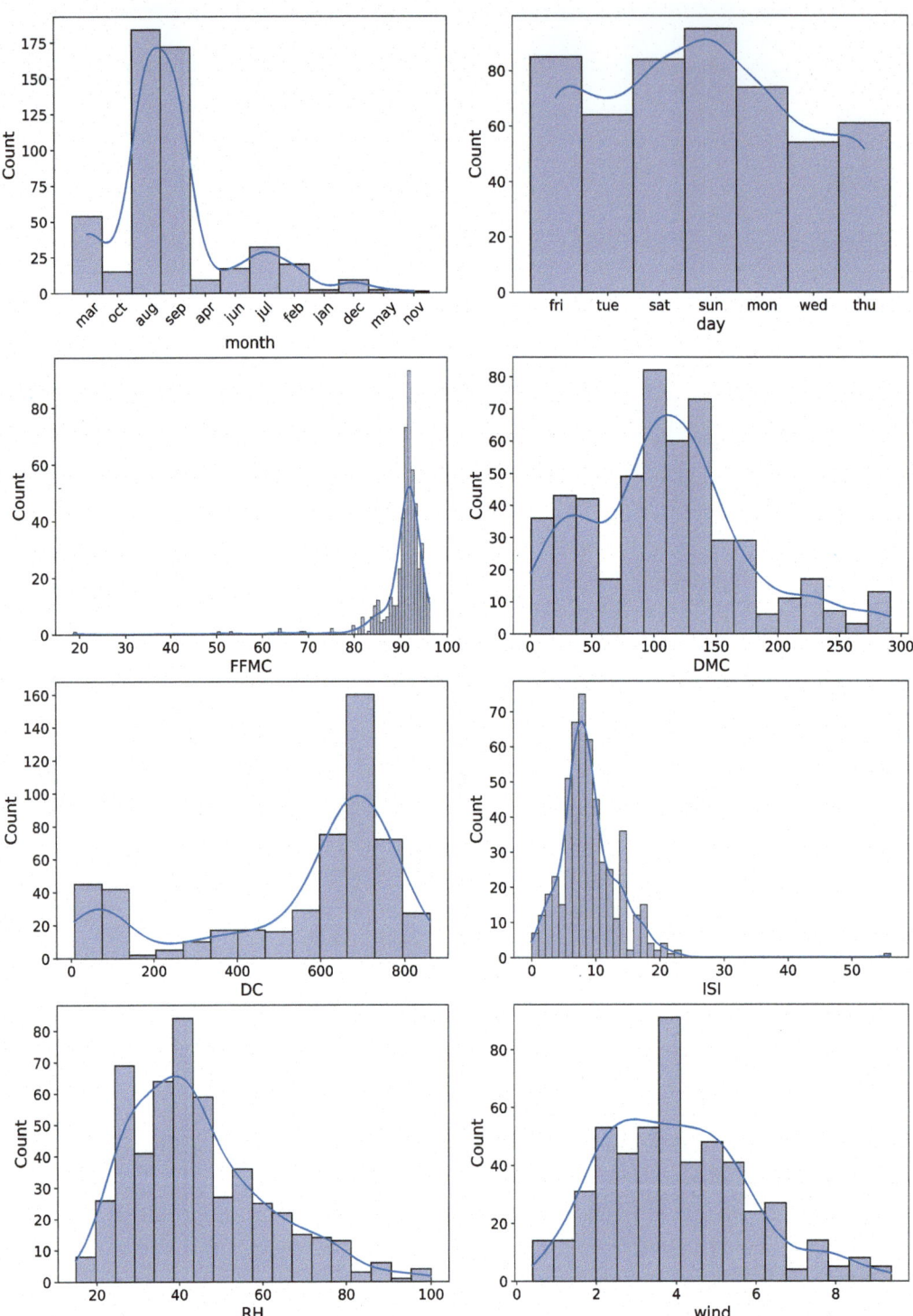

FIGURE 3.2 Histograms and smoothed functions of variables "month", "day", "FFMC", "DMC", "DC", "ISI", "RH", and "wind" of the Forest Fires dataset.

Finally, it is also important to observe the spread of the distribution. Variables "RH" and "DMC" are more spread than variables "FFMC" and "ISI", meaning that the occurrence of variables "FFMC" and "ISI" is more concentrated around specific values. Section 3.2 will present summary measures that help to numerically determine the shapes of distributions, including their means, variability (spread), presence of outliers, and level of flatness or peakness.

3.1.2 Contingency Tables

A useful tool to summarize the relationship between two categorical variables is a *contingency table*, also known as *cross tabulation*, *crosstab* or *two-way frequency table*. In a crosstab, the relationship between the frequency distribution of the two variables is presented in a table with one variable in the rows and the other in the columns of the table.

To illustrate this concept, consider the mammographic dataset from UCI. Table 3.3 presents a data dictionary for this dataset, highlighting the type of each variable, its domain, and the number of missing values for each variable.

Code 3.4 presents a script to generate the following contingency tables: "Shape" × "Severity"; "Margin" × "Severity"; and "Density" × "Severity". The goal is to investigate the relationship between variables "Shape", "Margin", and "Density" with the target variable "Severity". The script uses the `crosstab()` method from the `Pandas` library and, when run, generates the following output:

```
Shape and Severity:        Margin and Severity:       Density and Severity:
 Severity    0     1        Severity    0     1         Severity    0     1
Shape                      Margin                     Density
1.0        158    32       1.0        282    38       1.0          6     5
2.0        149    31       2.0          8    15       2.0         38    18
3.0         39    42       3.0         39    67       3.0        379   376
4.0         81   298       4.0         77   177       4.0          4     4
                           5.0         21   106
```

TABLE 3.3   Data Dictionary for the Mammographic Dataset

Variable Name	Definition (Meaning)	Variable Type: Domain	Number of Missing Values
BI-RADS	Breast Imaging Reporting and Data System. International system to evaluate, interpret, and report breast imaging exams.	Ordinal: [1,5]	2
Age	Patient age in years	Integer	5
Shape	Mass shape	Nominal: {Round = 1, Oval = 2, Lobular = 3, Irregular = 4}	31
Margin	Mass margin	Nominal: {Circumscribed = 1, Microlobulated = 2, Obscured = 3, Ill-defined = 4, Spiculated = 5}	48
Density	Mass density	Ordinal: {Mass density high = 1, Iso = 2, Low = 3, Fat-containing = 4}	76
Severity	Severity level	Binary: {Benign = 0, Malignant = 1}	0

CODE 3.4 Script to generate the contingency tables for variables "Shape", "Margin", and "Density" versus the target variable "Severity".

```
# Generate Contingency Tables for the Mammographic Dataset

import pandas as pd
from ucimlrepo import fetch_ucirepo

# fetch dataset (https://archive.ics.uci.edu/ml/datasets/Mammographic+Mass)
dmammo = fetch_ucirepo(id=161)["data"]["original"]

# Remove rows with missing values
dmammo.dropna(inplace=True)

# Print the contingency tables
var = ["Shape", "Margin", "Density"]
print("**Contingency Tables**")
for i in var:
    CT = pd.crosstab(dmammo[i], dmammo["Severity"])
    print("Variables", i, "and Severity:\n", CT)
```

As shown in Table 3.4, the contingency table is constructed by counting the number of objects in each frequency distribution category for the two variables, with rows showing one variable, columns the other, and the table values indicating the frequency of each category pair. The total numbers on the right-hand side and the bottom of the table are called *marginal totals*, and the number in the bottom right is the grand total.

3.1.2.1 Interpreting the Results

The interpretation of the results is straightforward; let us take the case of "Shape" × "Severity". The contingency table shows that there are 158 women with the mass shape "Round" that present a "Benign" diagnosis, and 32 women with the mass shape "Round" that present a "Malignant" diagnosis; there are 149 women with the mass shape "Oval" that present a "Benign" diagnosis, and 31 women with the mass shape "Oval" that present a "Malignant" diagnosis; there are 39 women with the mass shape "Lobular" that present a "Benign" diagnosis, and 42 women with the mass shape "Lobular" that present a "Malignant" diagnosis; and, finally, there are 81 women with the mass shape

TABLE 3.4 Contingency Table for the Pair "Shape" × "Severity" of the Mammographic Dataset

	Severity		
Shape	**Benign = 0**	**Malignant = 1**	**Total**
Round = 1	158	32	190
Oval = 2	149	31	180
Lobular = 3	39	42	81
Irregular = 4	81	298	379
Total	427	403	830

"Irregular" that present a "Benign" diagnosis, and 298 women with the mass shape "Irregular" that present a "Malignant" diagnosis. These results suggest that the irregular shape is a frequent indicator of a malignant tumor.

3.2 SUMMARY MEASURES

The frequency distribution is a useful tool for the identification of the range of values of a given variable and to build graphs that allow us to understand and characterize the data. In addition, it is also possible to calculate several measures that help us summarize and characterize distributions. These measures involve the calculation of the *center of the distribution*, known as *central tendency measures*, its *variability* (*variability* or *dispersion measures*), and its *shape* (*measures of shape*).

3.2.1 Central Tendency Measures

One of the most useful ways of summarizing a distribution is to find its *average*, that is, a measure of the *central tendency* of the data. The average represents a central or typical value of the distribution. The most common central tendency measures are the *mean*, *median*, *mode*, and *midpoint* (de Castro & Ferrari, 2016). To choose one of the four main central tendency measures to use in each application, it is necessary to know and understand their differences, advantages, and disadvantages. To structure this discussion, the following aspects will be considered: (i) sensitivity to outliers (extreme values); (ii) computation based on all values; (iii) existence; and (iv) main uses.

3.2.1.1 Mean

The *mean*, also known as *arithmetic mean* or *expected value*, is given by the sum of all values divided by the number of values:

$$Sample\,mean: \quad \bar{x} = \frac{1}{n}\sum_{i=1}^{n} x_i, \tag{3.1}$$

$$Population\,mean: \quad \mu = \frac{1}{N}\sum_{i=1}^{N} x_i, \tag{3.2}$$

where $x_i = 1, \ldots, n$, are the values of variable x for each object i in the sample, n is the number of objects in the sample, and N is the number of objects in the population.

Note: If it is not specified that it is a sample or the population, both equations can be used interchangeably.

The mean is sensitive to outliers, in the sense that outliers may significantly displace the mean from the general tendency of most of the data. It requires the computation over all values, always exists, and is recommended when the data distribution is approximately normal or there is a need to calculate other measures like variance, standard deviation, and the standardized score (z-score).

3.2.1.2 Median

The *median* is the central value (middle number) of a distribution, obtained by ordering all values and taking the middle one. If there is an even number of values, then take the average of both central values. The median will be represented here as $\tilde{x}$.

The median is not sensitive to outliers, requires the computation over all values, always exists, and is recommended when the data is skewed or has outliers.

3.2.1.3 Mode

The *mode* is the most frequent value in a distribution, usually represented by M. When more than one value occurs with the same highest frequency, it is said that the data or variable is *multimodal*.

The mode is not sensitive to outliers, requires reading all values, may not always exist or may have multiple values, and is recommended for categorical data, though it is not useful for continuous or multimodal data.

3.2.1.4 Midpoint

The *midpoint* is a value located halfway between the largest (x^L) and the smallest values (x^l) in a distribution:

$$midpoint = \left(x^L + x^l\right)/2. \tag{3.3}$$

The midpoint is sensitive to outliers, does not require the computation over all values, always exists, and is usually recommended when you need to know the middle point of a given range of values.

Code 3.5 contains the script to calculate the *mean, median,* and *midpoint* of numeric variables "FFMC" and "temp", and the *mode* of the nominal variables "month" and "day" of the Forest Fires dataset. Note that we are using the mean(), median(), and mode() methods from the Statistics library, but we calculated the midpoint for the numeric variables.

CODE 3.5   Code to calculate the *mean, median,* and *midpoint* of numeric variables "FFMC" and "temp", and the *mode* of the nominal variables "month" and "day" of the Forest Fires dataset.

```
# Calculating the mean and mode one by one using the Statistics library
# Numeric variables

import statistics as st

print('**Forest Fires Dataset**')
print('\n*Numeric Variable FFMC*')
print('Mean of variable FFMC: {:.2f}'.format(st.mean(dforest['FFMC'])))
print('Median of variable FFMC: {:.2f}'.format(st.median(dforest['FFMC'])))
midpoint = (max(dforest['FFMC'])+min(dforest['FFMC']))/2
print('Midpoint of variable FFMC: {:.2f}'.format(midpoint))

print('\n*Numeric Variable temp*')
print('Mean of variable temp: {:.2f}'.format(st.mean(dforest['temp'])))
print('Median of variable temp: {:.2f}'.format(st.median(dforest['temp'])))
midpoint = (max(dforest['temp'])+min(dforest['temp']))/2
print('Midpoint of variable temp: {:.2f}'.format(midpoint))
```

```
# Nominal variables
print('\n*Categorical Variables*')
print('Mode of nominal variable month: {v1}'
      .format(v1=st.mode(dforest['month'])))
print('Mode of nominal variable day: {v1}'
      .format(v1=st.mode(dforest['day'])))
```

Figure 3.3 shows the mean (18.89), median (19.30) and midpoint (17.75) of variable "temp" for the Forest Fires dataset. Note that as this variable has an approximately normal distribution, these central tendency measures have similar values. The script presented in Code 3.6 was used to plot this graph.

CODE 3.6   Script to plot the central tendency measures over the histogram for variable "temp".

```
# Plot the central tendency measures over the histogram

import statistics as st
import seaborn as sns
import matplotlib.pyplot as plt
from ucimlrepo import fetch_ucirepo

# fetch dataset (https://archive.ics.uci.edu/ml/datasets/forest+fires)
dforest = fetch_ucirepo(id=162)["data"]["original"]

var = "temp"  # Choose the target variable
mean = st.mean(dforest[var])
median = st.median(dforest[var])
midpoint = (max(dforest[var]) + min(dforest[var])) / 2
print("Mean, median and midpoint for temp:", mean, median, midpoint)

ax = sns.histplot(dforest, x=var, bins="auto", kde=True)

# Add a legend
plt.axvline(x=mean, color="r", linestyle="--", label="Mean", linewidth=2)
plt.axvline(x=median, color="g", linestyle="-", label="Median", linewidth=2)
plt.axvline(x=midpoint, color="m", linestyle=":", label="Midpoint", linewidth=2)
plt.legend()

# Show plot
plt.show()
```

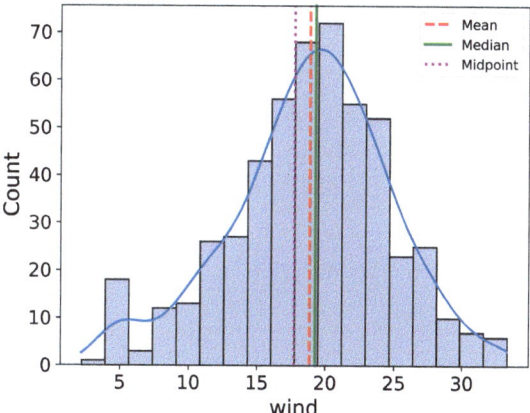

FIGURE 3.3   Mean, median, and midpoint of the "temp" variable distribution.

In addition to the four general central tendency measures described previously, there are five specific cases of average that also deserve attention: mean of a frequency distribution, weighted average, geometric mean, harmonic mean, and trimmed mean.

3.2.1.5 Mean of a Frequency Distribution

When data are summarized in a frequency distribution, it is considered that, in each class, all sample values are equal to the midpoint of the class. Since each class midpoint is repeated a number of times equal to the class frequency, the sum of all sample values is $\sum_i (f_i \cdot X_i)$, where f_i represents frequency and x_i, the class midpoint, is calculated as:

$$\overline{x} = \frac{\sum_{i=1}^{n} (f_i \cdot x_i)}{\sum_{i=1}^{n} f_i}. \tag{3.4}$$

3.2.1.6 Weighted Average

In some cases, values vary in importance, so you can weight them appropriately:

$$\overline{x} = \frac{\sum_{i=1}^{n} (w_i \cdot x_i)}{\sum_{i=1}^{n} w_i}, \tag{3.5}$$

where w_i is the weight associated with the value of variable i.

3.2.1.7 Geometric Mean

The geometric mean indicates the central tendency of an attribute using the product of their values instead of the sum:

$$\overline{x} = \left(\prod_{i=1}^{n} x_i \right)^{\frac{1}{n}}. \tag{3.6}$$

Geometric means are important in situations where multiplicative relationships or ratios are involved, and they have applications in finance, statistics, and various scientific fields. For example, it is often used to determine the performance results of an investment or portfolio because it takes into account the effects of compounding. It gives more weight to small observations and is less affected by extreme values compared to the arithmetic mean. This makes it a more reliable measure of central tendency for datasets with widely varying values.

3.2.1.8 Harmonic Mean

The harmonic mean is a type of average that is calculated by dividing the number of objects by the sum of the reciprocals of the objects:

$$\bar{x} = \frac{n}{\sum_{i=1}^{n} \frac{1}{x_i}}. \tag{3.7}$$

The harmonic mean gives more weight to smaller values in the dataset, which can be useful when dealing with rates or ratios. For instance, it is often used in finance to calculate average rates of return. In addition, when compared with the arithmetic mean, the harmonic mean tends to mitigate the impact of large outliers and aggravate the impact of small ones. This makes it a more reliable measure of central tendency for datasets with widely varying values. However, it is important to note that the harmonic mean can only be calculated for positive numbers and is equal to zero if any value in the dataset is zero.

3.2.1.9 Trimmed Mean

The sensitivity of the *mean* to outliers and the insensitivity of the *median* to many outliers led to the proposal of the *trimmed mean*, which orders the data values from smallest to largest, removes a predefined percentage of values from both ends, and then averages the resultant values:

$$\bar{x} = \frac{1}{n_t} \sum_{i=1}^{n_t} x_i, \tag{3.8}$$

where n_t is the number of remaining values after the removal of $r\%$ of the values from both ends of x_i, $\forall i$.

Code 3.7a presents a script to calculate the mean of a frequency distribution stored in a dataframe. The code appends one column with the midpoint of each bin and another with the numerator of Eq. (3.4) to the dataframe. The script in Code 3.7b uses methods from the NumPy and SciPy libraries to calculate the weighted, geometric, and harmonic means.

CODE 3.7 (a) Scripts to calculate the mean of a frequency distribution and (b) the weighted, geometric, harmonic, and trimmed means of a variable.

```
# (a) Calculating the mean of a frequency distribution (Eq. 3.4)
# Create a DataFrame from the frequency distribution data

import pandas as pd

data = {
    "Bins": ["(16.65, 19.98]", "(19.98, 23.31]", "(13.32, 16.65]",
             "(23.31, 26.64]", "(9.99, 13.32]", "(26.64, 29.97]",
             "(3.33, 6.66]", "(6.66, 9.99]", "(29.97, 33.3]",
             "(0.0, 3.33]"],
    "Frequency": [128, 119, 75, 69, 47, 30, 20, 15, 13, 1]}
df = pd.DataFrame(data)

# Calculate the midpoint of each bin (interval)
df["Midpoint"] = (
    # Get first float from interval
    df["Bins"].str.split(", ").str[0].str.replace("(", "").astype(float) +
```

```
    # Get second float from interval
    df["Bins"].str.split(", ").str[1].str.replace("]", "").astype(float)
) / 2
# Multiply the midpoint by the frequency to get the product
df["Product_fx"] = df["Midpoint"] * df["Frequency"]

# Sum the products and frequencies
sprod = df["Product_fx"].sum()
sfreq = df["Frequency"].sum()

# Calculate the mean
mean = sprod / sfreq
print(df)
print(f"Mean of the frequency distribution: {mean:.2f}")

# (b) Calculate the weighted average (Eq. 3.5), geometric (Eq. 3.6)
# harmonic (Eq. 3.7), and trimmed (Eq. 3.8) means

import numpy as np
import scipy.stats as spy

variables = ["FFMC", "temp"]
for var in variables:
    weights = np.random.randn(len(dforest[var]))
    wavg = np.average(dforest[var], weights=weights)
    gavg = spy.gmean(dforest[var])   # From Scipy library
    havg = spy.hmean(dforest[var])   # From Scipy library
    tavg = spy.trim_mean(dforest[var], 0.05)   # 5% trim

    print(f"Weighted average of variable {var}: {wavg:.2f}")
    print(f"Geometric mean of variable {var}: {gavg:.2f}")
    print(f"Harmonic mean of variable {var}: {havg:.2f}")
    print(f"Trimmed mean of variable {var}: {tavg:.2f}\n")
```

3.2.2 Comparing the Central Tendency Measures

Table 3.5 summarizes the main central tendency measures for numerical and categorical data. They are compared in terms of sensitivity to outliers, the need for computing with all values in the distribution, their existence, and their main uses.

Code 3.8 presents a script to generate all central tendency measures for some numeric variables of the Forest Fires dataset. The mean(), median(), max(), min(), and average() methods in Numpy were used, together with the gmean(), hmean(), and trim_mean() methods in Scipy. The weights in the weighted mean were taken as the values in the "area" variable.

CODE 3.8 Script to generate the central tendency measures for some variables of the Forest Fires dataset. The weights in the weighted mean were taken as the values in the "area" variable.

```
# Central Tendency Measures for the Forest Fires Dataset
# Columns of interest: 'FFMC','DMC','DC', 'ISI', 'temp', 'RH', 'wind', 'rain'

import numpy as np
import scipy.stats as spy
from ucimlrepo import fetch_ucirepo
```

```python
# fetch dataset 2
# https://archive.ics.uci.edu/ml/datasets/forest+fires
dforest = fetch_ucirepo(id=162)["data"]["original"]
# Dictionary to store the results
CTM = {}

variables = ["FFMC", "DMC", "DC", "ISI", "temp", "RH", "wind", "rain"]
for var in variables:
    # Add the results to the dictionary
    CTM[var] = {
        "Mean": np.mean(dforest[var]),
        "Median": np.median(dforest[var]),
        "Midpoint": (np.max(dforest[var]) + np.min(dforest[var])) / 2,
        "Weighted Mean": np.average(dforest[var], weights=dforest["area"]),
        "Geometric Mean": spy.gmean(dforest[var]),
        "Harmonic Mean": spy.hmean(dforest[var]),
        "Trimmed Mean": spy.trim_mean(dforest[var], proportiontocut=0.1),
    }

# Print the results
for key, value in CTM.items():
    print(key)
    for stat_name, stat_value in value.items():
        print(f"\t{stat_name}: {stat_value:.2f}")
```

The results are saved in a dictionary data type, and then plot one variable at a time, as shown in the sequence:

TABLE 3.5   Comparison of the Different Central Tendency Measures

Measure	Sensitivity to Outliers	Computation	Existence	When to Use
Mean	High	All values	Always	Normal distributions; variation measures are needed; there are no extreme values
Median	No	All values	Always	Skewed distributions; there are extreme values
Mode	No	Some values	Not always or multiple	Categorical data; when need to find the most frequent value
Midpoint	High	Extreme values	Always	Middle point is desired
Weighted mean	High	All values	Always	Different values have different importance in the average
Geometric mean	Low	All values	Always	Skewed distributions; there are extreme values; average rates of change or growth over time, especially when dealing with percentages or ratios
Harmonic mean	Low	All values	Always	There are extreme values; average rates, ratios, or proportions
Trimmed mean	No	Some values	Always	There are extreme values; skewed distributions

FFMC	DMC	DC
Mean: 90.64	Mean: 110.87	Mean: 547.94
Median: 91.60	Median: 108.30	Median: 664.20
Midpoint: 57.45	Midpoint: 146.20	Midpoint: 434.25
Weighted Mean: 91.74	Weighted Mean: 133.99	Weighted Mean: 608.52
Geometric Mean: 90.37	Geometric Mean: 85.49	Geometric Mean: 418.49
Harmonic Mean: 89.82	Harmonic Mean: 44.22	Harmonic Mean: 194.02
Trimmed Mean: 91.45	Trimmed Mean: 106.52	Trimmed Mean: 578.69
ISI	temp	RH
Mean: 9.02	Mean: 18.89	Mean: 44.29
Median: 8.40	Median: 19.30	Median: 42.00
Midpoint: 28.05	Midpoint: 17.75	Midpoint: 57.50
Weighted Mean: 9.21	Weighted Mean: 21.70	Weighted Mean: 38.19
Geometric Mean: 0.00	Geometric Mean: 17.74	Geometric Mean: 41.50
Harmonic Mean: 0.00	Harmonic Mean: 16.08	Harmonic Mean: 38.90
Trimmed Mean: 8.73	Trimmed Mean: 19.09	Trimmed Mean: 42.71
wind	rain	
Mean: 4.02	Mean: 0.02	
Median: 4.00	Median: 0.00	
Midpoint: 4.90	Midpoint: 3.20	
Weighted Mean: 4.13	Weighted Mean: 0.01	
Geometric Mean: 3.59	Geometric Mean: 0.00	
Harmonic Mean: 3.12	Harmonic Mean: 0.00	
Trimmed Mean: 3.90	Trimmed Mean: 0.00	

3.2.2.1 Interpreting the Results

The results themselves are only numbers; therefore, it is very important to interpret them to extract their meaning and insights from a contextual perspective. One possible way of interpreting these results is as follows:

- For "FFMC", the mean and median are very close, indicating a symmetric distribution. The midpoint is significantly lower than the other measures, suggesting that there might be a left skew and some outliers in the dataset. The trimmed mean is close to the mean and median, indicating that after removing some extreme values, the distribution becomes more symmetric and with shorter tails.

- For "DMC", the mean is slightly greater than the median, indicating a slightly right-skewed distribution. The geometric and harmonic means are much lower than the other measures, suggesting that there might be some outliers or a positively skewed distribution. The trimmed mean is closer to the median than to the mean, indicating that there might be some high outliers affecting the mean.

- For "DC", the mean is lower than the median, indicating a left-skewed distribution. The geometric and harmonic means are lower than the other measures, suggesting that there might be some lower outliers in the dataset. The trimmed mean is close to the median, indicating that there are not many outliers affecting the mean.

- For "ISI", the mean and median are quite close, indicating a symmetric distribution. The geometric and harmonic means are both 0, indicating that there might be some zero values in the dataset. The trimmed mean is close to the mean and median, indicating that after removing some extreme values, the distribution becomes more symmetric and with shorter tails.

- For "temp", the mean and median are close, indicating a symmetric distribution. The geometric and harmonic means are also close to the mean and median, indicating a more symmetric distribution. The trimmed mean is close to the mean and median, indicating that after removing some extreme values, the distribution becomes more symmetric and with shorter tails.

- For "RH", the mean is slightly higher than the median, indicating a slightly right-skewed distribution. The weighted mean is lower than the other two measures, indicating that some values have a smaller impact on the mean due to their weights. The geometric and harmonic means are close to the mean and median, indicating a more symmetric distribution. The trimmed mean is closer to the median than to the mean, indicating that there might be some high outliers affecting the mean.

- For "wind", the mean and median are quite close, indicating a symmetric distribution. The geometric and harmonic means are both lower than the other measures, suggesting that there might be some outliers in the dataset. The trimmed mean is close to the mean and median, indicating that after removing some extreme values, the distribution becomes more symmetric and with shorter tails.

- For "rain", the mean and median are 0 or very low, indicating that most of the values are either 0 or close to 0. The midpoint is much greater than the mean and median, indicating a highly skewed distribution. The weighted mean and the trimmed mean are also very low, indicating that most values have little impact on the mean. The geometric and harmonic means are both 0, indicating that there might be some zero values in the dataset.

In most cases, the weighted mean is (slightly) greater than the mean and median, suggesting that some values have a greater impact on the mean due to their weights. This is because the weighted mean was calculated by taking the "area" as the weights, and this variable has many values equal to 0, while the non-zero values represent the burnt area of the forest.

3.2.3 Variability Measures

Variability measures, also called *dispersion measures*, provide numeric indices about the spread of the data, that is, the extent to which the values are spread out from the average. The most common variability measures are the *range, interquartile range, semi-interquartile range, variance, standard deviation*, and the *variation coefficient*.

3.2.3.1 Range

The *range, R*, also called *amplitude*, is simply calculated by subtracting the largest (x^L) from the smallest value (x^l) in a distribution:

$$R = x^L - x^l. \tag{3.9}$$

Note that although variability is influenced by the whole dataset, the range only considers the two extreme observations to calculate its value and thus, is highly influenced by outliers. It presents the size of the data distribution interval. Usually, a larger range indicates larger variability, and a smaller range indicates less variability.

3.2.3.2 Interquartile Range

The *interquartile range*, *IQR*, is a measure of the spread in the center half of the distribution. One form of measuring it is by ordering the values from smallest to largest and dividing them into *quartiles* (Q_1, Q_2, and Q_3), each one of them containing 25% of the values in the dataset. Therefore, *IQR* can be calculated by simply taking Q_3 minus Q_1:

$$IQR = Q_3 - Q_1. \tag{3.10}$$

Similarly to the trimmed mean, *IQR* also discards part of the extreme values (25% of each extreme), and thus, it is less sensitive to outliers and useful for describing spread in skewed distributions. A more complete description of the quartiles will be provided in Section 3.2.5.

3.2.3.3 Semi-Interquartile Range

The *semi-interquartile range*, *sIQR*, is simply the interquartile range divided by 2:

$$sIQR = (Q_3 - Q_1) / 2. \tag{3.11}$$

Its importance lies in the fact that, for symmetric distributions, the median plus or minus the *sIQR* contains half of the values in the distribution.

3.2.3.4 Variance

The *variance* is a way of measuring variability in terms of how close the data values are to the mean, that is, the average of the sum of the squared deviations of values from the mean:

$$Sample\ variance: \quad s^2 = \frac{1}{n-1} \sum_{i=1}^{n} (x_i - \overline{x})^2, \tag{3.12}$$

$$Population\ variance: \quad \sigma^2 = \frac{1}{N} \sum_{i=1}^{N} (x_i - \mu)^2. \tag{3.13}$$

As the variance depends on the mean, it is expected that its calculus varies between a sample and a population and also makes it susceptible to extreme values. The sum of the differences between each value and the mean forced the use of the square as a mechanism to maintain only the magnitude of the deviation and avoid the counteraction of positive and negative deviations.

3.2.3.5 Standard Deviation

The *standard deviation*, *std*, is simply the square root of the variance:

$$Sample\ std : s = \sqrt{\frac{1}{n-1}\sum_{i=1}^{n}(x_i - \overline{x})^2}\,, \tag{3.14}$$

$$Population\ std : \sigma = \sqrt{\frac{1}{N}\sum_{i=1}^{N}(x_i - \mu)^2}\,. \tag{3.15}$$

As the variance takes the square of the deviations, it is measured in the square of the x unit. Thus, the standard deviation takes the square root of the variance and is measured using the same unit as x. Its characteristics are the same as those of variance.

3.2.3.6 Coefficient of Variation

The *coefficient of variation*, *CV*, is presented as the percentile ratio between the standard deviation and the mean:

$$CV = \frac{s}{\overline{x}} \cdot 100\% \quad CV = \frac{\sigma}{\mu} \cdot 100\%, \tag{3.16}$$

CV is useful to compare the variability of datasets with different units or scales and when the mean changes over time or is close to zero.

3.2.4 Comparing the Variability Measures

Table 3.6 provides a comparison of the six variability measures described previously in terms of their sensitivity to outliers, the use of all data values in their computation, and presents some general comments on when to use them.

TABLE 3.6   Comparison of the Different Variability Measures

Measure	Sensitivity to Outliers	Computation	Comments
Range	Yes	Extreme values	Sensitive to extreme values and does not take into account the data distribution
IQR	No	Some values	Not sensitive to extreme values and is suitable for skewed data
sIQR	No	Some values	Not sensitive to extreme values and is suitable for skewed data
Variance	Yes	All values	Sensitive to extreme values and with unit measured as the square of the x unit
Standard deviation	Yes	All values	Sensitive to extreme values and measured in the same unit as x
Coefficient of variation	Yes	All values	Sensitive to extreme values and suitable for data with a mean close to zero

Code 3.9 presents a script to calculate the variability measures and applies it to the "*FFMC*" variable of the Forest Fires dataset. Note that this script uses methods from the Numpy library. Running this code leads to the following results:

```
*Variability Measures*
Range of variable FFMC: 77.50
IQR of variable FFMC: 2.70
sIQR of variable FFMC: 1.35
Variance of variable FFMC: 30.41
Standard deviation of variable FFMC: 5.51
Variation coefficient of variable FFMC: 6.08
```

3.2.4.1 Interpreting the Results

Again, once the results have been obtained, it is necessary to interpret them. One possible interpretation for these results is as follows:

- The range of the "*FFMC*" values is 77.50, which means that the difference between the highest and lowest "*FFMC*" values is 77.50.

- The interquartile range (*IQR*) of "*FFMC*" is 2.70, meaning that 50% of all values lie within an interval of range 2.70.

- The *sIQR* represents the spread of the middle 50% of the "*FFMC*" values around the median, and is equal to 1.35, which is half of the *IQR* value found.

- By knowing that '*FFMC*' $\in [18.7, 96.20]$, a variance of 30.41 indicates that the "*FFMC*" values are spread out over a wide range.

- A coefficient of variation (*CV*) equals to 6.08 is a relatively high value. A *CV* greater than 1 usually indicates high variability in the data.

Overall, these results suggest that the "*FFMC*" values in the UCI Forest Fires dataset are moderately spread out with a high coefficient of variation.

CODE 3.9 Script to calculate the *range, IQR, sIQR, variance, standard deviation*, and *CV* of numeric variable "FFMC" of the Forest Fires dataset.

```python
# Calculate the variability measures range (Eq. 3.9),
# IQR (Eq. 3.10), sIQR (Eq. 3.11), variance (Eq. 3.12),
# std (Eq. 3.14), and CV (Eq. 3.16) using Numpy

import numpy as np
from ucimlrepo import fetch_ucirepo

# fetch dataset
# https://archive.ics.uci.edu/ml/datasets/forest+fires
dforest = fetch_ucirepo(id=162)["data"]["original"]

var = "FFMC"
drange = np.max(dforest[var]) - np.min(dforest[var])
Q1, Q3 = np.percentile(dforest[var], [25, 75])
IQR = Q3 - Q1
```

```
sIQR = IQR / 2
dvar = np.var(dforest[var])
dstd = np.std(dforest[var])
CV = dstd / np.mean(dforest[var]) * 100

print("*Variability Measures*")
print(f"Range of variable FFMC: {drange:.2f}")
print(f"IQR of variable FFMC: {IQR:.2f}")
print(f"sIQR of variable FFMC: sIQR{sIQR:.2f}")
print(f"Variance of variable FFMC: {dvar:.2f}")
print(f"Standard deviation of variable FFMC: {dstd:.2f}")
print(f"Variation coefficient of variable FFMC: {CV:.2f}")
```

3.2.5 Relative Position Measures

So far, we have discussed summary measures that allow us to assess the center and variability of a distribution. There are situations, however, in which you may want to know how a given value, e.g., a score, compares with others. For example, if you scored 6.3 in an exam, but the average score was 8.2, then your performance was relatively poor in relation to the group that took the exam. Measures that can be used to compare the relative performance of a value, that is, how it compares in relation to others, are called *relative position measures*. This section introduces the *z-score* and the *quantiles* as measures that help us compare relative performances.

3.2.5.1 *z-Score*

One way to locate a particular value x in a data set is to compute its distance from the mean in units of standard deviation. A z-score, or *standardized score*, can be found by converting a value to a standardized scale and corresponds to the number of standard deviations that a given value of x is above or below the mean:

$$\textit{Sample z-score}: \quad z = \frac{x - \bar{x}}{s}, \tag{3.17}$$

$$\textit{Population z-score}: \quad z = \frac{x - \mu}{\sigma}, \tag{3.18}$$

where $\bar{x}$ is the sample mean and μ is the population mean.

If the z-score is positive, this means that the value of x is greater than the mean, and if $z < 0$, then the value of x is smaller than the mean. In practical terms, the z-score indicates if a given value, e.g., a mark on a test or a salary, is above or below the mean in a given sample. It also measures how much greater or smaller it is than the mean. Therefore, the z-score plays an important role in assessing the relative performance of a given value, measuring direction and proportion.

If the z-score is known, then x can be retrieved by using the corresponding inverse equations:

$$\textit{Sample}: \quad x = \bar{x} + s \cdot z, \tag{3.19}$$

$$\textit{Population}: \quad x = \mu + \sigma \cdot z. \tag{3.20}$$

3.2.5.2 Quantiles and Quartiles

While the z-score compares a value x with the sample or population mean, it is sometimes necessary to divide a set of numerical data into equally sized groups and find its position in relation to these groups.

The *quantiles* are points taken at regular intervals from the cumulative frequency distribution of a variable; that is, they are cut-off points that separate a variable into smaller groups with equal numbers of values. To calculate them, just order the data and divide them into q subsets of the same cardinality. For example, suppose you want to divide the set of values of an attribute into $q = 4$ quantile intervals. The result is the *quartiles*, that is, the three values that divide the data into four subsets, each containing a quarter of the data. Just as the median divides the data into two subsets, each containing half of the values, the three quartiles, represented by Q_1, Q_2, and Q_3, divide the ordered values into four subsets, each containing a quarter of the data:

- **First quartile (Q_1):** divides the 25% lowest ordered values from the remaining 75%.

- **Second quartile (Q_2):** divides the 50% lowest ordered values from the remaining 50%; that is, it is the same as the median.

- **Third quartile (Q_3):** divides the 75% lowest ordered values from the remaining 25%.

Note that Q_1 is the median of the lower half, while Q_3 is the median of the upper half of the data.

The importance of quantiles lies in the fact that they are values that delimit consecutive subsets of values. In other words, the k-th quantile of a variable is the value x such that the probability of the variable being less than x is at most k/q, where q is the number of intervals chosen to divide the variable.

To illustrate the relative position measures, consider again the case of variable "temp" in the Forest Fires dataset. Six different temperature values were chosen [5, 10, 15, 20, 25, 30], and their respective z-scores were calculated:

```
Z-score for temp value 05: -2.39
Z-score for temp value 10: -1.53
Z-score for temp value 15: -0.67
Z-score for temp value 20: 0.19
Z-score for temp value 25: 1.05
Z-score for temp value 30: 1.91
Mean temp: 18.89 Std temp: 5.80
```

Figure 3.4a shows the frequency distribution of variable "temp" and the six values for which the z-scores presented above were calculated. The negative and positive z-scores can be observed in the picture. Figure 3.4b shows a graph called boxplot, highlighting the minimal and maximal values of the distribution in the extremes of the whiskers and the quartiles in the box. This type of visual will be described in detail in Chapter 5.

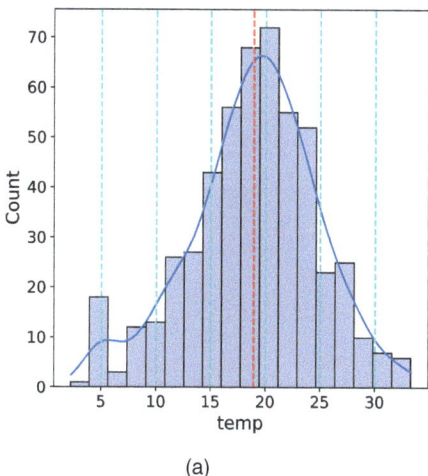
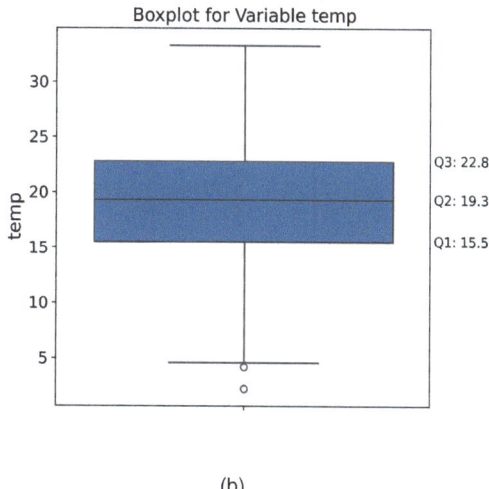

(a)   (b)

FIGURE 3.4   Relative position measures. (a) Variable "temp" frequency distribution with the mean plotted in red and different values of temperature plotted in cyan. (b) Box plot with Q_1, Q_2, and Q_3.

3.2.6 The `describe()` Method from Pandas

In the scripts presented previously, we showed how to calculate, one by one, various summary measures for numeric and categorical data. Code 3.10 introduces the method `describe()` from the Pandas library that provides, all at once, various summary measures for numerical and categorical data. When executed, this code generates the following result:

```
Forest Fires Dataset

Numerical variables
          X      Y    FFMC    DMC      DC    ISI    temp      RH    wind    rain     area
count 517.00 517.00 517.00 517.00 517.00 517.00 517.00 517.00 517.00 517.00    17.00
mean    4.67   4.30  90.64 110.87 547.94   9.02  18.89  44.29   4.02   0.02    12.85
std     2.31   1.23   5.52  64.05 248.07   4.56   5.81  16.32   1.79   0.30    63.66
min     1.00   2.00  18.70   1.10   7.90   0.00   2.20  15.00   0.40   0.00     0.00
25%     3.00   4.00  90.20  68.60 437.70   6.50  15.50  33.00   2.70   0.00     0.00
50%     4.00   4.00  91.60 108.30 664.20   8.40  19.30  42.00   4.00   0.00     0.52
75%     7.00   5.00  92.90 142.40 713.90  10.80  22.80  53.00   4.90   0.00     6.57
max     9.00   9.00  96.20 291.30 860.60  56.10  33.30 100.00   9.40   6.40  090.84


Nominal variable: month          | Nominal variable: day
count        517                 | count        517
unique        12                 | unique         7
top          aug                 | top          sun
freq         184                 | freq          95
Name: month, dtype: object       | Name: day, dtype: object
```

CODE 3.10 Using the `describe()` method from the `Pandas` library to provide a descriptive summary of the Forest Fires dataset.

```
# Summarizing the data using the describe() method from the Pandas library

import pandas as pd
from ucimlrepo import fetch_ucirepo

# fetch dataset
# https://archive.ics.uci.edu/ml/datasets/forest+fires
dforest = fetch_ucirepo(id=162)["data"]["original"]

print("Forest Fires Dataset\n")
print("Numerical variables \n", dforest.describe().round(2))
print("\nNominal variable: month \n", dforest["month"].describe())
print("\nNominal variable: day \n", dforest["day"].describe())
```

3.2.7 Measures of Shape

The *shape* of a distribution brings important information about the underlying data, such as where the data are accumulated, the presence or absence of outliers, and if the distribution is more or less skewed and more or less spread.

When talking about the shape, location, and variability of a probability distribution, it is usual to use the concept of *moment*. The moment is a quantitative measure associated with the central tendency and dispersion of a frequency distribution. The *n*-th moment, μ, of a frequency distribution is given by:

$$\mu = \frac{E\left[(x - \bar{x})^n\right]}{\sigma^n}, \tag{3.21}$$

where $E[.]$ is the expected value and σ is the standard deviation. The mean and variance are known as *raw moments*, and the skewness and kurtosis that will be discussed in this section are known as *standardized moments*.

3.2.7.1 Skewness

Skewness is a measure of the *asymmetry* (lack of symmetry) of a distribution, allowing us to quantify the shape, in terms of direction and length, of its tail. A *positively skewed*, or *right-skewed*, distribution has a long tail to its right, while a *negatively skewed*, or *left-skewed*, distribution has a long tail to its left. Therefore, in positively skewed distributions, the mean is usually greater than the median, which is greater than the mode. By contrast, in negatively skewed distributions, the mean is usually smaller than the median, which is smaller than the mode.

There are different forms of calculating the sample skewness. The *Fischer-Pearson skewness coefficient*, γ, is given by (Zwillinger & Kokoska, 2000):

$$\gamma = \frac{m_3}{m_2^{3/2}}, \quad m_i = \frac{1}{n}\sum_{i=1}^{n}(x_i - \bar{x})^i, \tag{3.22}$$

where $\bar{x}$ is the mean of $x_i = i, ..., n$, and n is its length.

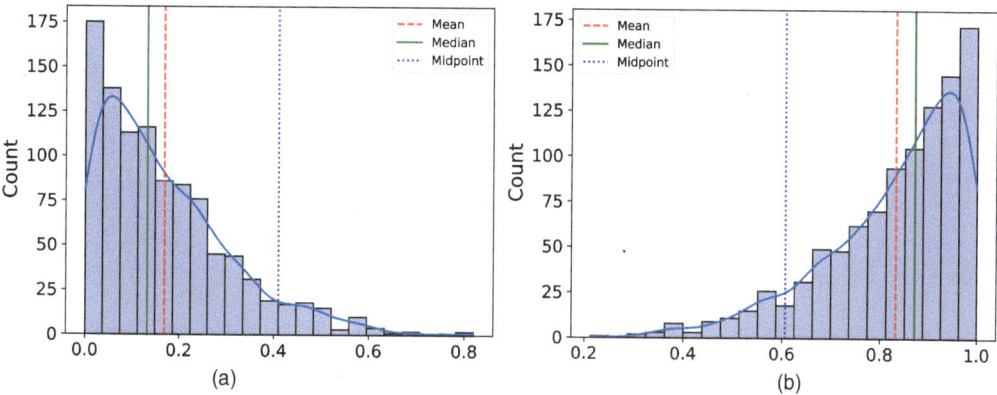

FIGURE 3.5 Skewed distributions with the values of mean, median, and mode plotted. (a) Right-skewed distribution. (b) Left-skewed distribution.

There are other forms of calculating skewness, such as the *Person mode skewness*, also known as the *Pearson first skewness coefficient* (Fiori & Zenga, 2009):

$$\gamma = \frac{\bar{x} - mode}{\sigma}, \tag{3.23}$$

where σ is the standard deviation of variable x and $\bar{x}$ is its mean.

The Pearson first skewness coefficient ranges over the interval [–1,1], where –1 means a perfect negative linear relationship, 0 means there is no linear relationship, and +1 means a perfect linear positive relationship between the mean and the mode.

Figure 3.5 shows two asymmetric distributions generated with a *beta distribution* from the Numpy library. Each distribution contains 1,000 data points, and their mean, median, and mode were calculated using the Statistics library and plotted in the respective figures.

Code 3.11 was used to generate the data, calculate the central tendency measures and the skewness using the Fischer-Pearson and the First Skewness coefficients, and plot the results. The numeric results obtained were:

```
Right-skewed distribution:
Mean, median, and midpoint: 0.17 0.13 0.40
Skewness (Fischer-Pearson Coefficient): 1.06
Skewness (First Skewness Coefficient): -1.67

Left-skewed distribution:
Mean, median, and midpoint: 0.83 0.86 0.57
Skewness (Fischer-Pearson Coefficient): -1.14
Skewness (First Skewness Coefficient): 1.81
```

CODE 3.11 Scripts to generate skewed distributions using a beta distribution from Numpy. (a) Right-skewed distribution. (b) Left-skewed distribution.

```
# (a) Skewness and Skewed distributions
# Generate random data with a right-skewed distribution
```

```python
import statistics as st
import numpy as np
from scipy.stats import skew
import seaborn as sns
import matplotlib.pyplot as plt

data = np.random.beta(a=1, b=5, size=1000) # Beta distribution
mean = st.mean(data)
median = st.median(data)
midpoint = (max(data) + min(data)) / 2  # Calculate the midpoint
print(f"Mean, median, and midpoint: {mean:.2f} {median:.2f} {midpoint:.2f}")
print(f"Skewness (Fischer-Pearson Coefficient): {skew(data):.2f}")
print(f"Skewness (First Skewness Coefficient): {(mean - midpoint) /
np.std(data):.2f}")

ax = sns.histplot(data, bins="auto", kde=2)
plt.axvline(x=mean, color="r", linestyle="--", label="Mean")
plt.axvline(x=median, color="g", linestyle="-", label="Median")
plt.axvline(x=midpoint, color="b", linestyle=":", label="Midpoint")
plt.legend()

# Show plot
plt.show()

# (b) Skewness and Skewed distributions
# Generate random data with a left-skewed distribution

import statistics as st
import numpy as np
from scipy.stats import skew
import seaborn as sns
import matplotlib.pyplot as plt

data_neg = np.random.beta(a=5, b=1, size=1000) # Beta distribution
mean = st.mean(data_neg)
median = st.median(data_neg)
midpoint = (max(data_neg) + min(data_neg)) / 2 # Calculate the midpoint
print(f"Mean, median, and midpoint: {mean:.2f} {median:.2f} {midpoint:.2f}")
print(f"Skewness (Fischer-Pearson Coefficient): {skew(data_neg):.2f}")
print(f"Skewness (First Skewness Coefficient): {(mean - midpoint) /
np.std(data_neg):.2f}")

ax = sns.histplot(data_neg, bins="auto", kde=2)
plt.axvline(x=mean, color="r", linestyle="--", label="Mean")
plt.axvline(x=median, color="g", linestyle="-", label="Median")
plt.axvline(x=midpoint, color="b", linestyle=":", label="Midpoint")
plt.legend()

# Show plot
plt.show()
```

3.2.7.2 Kurtosis

Kurtosis is a measure of the *tailedness* of the distribution and is useful to analyze the peak, the tails of the curve, and the presence of outliers. The distribution can have a steeper or flatter peak and a longer or shorter tail. A distribution with *negative kurtosis*, also called *platykurtic*, is one that usually has a flatter peak and shorter tail, meaning that it produces less extreme values than normal distributions. By contrast, a distribution with a *positive kurtosis*, also called *leptokurtic*, usually has a longer tail and steeper peak, producing more outliers than a normal distribution. Distributions with close to zero or zero kurtosis, like the normal distribution, are called *mesokurtic* distributions.

Similarly to skewness, there are different forms of calculating kurtosis, β, such as the so-called *fourth standardized moment* defined as:

$$\beta = \frac{E(x - \bar{x})^4}{\sigma^4} \tag{3.24}$$

where σ is the standard deviation of x, $\bar{x}$ is the average of x, and $E(.)$ is the expected value.

For a sample with n values, the so-called *excess kurtosis* is given by:

$$\beta = \frac{m_4}{(s^2)^2} - 3 = \frac{\frac{1}{N} \sum_{i=1}^{N} (x_i - \bar{x})^4}{(s^2)^2} - 3, \tag{3.25}$$

where $\bar{x}$ is the mean of x, m_4 is the *fourth standardized moment* of x, and s^2 is the variance of x.

To illustrate kurtosis, Figure 3.6 presents a normal distribution with β = 0.01, a uniform distribution with β = −1.2, a Laplace distribution with β = 3.19, and a Wigner semicircle

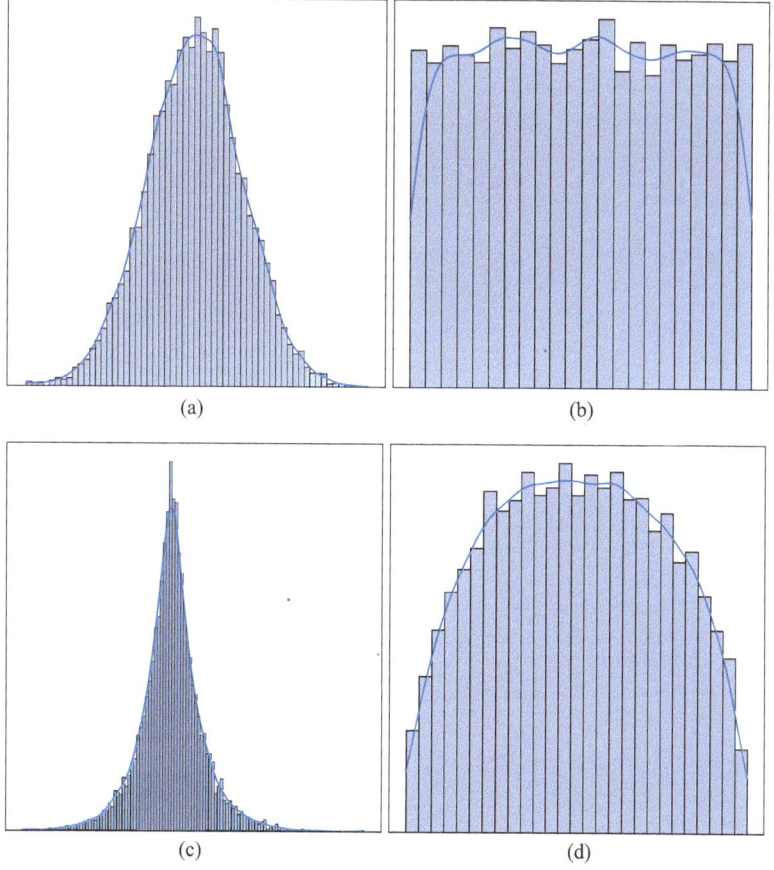

FIGURE 3.6   Four different data distributions with varying levels of kurtosis. (a) Normal distribution: kurtosis = 0.02. (b) Uniform distribution: kurtosis = −1.19. (c) Laplace distribution: kurtosis = 2.73.(d) Wiegner Semicircle distribution: kurtosis = −1.01.

distribution with $\beta = -1.0$. As discussed, the normal distribution is mesokurtic and has a kurtosis of approximately zero; the uniform and semicircle distributions are platykurtic and have negative kurtosis, and the Laplace distribution is leptokurtic with a positive kurtosis. It is also possible to observe that the semicircle distribution, though not as flat as the uniform distribution, has a negative kurtosis value, because it smooths the data toward its ends without presenting a long tail like the normal distribution, which is indicative of extreme values.

Code 3.12 describes how to generate data distributions to explore different levels of kurtosis. In this script, we used the Scipy method to calculate kurtosis spy.kurtosis(), and the Seaborn histplot() function to plot the graphs. Some distributions were generated using the rvs(), which is a Scipy method that generates a random value of a given type.

CODE 3.12   Script to generate the four data distributions presented in Figure 3.6 to illustrate the different shapes and calculus of kurtosis.

```python
# Kurtosis: mesokurtic, platykurtic and leptokurtic distributions

import numpy as np
from scipy.stats import norm, laplace, semicircular, kurtosis
import seaborn as sns
import matplotlib.pyplot as plt

# Set up sub-plots layout
fig, ((ax1, ax2), (ax3, ax4)) = plt.subplots(2, 2, figsize=(13, 13),
layout="constrained")

# Normal distribution (Mesokurtic)
dnorm = norm.rvs(size=10000)
knorm = kurtosis(dnorm)
print(f"Kurtosis: {knorm:.2f}")
sns.histplot(dnorm, bins="auto", kde=2, ax=ax1)
ax1.set_title(f"Normal Distribution - Kurtosis: {knorm:.2f}")

# Uniform distribution (Platykurtic)
dunif = np.random.uniform(0.01, 0.10, 10000)
kunif = kurtosis(dunif)
print(f"Kurtosis: {kunif:.2f}")
sns.histplot(dunif, bins="auto", kde=2, ax=ax2)
ax2.set_title(f"Uniform Distribution - Kurtosis: {kunif:.2f}")

# Laplace distribution (Leptokurtic)
dlap = laplace.rvs(loc=0, scale=1, size=10000)
klap = kurtosis(dlap)
sns.histplot(dlap, bins="auto", kde=2, ax=ax3)
ax3.set_title(f"Laplace Distribution - Kurtosis: {klap:.2f}")

# Wigner semicircle distribution
dwigner = semicircular.rvs(size=10000)
kwigner = kurtosis(dwigner)
sns.histplot(dwigner, bins="auto", kde=2, ax=ax4)
ax4.set_title(f"Wigner Semicircle Distribution - Kurtosis: {kwigner:.2f}")

# Show plot
plt.show()
```

Code 3.13 presents a script to calculate the skewness and kurtosis for variables "FFMC", "DMC, "DC", "ISI", "temp", "wind", and "rain" of the UCI Forest Fires dataset. The script uses the `skew()` and `kurtosis()` methods of the `Scipy` library. When run, this code generates the following output:

```
FFMC Skewness: -6.58                temp Skewness: -0.33
FFMC Kurtosis: 67.07 (Leptokurtic)  temp Kurtosis: 0.14 (Leptokurtic)
DMC Skewness: 0.55                  RH Skewness: 0.86
DMC Kurtosis: 0.20 (Leptokurtic)    RH Kurtosis: 0.44 (Leptokurtic)
DC Skewness: -1.10                  wind Skewness: 0.57
DC Kurtosis: -0.25 (Platykurtic)    wind Kurtosis: 0.05 (Mesokurtic)
ISI Skewness: 2.54                  rain Skewness: 19.82
ISI Kurtosis: 21.46 (Leptokurtic)   rain Kurtosis: 421.30 (Leptokurtic)
```

3.2.7.3 Interpreting the Results

These results can be interpreted as follows:

- For the "FFMC" variable, the skewness is negative, indicating a left-skewed (negatively skewed) distribution. The kurtosis is very high, indicating a leptokurtic distribution, that is, a distribution with a sharp peak and a long tail.

- The "DMC" variable has a small positive skewness, indicating that the distribution is right-skewed (positively skewed). The kurtosis is also leptokurtic, but with a small kurtosis, indicating a short tail.

- For the "DC" variable, the skewness is negative, indicating a left-skewed distribution. The kurtosis is platykurtic, indicating that the distribution is flatter than a normal distribution and has shorter tails.

- For the "ISI" variable, the skewness is positive, indicating a right-skewed distribution. The kurtosis is very high and, similarly to the "FFMC" case, indicates a distribution with a sharp peak and long tail.

- The "temp" variable has a small negative skewness, indicating a slightly left-skewed distribution. The kurtosis is also leptokurtic, but with a small value indicating an almost normal distribution.

- For the "RH" variable, the skewness is positive, and kurtosis is also leptokurtic, indicating that the distribution has a peak and a tail. Its numbers have similar orders of magnitude when compared with "DMC", and its shape also presents similar patterns.

- For the "wind" variable, the skewness value indicates a right-skewed distribution, and its close-to-zero kurtosis value indicates an almost normal distribution.

- The "rain" variable has a very high skewness, indicating a highly right-skewed distribution. The kurtosis is also very high, indicating a leptokurtic distribution with a sharp peak and long tails.

In summary, the "FFMC", "DMC", "ISI", and "RH" variables have leptokurtic distributions with a sharp peak and long tails; the DC variable has a platykurtic distribution with a flatter shape and shorter tails; and the "temp" and "wind" variables have almost mesokurtic distributions with kurtosis close to zero. The "rain" variable has a highly right-skewed leptokurtic distribution, indicating that the distribution has a sharp peak, long tails, and strong positive skewness.

CODE 3.13 Script to calculate the skewness and kurtosis for variables "FFMC", "DMC", "DC", "ISI", "temp", "RH", "wind", and "rain" of the UCI Forest Fires dataset.

```python
# Calculate the Skewness and Kurtosis for the Forest Fires variables

import pandas as pd
from scipy.stats import skew, kurtosis
from ucimlrepo import fetch_ucirepo

# fetch dataset
# https://archive.ics.uci.edu/ml/datasets/forest+fires
dforest = fetch_ucirepo(id=162)["data"]["original"]

# Select the variables of choice
variables = ["FFMC", "DMC", "DC", "ISI", "temp", "RH", "wind", "rain"]

# Skewness and kurtosis for each variable
skewness = dforest[variables].skew()
kurt = dforest[variables].kurtosis()

# Print the results and classify the kurtosis
for var in skewness.index:
    print(f"{var} Skewness: {skewness[var]:.2f}")
    if kurt[var] > 0:
        print(f"{var} Kurtosis: {kurt[var]:.2f} (Leptokurtic)")
    elif kurt[var] < 0:
        print(f"{var} Kurtosis: {kurt[var]:.2f} (Platykurtic)")
    else:
        print(f"{var} Kurtosis: {kurt[var]:.2f} (Mesokurtic)")
```

To conclude this section, let us return to the concept of moment presented in Eq. (3.21). It is interesting to observe that the moment's structure makes it dimensionless, that is, independent of scale. For $n = 1$ there is the *first moment*, which corresponds to the *z*-score; $n = 2$ corresponds to the distribution variance; $n = 3$ results in a measure of *skewness*; and $n = 4$ leads to kurtosis.

3.3 THE NORMAL DISTRIBUTION

The *normal distribution*, also known as the *Bell curve* or the *Gaussian distribution*, is one of the most important and widely used distributions in statistics. It is a symmetric distribution characterized by its mean, μ, and standard deviation, σ. Although the normal distribution is the most well-known bell-shaped curve, there are many other probability distributions, such as the *Student's t-distribution*, the *chi-squared distribution*, the *lognormal distribution*, the *beta distribution*, and the *exponential distribution*, among others, that have a normal shape depending on their parameters.

The formula for the probability density function of the normal distribution is:

$$y = f(x) = \frac{1}{\sigma\sqrt{2\pi}} \exp^{-\frac{1}{2}\left(\frac{x-\mu}{\sigma}\right)^2}.$$

(3.26)

Figure 3.7a illustrates the normal distribution with different values for the mean μ and standard deviation σ, and $x = [-5, 5]$. Note that the mean determines where the distribution peak is located, $\mu = \{-1, 0, 1\}$, and the standard deviation determines its spread, $\sigma = \{0.5, 1.0, 1.5\}$. Figure 3.7b shows a normal distribution with $\sigma = 1$ and $\mu = 0$, with vertical lines at $\sigma = \{-3, -2, -1, 0, 1, 2, 3\}$. For such normal distributions, the *empirical rule* 68–95–99.7 is known, as follows:

- Approximately 68% of all values are within one standard deviation from the mean;

- Approximately 95% of all values are within two standard deviations from the mean;

- Approximately 99.7% of all values are within three standard deviations from the mean.

In summary, the following important features define normal distributions (Lane et al., 2003):

- They are symmetric around their mean.

- The mean, median, and mode of a normal distribution are equal.

- The area under the normal curve is equal to 1.0. This property means that the total probability of all possible outcomes is 1.

- Normal distributions are denser in the center and less dense in the tails.

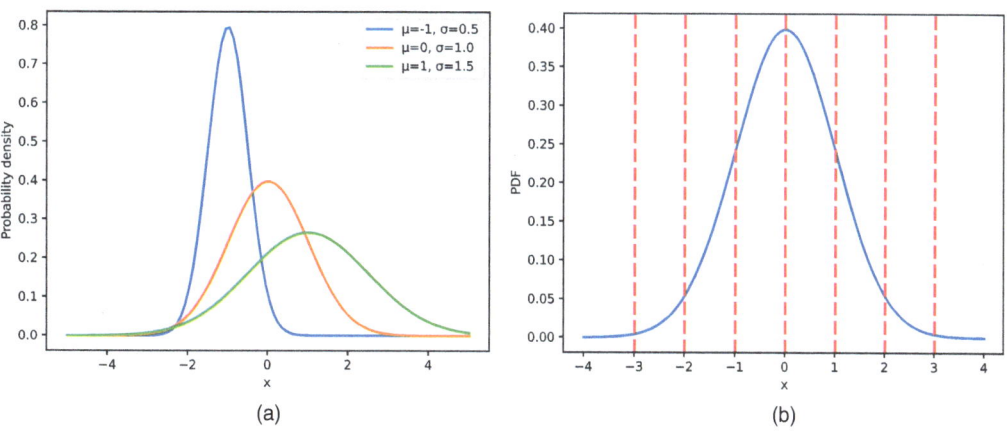

(a) (b)

FIGURE 3.7 Normal distributions. (a) Varying means and standard deviations: $\mu = \{-1, 0, 1\}$ and $\sigma = \{0.5, 1.0, 1.5\}$. (b) Plot with $\sigma = \{-3, -2, -1, 0, 1, 2, 3\}$.

- Normal distributions are characterized by their mean and standard deviation.

- Normal distributions obey the empirical rule 68–95–99.7.

Code 3.14 presents the scripts to generate the plots in Figure 3.7. In these scripts, the probability density function of the normal distributions was calculated in variable y and plotted using the `plot()` method from Matplotlib.

CODE 3.14   Scripts to generate normal distributions. (a) Distributions for $\mu = \{-1, 0, 1\}$ and $\sigma = \{0.5, 1.0, 1.5\}$. (b) Distribution for $\mu = 0$, $\sigma = 1.0$, and vertical lines in $\sigma = \{-3, -2, -1, 0, 1, 2, 3\}$.

```python
# (a) Plot Normal Distributions

import numpy as np
import matplotlib.pyplot as plt

# Define an array of mean and standard deviation values
vmu = np.array([-1, 0, 1])
vsigma = np.array([0.5, 1, 1.5])

# Create an array of x-values
x = np.linspace(-5, 5, 100)

# Loop through the mean and standard deviation values and plot the normal
# distributions
for mu, sigma in zip(vmu, vsigma):
    y = (1 / (sigma * np.sqrt(2 * np.pi))) * np.exp(-((x - mu) ** 2) / (2 * sigma**2))
    plt.plot(x, y, label=f"μ={mu}, σ={sigma}")

# Add a legend and axis labels
plt.legend()
plt.xlabel("x")
plt.ylabel("Probability density")
plt.title("Normal Distributions")

# Show plot
plt.show()

# (b) Plot a Normal Distribution detaching σ = {-3,-2,-1,0,1,2,3}

import numpy as np
import matplotlib.pyplot as plt

# Define the range of x values (which correspond to z-scores)
x = np.linspace(-4, 4, 1000)

# Calculate the probability density function (PDF) for the normal
# distribution
y = (1 / (np.sqrt(2 * np.pi))) * np.exp(-(x**2) / 2)

# Set up the plot, plot the PDF and vertical lines
fig, vax = plt.subplots()
vax.plot(x, y)
std = 1
mean = 0
```

```
for i in range(-3, 4):
    vax.axvline(mean + i , color="r", linestyle="--")

# Add a legend and labels to the plot
vax.set_xlabel("x")
vax.set_ylabel("PDF")
vax.set_title("Normal Distribution with Standard Deviation Lines")

# Show plot
plt.show()
```

The normal distribution with $\mu = 0$ and $\sigma = 1$ is called the *standard normal distribution* and is abbreviated by $N(0,1)$. If x is a value from the normal distribution $N(0,1)$, then the standard score of x is the z-score presented in Eq. (3.17) and corresponds to the number of standard deviations that a given value of x is above or below the mean.

In practical terms, normal distributions are important because there is a vast amount of natural and social phenomena where they can be observed. For instance, the height of adults in a given region, the age of students in a classroom, the weight of the same fruits harvested in a plantation, the IQ scores, blood pressure, and sugar level of people all follow a normal distribution.

3.4 MEASURES OF ASSOCIATION

Until now, we have been discussing measures to assess the central tendency, variability, and shape of the frequency distribution of a given variable. It is now time to measure the *association* between two variables. As in the previous cases, there are different *measures of association* that can be used to calculate the *strength* and *direction* of the relationship between two variables. Three important aspects must be considered: the type of distribution, the range of the association, and the variable time.

First, if the measure makes any assumption about the underlying data distribution, then it is said to be *parametric*. For example, some measures assume that the data has a normal distribution and should only be applied if the variables have this type of distribution. This can be verified by a visualization method (e.g., the respective histogram or density function) or by using specific techniques that determine numerically if a given distribution is normal or not.

Second, it is important to know and understand the range of each measure of association. Most of them are within the [–1, 1] range, where –1 indicates a perfect negative correlation, 0 indicates no correlation, and +1 indicates a perfect positive correlation. Two variables are negatively correlated when one variable increases and the other decreases, and vice versa; they are positively correlated if they either increase or decrease simultaneously; and when there is no correlation, it means that the change of one variable does not exert any influence in the change of the other.

Lastly, the type of variable influences the measure of association that can be used. There are measures capable of dealing with the main types of numerical and categorical variables, including binary, continuous, nominal, and ordinal. Some of them even assume that one variable is of one type and the other is of another type.

3.4.1 Covariance

The first measure to be presented for calculating the degree of association between two variables is the so-called *covariance*, which measures how much one variable changes in relation to another. If two variables deviate from their respective means in a similar way, it is possible to say that they are *covariant*, that is, there is a *statistical correlation* between their "fluctuations".

Assume a dataset with n pairs (x_i, y_i), $i = 1, 2, \ldots, n$. The covariance, $cov(x,y)$, between two random variables x and y is given by:

$$cov(x, y) = \frac{1}{n} \sum_{i=1}^{n} (x_i - \bar{x})(y_i - \bar{y}), \qquad (3.27)$$

where $\bar{x}$ and $\bar{y}$ are the means of x and y, respectively.

While the mean, variance, and standard deviation operate in a single variable, covariance takes into account two variables simultaneously.

Note: if covariance is calculated for one variable and itself, then the result is the variance.

The concept of covariance can be extended to a space of multiple dimensions by means of the *covariance matrix*, represented by Σ, whose element ij corresponds to the covariance between the elements i and j in the dataset:

$$\Sigma_{ij} = cov(x_i, x_j), \quad \forall i, j. \qquad (3.28)$$

The resultant covariance matrix is a squared and symmetric matrix whose main diagonal contains the variances, and the covariances are placed out of the diagonal.

Code 3.15 presents a script to calculate the covariance matrix of the numeric variables of the Forest Fires dataset. After loading the data, the desired features are selected, and the output is formatted to two decimal places. Then, the method `cov()` in `Pandas` is used to calculate the covariance. Running this script generates the covariance matrix shown below. Note that the covariance may assume any positive or negative values, depending on the input variables' scale.

	X	Y	FFMC	DMC	DC	ISI	temp	RH	wind	rain
X	5.35	1.54	-0.27	-7.17	-49.31	0.07	-0.69	3.22	0.08	0.04
Y	1.54	1.51	-0.31	0.61	-30.87	-0.14	-0.17	1.25	-0.04	0.01
FFMC	-0.27	-0.31	30.47	135.27	452.59	13.38	13.83	-27.11	-0.28	0.09
DMC	-7.17	0.61	135.27	4101.95	10838.50	89.10	174.64	77.12	-12.09	1.42
DC	-49.31	-30.87	452.59	10838.50	61536.84	259.19	714.75	-158.64	-90.43	2.63
ISI	0.07	-0.14	13.38	89.10	259.19	20.79	10.44	-9.86	0.87	0.09
temp	-0.69	-0.17	13.83	174.64	714.75	10.44	33.72	-49.97	-2.36	0.12
RH	3.22	1.25	-27.11	77.12	-158.64	-9.86	-49.97	266.26	2.03	0.48
wind	0.08	-0.04	-0.28	-12.09	-90.43	0.87	-2.36	2.03	3.21	0.03
rain	0.04	0.01	0.09	1.42	2.63	0.09	0.12	0.48	0.03	0.09

CODE 3.15 Script to calculate the covariance matrix of the numerical variables of the Forest Fire dataset.

```python
# Calculate and print the Covariance Matrix of the Forest Fires dataset

import pandas as pd
from scipy import stats
from ucimlrepo import fetch_ucirepo

# fetch dataset
# https://archive.ics.uci.edu/ml/datasets/forest+fires
dforest = fetch_ucirepo(id=162)["data"]["original"]

# Select the desired numeric features
features = ["X", "Y", "FFMC", "DMC", "DC", "ISI", "temp", "RH", "wind", "rain"]

# Compute the covariance matrix and format to two decimal places
pd.options.display.float_format = "{:.2f}".format
Mcov = dforest[features].cov()

# Print the covariance matrix
print(Mcov)
```

3.4.2 Correlation

Correlation is a terminology used to express the degree of association or dependence of two random variables, providing a sort of predictive relationship between them. There are different forms of calculating the correlation between variables, and some of them will be explored here (Rayward-Smith, 2007; Prematunga, 2012).

3.4.2.1 Pearson Correlation Coefficient

By looking at Eq. (3.27), it is possible to observe that covariance will be sensitive to the scales of x and y, and so it will be difficult to use it as a measure to directly compare different pairs of variables. As a consequence, and due to the other aspects that influence the measures of association discussed above, the Pearson Correlation Coefficient (*PCC*) was devised:

$$\rho(x,y) = \frac{cov(x,y)}{\sigma(x)\cdot\sigma(y)}, \tag{3.29}$$

where $cov(x,y)$ is the covariance, and $\sigma(x)$ and $\sigma(y)$ are the standard deviations of x and y, respectively.

Note: the PCC, $\rho(x,y)$, is the normalized covariance and measures the linear relationship between two variables.

When applied to a sample, it can be represented by the letter r and is known as the *Sample Pearson Correlation Coefficient*:

$$r = \frac{\sum_{i=1}^{n} (x_i - \bar{x})(y_i - \bar{y})}{\sqrt{\sum_{j=1}^{n} (x_j - \bar{x})^2} \cdot \sqrt{\sum_{j=1}^{n} (y_j - \bar{y})^2}}. \tag{3.30}$$

The *PCC* value $r \in [-1,1]$, where 1 means a *totally positive correlation*, 0 means no correlation, and −1 means a *totally negative correlation*. A value of 1 means that a linear equation perfectly describes the relationship between the variables, with the two increasing or decreasing simultaneously; a value of −1 indicates the opposite, that is, when one attribute increases, the other decreases.

3.4.2.2 Spearman Rank Correlation Coefficient

Spearman rank correlation coefficient (*SRCC*) is a nonparametric measure of the strength and direction of the relationship between two variables that is based on their ranks instead of on their actual values. For a sample of size n, the scores x_i and y_i are converted into the ranks $R(x_i)$ and $R(y_i)$, and *SRCC* is given by:

$$r_s = \rho\big(R(x), R(y)\big) = \frac{cov\big(R(x), R(y)\big)}{\sigma\big(R(x)\big) \cdot \sigma\big(R(y)\big)}, \tag{3.31}$$

where $\rho(.,.)$, $cov(.,.)$, and $\sigma(.)$ act upon the rank variables.

If all n ranks are distinct integers, then *SRCC* is calculated by:

$$r_s = 1 - \frac{6 \cdot \sum_{i=1}^{n} d_i^2}{n(n^2 - 1)}, \tag{3.32}$$

where $d_i = R(x_i) - R(y_i)$. *SRCC* also ranges over the interval $[-1, 1]$ and allows for the same interpretation discussed previously.

3.4.2.3 Kendall's Rank Correlation Coefficient

Kendall's rank correlation coefficient, also known as Kendall's τ, is also a nonparametric measure of the strength and direction of the relationship between the ranks of two variables. Assume that all values of x_i and y_i are unique, and that there are (x_i, y_i), $i = 1, \ldots, n$ pairs. A pair is *concordant* if either both $x_i > x_j$ and $y_i > y_j$, or both $x_i < x_j$ and $y_i < y_j$; otherwise, it is *discordant*. Kendall's rank correlation coefficient (*KRCC*) is given by:

$$\tau = \frac{(n_c - n_d)}{n(n-1)/2}, \tag{3.33}$$

where n_c is the number of concordant pairs, n_d is the number of discordant pairs, and the denominator, $n(n - 1)/2$, is the number of possible pairs. *KRCC* also ranges over the interval $[-1, 1]$ and allows for the same interpretation as discussed previously.

3.4.2.4 Chi Square (χ^2)

The *Pearson χ^2 test* (or *Pearson chi-square test*) is a nonparametric test to evaluate the association between categorical variables. It assumes that the variables being compared are independent, and its output ranges from 0 to positive infinity. It is calculated by comparing the observed frequencies, O_i, with the expected frequencies, E_i:

$$\chi^2 = \sum_{i=1}^{n} \frac{(O_i - E_i)^2}{E_i},$$
(3.34)

where O_i is the number of objects of type i, E_i is the number of expected counts of type i, and n is the total number of objects.

3.4.2.5 Cramer's V (φ_c)

Cramer's phi is used to measure only the strength of association between two non-binary categorical variables, more specifically, variables that have more than two categories:

$$V = \varphi_c = \frac{\chi^2 / n}{min(k-1, r-1)},$$
(3.35)

where k is the number of columns in the contingency table (Section 3.1.2) and r is its number of rows. φ_c output ranges from 0 to 1, where 0 means no association, and 1 means a perfect association between the variables.

3.4.2.6 Point-Biserial Correlation Coefficient

The point-biserial correlation coefficient (*PBCC*), represented by r_{pb}, is also a nonparametric measure of the strength and direction of the relationship between two variables, but it is used only when one of the variables is binary and the other is continuous (Brown, 2001). Assume that variable y is the binary variable assuming values 0 or 1, and divide the dataset into group 1 that receives the value 1 for y, and group 2 that receives the value 0 for y, r_{pb} is given by:

$$r_{pb} = \frac{M_1 - M_0}{s} \cdot \sqrt{p \cdot q},$$
(3.36)

where M_1 is the mean of the continuous variable x for all data points in group 1, M_0 is the mean of the continuous variable x for all data points in group 2, p is the number of data points in group 1 for variable x, q is the number of data points in group 2 for variable x, and s is the standard deviation of variable x.

When r_{pb} is positive, an increase in the continuous variable implies that the binary variable increases, and when r_{pb} is negative, an increase in the continuous variable implies a decrease in the binary variable.

3.4.3 Comparing the Correlation Measures

Table 3.7 summarizes the different correlation measures presented, taking into account if they assume a particular type of data distribution, their range, the types of variables they deal with, and some directions on when to use each one of them.

TABLE 3.7 Comparison of the different correlation measures; PCC: Pearson Correlation Coefficient; SRCC: Spearman Rank Correlation Coefficient; KRCC: Kendall's Rank Correlation Coefficient; PBCC: Point Biserial Correlation Coefficient

Measure	Parametric	Range	Types of Variables	When to Use
PCC	Yes	[−1, 1]	Continuous	Normally distributed data; linearly related variables; interval or ratio scale variables
SRCC	No	[−1, 1]	Ordinal or continuous	Monotonic, but not necessarily linear relationship; not normally distributed variables
KRCC	No	[−1, 1]	Ordinal	The distance between the variables cannot be measured; ranked variables not necessarily normal
χ^2	No	[0, ∞)	Categorical	The values of the variables are frequency or counts
Cramer's V	No	[0, 1]	Categorical	Categorical variables with more than two levels
PBCC	Yes	[−1, 1]	Continuous with binary	A continuous variable with one binary outcome; the continuous variable is normal; linear relationship among the variables

Code 3.16 presents the scripts to calculate the correlation coefficients described in this section. Code 3.16(a) shows the use of the `corr()` method in Pandas to calculate the Pearson, Spearman Rank, and Kendall's correlation coefficients for the Forest Fires numerical variables. In Code 3.16(b), the `contingency()` method in the Stats library was used to calculate χ^2, and the *KRCC* was determined from χ^2. The PBCC was determined using the `pointbiserialr()` function from Scipy Stats.

CODE 3.16 Scripts to calculate the correlation coefficients are presented. (a) *PCC*, *SRCC*, and *KRCC*. (b) χ^2, φ_c, and *PBCC*. PCC, Pearson correlation coefficient; SRCC, Spearman rank correlation coefficient; KRCC, Kendall's rank correlation coefficient.

```python
# (a) Calculate Correlation Coefficients: PCC, SRCC and KRCC
# for the numerical variables of the Forest Fires dataset

import pandas as pd
from scipy.stats import pearsonr, spearmanr, kendalltau
from ucimlrepo import fetch_ucirepo

# fetch dataset
# https://archive.ics.uci.edu/ml/datasets/forest+fires
dforest = fetch_ucirepo(id=162)["data"]["original"]
pd.options.display.float_format = "{:.2f}".format

# Calculate PCC, SRCC, KRCC
print("**Forest Fires Dataset: PCC, SRCC, KRCC**")
PCC = dforest.corr(method="pearson", numeric_only=True)
print("Pearson Correlation Coefficient (PCC)\n", PCC)
SRCC = dforest.corr(method="spearman", numeric_only=True)
print("\nSpearman Rank Correlation Coefficient (SRCC)\n", SRCC)
```

```
KRCC = dforest.corr(method="kendall", numeric_only=True)

print("\nKramers Rank Correlation Coefficient (KRCC)\n", KRCC)


# (b) Calculate Correlation Coefficients: Chi-square, Cramer's V and Point Biserial
# for the categorical variables of the Mammographic dataset
import pandas as pd
import numpy as np
from scipy import stats
from ucimlrepo import fetch_ucirepo
from scipy.stats import pointbiserialr

# fetch dataset
# https://archive.ics.uci.edu/ml/datasets/Mammographic+Mass
dmammo = fetch_ucirepo(id=161)["data"]["original"]
cols = ["BI-RADS", "Age", "Shape", "Margin", "Density", "Severity"]
dmammo = dmammo[cols]
dmammo.dropna(inplace=True) # Remove rows with missing values

# Chi-square and Cramer's V
cvars = ["Shape", "Margin", "Density", "Severity"] # Categorical variables
chis = pd.DataFrame()
phi = pd.DataFrame()
for var1 in cvars:
    for var2 in cvars:
        if var1 != var2:
            chi2, pval, dof, exp_freq = stats.chi2_contingency(pd.
            crosstab(dmammo[var1], dmammo[var2]))
            chis.loc[var1, var2] = chi2
            phi.loc[var1, var2] = np.sqrt(chi2 / (dmammo.shape[0] * (min(exp_freq.
            shape) - 1)))
        else:
            chis.loc[var1, var2] = np.nan
            phi.loc[var1, var2] = np.nan

print("\n**Mammographic Dataset: Chi-Square, Krammers V, PBCC**\n")
print("Chi-Square Correlation Coefficient (chi^2)\n", chis)
print("\nKramers V Correlation Coefficient (phi)\n", phi)

# Point Biserial Correlation between Age and Severity
PBCC, pval = pointbiserialr(dmammo["Severity"], dmammo["Age"])
print(f"\nPBCC between Age and Severity: {PBCC:.2f}")
```

Running the scripts in Code 3.16a generates the outputs presented in the following matrices. Note that the correlation matrices are symmetric, and their main diagonals are always 1, because the correlation of a variable with itself is maximally positive. By looking at these tables, it is possible to observe that the highest *PCC* was equal to 0.68 for the "DMC"-"DC" variables, and the highest *SRCC* and *KRCC* were equal to 0.78 and 0.62, respectively, for the "FFMC"-"ISI" variables. Although there is a disagreement between the *PCC* and *SRCC/KRCC* coefficients, these are high positive correlation values, indicating that the variables in the pairs have a strong correlation in the same direction. By contrast, these three correlation coefficients (*PCC*, *SRCC*, and *KRCC*) agreed that the variables "temp" and "RH" were the most negatively correlated variables in the dataset, with values of −0.53, −0.52, and −0.38, respectively.

```
**Forest Fires Dataset: PCC, SRCC, KRCC**
```

Pearson Correlation Coefficient (PCC)

	X	Y	FFMC	DMC	DC	ISI	temp	RH	wind	rain	area
X	1.00	0.54	-0.02	-0.05	-0.09	0.01	-0.05	0.09	0.02	0.07	0.06
Y	0.54	1.00	-0.05	0.01	-0.10	-0.02	-0.02	0.06	-0.02	0.03	0.04
FFMC	-0.02	-0.05	1.00	0.38	0.33	0.53	0.43	-0.30	-0.03	0.06	0.04
DMC	-0.05	0.01	0.38	1.00	0.68	0.31	0.47	0.07	-0.11	0.07	0.07
DC	-0.09	-0.10	0.33	0.68	1.00	0.23	0.50	-0.04	-0.20	0.04	0.05
ISI	0.01	-0.02	0.53	0.31	0.23	1.00	0.39	-0.13	0.11	0.07	0.01
temp	-0.05	-0.02	0.43	0.47	0.50	0.39	1.00	-0.53	-0.23	0.07	0.10
RH	0.09	0.06	-0.30	0.07	-0.04	-0.13	-0.53	1.00	0.07	0.10	-0.08
wind	0.02	-0.02	-0.03	-0.11	-0.20	0.11	-0.23	0.07	1.00	0.06	0.01
rain	0.07	0.03	0.06	0.07	0.04	0.07	0.07	0.10	0.06	1.00	-0.01
area	0.06	0.04	0.04	0.07	0.05	0.01	0.10	-0.08	0.01	-0.01	1.00

Spearman Rank Correlation Coefficient (SRCC)

	X	Y	FFMC	DMC	DC	ISI	temp	RH	wind	rain	area
X	1.00	0.49	-0.06	-0.08	-0.07	-0.01	-0.05	0.07	0.03	0.11	0.06
Y	0.49	1.00	-0.01	0.00	-0.11	-0.01	-0.04	0.05	-0.01	0.08	0.05
FFMC	-0.06	-0.01	1.00	0.51	0.26	0.78	0.59	-0.32	-0.04	0.10	0.03
DMC	-0.08	0.00	0.51	1.00	0.56	0.43	0.50	0.03	-0.11	0.12	0.07
DC	-0.07	-0.11	0.26	0.56	1.00	0.10	0.31	0.03	-0.21	0.01	0.06
ISI	-0.01	-0.01	0.78	0.43	0.10	1.00	0.42	-0.18	0.14	0.12	0.01
temp	-0.05	-0.04	0.59	0.50	0.31	0.42	1.00	-0.52	-0.18	0.03	0.08
RH	0.07	0.05	-0.32	0.03	0.03	-0.18	-0.52	1.00	0.04	0.18	-0.02
wind	0.03	-0.01	-0.04	-0.11	-0.21	0.14	-0.18	0.04	1.00	0.12	0.05
rain	0.11	0.08	0.10	0.12	0.01	0.12	0.03	0.18	0.12	1.00	-0.06
area	0.06	0.05	0.03	0.07	0.06	0.01	0.08	-0.02	0.05	-0.06	1.00

Kramers Rank Correlation Coefficient (KRCC)

	X	Y	FFMC	DMC	DC	ISI	temp	RH	wind	rain	area
X	1.00	0.40	-0.04	-0.06	-0.05	-0.01	-0.04	0.05	0.02	0.09	0.05
Y	0.40	1.00	-0.01	0.00	-0.08	-0.01	-0.03	0.04	-0.01	0.07	0.04
FFMC	-0.04	-0.01	1.00	0.37	0.17	0.62	0.44	-0.22	-0.02	0.08	0.02
DMC	-0.06	0.00	0.37	1.00	0.44	0.30	0.36	0.02	-0.08	0.10	0.05
DC	-0.05	-0.08	0.17	0.44	1.00	0.06	0.19	0.02	-0.14	0.01	0.04
ISI	-0.01	-0.01	0.62	0.30	0.06	1.00	0.29	-0.13	0.10	0.10	0.01
temp	-0.04	-0.03	0.44	0.36	0.19	0.29	1.00	-0.38	-0.13	0.02	0.06
RH	0.05	0.04	-0.22	0.02	0.02	-0.13	-0.38	1.00	0.02	0.15	-0.02
wind	0.02	-0.01	-0.02	-0.08	-0.14	0.10	-0.13	0.02	1.00	0.10	0.04
rain	0.09	0.07	0.08	0.10	0.01	0.10	0.02	0.15	0.10	1.00	-0.06
area	0.05	0.04	0.02	0.05	0.04	0.01	0.06	-0.02	0.04	-0.06	1.00

To experiment with the χ^2, φ_c, and *PBCC*, the mammographic dataset was chosen because it contains integer, nominal, and binary variables. χ^2 and φ_c will be calculated between variables "Shape", "Margin", "Density", and "Severity", and the PBCC will be calculated between the "Age" and the "Severity". Note that χ^2 and φ_c are not determined for a variable and itself, which will result in a NaN display. Code 3.16b generates these outputs, where it is possible to observe a high correlation between the "Shape" and "Margin" variables according to χ^2, a strong positive correlation for φ_c between variables "Shape"-"Severity" and "Margin"-"Severity", while there is almost no correlation for the "Shape"-"Density" and "Margin"-"Density" pairs according to ϕ_c. The point-based correlation coefficient showed a strong positive correlation between "Age" and "Severity" in the case of mammographic cancer.

```
**Mammographic Dataset: Chi-Square, Krammers V, PBCC**
Chi-Square Correlation Coefficient (chi^2)
          Margin   Density   Severity    Shape
Shape     525.12    20.78     284.81      NaN
Margin       NaN    17.79     291.39    525.12
Density    17.79      NaN       6.56     20.78
Severity  291.39      6.56       NaN    284.81

Kramers V Correlation Coefficient (phi)
          Margin   Density   Severity    Shape
Shape       0.46     0.09       0.59      NaN
Margin       NaN     0.08       0.59     0.46
Density     0.08      NaN       0.09     0.09
Severity    0.59     0.09        NaN     0.59
PBCC between Age and Severity: 0.46
```

3.4.3.1 Interpreting the Results

To start our interpretation of the correlation analysis, let us consider the PCC results for the Forest Fires dataset presented above. In this case, it is possible to observe that variables "FFMC", "DMC", "DC", and "temp" are all moderately positively correlated with one another, with correlation coefficients ranging from 0.33 to 0.68. These variables all relate to the moisture content and temperature of the forest, and it makes sense that they would be positively correlated with one another. Variables "RH" and "temp" are negatively correlated, with a correlation coefficient of −0.53, indicating a negative linear relationship between them, which would be expected, because as the temperature rises, the relative humidity typically decreases. Finally, the variable "area", which represents the burnt forest area (in ha), has a weak positive correlation with all other variables, with correlation coefficients ranging from 0.01 to 0.1, indicating that there is no strong linear relationship between the burnt area and the other variables in the dataset.

To graphically illustrate and interpret correlations, consider Figure 3.8, which shows the *scatter plots* for some pairs of variables. Figure 3.8a shows the scatter plots between the "DMC"-"DC" and "FFMC"-"ISI" variables, both with $PCC > 0.5$, which can be considered a strong positive correlation. Note that, although there are some outliers in "FFMC" ("FFMC" < 60), for "FFMC" ≥ 80, there is a strong positive correlation for the pair "FFMC"-"ISI". This is an intuitive association between these variables, because "FFMC" is the fine fuel moisture code, which is an indicator of the ease of ignition and flammability of the moisture content of fine fuels, and "ISI" is the initial fire spread index. Thus, the easier the ignition of fire, the faster the fire spread. For the pair "DMC"-"DC" the plot shows a clear increase in one variable following the increase of the other. Again, this is an intuitive association, because "DMC" is a numerical rating of the moisture content of the forest floor and "DC" is a numerical rating of the moisture content of deep organic layers in the soil. In both cases, higher values indicate lower moisture. Thus, it is expected that lower moisture (high rating values) in deep organic layers in the soil is positively correlated with the moisture level of the forest floor.

In the case of Figure 3.8b, it can be observed that the pair "temp"-"RH" has a strong negative correlation ($PCC < -0.5$), that is, an increase in the temperature promotes a decrease in the relative humidity ("RH"). Concerning the pair "temp"-"wind", the negative correlation can be observed more easily only for higher temperature values; more specifically, for temperatures greater than 23°C, the wind starts decreasing.

Finally, in Figure 3.8c it can be observed that there is almost no correlation between the pairs "wind"-"area", and "rain"-"DC". The association between "rain" and the "DC" seems counterintuitive because we could expect that the rain increases the moisture content of deep organic layers in the soil. Thus, this association result requires a more profound analysis. First, it is important to recognize that "DC" is influenced not only by rain but also by other factors, such as temperature, soil type, and evaporation rate. Also, the "DC" variable may have a lag in relation to the "rain" variable because the variable "rain" considers the

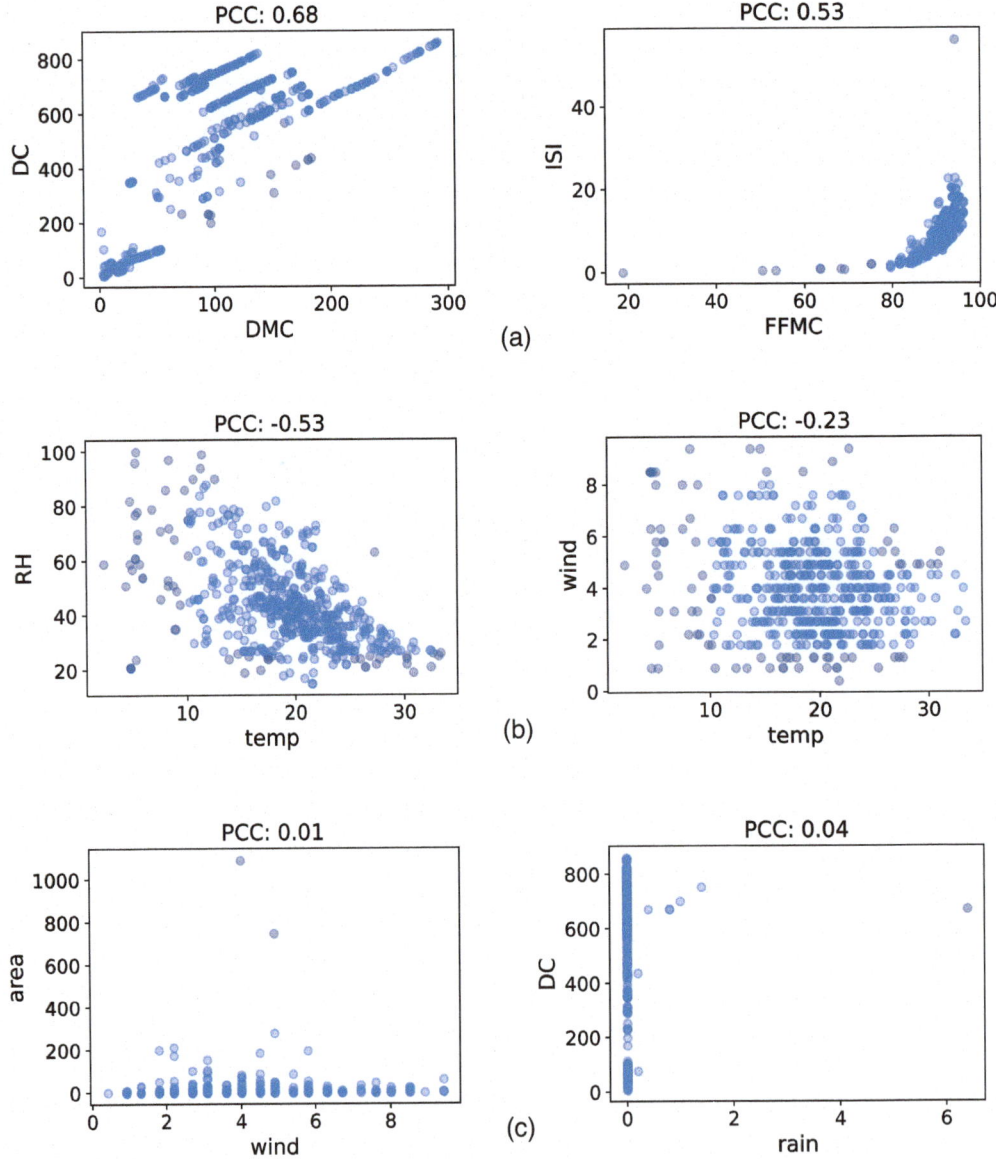

FIGURE 3.8 Scatterplots between pairs of variables from the Forest Fires dataset. (a) Positive correlations. (b) Negative correlations. (c) Almost no correlation.

amount of rain in the 24 h before the data is collected, and the moisture in the deep soil layers due to rain may take longer to be detected.

3.5 LINEAR REGRESSION

The association measures introduced previously aim at describing relationships among variables. It was discussed that the covariance measures the level of change in one variable in relation to another, and correlation measures the dependence of two variables, providing a predictive relationship between them.

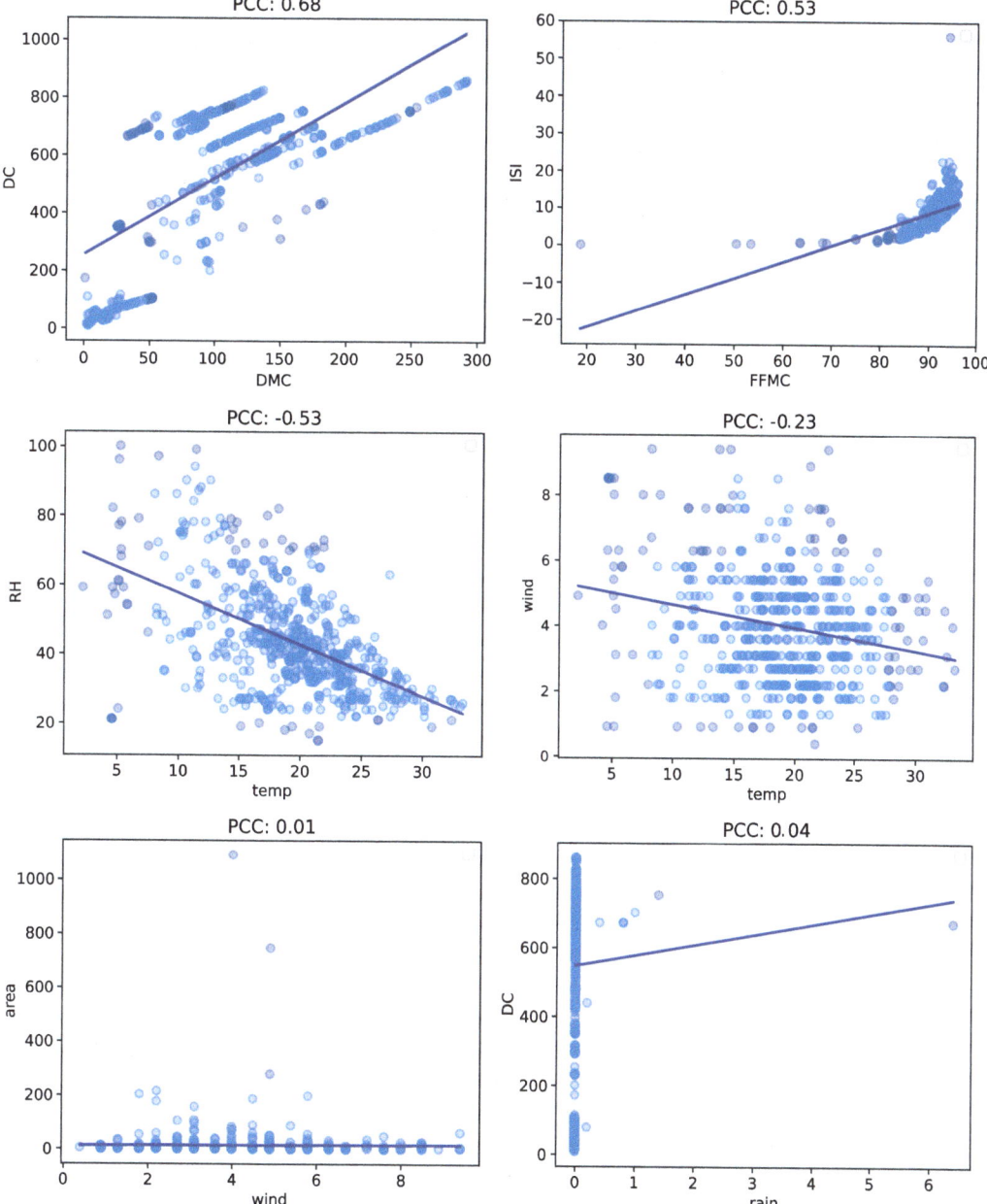

FIGURE 3.9   Scatterplots between pairs of variables from the Forest Fires dataset with the linear regressors plotted.

Assuming one of the variables is the independent variable (x) and the other (y) is the dependent one, it is possible to summarize the relationship between the variables by finding a curve that best approximates (fits) the data. This process is known as *regression analysis*, and if the curve (regressor) is a *line*, it is called *linear regression* (Peck et al., 2008; Watkins, 2016).

The standard form of a linear regression is:

$$y = a + b \cdot x, \tag{3.37}$$

where a is called the *intercept* and corresponds to the value where the line intercepts the y-axis, b is the *slope* of the line, y is the dependent variable, and x is the independent variable.

It is out of the scope of this book to discuss how to find the coefficients a and b that solve the linear equation in Eq. (3.37) in optimality, but Figure 3.9 shows the scatterplots of Figure 3.8 with the respective linear regressors included. Note that the regressors are the lines that better approximate the data distributions, and their slope indicates the type of correlation between the variables.

3.6 EXERCISES

3.6.1 Research Topics and Questions

1. Discuss the implications of different shapes of distributions and the use of contingency tables. How do these aspects influence our understanding of the data?

2. Explore the meaning of central tendency and variability measures. How do these measures help us understand the "typical" values and the spread of data?

3. Discuss the reasons behind the prevalence of the normal distribution in natural and social sciences. Why is it considered the "default" distribution for many phenomena?

4. Discuss the use of linear regression for understanding relationships between variables. Does correlation imply causation?

3.6.2 Quizzes

1. What is one of the first steps when analyzing a data set?

    a. Building a classification model.

    b. Characterizing the dataset structure and variables.

    c. Collecting more data.

    d. Conducting hypothesis testing.

2. In a survey collecting information about people's ages, which of the following is considered a variable?

 a. The age of the researcher.

 b. The color of the survey form.

 c. The participants' birthdates.

 d. The weather on the day of the survey.

3. What do summary measures provide in descriptive data analysis?

 a. Central tendencies, variability, and form of the data.

 b. Associations between variables.

 c. Frequency distributions.

 d. Outliers in the data.

4. If you have a dataset with outliers, which measure of central tendency is generally more robust and less affected by outliers?

 a. Mean.

 b. Midpoint.

 c. Median.

 d. Variance.

5. What does the interquartile range (IQR) measure?

 a. The range between the maximum and minimum values.

 b. The range between the first and third quartiles.

 c. The range between the median and mode.

 d. The range between the mean and median.

6. A higher standard deviation indicates what about the data?

 a. Greater spread or dispersion.

 b. Smaller spread or dispersion.

 c. No spread or dispersion.

 d. Perfect symmetry.

7. In measures of association, what does a positive correlation between two variables mean?

   a. One variable causes the other.

   b. There is no relationship between the variables.

   c. An increase in one variable is associated with an increase in the other.

   d. An increase in one variable is associated with a decrease in the other.

8. What does a histogram represent in descriptive data analysis?

   a. A graphical representation of frequency distributions.

   b. A measure of association between variables.

   c. A summary measure of central tendency.

   d. A scatterplot.

9. Which of the following is true about a positively skewed frequency distribution?

   a. The tail of the distribution is on the right side.

   b. The median is equal to the mean.

   c. The data is perfectly symmetrical.

   d. The mode is undefined.

10. What is the formula to calculate the range of a dataset?

   a. Range = Maximum − Minimum.

   b. Range = (Maximum + Minimum)/2.

   c. Range = Standard Deviation.

   d. Range = Median − Mean.

3.6.3 Computational Exercises

1. Create three different datasets:

   a. **A:** 1,000 random numbers following a uniform distribution between 0 and 1.

   b. **B:** 1,000 random numbers following a normal distribution with mean 50 and standard deviation 10.

   c. **C:** 1,000 random numbers following a skewed distribution, such as a gamma distribution with shape parameter 2.

Plot histograms for each dataset to visualize their shapes. Compare and contrast the shapes of the distributions.

2. For the "temp" variable of the Forest Fires dataset, include the values of the geometric and harmonic means in the graph and discuss their positions when compared with the other central tendency measures already plotted in Figure 3.3.

3. Calculate the *Pearson second coefficient of skewness* and compare it with the other two skewness coefficients presented (Fischer-Pearson skewness coefficient and First Skewness coefficient).

4. Generate a dataset of 1,000 random numbers following a normal distribution with mean 60 and standard deviation 15. Plot a histogram to visualize the distribution. Compute the percentage of data within one, two, and three standard deviations from the mean.

3.6.4 Case Studies

This section presents three case studies, for which the following tasks must be performed:

1. Present the data dictionary.

2. Perform a descriptive analysis of the data, including the distribution of each variable (using histograms), summary measures, and the shape of the distributions.

3. Create contingency tables for categorical variables.

4. Calculate measures of association (covariance and correlation) between variables.

5. Draw a linear regression line over the plot with the pairs of variables (scatter plot) and observe the type of correlation.

6. Interpret the results and provide insights.

CASE STUDY 1   Health Sciences – Cardiovascular Disease Dataset

https://www.kaggle.com/datasets/jocelyndumlao/cardiovascular-disease-dataset

Kaggle dataset description: This dataset contains information on heart disease patients from a multispecialty hospital in India. It offers access to valuable data on 1,000 individuals, including 12 key features commonly associated with heart disease. This dataset can be used to develop early detection methods and build predictive machine learning models for heart disease.

Objective: To understand the distribution of these health metrics in the patient population, identify any associations between them, and build simple linear regression models between pairs of variables.

CASE STUDY 2   Business – Superstore Sales Dataset

https://www.kaggle.com/datasets/rohitsahoo/sales-forecasting

Dataset description: Retail dataset of a global superstore for 4 years. A dataset containing information about order ID, order data, shipment date and mode, segment, country, and city.

Objective: To understand the sales trends and identify any patterns or associations.

CASE STUDY 3   Technology – Netflix User Behavior Data Analysis

https://www.kaggle.com/datasets/arnavsmayan/netflix-userbase-dataset

Kaggle dataset description: This dataset provides a simulated sample of Netflix user data, offering insights into user subscriptions, revenue, account details, and activity. Each record represents a unique user identified by an anonymized User ID. It includes details like subscription type (Basic, Standard, or Premium), monthly subscription revenue, join date, last payment date, and user location. Additional features shed light on user behavior, such as preferred device type (Smart TV, Mobile, etc.) and current account status (active or inactive). It is important to note that this is a synthetic dataset and does not reflect actual Netflix user information.

Objective: To understand user behavior, identify any patterns or associations, and predict user engagement.

## CHAPTER 4

Principles of Data Visualization

"The visual system is likely to have developed ways of detecting structure in the real world."

– Anne Treisman, Preattentive Processing in Vision, Computer Vision, Graphics, and Image Processing, *1985, p. 163.*

Drawings, illustrations, paintings, and photographs have been used by human society as effective means of conveying important information. Among the disciplines that have been developed to study these techniques, data visualization is of particular interest here. It is important to recognize that such disciplines emphasize specific techniques for communicating information. For instance, photography emphasizes color and light variation, while illustration omits unimportant details and highlights those aspects that are desired to be emphasized (Ebert, 2005).

Data visualization, by contrast, focuses on the visual representation of data in such a way that its values, structure, nature, type, and variability are accurately expressed by means of graphs. It aims to support the exploration and understanding of data, the identification of patterns, trends, distributions, correlations, and anomalies, the communication of insights, and aid in decision-making.

Before presenting the data visualization methods, there are three principles to be discussed in this chapter. The first one is related to the visual processing of information and the fact that there are datasets with the same summary measures but completely different visual representations. Second, it is important to recognize and understand that there are features in images that are noted before paying attention to a specific item. Third, and last, some visual characteristics help to explain how we organize and group visual elements. After covering these subjects, some guidelines for data visualization will be presented and the visualization methods will be introduced in the next chapter.

DOI: 10.1201/9781003570691-4

4.1 VISUAL PROCESSING

There is a trend in visualization called *perceptualization* of information, which means conveying data visualization techniques driven by characteristics of human perception, because the perceptual channels are the communication medium (Ebert, 2005). The human perceptual system involves the auditory, olfactory, visual, gustatory, and somatosensory systems. The perceptual systems receive physical stimuli and generate information that is transmitted to the brain, processed, and interpreted.

The visual system plays a key role in our capability of absorbing information from and navigating in the environment. The light detected by the eyes is converted into neural signals, processed by the brain, visually perceived, and then interpreted. From the key characteristics of vision, some perceptual properties are central to data and information visualization: *preattentive processing* and the *Gestalt principles* (Chen, 2017). In addition to these two visual properties, the fact that significantly different data may have the same or similar summary measures is the basis for this section.

This section starts by showing that data with significantly different distributions may have the same or very similar summary measures. In such cases, visualization plays a key role in complementing the analysis for data understanding. Then, it is discussed that some visual features are perceived without focused attention, a process called *preattentive processing*. Some important preattentive features are presented and illustrated using Python code snippets. Finally, some guidelines for visual perception, known as Gestalt principles, explaining how we naturally organize and group visual elements into meaningful patterns, are presented and illustrated. These concepts are important as design principles for effective data visualization graphs (Schwabish, 2021).

4.1.1 Can't See the Forest for the Trees

The previous chapter presented several summary measures aimed at characterizing the data and providing information about typical values, variability, form, and associations between variables. Although this information is very useful for the understanding of the data, it is usually insufficient for gaining full knowledge of the data distribution.

In 1973, a statistician named Francis Anscombe created four datasets, known as the *Anscombe's Quartet*, each with 11 pairs of values (*x,y*) each and identical summary statistics, but with different distributions and shapes (Anscombe, 1973). He wanted to highlight the fact that, although very useful as part of the exploratory data analysis process, the summary measures are insufficient, and sometimes misleading, to describe the data.

Code 4.1 presents a script to read the Anscombe's Quartet dataset, available as an example dataset from the `Seaborn` library, generate the data table with the summary measures (mean, standard deviation, and correlation) using `NumPy`, and plot the scatterplots using the `scatterplot()` method from `Seaborn`. It also calculates the regression lines using the `OLS()` method in the `Statsmodels.api` and plots the lines for each of the four datasets.

CODE 4.1   Script to generate the Anscombe's Quartet table with the summary measures (mean, standard deviation, correlation) and plot the scatterplots and regression lines for each of the four datasets.

```python
# Print the Anscombe's Quartet table with the summary measures (mean, std, corr, linear
# regression) for each dataset and plot the scatterplots of each of the four datasets

import seaborn as sns
import pandas as pd
import numpy as np
import statsmodels.api as sm
import matplotlib.pyplot as plt

# Uses the Seaborn library to load the Anscombe's data
danscombe = sns.load_dataset("anscombe")
pd.options.display.float_format = "{:.2f}".format

# Print the data and summary measures for each dataset
for dataset in ["I", "II", "III", "IV"]:
    df_subset = danscombe[danscombe.dataset == dataset]
    print(f"Dataset  {dataset}\n{df_subset}")
    print(f"Summary Measures for Dataset {dataset}:")
    print(f"Mean of x: {np.mean(df_subset.x):.2f}")
    print(f"Mean of y: {np.mean(df_subset.y):.2f}")
    print(f"Std of x: {np.std(df_subset.x):.2f}")
    print(f"Std of y: {np.std(df_subset.y):.2f}")
    print(f"Correlation between x and y: {np.corrcoef(df_subset.x, df_subset.y)
    [0,1]:.2f}")
    model = sm.OLS(df_subset.y, sm.add_constant(df_subset.x)).fit()
    print(f"Linear regression model: y = {model.params.iloc[0]:.2f} +
{model.params.iloc[1]:.2f}x\n")

# Plot the scatterplots and regression lines for each dataset
fig, axes = plt.subplots(2, 2, figsize=(10, 10))

for i, dataset in enumerate(["I", "II", "III", "IV"]):
    ax = axes.flatten()[i]
    df_subset = danscombe[danscombe.dataset == dataset]
    x = df_subset.x; y = df_subset.y
    model = sm.OLS(y, sm.add_constant(x)).fit()
    y_pred = model.predict(sm.add_constant(x))
    sns.scatterplot(x=x, y=y, ax=ax)
    sns.lineplot(x=x, y=y_pred, color="red", ax=ax)
    ax.set_title(f"Dataset {dataset}", fontsize=16)

# Show plot
plt.show()
```

Running Code 4.1 generates the output presented below with one dataset organized in each rectangle. When comparing the four datasets, it is observed that Datasets I, II, and III have the same x distribution and differ only in the y distribution, while Dataset IV has different x and y distributions, with x having a single value different from the others, that is, an outlier. Despite these differences, all datasets have the same summary measures and regression lines.

```
Dataset I
   dataset    x            y
0          I 10.00      8.04
1          I 8.00       6.95
2          I 13.00      7.58
3          I  9.00      8.81
4          I 11.00      8.33
5          I 14.00      9.96
6          I  6.00      7.24
7          I  4.00      4.26
8          I 12.00     10.84
9          I  7.00      4.82
10         I  5.00      5.68
Summary Measures for Dataset I:
Mean of   x: 9.00
Mean of   y: 7.50
Std of    x: 3.16
Std of    y: 1.94
Correlation between x and y: 0.82
Linear regression model: y = 3.00
 + 0.50x
```

```
Dataset II
   dataset    x            y
11         II 10.00      9.14
12         II  8.00      8.14
13         II 13.00      8.74
14         II  9.00      8.77
15         II 11.00      9.26
16         II 14.00      8.10
17         II  6.00      6.13
18         II  4.00      3.10
19         II 12.00      9.13
20         II  7.00      7.26
21         II  5.00      4.74
Summary Measures for Dataset II:
Mean of    x: 9.00
Mean of    y: 7.50
Std of     x: 3.16
Std of     y: 1.94
Correlation between x and y: 0.82
Linear regression model: y = 3.00
 + 0.50x
```

```
Dataset III
   dataset   x            y
22        III 10.00      7.46
23        III  8.00      6.77
24        III 13.00     12.74
25        III  9.00      7.11
26        III 11.00      7.81
27        III 14.00      8.84
28        III  6.00      6.08
29        III  4.00      5.39
30        III 12.00      8.15
31        III  7.00      6.42
32        III 5.00       5.73
Summary Measures for Dataset III:
Mean of x: 9.00
Mean of y: 7.50
Std of x: 3.16
Std of y: 1.94
Correlation between x and y: 0.82
Linear regression model: y = 3.00
 + 0.50x
```

```
Dataset IV
      dataset        x           y
33           IV 8.00       6.58
34           IV 8.00       5.76
35           IV 8.00       7.71
36           IV 8.00       8.84
37           IV 8.00       8.47
38           IV 8.00       7.04
39           IV 8.00       5.25
40          IV 19.00      12.50
41           IV 8.00       5.56
42           IV 8.00       7.91
43           IV 8.00       6.89
Summary Measures for Dataset IV:
Mean of    x: 9.00
Mean of    y: 7.50
Std of     x: 3.16
Std of     y: 1.94
Correlation between x and y: 0.82
Linear regression model: y = 3.00
 + 0.50x
```

Figure 4.1 shows the scatterplots and regression lines for Anscombe's Quartet. As can be observed, the scatterplots are completely different from one another, though all of them have the same summary measures.

An example similar to Anscombe's Quartet is the *Datasaurus Dozen*, a dataset consisting of 13 distinct datasets, each with a different shape but practically the same summary measures. This dataset was created by Alberto Cairo as another illustration of the need to

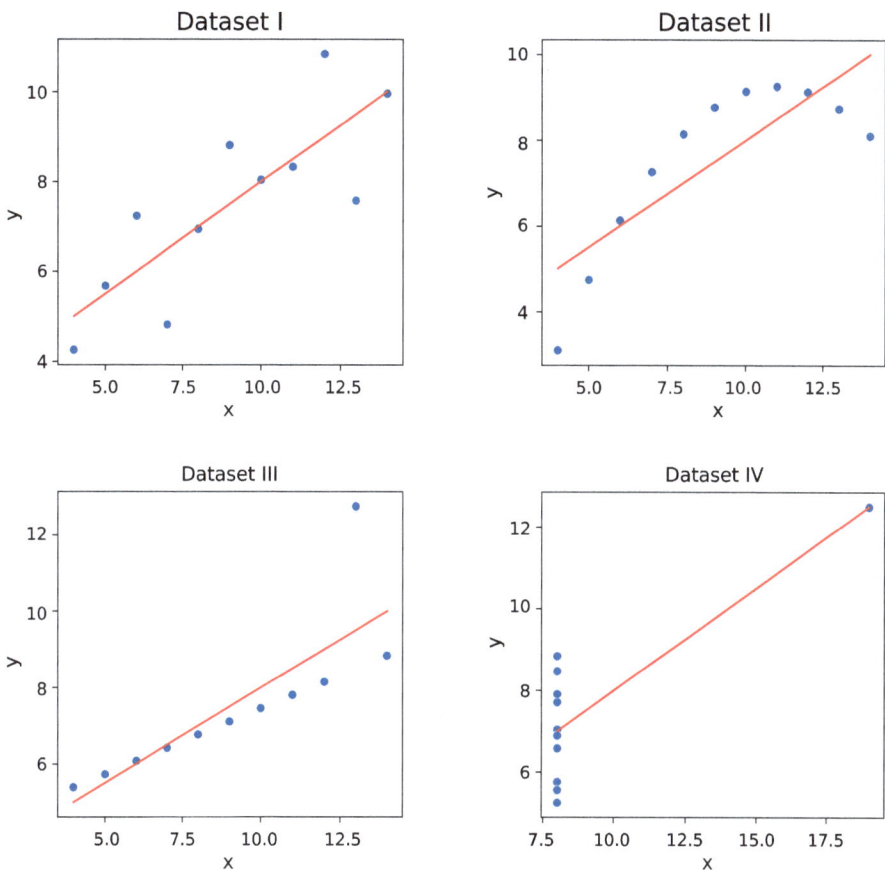

FIGURE 4.1   Scatterplots and regression lines for the four datasets of Anscombe's Quartet.

use data visualization, in addition to the summary measures, to have a more comprehensive understanding of the data distribution (Cairo, 2016; Matejka & Fitzmaurice, 2017). The 13 datasets have different shapes, each one intuitively named as follows (Figure 4.2): dino, away, h_lines, v_lines, x_shape, star, high_lines, dots, circle, bullseye, slant_up, slant_down, and wide_lines.

Code 4.2 is similar to Code 4.1 but reads the Datasaurus Dozen dataset from a CSV file with a semicolon delimiter using the Pandas library. It then loops over the 13 datasets, calculating and printing the summary measures on the screen using the Numpy library, and calculates the regression lines using the OLS() method in the Statsmodels.api. It then plots the scatterplot() with Seaborn for each dataset and removes the unused subplots. When run, the script generates the output below for the "dino" dataset. The summary measures for the other datasets are practically the same, with minimal differences in a few calculations, sustaining the hypothesis that significantly different shapes can have the same summary measures.

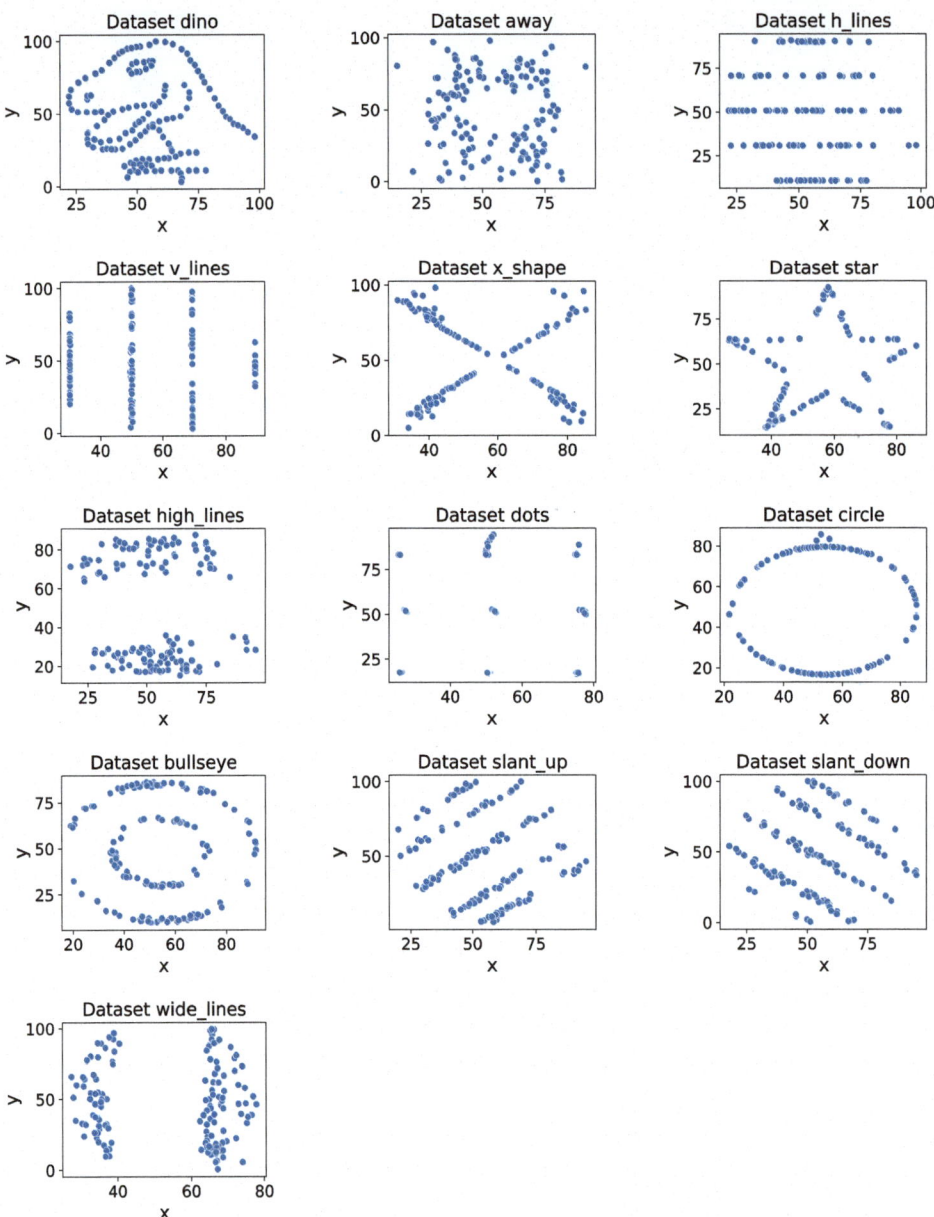

FIGURE 4.2   Scatterplots of the 13 datasets available in the Datasaurus Dozen.

```
Summary Measures for Dataset dino:
Mean of x: 54.26
Mean of y: 47.83
Std of x: 16.71
Std of y: 26.84
Correlation between x and y: -0.06
Linear regression model: y = 53.45 + -0.10x
```

CODE 4.2   Script to generate the Datasaurus Dozen table with the summary measures (mean, standard deviation, correlation, linear regression) and plot the scatterplots for each of the four datasets.

```python
# Print the Datasaurus Dozen table with the summary measures (mean, std, corr, linear
# regression) and plot the scatterplots of each dataset

import pandas as pd
import numpy as np
import statsmodels.api as sm
import matplotlib.pyplot as plt
import seaborn as sns

# Load the dataset using Pandas
dsaurus = pd.read_csv("datasaurus_dozen.csv", delimiter=';')
pd.options.display.float_format = "{:.2f}".format

# Print the data and summary measures for each dataset
for dataset in dsaurus.dataset.unique():
    print(f"Summary Measures for Dataset {dataset}:")
    df_subset = dsaurus[dsaurus.dataset == dataset]
    print(f"Mean of x: {np.mean(df_subset.x):.2f}")
    print(f"Mean of y: {np.mean(df_subset.y):.2f}")
    print(f"Std of x: {np.std(df_subset.x):.2f}")
    print(f"Std of y: {np.std(df_subset.y):.2f}")
    print(f"Correlation between x and y: {np.corrcoef(df_subset.x, df_subset.y)[0,
1]:.2f}")
    model = sm.OLS(df_subset.y, sm.add_constant(df_subset.x)).fit()
    print(f"Linear regression model: y = {model.params.iloc[0]:.2f} + {model.
params.iloc[1]:.2f}x\n")

# Plot the scatterplots for each dataset
fig, axes = plt.subplots(5, 3, figsize=(14, 18))

for i, dataset in enumerate(dsaurus.dataset.unique()):
    ax = axes.flatten()[i]
    df_subset = dsaurus[dsaurus.dataset == dataset]
    x = df_subset.x; y = df_subset.y
    sns.scatterplot(x=x, y=y, ax=ax)
    ax.set_title(f"Dataset {dataset}", fontsize=16)

for i in range(len(dsaurus.dataset.unique()), len(axes.flatten())):
    fig.delaxes(axes.flatten()[i])  # Remove unused subplots

# Show plot
plt.show()
```

4.1.2 Preattentive Processing

Preattentive processing refers to the automatic and rapid cognitive processing of visual features that occurs before attention is focused on a specific object or location (Treisman, 1985; Albustin et al., 2010; Schwabish, 2021). *Preattentive features*, such as color, shape, orientation, and size, are those basic visual properties that are processed automatically, without conscious effort or attention. By understanding preattentive features, data analysts can create effective data visualization designs that make use of them to convey information more efficiently and accurately to the audience.

In this context, visual analysis can be divided into an early *preattentive* level of processing and *focused attention*, which is necessary to integrate all the separate features into coherent information. Experiments revealed that tasks that can be performed on large multielement displays in up to 200–250 ms are considered preattentive, that is, can be processed without focused attention (Treisman, 1985; Healey et al., 1995). This is justified by the fact that eye movements need at least this amount of time to start, and perception within this time frame involves the information available in a single glimpse. These results suggest that the search for some visual primitives is automatic and parallel, while the absence of such primitives requires a serial search and focused attention (Cairo, 2016; Matejka & Fitzmaurice, 2017).

Various studies have explored preattentive visual stimuli. A standard technique involves measuring the response time to identify a target item within a set of distracting elements. If a stimulus is preattentive, the response time should remain unaffected by the presence of distractors. Additionally, identifying preattentive elements or features can involve briefly introducing a unique item amidst a set of similar items and observing if the viewer perceives it within the 200–250 ms timeframe (Ebert, 2005).

Understanding how our visual system processes and analyzes an image is a central aspect in the planning, design, and selection of data visualization techniques. Studying preattentive processing allows us to answer questions like (Chen, 2017):

- What types of features are perceived immediately?

- Which visual characteristics are discriminatory?

- What are the features or elements that can confuse the viewers?

- What data (information) or features should be highlighted from a graph?

Several authors have tried to determine the main features that are detected preattentively, but this depends on the expected use of these features, the target items to be detected, the presence of distractors and background, and other factors (Healey et al., 1995). The main preattentive features for data visualization to be stressed here are shape, line width, color, size, markings, orientation, position, 3D depth cues, length, curvature, density, closure, and texture.

This section provides a brief description of each of these preattentive features with some plots illustrating them with abstract images and the code snippet used to generate them. These code snippets are part of a longer script containing all of them and are available at the book's GitHub.

4.1.2.1 Shape

The preattentive processing of shape is a basic visual property that enables us to swiftly detect similarities and differences between items based on their shape, without requiring conscious effort or attention. For instance, in a picture with squares and circles, one can quickly differentiate one from the other based on their shapes. Similarly, using different shapes for different forms or categories, or using a shape that is indicative of the data

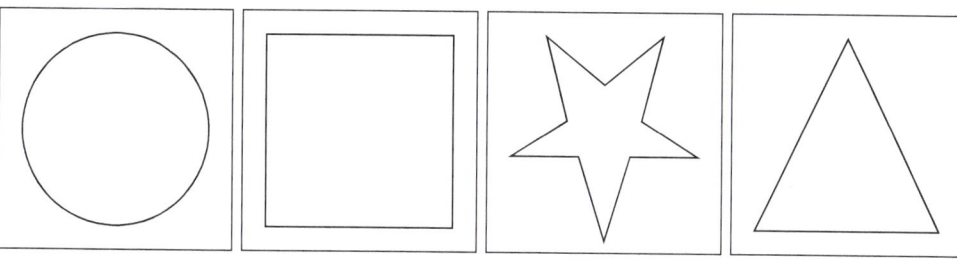

```python
# Shape
import numpy as np
import matplotlib.pyplot as plt
from matplotlib import patches

fig, axs = plt.subplots(1, 4, figsize=(8, 2), constrained_layout=True)
shapes = ['circle', 'square', 'star', 'triangle']
for i, ax in enumerate(axs):
    shape = shapes[i]
    # Create shapes using patches
    if shape == 'circle':
        shape_obj = patches.Circle((0.5, 0.5), radius=0.4, fill=False)
    elif shape == 'square':
        shape_obj = patches.Rectangle((0.1, 0.1), 0.8, 0.8, fill=False)
    elif shape == 'star':
        x = [0.5, 0.61, 0.9, 0.66, 0.75, 0.5, 0.25, 0.34, 0.1, 0.39]
        y = [0.05, 0.4, 0.4, 0.55, 0.9, 0.7, 0.9, 0.55, 0.4, 0.4]
        shape_obj = patches.Polygon(np.column_stack((x, y)), closed=True,
fill=False)
    elif shape == 'triangle':
        x = [0.1, 0.5, 0.9, 0.1]
        y = [0.1, 0.9, 0.1, 0.1]
        shape_obj = patches.Polygon(np.column_stack((x, y)), closed=True,
fill=False)
    # Add the shape to the plot
    ax.add_patch(shape_obj)
    ax.set_xlim(0, 1)
    ax.set_ylim(0, 1)
    ax.set_xticks([]); ax.set_yticks([])
plt.suptitle('Shape', fontsize=16, y=1.15)
```

FIGURE 4.3   Plots illustrating the preattentive feature of shape, and the code snippet used to generate the shapes.

(e.g., a circle for data on a map), can help viewers quickly identify patterns. Figure 4.3 shows four different shapes generated with a simple code snippet and the Matplotlib library. By looking at the plots, although we note that they are all lines, we can quickly recognize their differences in shapes.

4.1.2.2 Line Width

The preattentive processing of line width allows us to quickly detect variations in thickness, such as the presence of a thicker or thinner line in a group of otherwise similar lines. Variation in line width can be used to represent different quantities, relevance, and values, to emphasize certain parts of an image, or to promote a sense of depth or movement. For instance, in a graph with lines, the thicker ones may represent those reinforced by a given process or mechanism. Figure 4.4 shows four lines generated with increasing (from left to right) width using the `plot()` function from the `Matplotlib` library. A quick look at them allows us to observe that they appear in an increasing order of width from left to right.

4.1.2.3 Color

Color is a powerful visual tool to encode data and convey different meanings, such as categories, magnitude, visual hierarchy, and even emotions. Using different hues, saturations, and brightness levels can help differentiate between categories or show patterns in the data. For example, in a pie chart describing fruits, we may use yellow for bananas, green for avocados, red for apples, etc. In addition to its functional uses, the preattentive processing of color can also be used to create visually pleasing designs. Figure 4.5 shows the plots

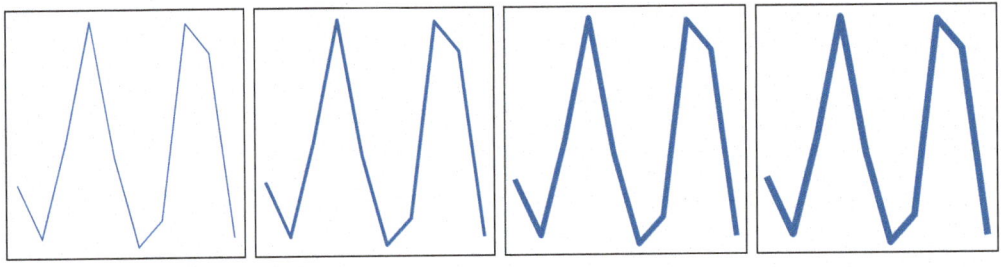

```python
# Line Width
fig, axs = plt.subplots(1, 4, figsize=(8, 2), constrained_layout=True)
line_widths = [1, 2, 3, 4]
x = np.arange(10)
y = np.random.rand(10)
for ax, lw in zip(axs, line_widths):
    ax.plot(x, y, linewidth=lw)
    ax.set_xticks([]); ax.set_yticks([])
plt.suptitle('Line Width', fontsize=16, y=1.15)
```

FIGURE 4.4   Plots illustrating the preattentive feature of line width, and the code snippet used to generate the lines with different widths.

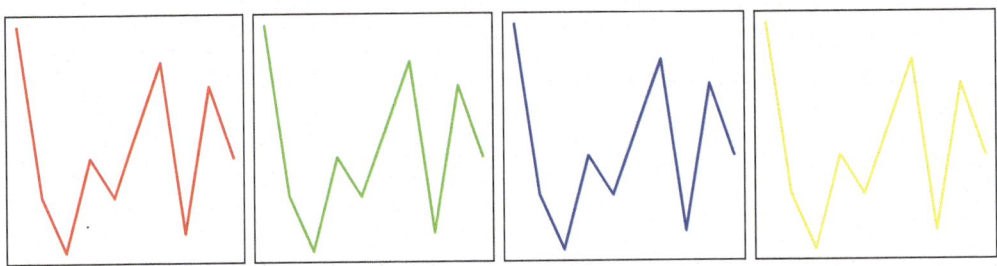

(Continued)

```
# Color
fig, axs = plt.subplots(1, 4, figsize=(8, 2), constrained_layout=True)
colors = [[1, 0, 0], [0, 1, 0], [0, 0, 1], [1, 1, 0]]
x = np.arange(10)
y = np.random.rand(10)
for ax, c in zip(axs, colors):
    ax.plot(x, y, color=c)
    ax.set_xticks([]); ax.set_yticks([])
plt.suptitle('Color', fontsize=16, y=1.15)
```

FIGURE 4.5 (*Continued*) Plots illustrating the preattentive feature of colors, and the code snippet used to generate the lines with different colors.

of four lines with different colors and the code snippet used to generate them. Again, their color differences are immediately observed without the need for any conscious effort.

4.1.2.4 Size

Size is a preattentive feature that exerts a similar effect in vision as that exerted by the line width, that is, to detect differences quickly and automatically in items (e.g., objects, data points, font sizes, etc.). Differences in size can draw attention to specific data points, indicate hierarchy, emphasize specific items, or convey information about the magnitude of the data. Variation in size can be used to represent different quantities or values, where larger sizes may indicate higher values or importance, while smaller sizes may indicate lower values or importance. Figure 4.6 shows four plots with ten random data points each generated with increasing (from left to right) sizes using the scatter() function from the Matplotlib library.

4.1.2.5 Markings

The preattentive processing of markings (e.g., stripes, dots, crosses, stars, hatchings, etc.) includes various visual properties, such as texture, shading, and patterns. These properties allow us to swiftly detect differences and similarities between objects or regions, such as the presence of a repeating pattern in a group of otherwise random shapes. The presence

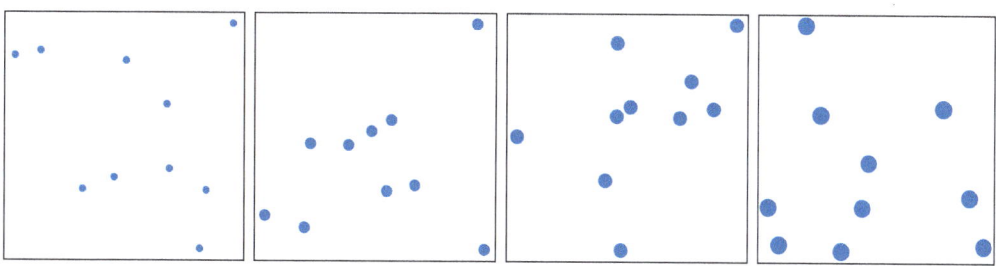

```
# Size
fig, axs = plt.subplots(1, 4, figsize=(8, 2), constrained_layout=True)
sizes = [10, 30, 50, 80]
for ax, s in zip(axs, sizes):
    ax.scatter(np.random.rand(10), np.random.rand(10), s=s)
    ax.set_xticks([]); ax.set_yticks([])
plt.suptitle('Size', fontsize=16, y=1.15)
```

FIGURE 4.6 Plots illustrating the preattentive feature of size, and the code snippet used to generate the data points with different sizes.

or absence of certain markings, such as dots or squares, can be used to represent different categories or values. Figure 4.7 shows four identical lines plotted with different markings, allowing us to differentiate them. Note that similar markings, such as the "+" and the "×" signs, require more attention from us to be differentiated.

4.1.2.6 Orientation

Differences in orientation can help us differentiate between items (e.g., data points, lines, objects, etc.) or extract information about the data. For example, using vertical bars in a bar chart can help differentiate between categories, while using horizontal bars can emphasize the magnitude of the data. Angles and direction can be used to convey information, such as trends, movement, sense of depth, or changes in values. Figure 4.8 shows the four plots containing lines with different angles in relation to the *x*-axis and the code snippet that

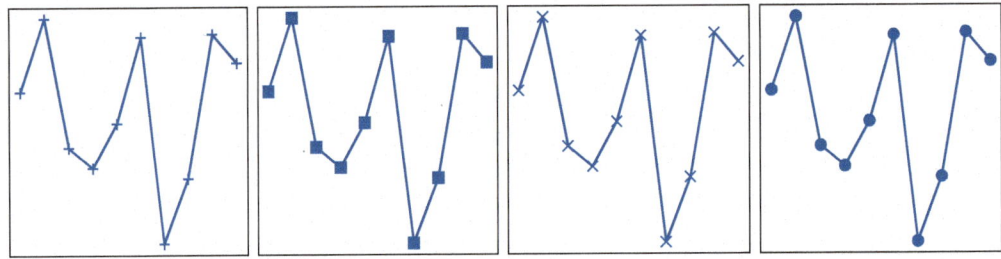

```python
# Markings
fig, axs = plt.subplots(1, 4, figsize=(8, 2), constrained_layout=True)
marks = ['+', 's', 'x', 'o']
x = np.arange(10)
y = np.random.rand(10)
for ax, mark in zip(axs, marks):
    ax.plot(x, y, marker=mark)
    ax.set_xticks([]); ax.set_yticks([])
plt.suptitle('Markings', fontsize=16, y=1.15)
```

FIGURE 4.7   Plots illustrating the preattentive feature of markings, and the code snippet used to generate the identical lines with different markings.

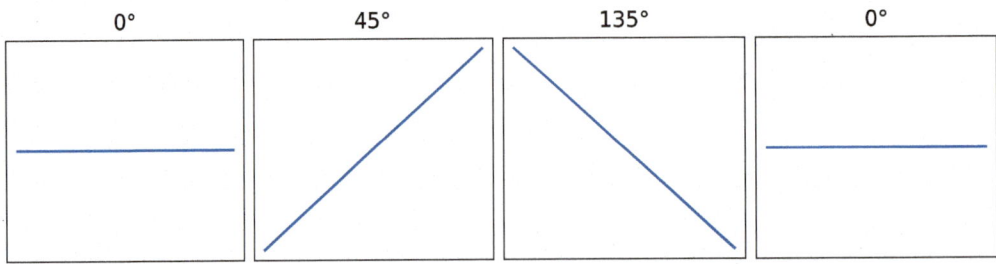

(Continued)

```
# Orientation
fig, axs = plt.subplots(1, 4, figsize=(8, 2), constrained_layout=True)
orientations = [0, 45, 135, 0]
for ax, o in zip(axs, orientations):
    angle = np.deg2rad(o)
    x = np.array([0, np.cos(angle)])
    y = np.array([0, np.sin(angle)])
    ax.plot(x, y)
    ax.set_xticks([]); ax.set_yticks([])
    ax.set_title(f'{o}°')
plt.suptitle('Orientation', fontsize=16, y=1.15)
```

FIGURE 4.8 (*Continued*) Plots illustrating the preattentive feature of orientation, and the code snippet used to generate the lines with different orientations (angles).

uses the `deg2rad()` method from `Numpy` and `plot()` from `Matplotlib`. These plots may give us the impression that the line is rotating counterclockwise.

4.1.2.7 Position
Preattentive processing of position allows us to quickly detect changes in location, such as the presence of a dot or other object that is slightly displaced from the others. The spatial location of visual elements can also be used to guide the viewer's attention or encode information, such as ranking, hierarchy, or relationship (grouping). Figure 4.9 shows four plots with ten data points each generated in random positions using the `scatter()` function from the `Matplotlib` library. In this example, even without focused attention, we observe that the dots in each frame have different positions.

4.1.2.8 3D
Preattentive processing of 3D (three-dimensional) properties allows us to detect the depth and spatial relationships between objects, such as the presence of an object that appears to be closer or farther away than the others, without the need for focused attention. Perspective, lighting, size, or shading can be used to create the illusion of depth and convey information,

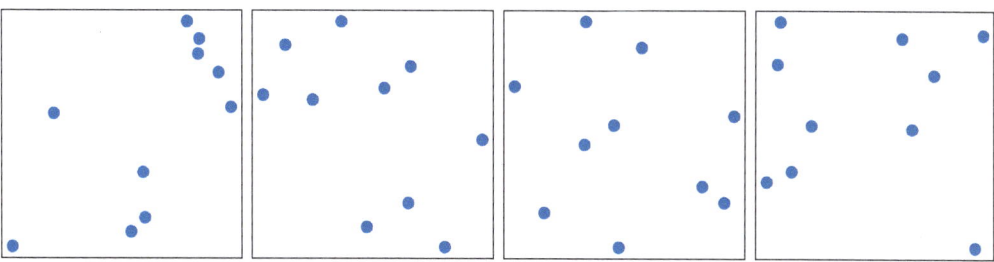

```
# Position
fig, axs = plt.subplots(1, 4, figsize=(8, 2), constrained_layout=True)
for ax in axs:
    ax.scatter(np.random.rand(10), np.random.rand(10))
    ax.set_xticks([]); ax.set_yticks([])
plt.suptitle('Position', fontsize=16, y=1.15)
```

FIGURE 4.9 Plots illustrating the preattentive feature of position, and the code snippet used to generate the data points with different positions in the space.

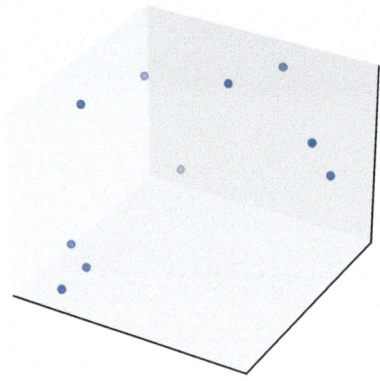

```
# 3D
fig = plt.figure()
ax = fig.add_subplot(111, projection='3d')
ax.scatter(np.random.rand(10), np.random.rand(10), np.random.rand(10))
ax.set_xticks([]); ax.set_yticks([]); ax.set_zticks([])
ax.set_title('3D', fontsize=16, y=1.15)
```

FIGURE 4.10   Plot illustrating the preattentive feature of 3D, and the code snippet used to generate the data points in the 3D space.

such as relationships between variables. Figure 4.10 shows a plot with ten data points generated in a 3D scatterplot using the scatter() function from the Matplotlib library. The perception we have when we first look at this image is that the points are floating in the 3D space, but focused attention shows that they are plotted on a 2D plane.

4.1.2.9 Length
Length is another preattentive visual property that can be used to create visual contrast, differences, importance, and proportions. The perception of differences in length normally occurs automatically and rapidly, without conscious effort or attention. It can be used in visual communication to quickly draw attention to important information or to create a visual hierarchy. For example, in a graph, longer bars may indicate larger values or quantities; in a map, longer lines may indicate longer distances; in a drawing, longer items may convey a sense of flow, etc. Figure 4.11 shows four plots containing lines with increasing lengths from left to right, and the code snippet that uses the plot() function from Matplotlib. A quick look at these figures from left to right results in the perception of their increase in length and complexity.

4.1.2.10 Curvature
Curvature is another preattentive feature that leads to a fast detection of changes in the degree of curvature, bending, or angularity of a shape or line, such as the presence of a more or less curved line in a group of otherwise similar lines. The degree of curvature in a line or shape can be used to represent different quantities or values, for instance, a smaller or larger number of peaks in a function. Figure 4.12 shows four plots illustrating sinusoidal curves with different curvatures and the code snippet to generate them using the sin()

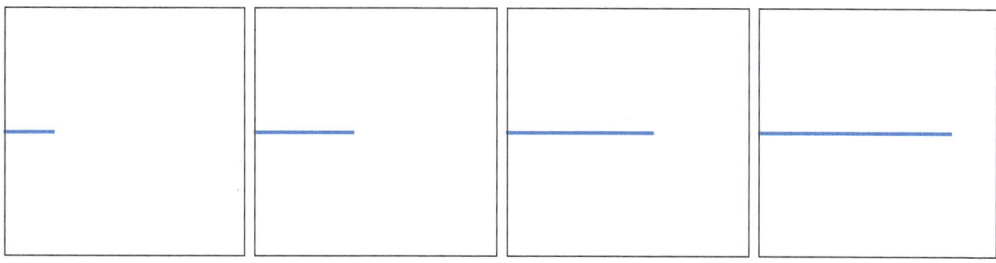

```
# Length
fig, axs = plt.subplots(1, 4, figsize=(8, 2), constrained_layout=True)
lengths = [0.2, 0.4, 0.6, 0.8]
for ax, l in zip(axs, lengths):
    ax.plot([0, l], [0.5, 0.5], linewidth=2)
    ax.set_xlim(0, 1)
    ax.set_ylim(0, 1)
    ax.set_xticks([]); ax.set_yticks([])
plt.suptitle('Length', fontsize=16, y=1.15)
```

FIGURE 4.11   Plots illustrating the preattentive feature of length, and the code snippet used to generate four lines with different shapes and lengths.

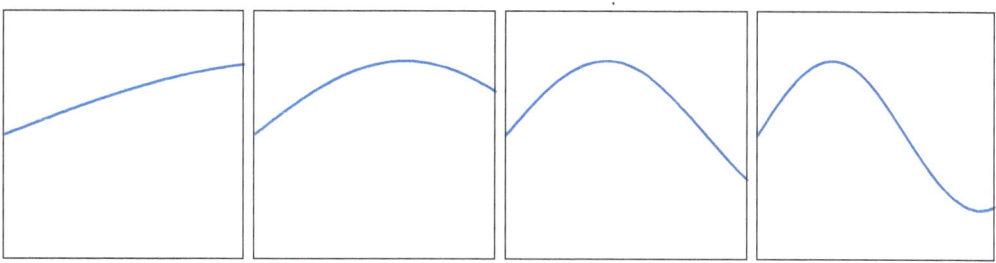

```
# Curvature
fig, axs = plt.subplots(1, 4, figsize=(8, 2), constrained_layout=True)
curvatures = [0.2, 0.4, 0.6, 0.8]
x = np.linspace(0, 1, 100)
for ax, c in zip(axs, curvatures):
    y = np.sin(2 * np.pi * c * x) * 0.3 + 0.5  # Adjust curvature
    ax.plot(x, y, linewidth=2)
    ax.set_xlim(0, 1)
    ax.set_ylim(0, 1)
    ax.set_xticks([]); ax.set_yticks([])
plt.suptitle('Curvature', fontsize=16, y=1.15)
```

FIGURE 4.12   Plots illustrating the preattentive feature of curvature, and the code snippet used to generate four sinusoidal curves with different curvatures.

function in Numpy and the plot() function from Matplotlib. In this case, an initial quick look may bring an interpretation of frequency, i.e., that the curves increase in frequency from left to right.

4.1.2.11 Density

The preattentive processing of density occurs automatically and rapidly, without conscious effort or attention, and can be used in visual communication to create contrast and emphasize importance or relevance. This feature can be swiftly detected by the presence of varying numbers of objects (e.g., data points or shapes) in a given region of the space, representing different quantities or values. For instance, in a chart or graph, a higher density of data points can be used to represent a larger quantity, a more significant trend, or a more exciting or energetic area. By making use of the preattentive processing of density, designers can create effective visual designs that convey information quickly and efficiently to the viewer. Figure 4.13 shows four plots with an increasing number of data points randomly placed in the space. It uses the `scatter()` function in `Matplotlib`, and the denser plots seem to be more cluttered and chaotic than the less dense ones.

4.1.2.12 Closure

Closure is a feature related to our capability of completing (closing) an object or a shape that is incomplete, that is, one that has some parts missing. The preattentive processing of closure is also automatic, not requiring conscious effort. For example, when looking at any shape, e.g., a circle or a square, with a small part missing, our brain automatically and preattentively perceives whether the shape is incomplete and fills these gaps. Preattentive processing of closure can be used in visual communication to create recognizable symbols and logos. For instance, a simple outline of an apple with a bite taken out of it can be preattentively recognized as the Apple Inc. logo. By making use of the preattentive processing of closure, designers can create effective visual designs that convey information quickly and efficiently to the viewer. Figure 4.14 shows four plots with an increasing number of lines until the fourth plot, from left to right, containing a square. In this example, we have the

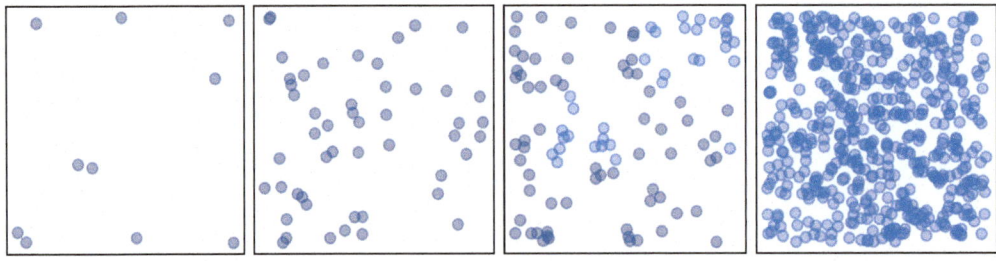

```
# Density
fig, axs = plt.subplots(1, 4, figsize=(8, 2), constrained_layout=True)
densities = [10, 50, 100, 500]
for ax, d in zip(axs, densities):
    x = np.random.rand(d)
    y = np.random.rand(d)
    ax.scatter(x, y, alpha=0.5)
    ax.set_xticks([]); ax.set_yticks([])
plt.suptitle('Density', fontsize=16, y=1.15)
```

FIGURE 4.13 Plots illustrating the preattentive feature of density, and the code snippet used to generate a varying number of data points in each plot.

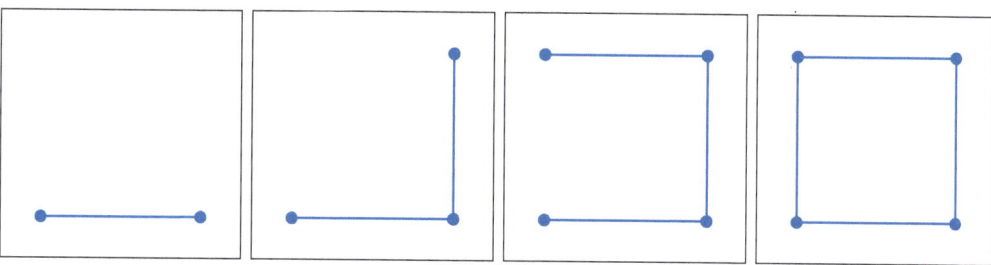

```
# Closure
fig, axs = plt.subplots(1, 4, figsize=(8, 2), constrained_layout=True)
for i, ax in enumerate(axs):
    x = [0, 1, 1, 0, 0][:i+2]
    y = [0, 0, 1, 1, 0][:i+2]
    ax.plot(x, y, '-o')
    # adjust scale of plot
    ax.set_xlim([-0.25, 1.25]), ax.set_ylim([-0.25, 1.25])
    ax.set_xticks([]); ax.set_yticks([])
plt.suptitle('Closure', fontsize=16, y=1.15)
```

FIGURE 4.14   Plots illustrating the preattentive feature of closure, and the code snippet used to generate a sequence of lines in each plot such that, from left to right, each plot has one more line until the square is closed.

perception of movement, as if the picture is being constructed until it becomes complete in the last plot. The code snippet to generate these figures is also presented, using the plot() function from Matplotlib.

4.1.2.13 Texture

In data visualization, texture is the visual quality of an object related to its roughness, pattern, or smoothness. It can be created using a variety of techniques, for example, using different line styles, brushes, patterns, and even special effects. Differences in texture can help distinguish between data points or objects, create visual hierarchies, or convey information about the data. For example, using different textures for different categories can help viewers quickly identify and differentiate patterns. Like the other features described here, the texture is usually processed preattentively, without the need for focused attention. Figure 4.15 shows four identical lines, each with a different line pattern. By looking at them, one can automatically tell they are different, though they have the same shape. If we imagine that we are touching them, our brain tends to create a different feeling for each of them, because our brain associates the touch feel with the line texture.

To summarize, the preattentive features can be combined or used in isolation to promote the desired visual effects that will be employed to effectively communicate the information, for example, an analytical report. Thinking about and planning which preattentive features will be used in the chosen visualization methods is of primary importance and will contribute to the success of your data visualization project. Table 4.1 summarizes the preattentive features and how each one of them enables us to identify and differentiate visual elements.

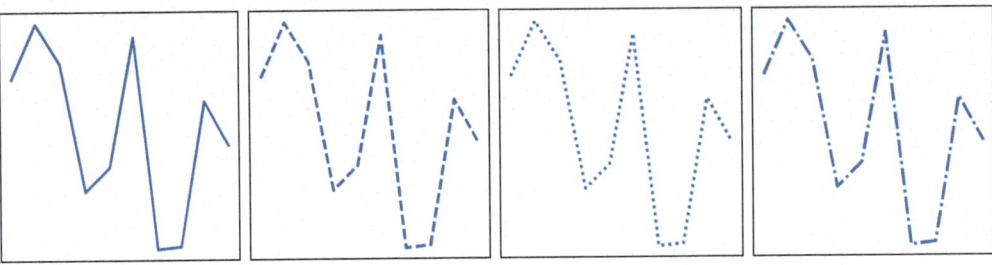

```python
# Texture
fig, axs = plt.subplots(1, 4, figsize=(8, 2), constrained_layout=True)
lins = ['-', '--', ':', '-.']
x = np.arange(10)
y = np.random.rand(10)
for ax, lin in zip(axs, lins):
    ax.plot(x, y, linestyle=lin)
    ax.set_xticks([]); ax.set_yticks([])
plt.suptitle('Texture', fontsize=16, y=1.15)
```

FIGURE 4.15 Plots illustrating the preattentive feature of texture, and the code snippet used to generate four random curves with different line textures.

4.1.3 Gestalt Principles and Data Visualization Methods

The *Gestalt principles* were developed early in the 20th century by a group of German psychologists to study the perception of visual forms, providing a set of theories to describe the way people perceive and organize visual information. They account for a holistic and non-additive approach to studying objects from the point of view of the whole, instead of as a sum of parts (Wagemans et al., 2012; Mennan, 2009). In the present context, seven Gestalt principles are relevant, as they can be applied in the creation of more effective and appealing data visualization graphics: *continuity, proximity, similarity, closure, symmetry, figure-ground (figure-field)*, and *common fate*.

The Gestalt principles of visual organization operate in conjunction with one another and enhance their combined impact on most visualization methods. They imply that the formation of shapes and patterns is guided by inherent and universal principles. As the Gestalt principles are based on our visual perception, bearing them in mind helps us create data visualizations that are more appealing and intuitive.

The Gestalt principles and the preattentive features complement one another as concepts necessary for an effective data visualization design. On the one hand, the preattentive features are employed to quickly draw attention to specific parts or items in a graph, before focal attention takes place. They serve as guidelines for planning which features will be used in each graph to convey the desired information to the reader. On the other hand, the Gestalt principles are used to group and organize visual items in a way that they can be easily and intuitively interpreted and understood by the reader. Therefore, their combination results in a more effective and engaging data visualization project.

TABLE 4.1   Summary of the Preattentive Features Reviewed and Their Descriptions

Preattentive Feature	Description
Shape	Enables effortless and automatic detection of similarities and differences based on form.
Line width	Allow the rapid identification of variations in thickness within a group of similar lines.
Color	Utilizes encoding to convey data, including categories, magnitude, visual hierarchy, and emotions.
Size	Facilitates quick and automatic detection of differences in items, similar to the effect of line width.
Markings	Allow a swift detection of differences and similarities, such as the identification of repeating patterns among random shapes.
Orientation	Assists in item differentiation and extraction of information from data points, lines, objects, etc.
Position	Allows a swift detection of location changes, such as the displacement of an item or object.
3D	Enables the perception of depth and spatial relationships without focused attention.
Length	Creates visual contrast, differences, importance, and proportions.
Curvature	Allows the rapid detection of changes in shape curvature, bending, or angularity.
Density	Utilized in visual communication for contrast and emphasis on importance or relevance.
Closure	Relates to our ability to mentally complete an incomplete object or shape.
Texture	Pertains to the visual quality of objects, including roughness, pattern, and smoothness that enable a fast distinction among them.

This section describes the seven Gestalt principles listed above as applied to some random datasets and to some of the datasets presented in Section 2.4. Preattentive features will be used and discussed so that the reader observes how they were considered in and contributed to the plots presented. Each of the data visualization techniques presented will be described in more detail later in the chapter because the focus here is on the Gestalt principles only.

All the graphs shown were generated using Python code snippets written to illustrate the Gestalt principles and, as these code snippets involve many lines, they will be presented in Appendix B.

4.1.3.1 Principle of Continuity

The principle of continuity states that objects that are arranged in a smooth, continuous way are more likely to be perceived as a single object, even if their pattern is interrupted. The *line chart*, the *Sankey diagram*, and the *scatterplot* are good examples of the principle of continuity in the use of Gestalt theory in data visualization. To illustrate, Figure 4.16 shows a line chart connecting data points showing a continuous trend over time; a flowchart, known as the Sankey diagram, which uses a series of arrows to show the flow of data through a system, indicating a continuous flow; and the scatterplot with a trend line showing the relationship between two variables, indicating a connection or trend. Several preattentive features were used in these graphs, for instance, the scatterplot used density, color, and orientation to convey information, while the other two graphs explored curvature, markings, and closure.

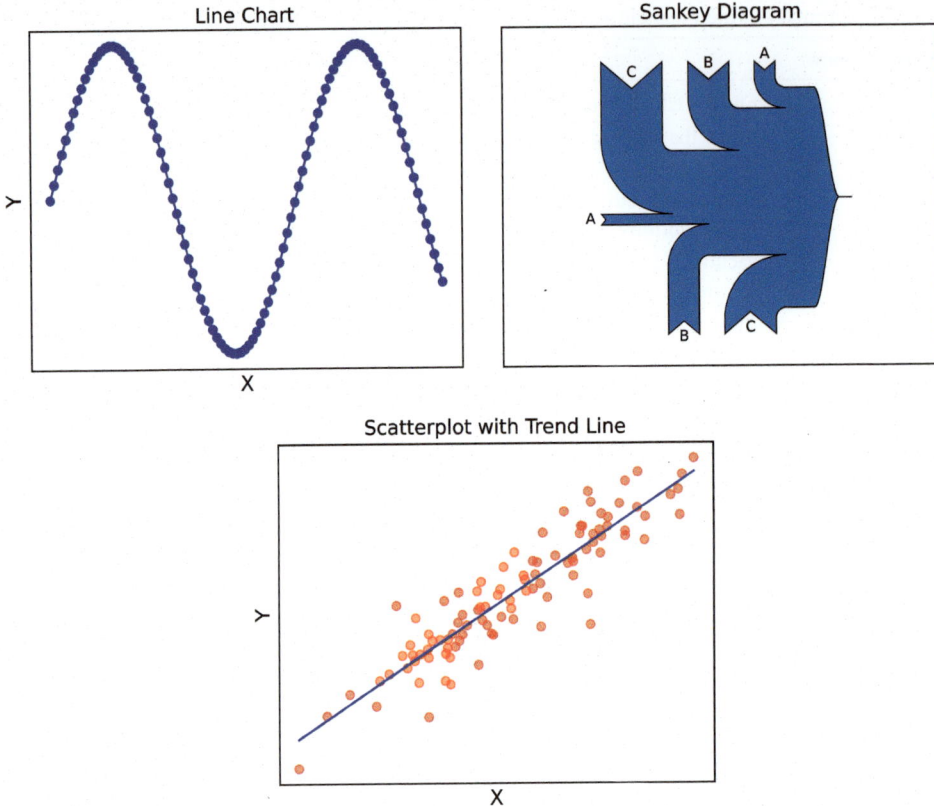

FIGURE 4.16 Data visualization graphs showing the principle of continuity: line chart, Sankey diagram, and scatterplot.

4.1.3.2 Principle of Closure

The principle of closure states that incomplete objects are perceived as complete because our brain tends to fill the gaps to create the complete image. Note that closure is also a pre-attentive feature and thus plays a key role not only in the quick filling of gaps or completion of shapes, but also in the organization of the information to be conveyed.

Examples of data visualization methods that account for the principle of closure are *pie charts*, *word clouds*, and *treemaps*. Pie charts are a classic example of the closure principle because the chart is a circle divided into slices, which are individually perceived as complete shapes, but that, altogether, form one unique circle. In word clouds, the viewer sees a collection of words arranged in a particular pattern or shape, though the words are not complete shapes themselves. In treemaps, the viewer perceives each rectangle as a complete shape, even though it is only a partial segment of the overall rectangle that contains it.

These cases are illustrated in Figure 4.17. Different shades of blue were used in the pie chart and treemap, and we can also emphasize the word cloud that was plotted within a comment mask, forcing the cloud to have the shape of a comment balloon.

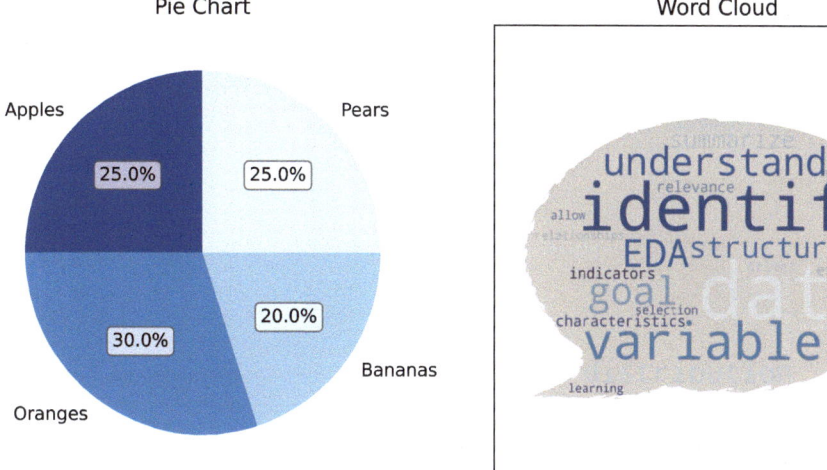

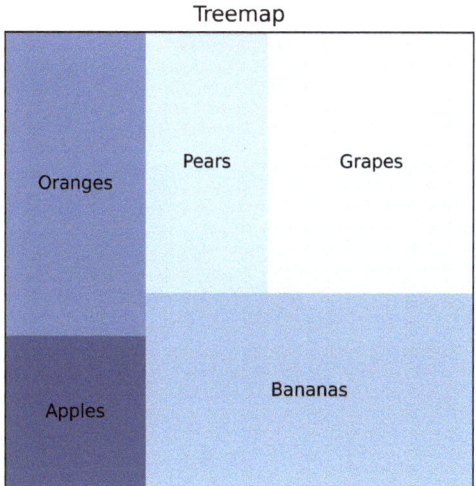

FIGURE 4.17   Data visualization graphs illustrating the Gestalt principle of closure: pie chart, word cloud, and treemap.

4.1.3.3 Principle of Proximity

The principle of proximity proposes that objects that are close to one another tend to be perceived as a group or a pattern. In data visualization, the *heatmap*, the *scatterplot*, and the *bar chart* are good examples of methods that account for the principle of proximity. The heatmap is a graph in which the values of a matrix are represented by colors, which are a preattentive feature, and neighboring cells in the matrix convey a sense of organization and relationship. The scatterplot places similar data values close to one another, grouping them in the plot. In a bar chart, related data values are placed close together in the bars, allowing a visual association among them.

Figure 4.18 illustrates a heatmap showing the correlation among the variables in the UCI Forest Fires dataset, where neighboring regions of similar colors indicate similar correlation values. The scatterplot displays the "temperature" versus the "RH", with data

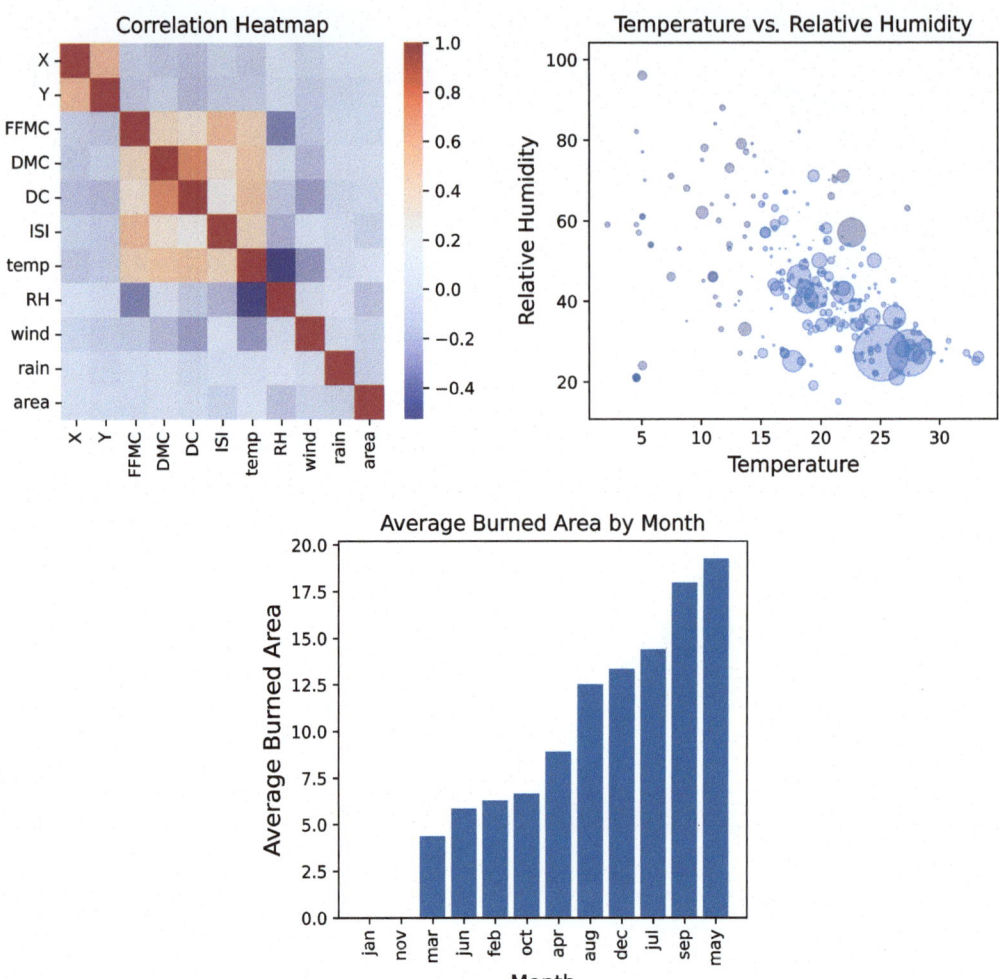

FIGURE 4.18 Data visualization graphs illustrating the Gestalt principle of proximity using the UCI Forest Fires dataset: heatmap, bubble chart, and bar chart.

points sized proportionally to the area burned. It can be observed that an increase in the temperature leads to an increase in the area burned, and this is highlighted by the pre-attentive feature of size. The bar chart plotted the months in ascending order based on the average burned area, showing that months with similar average burned areas can be plotted together, bringing in the Gestalt principles of proximity and continuity.

4.1.3.4 Principle of Similarity

The principle of similarity proposes that objects that share similar characteristics, such as color or form, tend to be perceived as a group or a pattern. Examples of data visualization techniques that account for the similarity principle in Gestalt theory include a *line chart* in which lines representing different categories have the same style, a *bar chart* in which the bar patterns or colors indicate the same group or category, and a *scatterplot* with different markers representing different categories of categorical variables.

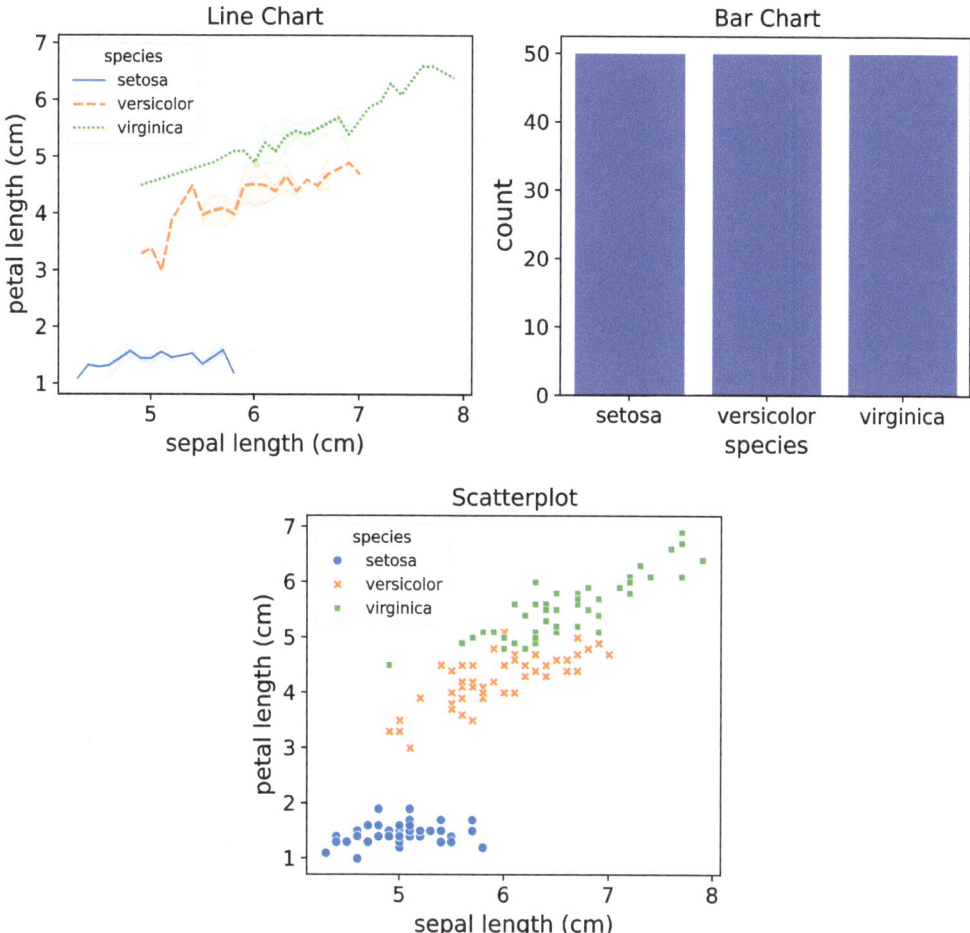

FIGURE 4.19   Data visualization graphs illustrating the Gestalt principle of similarity using the Iris dataset of Fischer: line chart, stacked bar chart, and scatterplot.

Figure 4.19 illustrates these three types of graphs. In all cases, the Iris dataset by Fischer was used, along with `Seaborn` library, and the variables were categorized based on the three iris classes: setosa, virginica, and versicolor. In the line chart, one line drawing a parallel between the sepal and petal lengths in centimeters (cm) was plotted with a different style for each Iris species. The principle of similarity is expressed here by the trend and proximity of the curves for the versicolor and virginica species. The bar chart shows one bar with the count of values for each Iris species, and the similarity here is expressed by the bars of the same size. The scatterplot shows the sepal versus petal length in centimeters (cm), plotted with different shapes and colors for each Iris species, and despite that, similarity is observed through the proximity and trend of the versicolor and virginica species. All these graphs show the principle of similarity in Gestalt theory based on the grouped plant species. In these graphs, the following preattentive features were used: shape, color, size, markings, orientation, position, length, density, and texture.

4.1.3.5 Principle of Symmetry

The principle of symmetry states that objects that are symmetrical, or have a balanced appearance, tend to be perceived as a group or a pattern. Some data visualization graphs that can be used to explore this principle are the *boxplot* with boxes symmetrically placed around the median (Q_2), the *radar chart* displaying multivariate data as a bidimensional chart with quantitative variables, and the *mirrored bar chart* with two sets of bars with mirrored values displayed.

Figure 4.20 illustrates a boxplot showing sepal length values in centimeters (cm) for each Iris species, a bar chart with values mirrored around the petal width for each Iris species, and a radar chart with values symmetrically arranged around the center point. In the mirrored bar chart, color and size allow differentiation between the plant species, while the radar chart uses texture to differentiate the lines (plant species). The boxplots show symmetrical distributions for all plant varieties. The mirrored bar chart forces the symmetry by reflecting the bars around the 0 value, and the symmetry of the radar chart is observed mainly in the versicolor and virginica cases, for which the radars are symmetrical around the center of the radar.

4.1.3.6 Principle of Figure-Ground

The principle of *figure-ground*, also called *figure-field*, states that objects are perceived as either being in the foreground or the background. One way of forcing this principle is by using contrasting colors in the background and foreground of an image, for instance, black and white, blue and orange, green and purple, red and green, yellow and purple, pink and green, and others. However, many of these pairs are not suitable for technical and scientific works, and thus, the recommendation is to use colors with parsimony.

There are some graph types, however, that naturally account for the principle of figure-ground, such as the *bubble chart*, in which larger data points stand out against a more neutral background, and the *choropleth maps* that use colors to represent geographic data, such as population density, poll results, and political preferences. Figure 4.21 illustrates the use of a scatterplot with contrasting colors that offer a perception of depth in the image, a bubble chart showing the life expectancy of the continents in relation to the GDP per capita, and a choropleth map with a color scale indicating the world population.

4.1.3.7 Principle of Common Fate

The principle of common fate proposes that objects that move together or change similarly tend to be perceived as a group or a pattern. In this case, graphs that allow visualizing data obeying this principle will have to embody a type or a sense of motion. To illustrate this principle, let us consider a *motion chart*, a *streamgraph*, and a *force-directed graph*. The motion chart is a visualization method that shows how data changes over time; the streamgraph is a stacked area graph that shows the changes in a set of data over time; and the force-directed graph is a network visualization that shows the relationships of nodes in a graph. In all cases, there is a sense of common fate in the data.

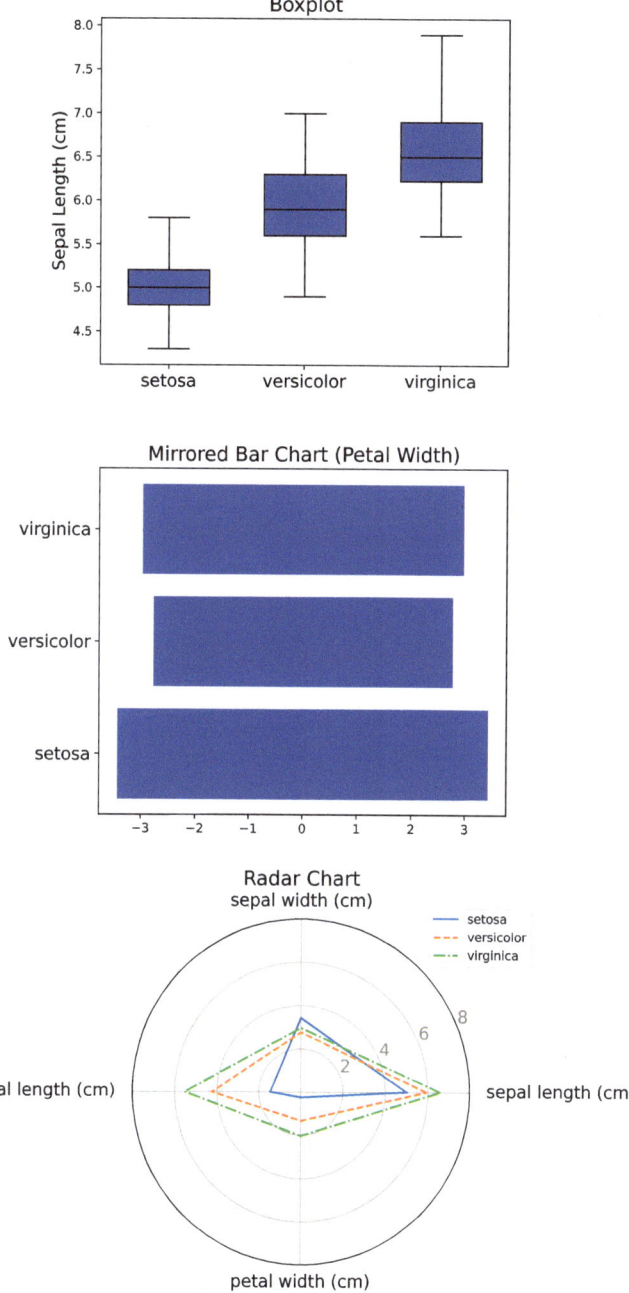

FIGURE 4.20 Data visualization graphs illustrating the Gestalt principle of symmetry using the Iris dataset of Fischer: boxplot, mirrored bar chart, and radar chart.

Figure 4.22 shows these three graphs. At the top of the figure, there is a motion chart with the Gapminder data and a scroll that allows you to observe the data movement over the years, starting in 1952 and ending in 2002. It can be observed that the data moves in a block but maintains its overall structure through time. The sample streamgraph uses

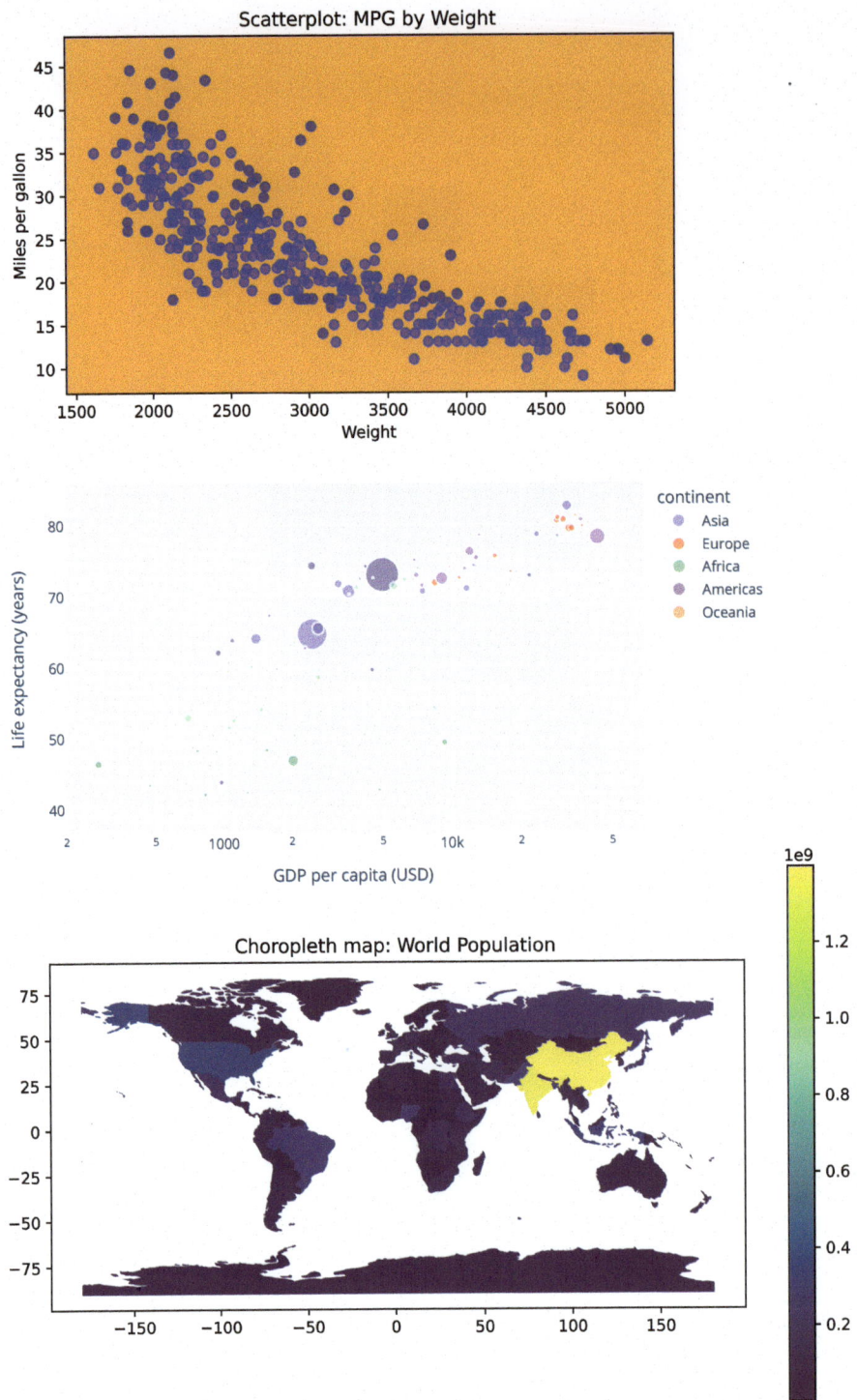

FIGURE 4.21   Data visualization graphs illustrating the Gestalt figure-ground principle using the Auto-mpg, the Gapminder, and the Naturalearth_lowres datasets: scatterplot, bubble chart, and choropleth map.

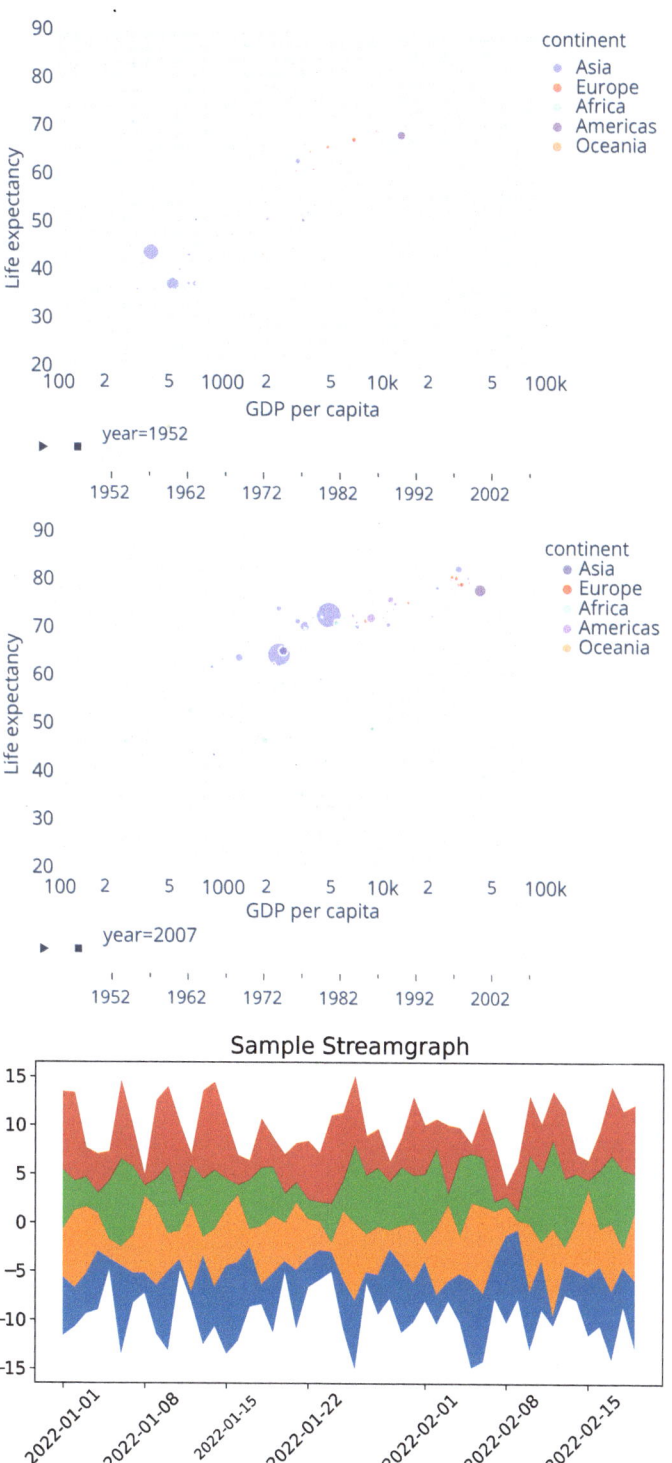

FIGURE 4.22 Data visualization graphs illustrating the Gestalt principle of common fate using the Gapminder and the Karate Club Graph dataset: motion chart, streamgraph, and force-directed graph.

(Continued)

Force-Directed Graph with Common Fate Illustration

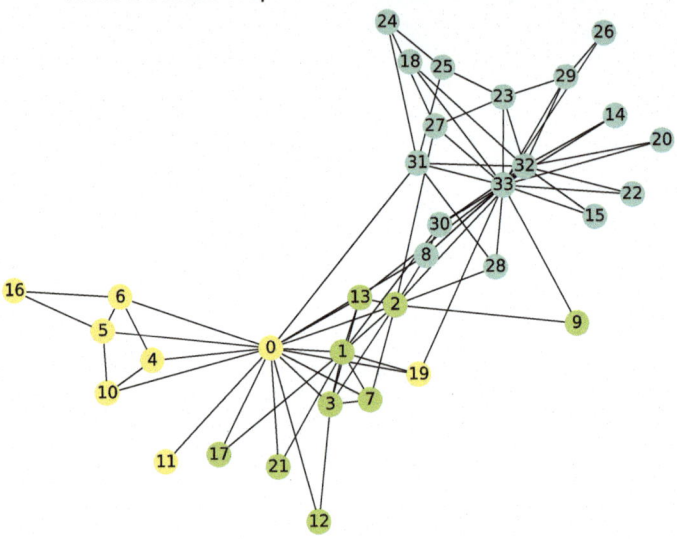

FIGURE 4.22 (*Continued*)   Data visualization graphs illustrating the Gestalt principle of common fate using the Gapminder and the Karate Club Graph dataset: motion chart, streamgraph, and force-directed graph.

four randomly generated sets of data with 50 days starting on 01/01/2022 and then plots the area graph conveying the notion of movement over time. Lastly, to illustrate the Gestalt principle of common fate using the Karate Club graph dataset, we colored nodes based on their community membership. Nodes that share a common fate, meaning they belong to the same community, were grouped together and colored with the same color.

Table 4.2 summarizes the Gestalt principles reviewed and their description.

4.2 DESIGN PRINCIPLES FOR DATA VISUALIZATION

Structured data requires a data model that describes the objects, their relations, and properties. As such, it is common to have them presented in tables and spreadsheets, making them some of the most used data visualization methods. As described in Section 4.2.1,

TABLE 4.2   Summary of the Gestalt Principles Reviewed and Their Descriptions

Gestalt Principle	Description
Continuity	Objects that are arranged in a smooth, continuous way are more likely to be perceived as a single object, even if their pattern is interrupted.
Closure	Incomplete objects are perceived as complete because our brain tends to fill the gaps to create the complete image.
Proximity	Objects that are close to one another tend to be perceived as a group or a pattern.
Similarity	Objects that share similar characteristics, such as color or form, tend to be perceived as a group or a pattern.
Symmetry	Objects that are symmetrical, or that have a balanced appearance, tend to be perceived as a group or a pattern.
Figure-ground	Objects are perceived as either being in the foreground or the background.
Common fate	Objects that move together or change similarly tend to be perceived as a group or a pattern.

tables organize the data into rows and columns, where the rows usually correspond to the objects and the columns to their variables or features. The values of the variables or features are described by qualitative (e.g., texts) or quantitative (e.g., numbers) data. What characterizes a table are not the lines that may compose it, but the way the data is arranged. Tables are particularly useful for displaying data in the following situations (Few, 2012):

- When specific values must be identified with precision;
- When pairs of related values must be compared;
- When look-up and one-to-one comparisons must be made;
- When objects must be compared over various characteristics with different units of measure;
- When a single display must be used to present unit and summary data.

Figure 4.23 describes the main components of a data table and will be used to explain the design principles for visualizing data by means of tables.

Graphs, by contrast, usually display the values using visual objects within an area bounded by axes, which play the role of scales labeling and assigning values to the visual objects. Unlike tables, graphs do not always allow for an exact reading of the data presented but allow us to make relative and approximate comparisons of values. They are particularly useful when (Few, 2012):

- A set of quantitative values must be examined to find its general shape, pattern, or trend;
- A single unit of measure is sufficient to compare the different values;
- Specific patterns are sought, such as anomalous values and clusters;
- The volume of data is too large for a table but can be summarized in a graph.

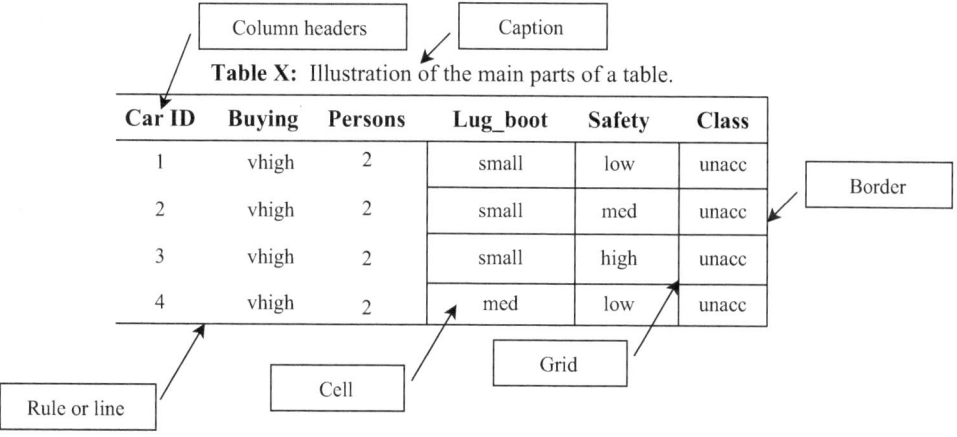

FIGURE 4.23   Main components of a data table.

Tables leverage the Gestalt principles of proximity and continuity to organize data into rows and columns. By grouping related information together and creating a sense of visual cohesion, tables make it easier to compare and analyze data. On the other hand, graphs utilize various techniques to represent and convey data visually. The Gestalt principle of similarity is often employed, where elements with common attributes, such as colors or shapes, are grouped together. This grouping helps to highlight patterns and relationships within the data. Additionally, the Gestalt principle of connection is employed in graphs, often using lines or curves to connect data points. These connections enable the visualization of trends, changes, and correlations.

Figure 4.24 contains an illustration of the main components of a graph and will be used to explain the design principles for visualizing data by means of graphs.

Table 4.3 summarizes the comparison between tables and graphs for visualizing data based on their characteristics, as described above. Note that, in general, the information carried by each one of them is complementary, and the choice of one over another may depend on many factors, including the availability of space in the document, the target audience, and the story to be told.

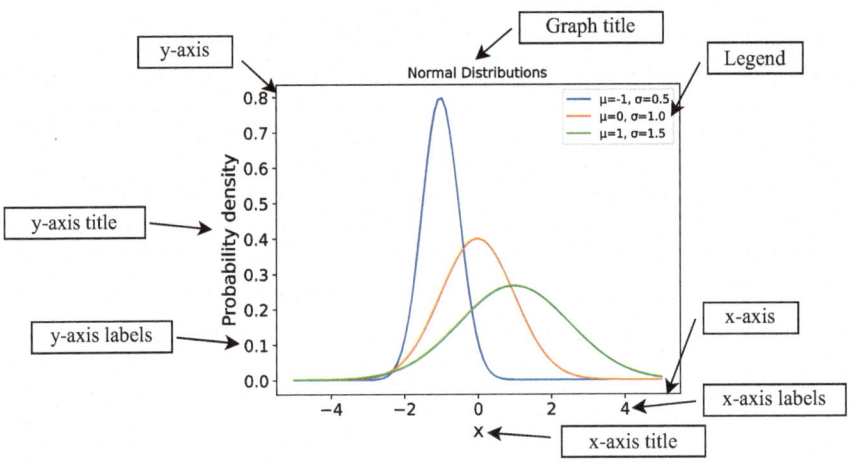

FIGURE 4.24   Main components of a graph.

TABLE 4.3   Comparison of the Suitability of Tables and Graphs for Data Visualization Based on Some of Their Characteristics

Characteristic	Tables	Graphs
Accuracy in identifying values	Yes	No
Easier identification of trends in data	No	Yes
Look-up and one-to-one comparisons	Yes	No
Comparison over multiple characteristics simultaneously	Yes	No
Display of unit and summary information	Yes	No
Large volumes of data	No	Yes
Fast identification of patterns, trends, and outliers	No	Yes

4.2.1 Tables

As the most commonly used visualization method and often the starting point for structured data analysis, it is important to list some guidelines for a suitable design and presentation of tables. In the book titled *Show Me the Numbers: Designing Tables and Graphs to Enlighten*, Few (2012) provided an extensive discussion on table design. He divided the process into five topics (delineating rows and columns, arranging data, formatting text, summarizing values, and giving page information) and 19 main practices, each with several sub-practices. He also discussed how many of these design rules obey some of the Gestalt principles described previously. Detailed guidelines were given for placing categorical and numeric values, organizing the sequence of values, orienting, and aligning text, formatting numbers and dates, selecting fonts and colors, summarizing and grouping data, and emphasizing specific items or values.

Wilke (2019) and Schwabish (2021) presented a more summarized approach to table design, arguing that tables are particularly susceptible to clutter. They introduced some guidelines to create effective table visualizations, from among which we describe the main ones here:

1. **Use lines only as table frames and to separate the title row**: do not use vertical lines and lines between data rows in the whole table.

2. **Offset the headers from the body**: highlight the column titles from the body of the table by using boldface text or lines.

3. **Use subtle dividers instead of heavy gridlines**: instead of using heavy borders or gridlines, use spaces, light lines, or light shades to highlight the rows.

4. **Right-align numbers**: by aligning numbers on the right and standardizing decimal places, it is much easier to read and compare the values. To follow this standard, the headers should also be right aligned.

5. **Left-align text**: as English and most languages are read from left to right, a left alignment for texts makes their reading more natural.

6. **Center-align columns with single characters or binary variables**: columns with a single character should be centered.

7. **Align the headers with their data**: headers of columns composed of numbers should be aligned right, headers of columns with text should be aligned left or centered, and columns with centered data should have their header centered.

8. **Select the appropriate level of precision**: the number of decimal places to be presented in a table must be necessary and sufficient to convey the information.

9. **Guide the reader with space between rows and columns**: white spaces underlie the Gestalt principle of proximity and are used in tables between rows and columns to group data that belong together, separating them from others.

10. **Remove unit repetition**: units can be presented in the title, subtitle, or column headers, avoiding cluttering when presented next to every number.

11. **Highlight specific values**: sometimes it is desired to highlight specific values in a table (e.g., the best performance or outliers) and this can be done using boldface letters, a gray or color shading, circling, or any other type of marker.

12. **Group similar data and highlight them**: there are cases when categories or values of a given variable can be grouped together, simplifying the presentation. The groups can be highlighted by increasing the space between the rows or using some color or shading scheme.

To illustrate the relevance of these design principles, consider the three versions of the same table presented in Table 4.4. These tables were generated by taking Table 2.10 removing the first column and the row that represents the continuity of rows.

Version 1 was purposefully designed without following the guiding principles, while Versions 2 and 3 followed some of the guidelines presented. Note that in Version 1, the column titles, apart from the fact that they are displayed in the first row, get mixed with the other rows; the gridlines make the table's visual appearance heavy and cluttered; and the alignments of numbers and texts make it difficult to read and compare them.

Version 2 conveys the same information as Version 1 in a more pleasant and easy-to-read format by removing the gridlines, aligning numbers and texts as suggested, and changing the values of variable "geometry" to lowercase letters. Version 3 takes Version 2, groups similar data, and introduces a line shading every two rows, helping the reader to identify the continent category. Note that the order of some columns was changed to position the category row as the first one, creating a hierarchy in the order of the information presented (first continent, then country, and then other information). If the variable (column) "geometry" was relevant for the organization, it could be moved to the first column and used to group the data as well.

In Version 3, two further comments deserve to be made. First, it is important to acknowledge that if you are using a table to describe a raw dataset, that is, a dataset as it is available in the database, you may not want to group any variable, because this grouping normally does not exist in the real database. Second, the shading used to differentiate the reading of different rows must be subtle, such that it does not make it difficult to distinguish between the shade and the text.

4.2.2 Graphs

It is possible to display the same data in various ways using different types of graphs and charts, with the choices being not only technical but also a subjective decision of the data analyst. Despite the subjectivity, similar to what happens with tables, there are some guidelines that, if followed, result in good practices in the design and visualization of graphs.

In the book titled *Handbook of Data Visualization* by Chen et al. (2008), the authors argue that successful graphic visualization requires an effective combination of *content*, *context*, *construction*, and *design*. They presented some scientific design choices in data visualization, dividing them into the choice of graphical form and graphical display options.

TABLE 4.4 Three Versions of Table 2.10 Highlighting the Importance of Some of the Guiding Principles for Table Design

Version 1

pop_est	continent	name	iso_a3	gdp_md_est	geometry
889,953	Oceania	Fiji	FJI	5496	MULTIPOLYGON
58,005,463	Africa	Tanzania	TZA	63177	POLYGON
603,253	Africa	W. Sahara	ESH	907	POLYGON
37,589,262	America	Canada	CAN	1736425	MULTIPOLYGON
328,239,523	America	USA	USA	21433226	MULTIPOLYGON
6,944,975	Europe	Serbia	SRB	51475	POLYGON
622,137	Europe	Montenegro	MNE	5542	POLYGON
1,794,248	Europe	Kosovo	−99	7926	POLYGON
1,394,973	America	Trinidad and Tobago	TTO	24269	POLYGON
11,062,113	Africa	S. Sudan	SSD	11998	POLYGON

Version 2

pop_est	continent	name	iso_a3	gdp_md_est	geometry
889,953	Oceania	Fiji	FJI	5496	MULTIPOLYGON
58,005,463	Africa	Tanzania	TZA	63177	POLYGON
603,253	Africa	W. Sahara	ESH	907	POLYGON
37,589,262	America	Canada	CAN	1736425	MULTIPOLYGON
328,239,523	America	USA	USA	21433226	MULTIPOLYGON
6,944,975	Europe	Serbia	SRB	51475	POLYGON
622,137	Europe	Montenegro	MNE	5542	POLYGON
1,794,248	Europe	Kosovo	−99	7926	POLYGON
1,394,973	America	Trinidad and Tobago	TTO	24269	POLYGON
11,062,113	Africa	S. Sudan	SSD	11998	POLYGON

Version 3

continent	name	pop_est	iso_a3	gdp_md_est	geometry
Oceania	Fiji	889,953	FJI	5496	MULTIPOLYGON
	Tanzania	58,005,463	TZA	63177	POLYGON
Africa	W. Sahara	603,253	ESH	907	POLYGON
	S. Sudan	11,062,113	SSD	11998	POLYGON
America	Canada	37,589,262	CAN	1736425	MULTIPOLYGON
	USA	328,239,523	USA	21433226	MULTIPOLYGON
	Trinidad and Tobago	1,394,973	TTO	24269	POLYGON
	Serbia	6,944,975	SRB	51475	POLYGON
Europe	Montenegro	622,137	MNE	5542	POLYGON
	Kosovo	1,794,248	−99	7926	POLYGON

4.2.2.1 Choice of Graphical Form

This is the first step in the design choices and depends upon the type of data available (e.g., discrete, continuous, ordinal, categorical, etc.), and the information to be conveyed (e.g., distributions, associations, amounts, proportions, evolution, flow, geospatial data, etc.). It is important to acknowledge that there is no single best choice, and there may be equally appropriate alternatives. Therefore, it is essential to plan and make some tests and comparisons.

4.2.2.2 Graphical Display Options

The second main design decision involves choosing the graphical display options, such as the scales, the position and order of appearance, the addition of information in the graphics, the use and properties of captions, legends, and annotations, the choice of size, frames, and aspect ratios, and the use of colors. Some details of each of these choices are provided in the sequence.

Scales: When dealing with categorical variables, the scale may reflect a desired information order; for example, if the categories are weekdays or months, it is natural to order them chronologically, or if the categories represent income levels, they can be placed in ascending or descending order. In the case of continuous variables, the endpoints, divisions, and tick marks must be determined, and, in most cases, a suitable choice can only be made after some experimentation. Wilkinson (2005) suggests simplicity, granularity, and coverage as the main properties to be accounted for while defining the scales.

Sorting and ordering: In many situations, there is a natural order in the values or categories of a variable, but there are cases with no natural order, mainly for categorical variables. In this scenario, the use of alphabetic ordering or a specific grouping (e.g., increasing income levels or acceleration rate) may be appropriate.

Adding model or statistical information: Placing regressors or smoothers over a graph is a common practice that helps us extract further information from a chart, such as its tendency, variability, and form. It is important, however, to be careful not to overload or clutter the chart with the added information.

Captions, legends, and annotations: The data analyst must define the standard for captions in terms of the information to be presented. For instance, the captions may simply describe the chart and data being presented, or they may fully explain the graph. In the former case, the reader will need to rely on the information available in the text to fully interpret the graph, and in the latter case, the caption plus the graphics may be enough for a suitable understanding of the data presented. There is always a compromise between the caption's extensiveness and the description presented in the text. The legends describe the symbols and/or colors that appear in the graphics, and it is recommended to be placed directly in the plot instead of in a separate legend (Tufte, 2001). Despite that, most software tools and libraries do not offer this possibility or use a separate legend as the default choice. Finally, annotations serve to explain and highlight specific properties or observations about the data but are not usually recommended because they tend to clutter the graph.

Positioning in text: When planning the layout of a text, it is important to consider where each figure and table will be placed in relation to the corresponding text. The common practice is to have both (figure/table and text description and call) on the same page to avoid the reader having to change pages to fully understand a given concept or result.

Some text editors, like MS Word, allow you to move these items naturally and freely, but others, like LaTeX, automatically place figures and tables based on the page layout.

Sizes and frames: A simple rule of thumb for the size of graphics is that they should be large enough for clear reading and understanding of the information being conveyed, but not too large to be disproportional to the text size and layout. In addition, most graphics must contain a surrounding frame to highlight them from the text. For captions, legends, and annotations, the font size is usually 1–2 points smaller than the font size of the main text, and it is also common to have the font size of the legends and annotations 1–2 points smaller than the font size of the caption. However, it is important to ensure that all of them are clearly readable, mainly after the document is printed.

Colors: Although the use of colors has a major impact on the graph and the information to be conveyed to the reader, it is one of the most difficult aspects to choose. It must be accounted for the fact that some people are color blind, some colors may have specific associations (e.g., red for prohibited and green for allowed), the preference for colors is subjective, and the fact that the printed colors may be different from the ones that appear on the screen.

In Schwabish (2021), the author proposed five guidelines for better data visualizations:

1. **Show the data**: highlight (only) those values that are of central importance for the story being told;

2. **Reduce the clutter**: focus on the necessary and sufficient visual elements to convey a specific message (result), and be parsimonious on colors, number precision, labels, annotations, etc.

3. **Integrate the graphics and text**: titles, labels, legends, and annotations are often as important as the graph itself; for example, instead of using legends, the data can be directly labeled.

4. **Avoid the spaghetti chart**: the excess use of colors, icons, bars, lines, textures, annotations, etc., can all make the reading and understanding of a chart more complicated, resulting in the so-called *spaghetti chart*.

5. **Start with gray**: starting with gray forces you to be more careful and conscious in the planning of colors and other visual elements.

4.3 EXERCISES

4.3.1 Research Topics and Questions

1. Discuss the implications of visual processing in data visualization. How does our perception influence our understanding of data?

2. Discuss the role of preattentive processing in data visualization. How does our brain's ability to process certain visual properties without conscious thought influence the effectiveness of data visualizations?

3. Investigate the application of Gestalt principles in data visualization and discuss how these principles guide the design of effective visualizations.

4. Discuss the advantages and disadvantages of tables and graphs in data visualization. When is it more appropriate to use one over the other?

5. Discuss how the structure and presentation of tabular data may impact clarity, transparency, and the potential for misinterpretation, raising questions about responsible data communication.

6. Explore the narrative potential of graphs in data visualization. Discuss how graphical representations tell stories about data, and consider the implications of using visual narratives to convey information, including questions about representation, bias, and the nature of storytelling.

7. Based on the Guidelines for Table Visualization, draw one table that violates some of these design principles and then draw the same table correcting the violations presented. Describe the visual gains of the corrected table.

8. Based on the Guidelines to Display Graphs, draw one graph that violates some of these design principles for graphs and then the same graph correcting the violations presented. Describe the visual gains of the corrected graph.

4.3.2 Quizzes

1. The Anscombe's Quartet is used to highlight what aspect of data visualization?

   a. The importance of color in data visualization.

   b. The limitations of summary statistics in describing data.

   c. The effectiveness of 3D depth cues in data visualization.

   d. The role of preattentive processing in data analysis.

2. What are "preattentive features" in data visualization?

   a. Features that require focused attention to be processed.

   b. Features that are processed automatically without conscious effort.

   c. Features related to data summarization.

   d. Features used in 3D data visualization.

3. How can preattentive processing help data analysts in creating effective data visualization designs?

   a. It helps in reducing the amount of data to be visualized.

   b. It allows for the use of complex visual elements.

    c. It enables viewers to quickly identify patterns and differences in data.

    d. It speeds up the process of data collection.

4. What is the main purpose of the Gestalt principles in data visualization?

    a. To confuse viewers with abstract shapes.

    b. To create visually appealing but inaccurate visualizations.

    c. To organize and group visual elements into meaningful patterns.

    d. To enhance preattentive processing.

5. How do preattentive features and Gestalt principles complement each other in data visualization?

    a. They serve the same purpose in visual analysis.

    b. They are unrelated and do not affect data visualization design.

    c. Preattentive features guide the selection of visual features, while Gestalt principles help organize and group visual items.

    d. Preattentive features and Gestalt principles are interchangeable terms in data visualization.

6. Which of the following is one of the Gestalt principles relevant to data visualization?

    a. Temperature.

    b. Similarity.

    c. Gravity.

    d. Sound.

7. What is the primary purpose of using appropriate design principles in table data visualization?

    a. To make the table visually appealing.

    b. To present data in a way that is easy to understand and interpret.

    c. To use as many colors and fonts as possible.

    d. To hide important data for added complexity.

8. Which of the following is a key design principle for effective table data visualization?

    a. Maximizing the use of decorative elements.

    b. Avoiding any form of data grouping.

    c. Providing clear headers and labels.

    d. Using as many different font styles as possible.

9. Why is it important to select an appropriate chart type for your data?

    a. To make the graph visually interesting.

    b. To confuse viewers with unfamiliar chart types.

    c. To accurately represent the data and facilitate understanding.

    d. To use as many chart types as possible in a single graph.

10. What is the benefit of providing clear and meaningful labels and titles in a graph?

    a. It makes the graph visually cluttered.

    b. It adds unnecessary complexity to the graph.

    c. It helps viewers understand the context and purpose of the graph.

    d. It distracts viewers from the data.

4.3.3 Computational Exercises

1. The Anscombe Quartet is a famous example of the limitations of summary statistics and the importance of visual data analysis. Based on the visual characteristics of each plot, discuss how the data points distribute themselves and the impact of removing the outliers from the data.

2. For the Iris dataset, create a scatter plot of any two variables (e.g., petal length vs sepal width) and apply Gestalt principles like continuity and closure to improve interpretation. Consider adding trendlines or highlighting clusters to reveal underlying patterns.

3. Design a visualization that leverages preattentive processing. Explain your design choices and how they align with the principles of preattentive processing.

4. Choose a Gestalt principle and create a data visualization that exemplifies this principle. Discuss why you chose this principle and how it is demonstrated in your visualization.

## CHAPTER 5

Data Visualization Methods

"The purpose of visualization is insight, not pictures."

– Ben Shneiderman, Extreme visualization: squeezing a billion records into a million pixels. Proceedings of the 2008 ACM SIGMOD international conference on Management of data, *2008, p. 3*

The rapid increase in volume and complexity of data requires not only an increase in our capability of extracting information from data but also efficient, accurate, and reproducible ways of communicating such information. This communication requires the use of visualization techniques and well-planned data storytelling that will guide your audience through the message that you want to convey. Data visualization, also called *datavis* or *dataviz*, is the representation of data in a pictorial or graphical format, using charts, graphs, maps, or other visual elements. Data visualization is important for many reasons:

- **Discover trends in data**: patterns in data may not be directly evident to us, but a suitable visual allows us to identify patterns and trends in data, such as correlations, maximal or minimal values, skewness, and outliers. For example, a histogram allows us to identify the format of a distribution, leading us to conclusions about flatness, tailedness, outliers, etc.

- **Make complex data understandable**: tabular or textual representations of data may be difficult to interpret, and the visualization may simplify such complexity by presenting data in a graphical format. For example, a scatterplot allows us to observe the correlations between variables and the presence of clusters of objects.

- **Provide perspectives on data**: a visual may bring some perspectives that are not obvious, including a multi-dimensional or a temporal view of the data, allowing us to compare variables, find relationships, and understand the context. For example, a line chart allows us to observe seasonality and other trends in data.

DOI: 10.1201/9781003570691-5

- **Save analytical time**: the visual representation of data may allow us to spot outliers, find clusters, identify trends, etc., all without the need to run sophisticated learning algorithms.

- **Allow us to tell a story (data storytelling)**: data visualization is a powerful tool for storytelling, because it enables the presentation of data in a compelling narrative format, making it much easier to communicate insights and findings to the audience.

This chapter presents, explores, and illustrates some of the most important data visualization techniques, and the next chapter will focus on some specific types of data, namely, time series, texts and documents, and graphs and networks. We use the term *graph* to generically refer to any type of graphical data visual used in the text.

There are different forms of organizing data visualization methods to present them consistently. To exemplify, in Ward et al. (2010), the authors organized the methods into spatial data, geospatial data, multivariate data, trees/graphs/networks, and documents; in Schwabish (2021), the author divided the chart types into comparing categories, time, distribution, geospatial, relationship, part-to-whole, qualitative, and tables; in Wilke (2019), the author organized the methods into visualizing amounts, distributions, proportions, associations, time series, trends, geospatial data, and uncertainty; and in Holtz and Healy (2018), the authors categorized the methods into distribution, correlation, ranking, part of a whole, evolution, map, and flow.

This book adopts a categorization that combines some of the proposals above, considering the type of data available and visualization generated by the graphs, as follows:

- **Distribution**: the graphs in this category aim to plot data distributions, which form the first set of descriptive analyses presented in Chapter 2. Examples of graphs in this category include the *histogram*, *violin plot*, and *box and whisker plot* (also called *boxplot*).

- **Associations**: graphs in the association category allow the plotting of relationships between two or more variables or categories. Examples include the *scatterplot* and *scatterplot matrix*, *heatmaps* and *correlograms*, and the *bubble chart*.

- **Amounts**: graphs that plot amounts allow us to compare different values of one or more variables. Examples include the *bar chart*, *radar chart*, and *word clouds*, which will be studied in the next chapter.

- **Proportions**: proportion graphs allow us to divide the data into parts proportionally to their contribution to a whole. As examples, there are *treemaps*, *pie charts*, *doughnut charts*, *sunbursts*, and *dendrograms*.

- **Evolution and flow**: evolution graphs, like *line plots* and *area charts*, show the evolution of numeric variables, and flow graphs, like the *Sankey* and *Gantt charts*, are used to plot data flows and networks.

- **Geospatial**: maps are used to plot geospatial data. Examples include *choropleth maps* and *bubble maps*.

It is important to note that the proposed categorization has fuzzy boundaries, in the sense that one graph may belong to more than one category. For example, consider the case of heatmaps that can be used to show the correlation (association) between variables, but also express the degree (amount) of correlation.

Furthermore, there are special types of data, such as *time series, texts and documents, trees, graphs, and networks*, that require specific preprocessing, and sometimes, special descriptive analysis and graphs to be visualized. Due to their specificity and relevance, these will be studied separately in the next chapter.

5.1 DISTRIBUTIONS

Chapter 3 introduced distributions as an important tool to visualize patterns and trends in a given variable. By looking at a data distribution, it is possible to identify outliers, kurtosis, skewness, and other important characteristics of the data. This section describes the following data visualization graphs to analyze distributions: *histograms, box and whisker plots* (*boxplots*), and *violin plots*.

5.1.1 Histogram

Purpose (when to use): to explore and visualize the distribution of a variable.

Common type of data: continuous data.

Interpretation: the histogram divides the range of data into bins and presents the frequency of occurrence (count) of each bin by its height, providing a general overview of the variable's distribution. Thus, the histogram interpretation involves assessing its overall pattern, center, spread, shape, outliers, gaps, modes, skewness, and kurtosis.

Examples of applications: to visualize any type of (continuous) variable, such as height, distance, weight, temperature, blood pressure, exam scores, income levels, etc.

The *histogram* is a useful visualization technique to explore the pattern of a single variable distribution, where the x-axis represents the range of values, and the y-axis represents the absolute or relative frequency of data points within each bin. Histograms allow the exploration of central tendency measures, such as the mean and median; dispersion measures, such as the standard deviation; and range, and shape, such as skewness and kurtosis. It also helps to identify outliers or unusual values and to reveal potential biases or errors in the data collection process.

Chapter 3 brought an extensive explanation about distributions and histograms. It was shown how to build frequency distributions for continuous and discrete variables, how to calculate the main summary measures for these distributions, how to interpret the shapes of distributions, and more. Chapter 3 is also filled with examples of histograms and how to interpret them and their measures. To illustrate, we are going to reproduce here the histograms in Figures 3.3 and 3.5a. Figure 5.1a shows the histogram for the variable "temp" of the UCI Forest Fires dataset, with the smooth density function plotted over the histogram and the limits of each bin plot on the x-axis. It can be noted that variable "temp" has a nearly normal distribution centered at approximately 20°C. Figure 5.1b shows

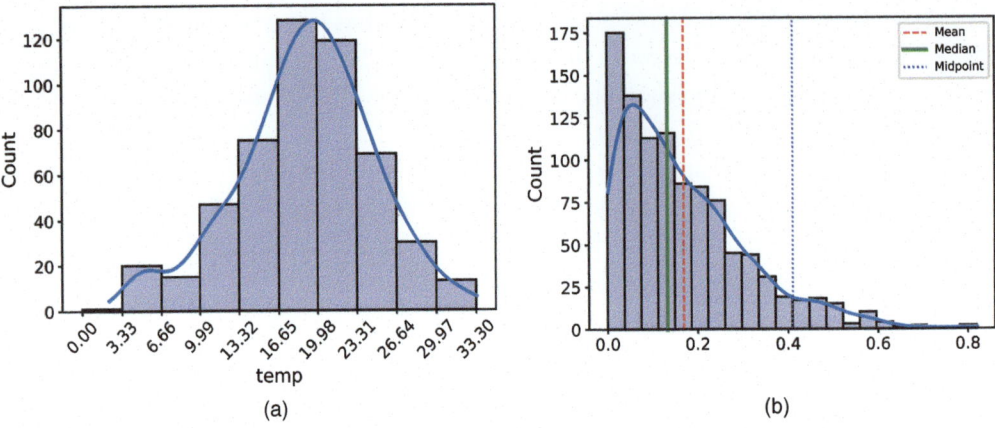

FIGURE 5.1 Histogram. (a) Variable 'temp' from the Forest Fires dataset. (b) Right-skewed randomly generated distribution.

a right-skewed distribution with its mean, median, and mode values plotted with different line colors and textures. The scale in the x-axis was left automatic because if we had chosen the bin limits, the values would appear cluttered in the picture unless we rotated the x-labels vertically, as was done in Figure 5.1c.

5.1.2 Boxplot (Box and Whisker Plot)

Purpose (when to use): to explore and visualize the distribution of a variable, or to compare the distribution of different variables, using the *five number summary* (FNS), which is an extension of the quartiles to include the minimal and maximal values of the variable: *min*, Q_1, Q_2, Q_3, *max*.

Common type of data: continuous data.

Interpretation: the boxplot is a diagram that shows the minimal value, the first quartile (Q_1), the median (Q_2), the third quartile (Q_3), and the maximal value of a variable, in addition to outliers. Thus, boxplots allow us to observe the data distribution, its shape, and the presence of outliers.

Examples of applications: to visualize the distribution of any type of (continuous) variable, such as height, distance, weight, temperature, blood pressure, exam scores, income levels, etc.

The FNS adds the minimal (*min*) and maximal (*max*) values of a variable to the quartiles to provide a more complete numeric description of the data distribution: *min*, Q_1, Q_2, Q_3, and *max*. From the FNS a graph called *boxplot*, or *box and whisker plot*, is designed using a box in the interquartile range (*IQR*), a horizontal line in the median, and whiskers going from the box to the minimal and maximal values, as illustrated in Figure 5.2.

Boxplots are a powerful tool to identify outliers in a single variable. Values greater than $Q_3 + \gamma * IQR$ or smaller than $Q_1 - \gamma * IQR$, where γ is a predefined *IQR* multiple, are

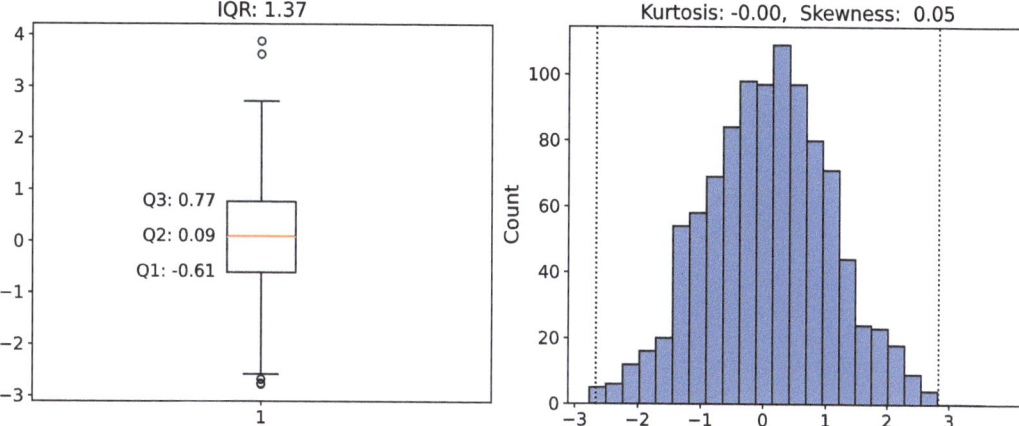

FIGURE 5.2 Boxplot and the data distribution used to generate it with the mean, median, mid-point, kurtosis, skewness, and IQR calculated and shown in the graphs.

considered anomalies and are plotted outside the whiskers. Most software packages use $\gamma = 1.5$ as a standard value to identify outliers. Figure 5.2 shows five outlier cases as small dots plotted above and below the whiskers, that is, the *max* and *min* values in the boxplot. The histogram also shows the upper and lower outlier thresholds as dashed vertical lines.

Code 5.1 shows the script to generate the boxplot and histogram of Figure 5.2. This script uses the Matplotlib and Numpy libraries. Note that the upper and lower outlier thresholds were calculated using $\gamma = 1.5$, and these values were added to the histogram so that the reader can observe, in the histogram itself, those values that exceed the predefined thresholds.

CODE 5.1 Script to generate a normal distribution, calculate its summary measures, and plot the histogram and its respective boxplot.

```
# Box plot and histogram for a normal distribution

import matplotlib.pyplot as plt
import numpy as np
import scipy.stats as spy
import seaborn as sns

# Generate the random sample data
np.random.seed()
data = np.random.normal(loc=0, scale=1, size=1000)

# Calculate the summary measures
q1, q2, q3 = np.percentile(data, [25, 50, 75])
iqr = q3 - q1
upper_whisker = q3 + 1.5* iqr; lower_whisker = q1 - 1.5*iqr
max_val = np.max(data); min_val = np.min(data)
midpoint = (max_val+min_val)/2
k = spy.kurtosis(data); s = spy.skew(data)

# Plot the boxplot and print the values (Q1, Q2, Q3) on the first subplot
fig, (ax1, ax2) = plt.subplots(nrows=1, ncols=2, figsize=(10,5))
```

```
bp = ax1.boxplot(data)
ax1.set_title(f"IQR: {iqr:.2f}", fontsize=16)
ax1.text(0.9, q1, f'Q1: {q1:.2f}', ha='right', va='center', fontsize=14)
ax1.text(0.9, q2, f'Q2: {q2:.2f}', ha='right', va='center', fontsize=14)
ax1.text(0.9, q3, f'Q3: {q3:.2f}', ha='right', va='center', fontsize=14)

# Plot the histogram on the second subplot
sns.histplot(data, bins='auto', ax=ax2)
plt.axvline(x=upper_whisker, color='k', linestyle=':')
plt.axvline(x=lower_whisker, color='k', linestyle=':')

plt.title(f"Kurtosis: {k:.2f},  Skewness: {s: .2f}")

# Show plot
plt.show()
```

Let us now expand the discussion about the interpretation of histograms and boxplots. To do so, let us look at Figure 5.3, which shows various shapes of distributions and their

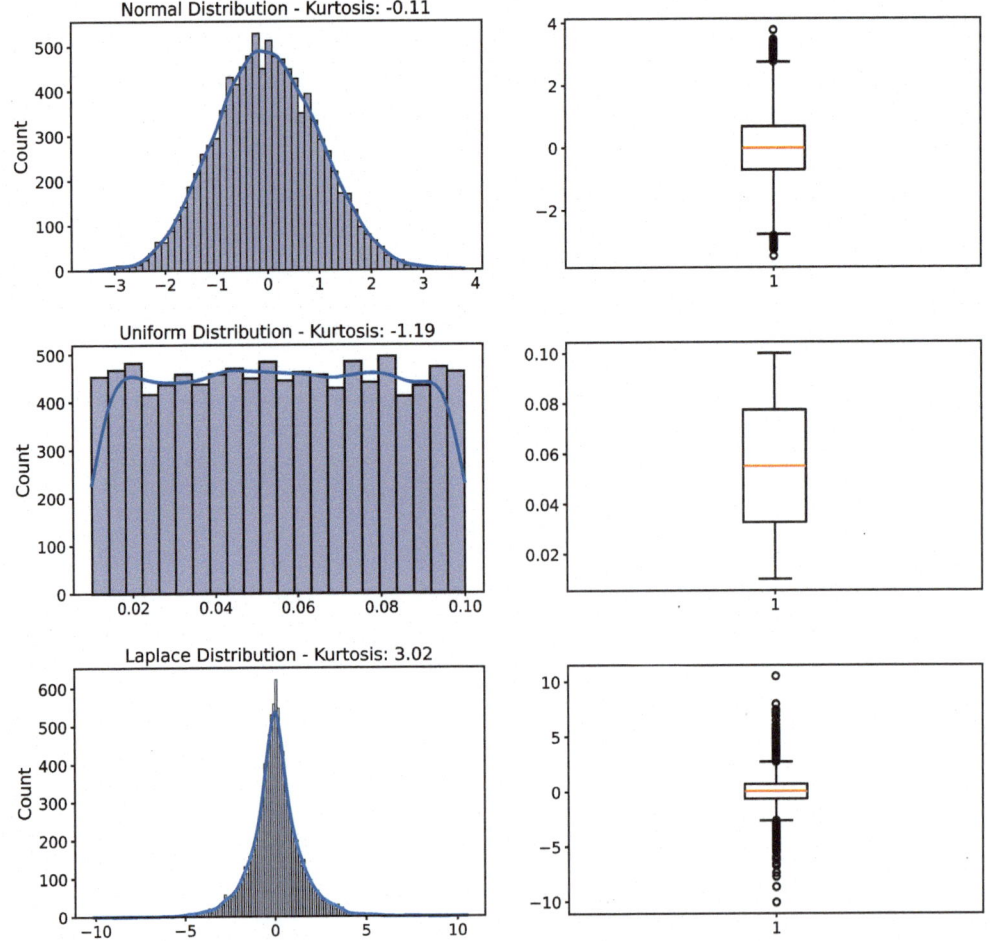

FIGURE 5.3 Histograms and boxplots of distributions with various forms: normal, uniform, Laplace, semicircle, right skewed, and left skewed.

(Continued)

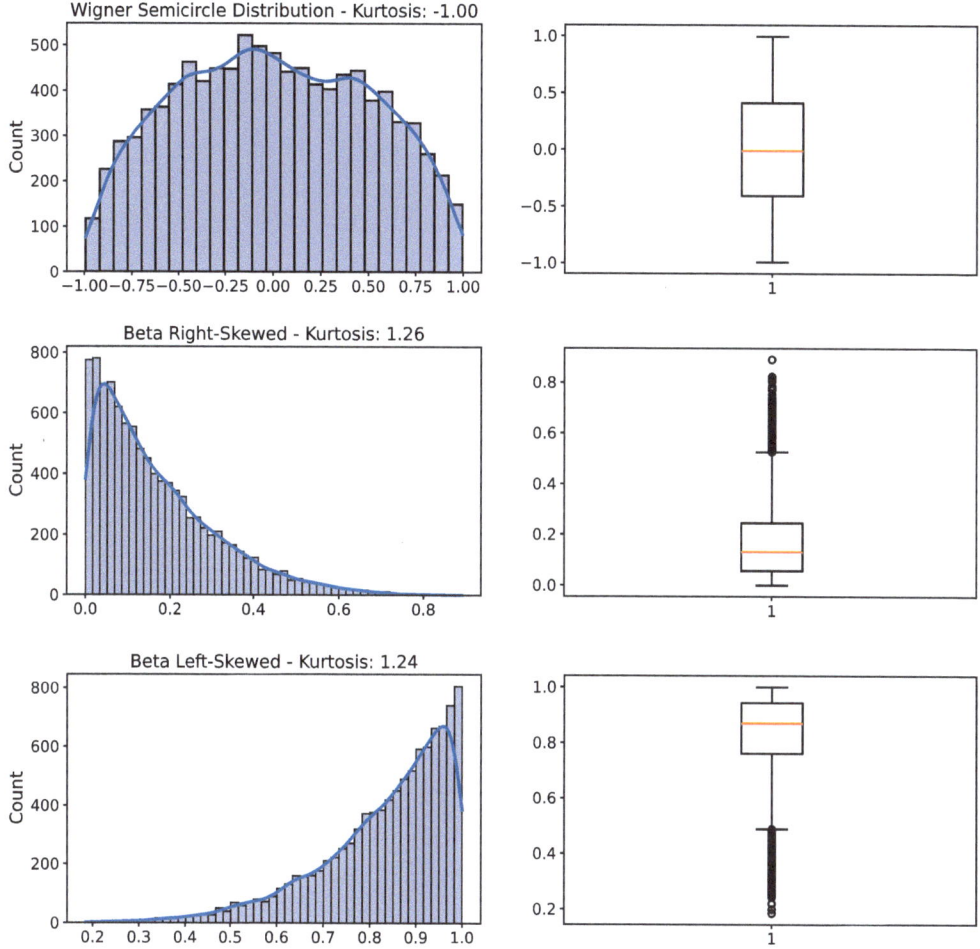

FIGURE 5.3 *(Continued)* Histograms and boxplots of distributions with various forms: normal, uniform, Laplace, semicircle, right skewed, and left skewed.

respective boxplots. The presence or absence of outliers is one of the first characteristics that attract our attention. It can be observed that longer tails result in more outliers, even in symmetric distributions. Note also that asymmetric distributions have asymmetric boxes and whiskers: right-skewed distributions tend to generate outliers greater than Q_3, while left-skewed distributions tend to generate outliers smaller than Q_1. The position of the median (Q_2) within the boxplot gives an idea of the spread of the middle 50% of the values.

5.1.3 Violin Plot

Purpose (when to use): to explore and visualize the distribution of a variable, or to compare the distribution of different variables, using a combination of the boxplot with a kernel density plot.

Common type of data: continuous data.

Interpretation: wider areas in the violin plot represent a larger density of data points, narrower areas mean fewer data points, and outliers appear out of the violin body. Thus, the violin plots allow us to observe the data distribution, its shape, and the presence of outliers.

Examples of applications: to visualize the distribution of any type of (continuous) variable, such as height, distance, weight, temperature, blood pressure, exam scores, income levels, etc.

Section 3.1 introduced frequency distributions and presented histograms as a tool to visualize their shapes. Histograms are plots that discretize the variable range to present the distribution in a series of connected bars. In the limit, these bars could be approximated by a *kernel density curve* that smoothly approximates the shape of the distribution.

A similar approach can be performed with the boxplot, that is, instead of showing the FNS (*min*, Q_1, Q_2, Q_3, *max*), the *violin plot* combines the boxplot with a kernel density estimation to show the shape of the distribution. This is illustrated in Figure 5.4 for histograms with similar distributions as the ones presented in Figure 5.3. Note that the violin plot mirrors the distribution on the top of an imaginary base (horizontal) line, generating the shape of the violin.

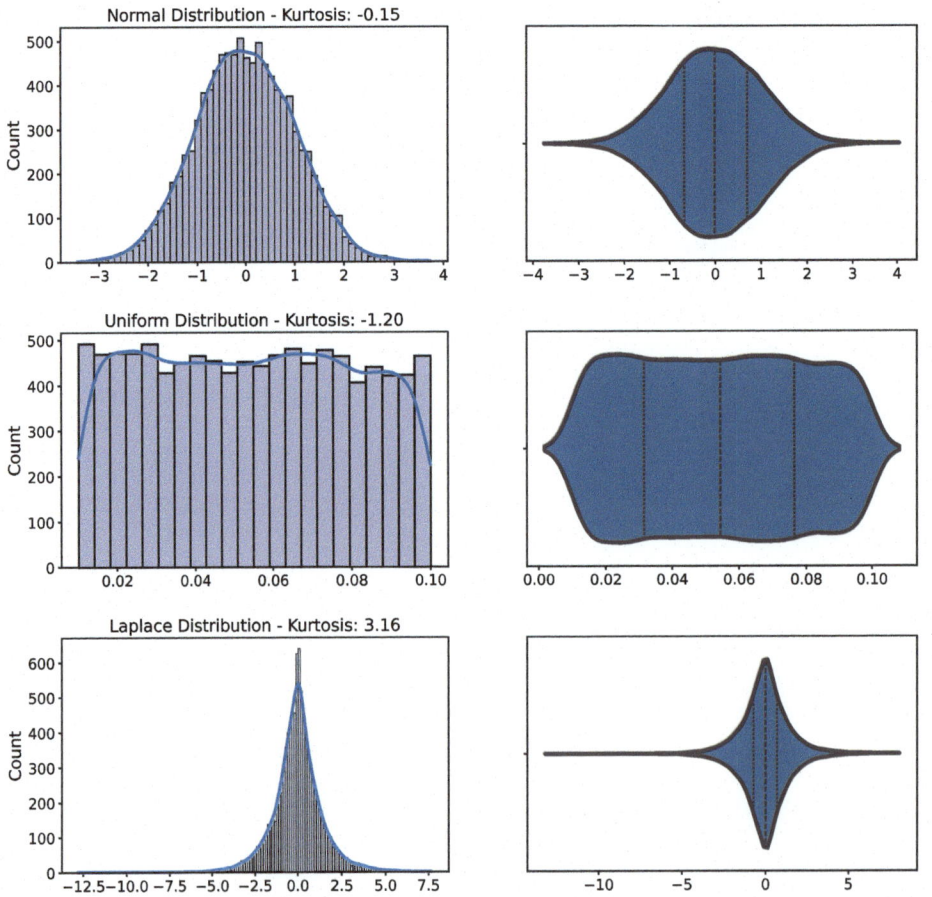

FIGURE 5.4   Violin plots for the distributions of Figure 5.3 with the quartiles drawn in dashed lines within the violins.

(*Continued*)

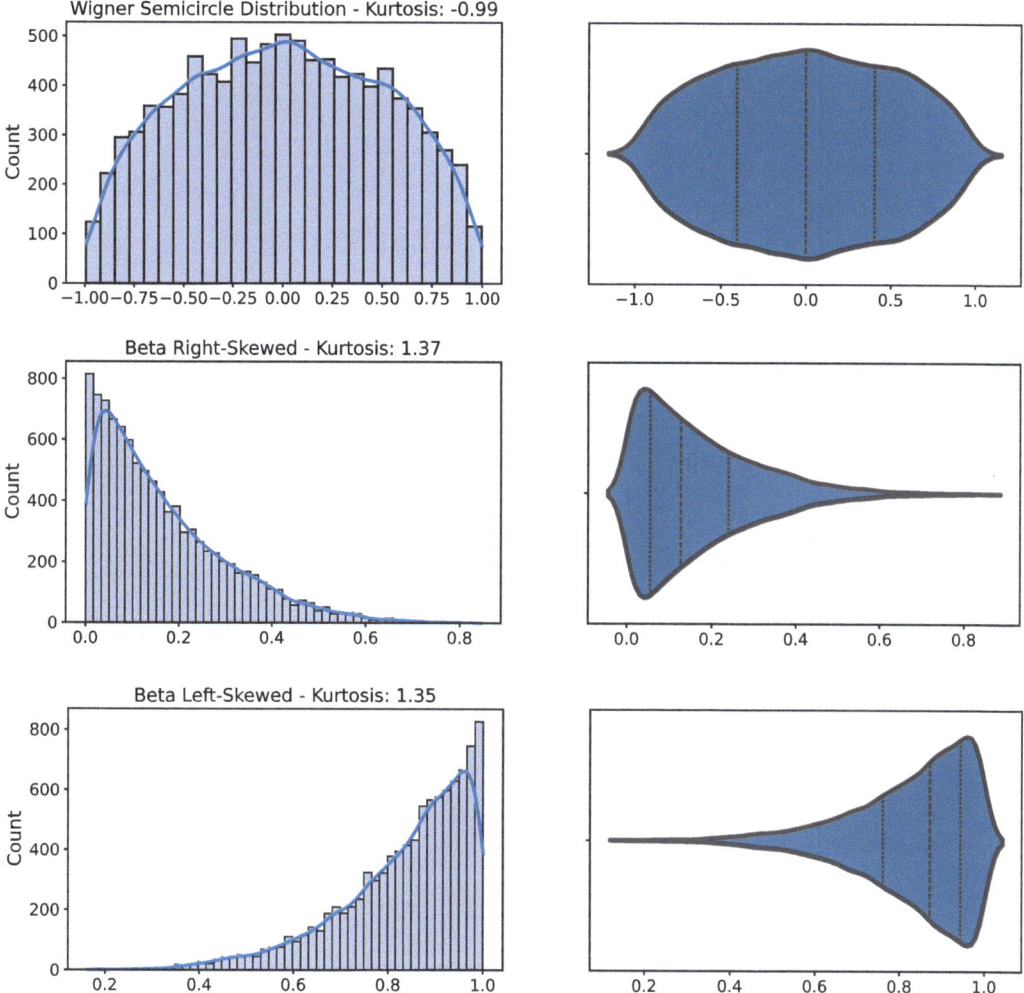

FIGURE 5.4 *(Continued)*   Violin plots for the distributions of Figure 5.3 with the quartiles drawn in dashed lines within the violins.

As a final remark about the use and interpretation of boxplots and violin plots, their application in the comparison of different data distributions is very helpful. For example, Figure 5.5a shows a graph with three boxplots, all measuring the sepal length against one of the Iris plant species, and includes the data points over the boxplots. Figure 5.5b presents the same data using violin plots. Both sets of plots show symmetric distributions with little or no tail, but with varying sepal lengths according to the plant species. Note that there is one sepal length value for the Iris-virginica species that is significantly smaller than the lower whisker in its respective boxplot. It was not small enough to be marked as an outlier neither in the boxplot nor in the violin plot.

Code 5.2 shows the script to generate the box and violin plots for the Iris dataset. It uses the methods `boxplot()` and `violinplot()` in the `Seaborn` graphic library and Scikit-learn to load the dataset. Note that the violins were plotted vertically to be compatible with the boxplots, and their *y*-axis scales were standardized. The method `stripplot()` was used to plot the data points within the boxplots and violins.

CODE 5.2   Script to generate the box and violin plots for the Iris dataset loaded from the Scikit-learn library.

```python
# Comparing the Box and Violin plots for the Sepal length of
# the Iris dataset grouped by plant species

import seaborn as sns
import matplotlib.pyplot as plt
from sklearn.datasets import load_iris

diris = load_iris()  # Load the Iris dataset from Scikit-learn
fig, axs = plt.subplots(nrows=1, ncols=2, figsize=(12, 6))

# Boxplot with data points
sns.boxplot(x=diris.target, y=diris.data[:, 0], ax=axs[0], width=0.6,
            boxprops=dict(edgecolor='black'),
            whiskerprops=dict(color='black', linestyle='-'),
            medianprops=dict(color='black'),
            capprops=dict(color='black', linestyle='-'))
sns.stripplot(x=diris.target, y=diris.data[:, 0], ax=axs[0], color='black')
axs[0].set_xticks([0, 1, 2])
axs[0].set_xticklabels(diris.target_names)
axs[0].set_ylabel('Sepal Length (cm)')
axs[0].set_ylim([3.6, 8.6])
axs[0].set_title('Boxplot with Data Points')

# Violinplot with data points
sns.violinplot(x=diris.target, y=diris.data[:, 0], ax=axs[1], inner=None)
sns.stripplot(x=diris.target, y=diris.data[:, 0], ax=axs[1], jitter=True,
color='black')
axs[1].set_xticks([0, 1, 2])
axs[1].set_xticklabels(diris.target_names)
axs[1].set_ylabel('Sepal Length (cm)')
axs[1].set_ylim([3.6, 8.6])
axs[1].set_title('Violinplot with Data Points')

# Show plot
plt.tight_layout()
plt.show()
```

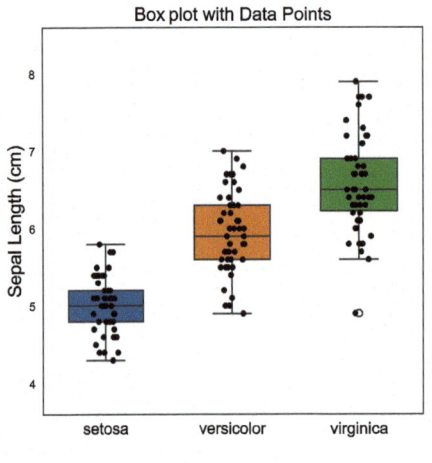

(a)

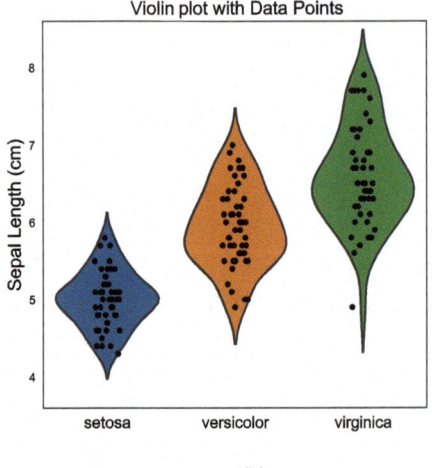

(b)

FIGURE 5.5   Boxplots (a) and violin plots (b) of the Iris dataset sepal length grouped by the plant species.

5.2 ASSOCIATIONS

In many situations, it is necessary to generate graphs that allow us to analyze the relationships between two or more variables. Sometimes these graphs only show the value of one variable in relation to another, and sometimes they show a measure calculated for both variables, for instance, their correlation. The association graphs to be presented here are the *scatterplot*, the *bubble chart*, the *scatterplot matrix*, and the *heatmaps*.

5.2.1 Scatter Plot

Purpose (when to use): to visualize the relationship (association) between two or three variables.

Common type of data: continuous data on both axes, and categorical data in the colors.

Interpretation: to analyze the type and strength of the relationship between two variables, for example, to identify if there is any type of correlation (weak/strong positive, negative, or no correlation) between the variables, and to identify trends, patterns, and changes in the data. As it plots one variable against another, it is also a useful tool to identify data clusters (groups) and outliers. A third variable, usually categorical, can be included in the scatterplot by using different colors for the dots.

Examples of applications: to visualize the relationship between weight and height, income and education level, inflation and tax rates, advertisement expenditure and sales revenue, etc.

A *scatterplot* is a data visualization graph that uses dots to represent the relationship between two quantitative variables. One variable, called the *explanatory variable*, is plotted on the *x*-axis, and the other variable, called the *response variable*, is plotted on the *y*-axis. It is also possible to include a third categorical variable, represented by different dot colors. Each dot represents an individual data point, and the colors, when used, represent the categories of the dots. Therefore, the data point is organized into two or three columns, one for each variable, and each data point is plotted on the graph using two coordinates, one for each variable, with various colors representing each category.

To illustrate the use of scatterplots to assess the relationship between pairs of variables, let us consider the UCI Forest Fires dataset used in the previous chapter for the study of correlation. The same plots of Figure 3.8 were used here, but we now added the regression lines to these plots. To do so, we basically included one line of code for each scatterplot as follows:

```
sns.regplot(x='explanatory variable', y='response variable', data=dataframe,
ax=axs[x_axis subplot, y_axis subplot]),
```

where the `regplot()` method is in `Seaborn`.

These scatterplots allow us to observe several important aspects of the relationship between these variables. Figure 5.6a shows plots between "DMC" × "DC" and "FFMC" vs "ISI" (initial spread index) with positive correlation coefficients. It can be observed, for

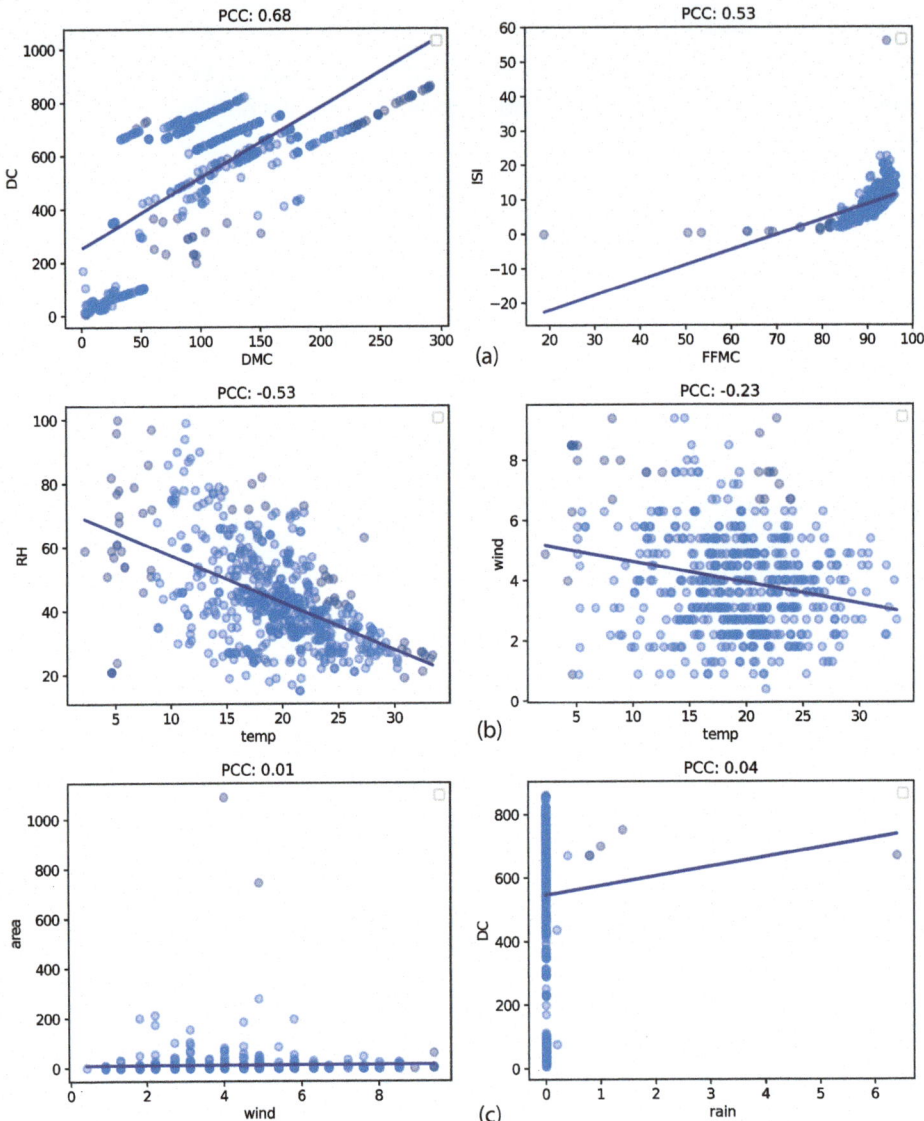

FIGURE 5.6   Scatter plots between pairs of variables from the Forest Fires dataset. (a) Positive correlations. (b) Negative correlations. (c) Almost no correlation.

instance, that the ISI increases with the moisture content of litter and other cured fine fuels ("FFMC"), and this increase becomes stronger for higher "FFMC" values. By contrast, the relative humidity ("RH") decreases as temperature ("temp") increases, with a denser amount of "RH" data points for higher "temp" values. When looking at "rain" vs "DC", an outlier is observed for "rain" = 6.4, drastically changing the angle of the regression line.

5.2.2 Bubble Chart

Purpose (when to use): to visualize the relationship (association) between three or four variables.

Common type of data: continuous data on both axes and bubble size, and categorical data in the colors.

Interpretation: as the bubble chart is an extension of the scatterplot with dots (bubbles) of varying sizes, its interpretation follows that of the scatterplot, adding the dot size as the value of the third or fourth variable.

Examples of applications: to visualize the relationship between three or four variables, like the price versus quality and market share of a given product; the relationship between income, education, and age; the fuel consumption versus acceleration, the number of cylinders, and horsepower of a vehicle; and the life expectancy versus the human development index, the continent, and CO_2 consumption, etc.

In its standard version, the *bubble chart* is an extension of the scatterplot with dots replaced by bubbles of varying sizes. These three variables are normally continuous, and a fourth categorical variable can be added as the bubble color, allowing us to visualize the relationship among four variables simultaneously.

Figure 5.7 shows one bubble chart for the Gapminder dataset and another for the Auto MPG dataset. In the first case, life expectancy is the response variable, the human development index (HDI) index is the explanatory variable, the different continents are represented by different colors, and bubble sizes indicate CO_2 consumption. This chart shows that the HDI index has a positive correlation with life expectancy, and although Africa has also increased in both indicators, it is still lower than the other continents. Furthermore, it is observed that Europe, Asia, and North America are ahead in these indicators but, at the same time, are producing more CO_2 per person. The graph also shows that all continents have approximately the same growth rate.

In the Auto MPG bubble chart, it can be observed that faster cars consume more fuel, have more cylinders, and more horsepower. The high positive correlation among these three variables sounds intuitive, though some outliers indicate the presence of fairly fast cars with low consumption and a low number of cylinders. At the same time, it can be observed that cars with six cylinders and a high horsepower value have disappointing performance in terms of acceleration. In such nonintuitive cases, it is important to investigate other car features, such as its weight, to understand why it presents these numbers.

Code 5.3 provides a script to generate the bubble charts for the Gapminder and the Auto MPG datasets, producing the graphs presented in Figure 5.7. It used the `scatterplot()` method in `Seaborn`, defining as `hue` the categorical variable chosen to color the bubbles, and as `size` the variable to determine the bubbles' sizes. The plots were also chosen to appear on a white grid, and the legends outside the plots. The titles were written to contain a full explanation of the role of each variable and appear with a font size slightly greater than the standard font size.

CODE 5.3   Script to generate the bubble charts with four variables for the Gapminder and Auto MPG datasets.

```
# Bubble charts with four variables for the Gapminder and Auto MPG datasets
```

```python
import pandas as pd
import matplotlib.pyplot as plt
import seaborn as sns
# Load the Gapminder dataset
dgapminder = pd.read_csv('gapminder.csv')

# Filter out missing values in 'lifeExp', 'hdi_index', and 'co2_consumption'
dgapminder = dgapminder.dropna(subset=['life_exp', 'hdi_index', 'co2_consump'])

# Set plot features
sns.set_style("whitegrid")
fig, (ax1, ax2) = plt.subplots(nrows=2, ncols=1, figsize=(10, 13))

# Create a bubble chart for the Gapminder dataset
sns.scatterplot(data=dgapminder, x="hdi_index", y="life_exp", hue="continent",
                size="co2_consump", sizes=(20, 500), alpha=0.7, ax=ax1)
ax1.set_xlabel("HDI Index", fontsize=14, labelpad=6.0)
ax1.set_ylabel("Life Expectancy", fontsize=14, labelpad=6.0)
ax1.set_title("Life Expectancy vs HDI Index by Continent (Bubble size is CO2
Consumption)", fontsize=16, pad=15.0)
ax1.legend(bbox_to_anchor=(1.05, 1), loc=2, borderaxespad=0.)

# Create a bubble chart for the Auto MPG dataset
dmpg = pd.read_csv('mpg.csv')
sns.scatterplot(data=dmpg, x="acceleration", y="mpg", hue="cylinders",
                size="horsepower", sizes=(20, 500), alpha=0.7, ax=ax2)
ax2.set_xlabel("Acceleration", fontsize=14, labelpad=6.0)
ax2.set_ylabel("MPG", fontsize=14, labelpad=6.0)
ax2.set_title("MPG vs Acceleration by Cylinders (Bubble size represents HP)",
fontsize=16, pad=15.0)
ax2.legend(bbox_to_anchor=(1.05, 1), loc=2, borderaxespad=0.)

# Adjust the layout to add space between subplots
plt.subplots_adjust(hspace=0.3)

# Show plot
plt.show()
```

5.2.3 Scatterplot Matrix (Pair Plot)

Purpose (when to use): to explore and visualize the relationship (association) between multiple variables simultaneously.

Common type of data: continuous data.

Interpretation: in a scatterplot matrix, the diagonal plots are usually histograms that show the distribution of each variable, and the off-diagonal plots are pairwise scatterplots showing the relationship between each pair of variables. Thus, it can be used to analyze the type and strength of the relationship between multiple variables, for example, to identify if there is any type of correlation (weak/strong positive, negative, or no correlation) between the variables, as well as to detect trends, patterns, and changes in the data. As it plots all-against-all variables, it is also a useful tool for identifying data clusters (groups) and outliers.

Examples of applications: to visualize the relationship between stock prices and financial indicators, physiological measurements and life quality, socioeconomic indicators and education level, etc.

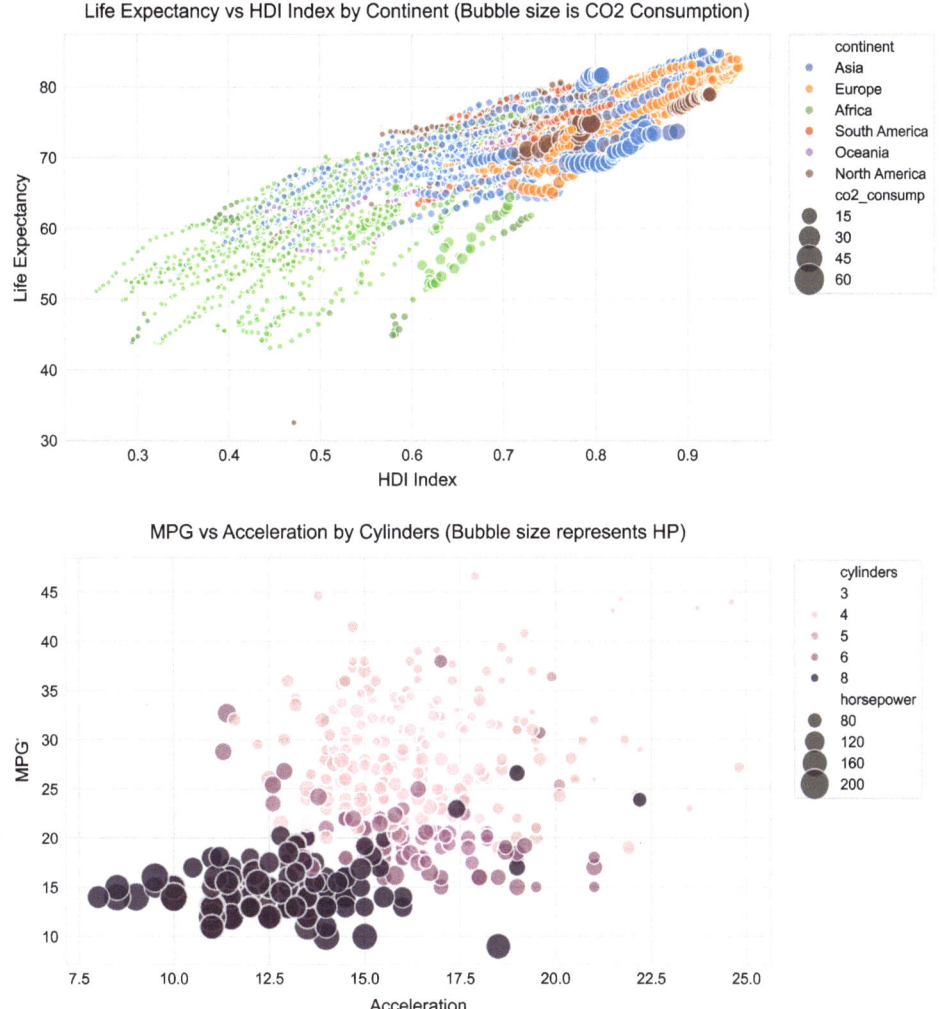

FIGURE 5.7 Four variable bubble charts for the Gapminder and Auto MPG datasets.

When the number of variables in a dataset increases, the sequential analysis of individual pairs of variables becomes more difficult. In such cases, a useful method is a *scatterplot matrix*, also called a *pair plot*, that is, a grid of scatterplots with m^2 cells, where m is the number of variables (i.e., dataset dimensionality). Every pairwise plot is shown twice, differing by a 90° rotation and in the same order as the horizontal and vertical orientations, leading to a symmetry along the diagonal (Ward et al., 2010). The diagonal plots are used to show the names, the histogram, or a density plot of the variables.

Figure 5.8 shows the scatterplot matrix for the Iris dataset of Fischer, plotting all possible combinations of the four features, with histograms along the diagonal. The pair plot allows for a visual inspection of the relationships between the different features, as well as the separability of the different species of iris. Figure 5.8a shows the scatterplot matrix with the variables' histogram on the main diagonal, while Figure 5.8b shows the scatterplot matrix with the kernel estimates on the main diagonal.

To generate the plots presented in Figure 5.8, we can use the `pairplot()` method in Seaborn, as shown in Code 5.4, which creates a grid of scatterplots and histograms, where each variable in the dataset is plotted against every other variable. By default, the diagonal of the grid is used to plot the histogram of each variable, as shown in Figure 5.8a, which uses the command `seaborn.pairplot("diris")`, where `diris` is the DataFrame generated by reading the iris.csv file using `Seaborn`. The `hue` parameter colors the plot based on a categorical variable, in this case, the variable "species", making it easier to see how different groups within the data are related. By assigning a hue variable, a semantic mapping is added, and the default marginal plot (histogram) is changed to a layered kernel

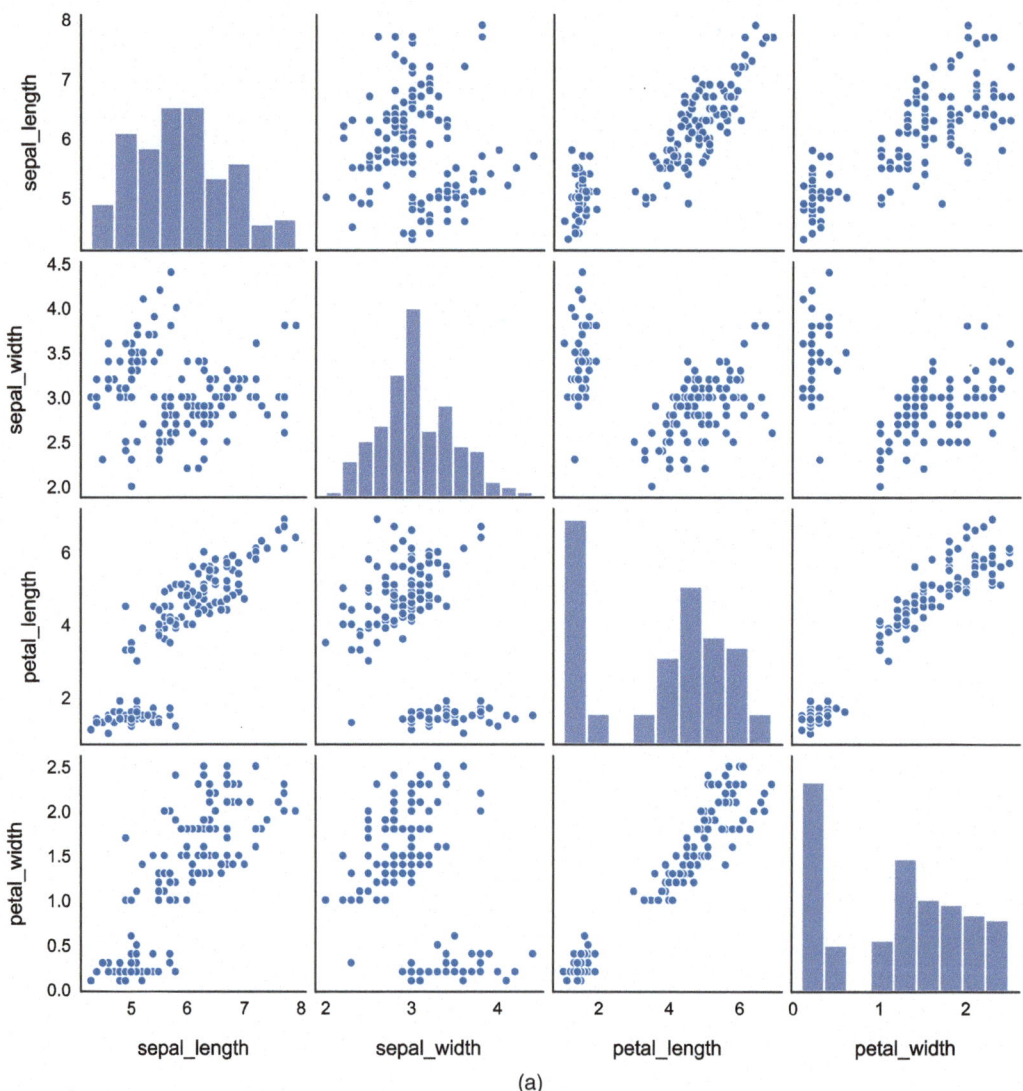

(a)

FIGURE 5.8 Scatterplot matrix of the Iris dataset of Fischer. (a) `seaborn.pairplot('diris')`. (b) `seaborn.pairplot('diris','hue'='species')`.

(Continued)

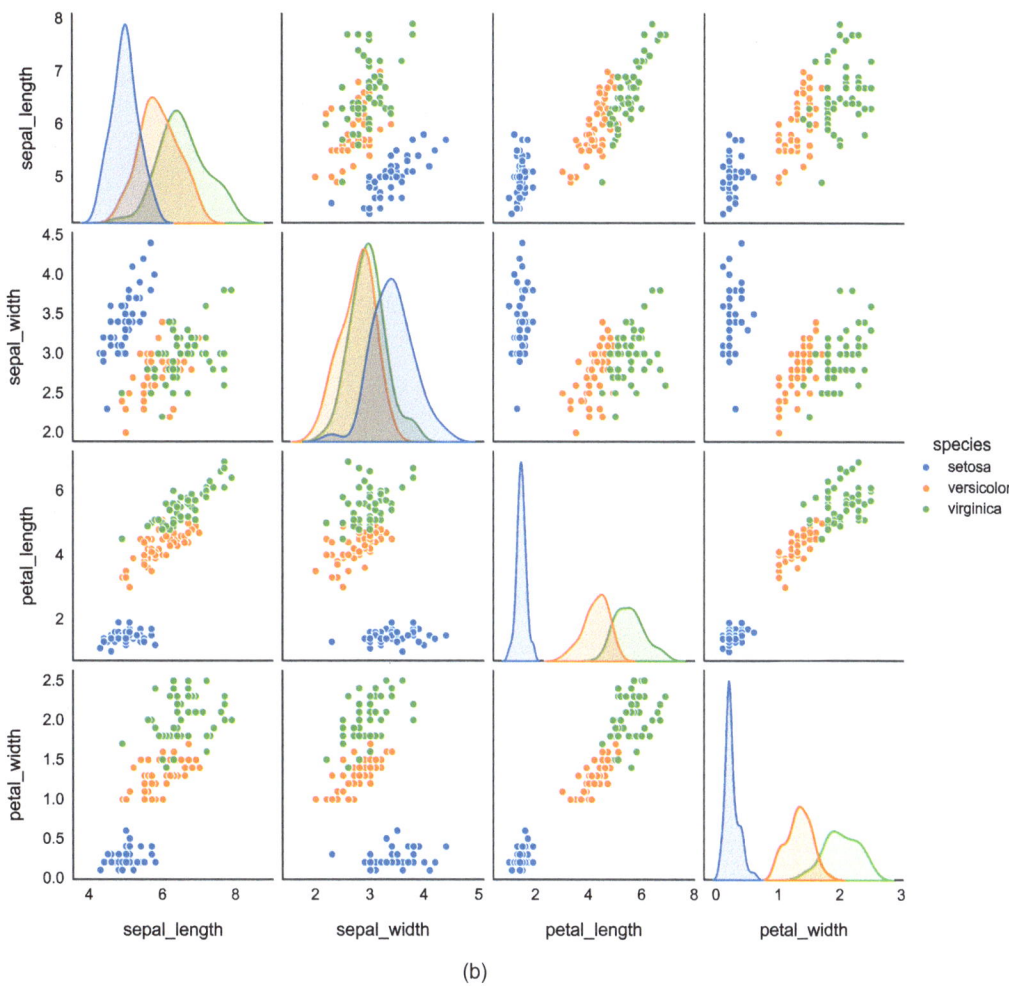

(b)

FIGURE 5.8 *(Continued)* Scatterplot matrix of the Iris dataset of Fischer. (a) `seaborn.pairplot('diris')`. (b) `seaborn.pairplot('diris','hue'='species')`.

density estimate, as illustrated in Figure 5.8b. Note that the setosa species is linearly separable from all the others, independently of the variable that is being observed.

CODE 5.4 Script to generate the scatterplot matrix with the histograms and kernel density estimates (KDE) on the main diagonal.

```python
# Scatterplot matrix for the Iris dataset
import seaborn as sns
import matplotlib.pyplot as plt
from sklearn.datasets import load_iris

# Load the Iris dataset from scikit-learn
iris = load_iris()

# Convert the dataset to a Pandas DataFrame
diris = sns.load_dataset('iris')
```

```
# Pairplot
sns.set_style("white")
grid1 = sns.pairplot(diris) # Distributions
grid2 = sns.pairplot(diris, hue='species') # Kernel density estimate (KDE)

# Show plot
plt.show()
```

5.2.4 Heatmaps and Correlograms

Purpose (when to use): to use colors to explore and visualize the magnitude of variables. If these magnitudes are the correlations between variables in a dataset showing the type and strength of their relationships, then the heatmap is known as a *correlogram*.

Common type of data: numerical, either discrete or continuous data.

Interpretation: they typically use a color gradient to represent the values of the data, where darker colors represent higher values and lighter colors represent lower values. It can be used to analyze the type (direction) and strength of the relationship between the variables, for example, to identify if there is any type of correlation (weak/strong positive, negative, or no correlation) between the variables. Positive correlations indicate that two variables tend to increase or decrease together, while negative correlations indicate that as one variable increases, the other tends to decrease.

Examples of applications: to visualize the relationship among stock prices and financial indicators, physiological measurements and life quality, the relationship of gene expression and diseases, socioeconomic indicators and education level, customer behavior and preferences, etc.

Scatterplot matrices that compare all variables against one another can become difficult to manage when the number of variables rises above four or five. In such cases, it is more beneficial to determine the level of association between variable pairs and visually represent this information instead of using the raw data. In descriptive statistics, a popular method for achieving this is by calculating correlation coefficients, as discussed in Chapter 3.

Simply put, a *heatmap* is a graph that uses color coding to represent the values of a table or matrix. The *correlogram*, also known as a *correlation matrix* or *correlation plot*, is a graphical representation of the pairwise correlations between variables in a dataset. Each cell in the matrix represents the correlation coefficient between two variables, with the cell's color indicating the strength and direction of the correlation.

Figure 5.9 shows the heatmaps for the Iris and Forest Fire datasets. These plots show the correlation value (strength) and signal (direction) in each cell, facilitating reading of the relationships between the variables. These plots are very simple to make using the heatmap() method in the Seaborn library, as shown in Code 5.5. Run the command sns.heatmap(df.corr(), annot=True, cmap="coolwarm"), where df is the dataframe containing the data, corr() calculates the correlations between the variables in df, annot=True forces the values to appear in the cells, and cmap="coolwarm" maps the data values to the color space from blue for negative values (cool) to red for positive values (warm). In Code 5.5, we inverted the cmap colors so that blue corresponds to positive correlations and red to negative ones.

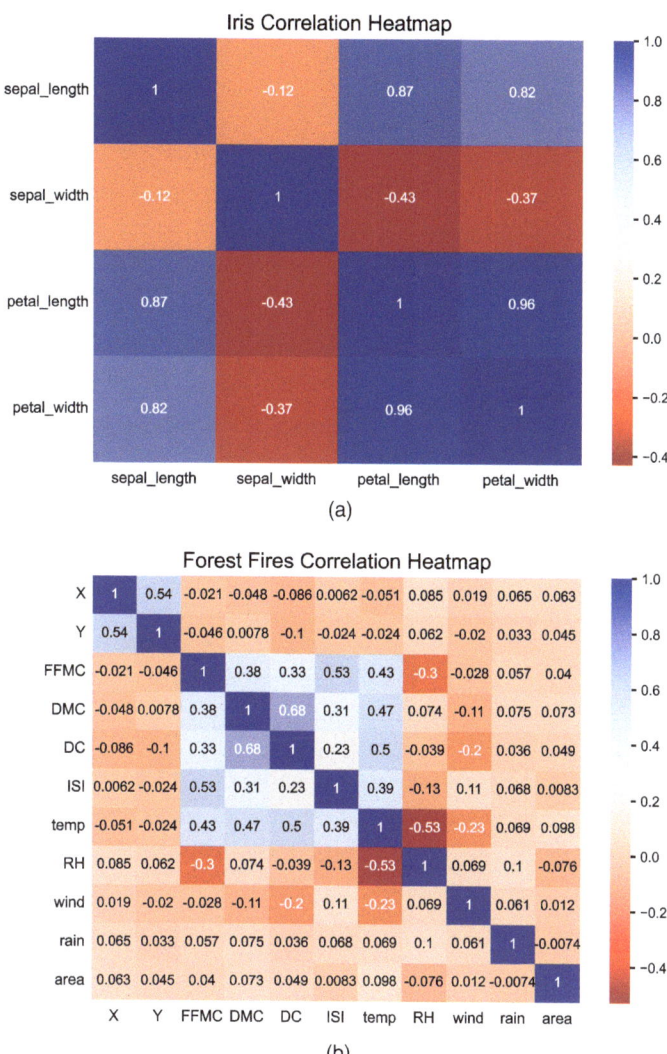

FIGURE 5.9   Heatmaps for the (a) Iris, and the (b) Forest Fires datasets.

CODE 5.5   Script to generate the correlograms for the Iris and Forest Fires datasets.

```python
# Correlation heatmaps (correlograms) for the Iris and Forest Fires datasets
import seaborn as sns
import matplotlib.pyplot as plt
from sklearn.datasets import load_iris
import pandas as pd
import numpy as np
from ucimlrepo import fetch_ucirepo

# Load the Iris dataset from scikit-learn
iris = load_iris()
diris = sns.load_dataset('iris')
diris = diris.drop(columns=['species'])

# Load the Forest Fires dataset
# https://archive.ics.uci.edu/ml/datasets/forest+fires
```

```python
dforest = fetch_ucirepo(id=162)["data"]["original"]
dforest = dforest.drop(columns=["month", "day"])

# Create a subplot grid with 2 rows and 1 column
fig, axs = plt.subplots(2, 1, figsize=(8, 12))

# Correlation heatmap for Iris dataset
corr_iris = diris.corr()
cmap_inverted = sns.color_palette("coolwarm", as_cmap=True)
cmap_inverted = cmap_inverted.reversed()
sns.heatmap(corr_iris, annot=True, cmap=cmap_inverted, ax=axs[0])
axs[0].set_title('Iris Correlation Heatmap', fontsize=16)

# Correlation heatmap for the Forest Fires dataset
corr_forest = dforest.corr()
sns.heatmap(corr_forest, annot=True, cmap=cmap_inverted, ax=axs[1])
axs[1].set_title('Forest Fires Correlation Heatmap', fontsize=16)

# Set tick labels font size & rotation
for ax in axs:
    ax.tick_params(axis='y', labelrotation=0.0)
    ax.tick_params(labelsize=11)

# Show plot
plt.show()
```

5.3 AMOUNTS

In many situations, the goal is to visualize the value of a given variable, for instance, the size of an item, the price of a stock, and the number of medals in a championship. In all cases, there are specific categories being studied, like size, prices, and prizes. These situations are called here as amounts because the goal is to visualize the values. Two types of graphs will be reviewed in this category: *bar charts* and *radar charts*.

5.3.1 Bar Chart

Purpose (when to use): to visualize data that can be clustered into discrete categories or groups, and to compare the magnitude of different variables or categories.

Common type of data: categorical or discrete data.

Interpretation: to analyze the relative magnitudes of the different categories or groups, to identify trends, patterns, and changes in the data, and to compare multiple variables or data series.

Examples of applications: to visualize the sales levels of different product categories, survey results, demographic data, financial data, etc.

A *bar chart* is similar to a line chart, except that each data point is replaced by a rectangle with a height proportional to the value. The rectangle is usually centered on the spatial attribute of the data, and its width is often uniform. When values are categorical or discrete and cannot be shown in a series, a *bar chart* may be a suitable alternative for the line chart. Similarly to the case of a line chart, it is possible to create multivariate bar charts by stacking the bars on top of each other in a form of superimposition easy to interpret.

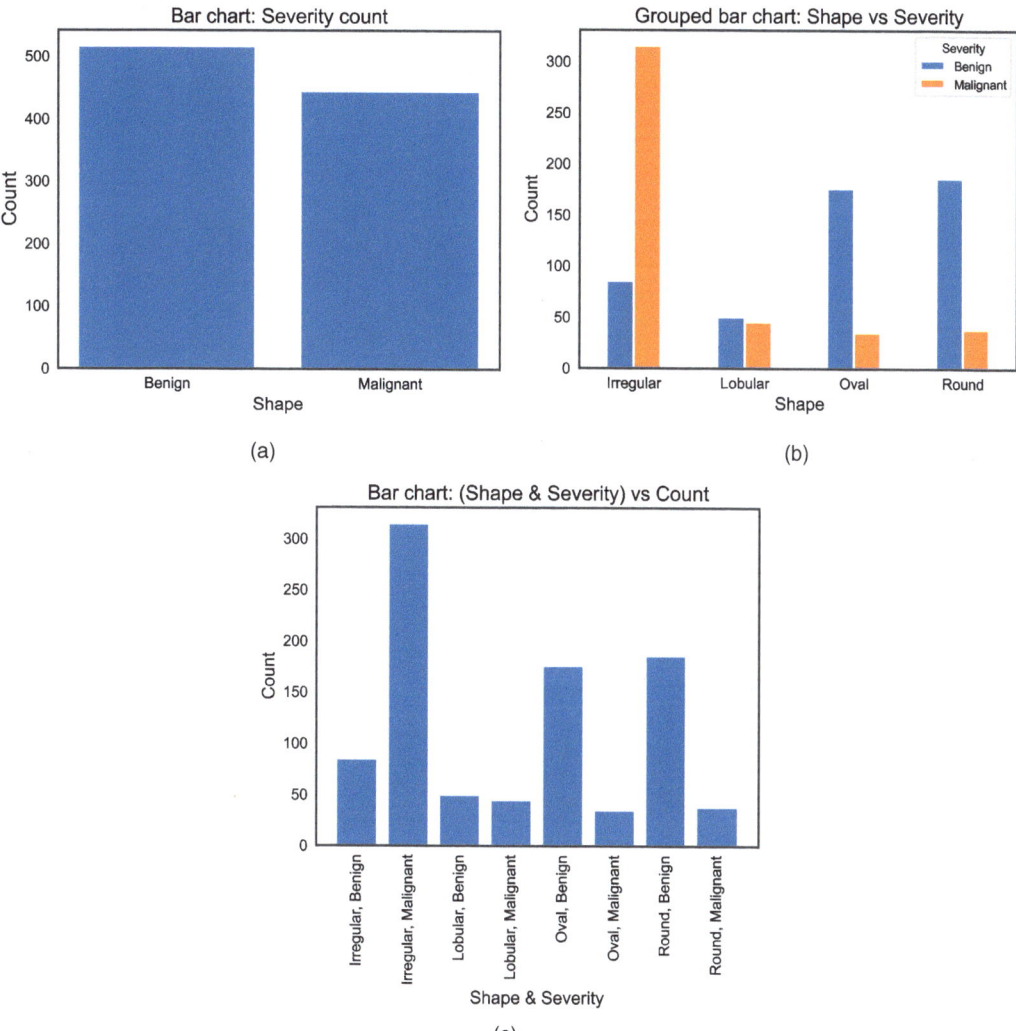

FIGURE 5.10 Bar charts for the mammographic dataset. (a) Frequency of occurrence (count) of each possible value of variable 'Severity'. (b) Count of variable 'Shape' grouped by severity level. (c) Same as in (b), but without grouping the bars.

Figure 5.10 illustrates bar charts to show (a) the count of variable "Severity", with values Benign and Malignant, and (b) the grouping of the variable "Shape" by its severity. Note that two different representations were chosen for plotting "Shape" in relation to severity (Figure 5.10b and c).

Code 5.6 presents the script to plot bar charts for variables "Severity" and "Shape" of the mammographic dataset. The first plot (Figure 5.10a) simply presents the frequency of occurrence of each possible value of variable "Severity" using the `bar()` method in `Matplotlib`, and the second graph (Figure 5.10b) uses the `plot()` method with parameter `kind = "bar"` to plot a chart with the count of variable "Shape" for each value of "Severity". Figure 5.10c shows the same graph as (b), but with a different presentation scheme. Note that plots (b) and (c) both used the `groupby()` method in `Pandas()` to group the data in the DataFrame `dmammo` in relation to the "Severity" values.

CODE 5.6 Script to generate the bar charts for the mammographic dataset: frequency of occurrence (count) of each possible value of variable 'Severity', count of variable 'Shape' grouped by severity level, and same as the previous one, but with a different representation.

```python
# Create the bar charts for Severity and Shape vs Severity
# of the mammographic dataset

import pandas as pd
import matplotlib.pyplot as plt
from ucimlrepo import fetch_ucirepo

# fetch dataset
# https://archive.ics.uci.edu/ml/datasets/Mammographic+Mass
dmammo = fetch_ucirepo(id=161)["data"]["original"]
# replace placeholders with labels
dmammo['Severity'] = dmammo['Severity'].map({0:'Benign', 1:'Malignant'})
dmammo['Shape'] = dmammo['Shape'].map({1.0:'Round', 2.0:'Oval', 3.0:'Lobular',
4.0:'Irregular'})

# 1. Calculate and plot the bar chart for 'Severity'
counts = dmammo['Severity'].value_counts().sort_index()
plt.bar(counts.index, counts.values) # Plot the bar chart
plt.title('Bar chart: Severity count')
plt.ylabel('Count'); plt.xlabel('Shape')
# Show plot
plt.show()

# 2. Plot a bar chart for 'Shape' in relation to 'Severity'
dmammo.groupby(['Shape', 'Severity']).size().unstack().plot(kind='bar', rot=0)
plt.title('Grouped bar chart: Shape vs Severity', fontsize=16)
plt.ylabel('Count'); plt.xlabel('Shape')
# Show plot
plt.show()

# 3. Calculate and plot the bar chart for 'Shape'&'Severity' vs 'Count'
counts = dmammo.groupby(['Shape', 'Severity']).size().reset_index(name='count')
plt.bar(range(len(counts)), counts['count'])  # Plot the bar chart
plt.title('Bar chart: (Shape & Severity) vs Count')
plt.xlabel('Shape & Severity'); plt.ylabel('Count')

# Format and rotate the ticks
plt.xticks(range(len(counts)), [', '.join(map(str, tpl)) for tpl in
                                counts[['Shape','Severity']].to_
records(index=False)], rotation=90)

# Show plot
plt.show()
```

5.3.2 Radar Chart

> **Purpose (when to use)**: to compare and visualize multiple series of continuous variables in a single radial chart.

> **Common type of data**: continuous data.

> **Interpretation**: the radar chart plots one or more series of values considering numerical variables over a radial graph, forming a polygon. In the radar chart, larger values are

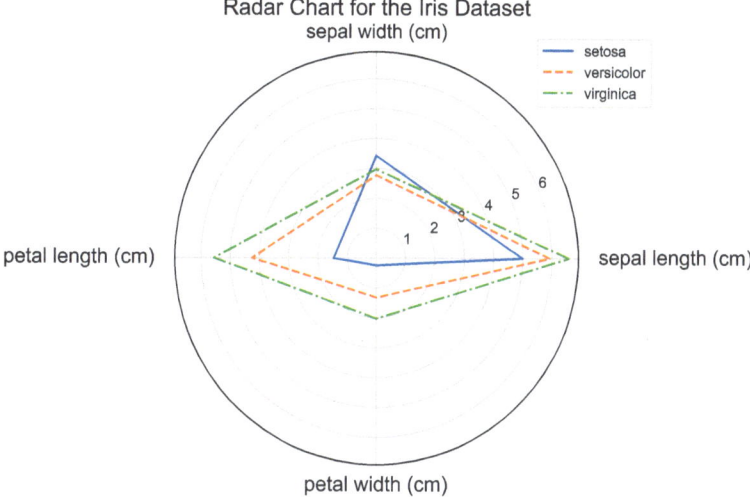

FIGURE 5.11   Radar chart for the Iris dataset.

farther from the radar center, allowing the comparison of different series in terms of amplitude. Furthermore, the shape and size of the polygon can be used to compare the different series.

Examples of applications: to compare brands considering their features, stocks in relation to their (fundamental) indicators, students in relation to their grades in each subject, animals in relation to their characteristics, etc.

Radar charts, also called *spider* or *web charts*, plot one or more series of values organized in a set of numerical variables over a radial graph, such that each variable has its own axis starting at the origin of the graph, and the values of all variables are connected, forming a polygon.

To illustrate, consider the graph in Figure 5.11. It shows the radar chart for the three species of Iris plant (Setosa, Virginica, and Versicolor) plotted in relation to their four variables: "sepal length"; "sepal width"; "petal length"; and "petal width". Each species was plotted with a different color and line style and the values for each variable were obtained by taking the mean of each variable for each plant species. As can be observed, the polygons for the Setosa and Virginica species have more similar shapes and sizes than the polygon for the Versicolor species, which shows a smaller average value for petal length and width. This analysis brings some light as to why the Versicolor species is linearly separable from the other two.

Code 5.7 generates the radar chart for the Iris dataset of Fischer. It starts by loading the dataset from the `Scikitlearn` library and setting up the plot figure using `Matplotlib`. It then calculates the angles for the radar chart plot using a polar plot and defines the line style for each Iris species. Then, the script calculates the mean values of each plant species for each of the four variables (features). Note that this code generates and draws the radar chart instead of using a specific method to plot the radar.

CODE 5.7   Script to generate and plot the radar chart for the Iris dataset.

```
# Radar Chart for the Iris dataset available at the Scikitlearn library
```

```
import matplotlib.pyplot as plt
import numpy as np
from sklearn.datasets import load_iris

# Load the Iris dataset from Scikitlearn and setup the radar chart
diris = load_iris()
fig = plt.figure(figsize=(10, 5))
axs = fig.add_subplot(polar=True)
angles = np.linspace(0, 2*np.pi, len(diris.feature_names), endpoint=False)
angles = np.concatenate((angles,[angles[0]]))
line = ['-','--','-.']

# For each Iris class, plot the mean values of its features as a line
for i in range(3):
    values = diris.data[diris.target == i].mean(axis=0)
    values = np.concatenate((values, [values[0]]))
    axs.plot(angles, values, label=diris.target_names[i], ls=line[i])
axs.set_xticks(angles[:-1])
axs.set_xticklabels(diris.feature_names)


axs.legend(bbox_to_anchor=(1.2, 1.05))
axs.set_title('Radar Chart for the Iris Dataset')

# Show plot
plt.show()
```

5.4 PROPORTIONS

There are situations where the goal is to investigate how a group or part can be divided into subgroups that represent parts of a whole, or proportions. A simple example is countries within continents, states within countries, and cities within states. We can also think of files within a folder, where subfolders represent subgroups of files stored in your PC or cloud. Proportion visualization allows us to visualize such clustered structures. The following proportion visualization methods will be reviewed here: *pie charts*; *doughnut charts*, and *treemaps*.

5.4.1 Pie Chart

Purpose (when to use): to explore and visualize the distribution of a variable that can be divided into a small number of different and mutually exclusive categories, where each category is a fraction (slice) of the whole.

Common type of data: categorical data.

Interpretation: each pie chart slice represents a category within the whole, and the larger the slice, the greater its value (proportion).

Examples of applications: to visualize the proportion of any categorical variable, such as colors in a painting, customers who buy each product type, marital status in a given area, etc.

The *pie chart* is a graph that represents the data values by an area in a circular shape, similar to a pie (or a pizza). Its circular nature makes it suitable for analyzing the proportion among categories of a variable, where each category is represented by a slice in the pie. However, it also makes it difficult for us to visualize small differences in sizes among the slices. This is the main reason why pie charts are employed for variables with a small number of categories, normally less than eight (Wong, 2010). When the number of categories (slices) is greater than eight, it is recommended to use stacked bar charts or grouped bar charts.

The slice sizes are presented as percentages or fractions. Thus, each slice, s_i, $i = 1, ..., m$ (m is the number of categories of the variable), of the whole sum of the pie chart is defined as $s_i/\Sigma(s_i)$. All pie slices add up to 100% if represented as percentages or 1 if represented as fractions. Sosulski (2019) offers some suggestions for the pie chart design: avoid pie charts when the slices have similar sizes; insert the labels directly in the pie slices; and use a whitespace (thin white line) to separate the slices.

Figure 5.12 shows the pie chart and grouped bar chart for the variable "Margin" of the Mammographic dataset and the variable "day" of the Forest Fires dataset. The percentage of each slice is shown within the slice and a default color palette was adopted. The grouped bar charts next to the pie charts were plotted to illustrate how our visual system interprets information differently in a pie chart and a bar chart. Human perception deals with

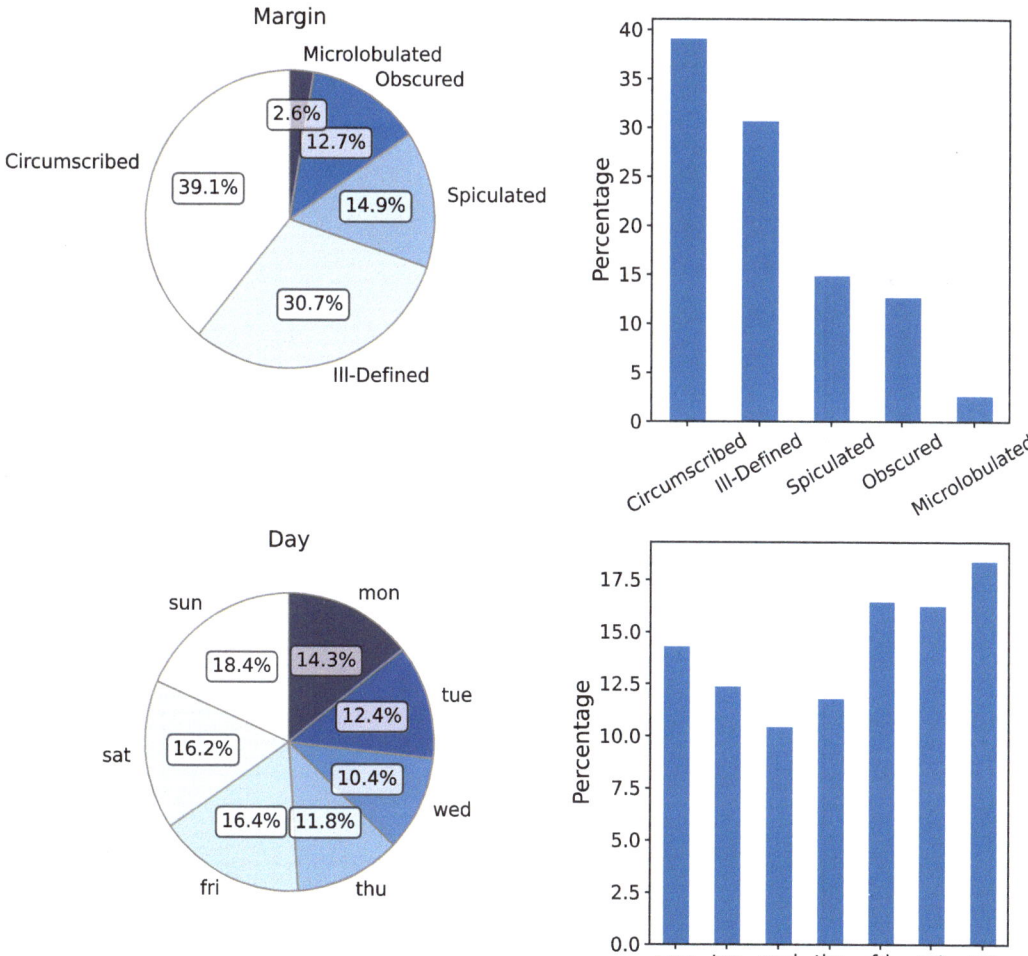

FIGURE 5.12   Pie chart and grouped bar chart for the variable 'Margin' of the Mammographic dataset, and the variable 'day' of the Forest Fires dataset.

distances more easily than with areas, so we perceive more accurately the differences in the bar heights than in the pie slices (Wilke, 2019).

Code 5.8 shows a script to generate the charts in Figure 5.12. It used the plot() method in Matplotlib and parameter kind set to "pie" and "bar", respectively. Note that the pie charts present the relative (percentage) contribution of each slice to the whole, while the bars only show the relative frequency of each variable category. The two different chart types illustrate well our capability of more accurately identifying the differences in the contributions of each category.

CODE 5.8   Script to generate the pie chart and grouped bar chart for the variable 'Margin' of the Mammographic dataset, and the variable 'day' of the Forest Fires dataset.

```python
# Pie Chart and Grouped Bar Chart for variables 'Margin' of the Mammographic
dataset, and
# 'Day' of the Forest Fires dataset - Code with percentage values for the grouped
bar chart

import pandas as pd
import matplotlib.pyplot as plt
from ucimlrepo import fetch_ucirepo

# fetch datasets
# https://archive.ics.uci.edu/ml/datasets/Mammographic+Mass
dmammo = fetch_ucirepo(id=161)["data"]["original"]
# https://archive.ics.uci.edu/ml/datasets/forest+fires
dforest = fetch_ucirepo(id=162)["data"]["original"]

# Create a figure with two subplots in each row
fig, ((pie1, bar1), (pie2, bar2)) = plt.subplots(nrows=2, ncols=2, figsize=(12, 12))

# replace placeholders with labels
mm_labeled = dmammo['Margin'].map({1:'Circumscribed', 2:'Microlobulated',
3:'Obscured', 4:'Ill-Defined', 5:'Spiculated'})

# Mammographic dataset - Pie chart
mm = mm_labeled.value_counts()
axes = mm.plot(kind='pie', autopct='%1.1f%%', startangle=90, ax=pie1)
## Format Pie Chart
pie1.set_title('Margin'); pie1.set_ylabel('')

# Mammographic dataset - Grouped bar chart
mm = mm_labeled.value_counts(normalize=True) * 100
mm.plot(kind='bar', ax=bar1, color='#1f77b4')
## Format Bar Chart
bar1.grid(False); bar1.legend().remove()
bar1.set_ylabel('Percentage'); bar1.set_xlabel('')

# Forest Fires dataset - Pie chart
ff = dforest['day'].value_counts()
ff_ordered = ff[['sun', 'sat', 'fri', 'thu', 'wed', 'tue', 'mon']]
axes = ff_ordered.plot(kind='pie', autopct='%1.1f%%', startangle=90, ax=pie2)
## Format Pie Chart
pie2.set_title('Day'); pie2.set_ylabel('')

# Forest Fires dataset - Grouped bar chart
ff = dforest['day'].value_counts(normalize=True) * 100
ff_ordered = ff[['mon', 'tue', 'wed', 'thu', 'fri', 'sat', 'sun']]
```

```
ff_ordered.plot(kind='bar', ax=bar2, color='#1f77b4')
## Format Bar Chart
bar2.grid(False); bar2.legend().remove()
bar2.set_ylabel('Percentage'); bar2.set_xlabel('')

# Show plot
plt.show()
```

5.4.2 Doughnut Chart

The *doughnut chart* is a variation of the pie chart in which the center of the pie is removed, resulting in a ring-like (doughnut) chart. Therefore, its purpose, type of data, interpretation, and examples of applications are the same as the pie chart. Examples of pie charts for the "margin" variable of the Mammographic dataset and the "day" variable of the UCI Forest Fires data are presented in Figure 5.13.

The script presented in Code 5.9 modifies Code 5.8 by adding the wedgeprops argument to the mm.plot() and ff.plot() methods in Matplotlib, such that the wedge objects in the pie chart could have their center removed with a predefined width. We have set different widths for the doughnut charts to illustrate the influence of this property in the final charts generated.

CODE 5.9   Script to generate the doughnut charts equivalent to the pie charts of Code 5.8.

```
# Doughnut chart for variables 'Margin' of the Mammographic dataset, and 'Day' of the
# Forest Fires dataset - Code with percentage values for the grouped bar chart

import pandas as pd
import matplotlib.pyplot as plt
from ucimlrepo import fetch_ucirepo

# fetch datasets
# https://archive.ics.uci.edu/ml/datasets/Mammographic+Mass
dmammo = fetch_ucirepo(id=161)["data"]["original"]
# https://archive.ics.uci.edu/ml/datasets/forest+fires
dforest = fetch_ucirepo(id=162)["data"]["original"]

# Create a figure with two subplots in each row
fig, (dnut1, dnut2) = plt.subplots(nrows=1, ncols=2, figsize=(12, 10))
```

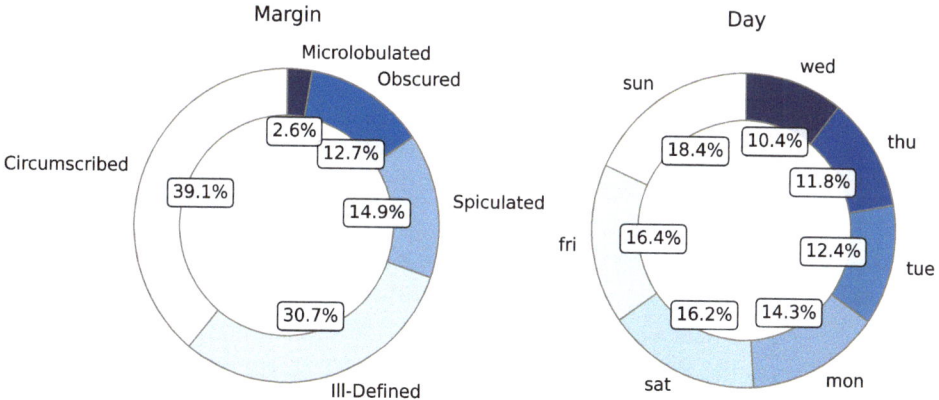

FIGURE 5.13   Doughnut charts equivalent to the pie charts presented in Figure 5.12.

```
# Mammographic dataset - Doughnut chart
## Replace placeholders with labels
mm = dmammo['Margin'].map({1:'Circumscribed', 2:'Microlobulated', 3:'Obscured',
4:'Ill-Defined', 5:'Spiculated'}).value_counts()
mm.plot(kind='pie', autopct='%1.1f%%', startangle=90, ax=dnut1,
        wedgeprops={'width': 0.3}, fontsize=14, colormap=plt.cm.Blues)
dnut1.set_title('Margin', fontsize=16); dnut1.set_ylabel('')
for ax in dnut1.texts[1::2]:
    ax.set_bbox(dict(fc='white', ec='black', alpha=0.875, boxstyle='Round'))
### Slightly adjust overlapping text
x, y = dnut1.texts[1::2][3].get_position()
dnut1.texts[1::2][3].set_position((x + 0.1, y - 0.05))

# Forest Fires dataset - Doughnut chart
ff = dforest['day'].value_counts()
ff.plot(kind='pie', autopct='%1.1f%%', startangle=90, ax=dnut2,
        wedgeprops={'width': 0.5}, fontsize=14, colormap=plt.cm.Blues)
dnut2.set_title('Day', fontsize=16); dnut2.set_ylabel('')
for ax in dnut2.texts[1::2]:
    ax.set_bbox(dict(fc='white', ec='black', alpha=0.875, boxstyle='Round'))

# Show plot
plt.show()
```

5.4.3 Treemap

Purpose (when to use): to explore and visualize hierarchical data in nested and mutually exclusive rectangles of varying sizes, where each category is a fraction (slice) of the whole.

Common type of data: data with a hierarchical structure and categories that can be divided into subcategories.

Interpretation: each rectangle represents a category within the whole, and the larger the rectangle, the greater its value (proportion). Color can be used to represent other values or variables.

Examples of applications: to visualize the proportion of hierarchical variables, such as continents, countries, and population; month, day, rain volume, etc.

Treemaps can be thought of as square versions of pie charts, in the sense that they use nested rectangles instead of pie slices, forming a larger square (or rectangle) to display different categories. The size of the rectangles corresponds to their relevance in the plot, and color can be used to provide another categorization. Originally, treemaps were proposed to visualize the file structure in a hard disk, aiming at determining how space was used (Johnson & Shneiderman, 1991).

To illustrate treemaps and compare them with pie charts, let us take the same example used previously. Figure 5.14 shows the corresponding treemaps for the variable "Margin" of the mammographic dataset and "day" of the Forest Fires dataset. In the rectangles of the treemaps, we display the absolute and relative sizes of each category of variables, "Margin" and "day". As this data is not hierarchical, variable "parent" has no value for the "microlobulated" category. A discussion about hierarchical data will be provided in Section 6.3.

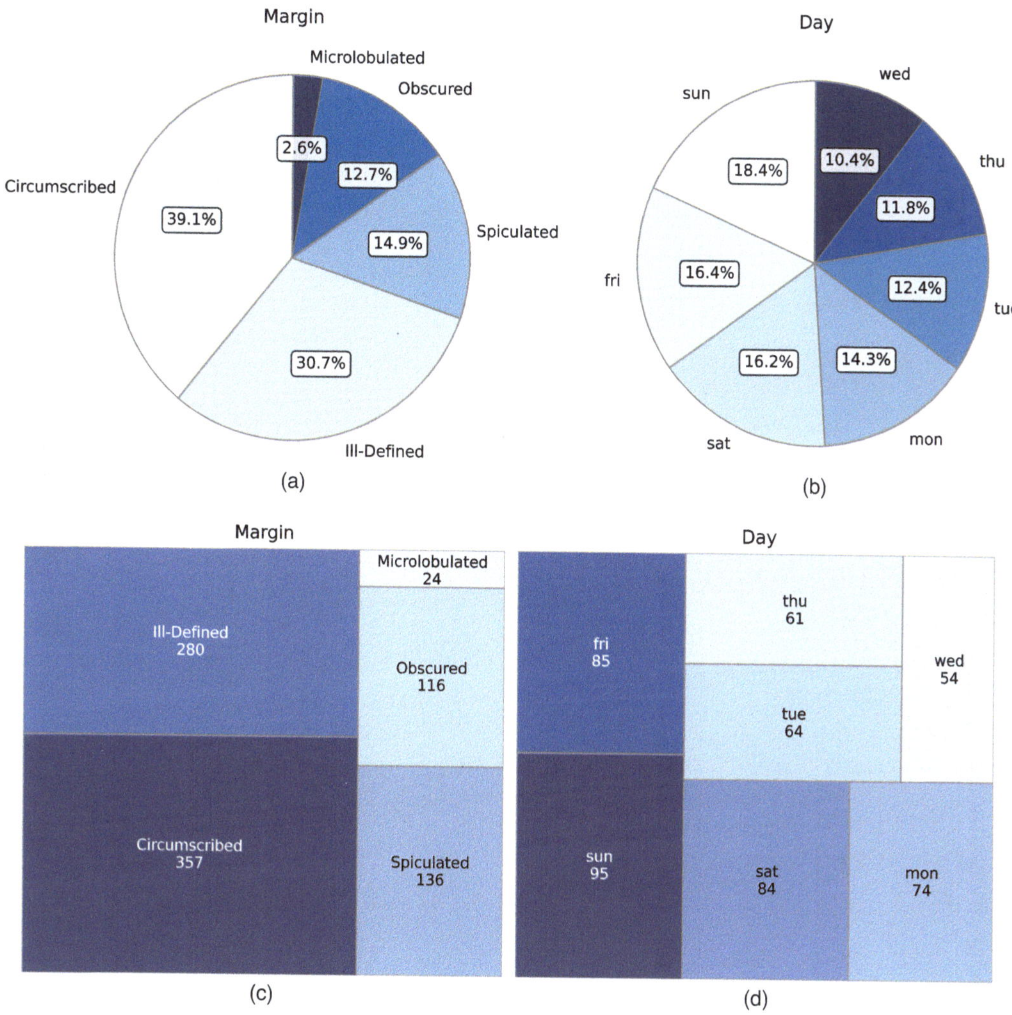

FIGURE 5.14 (a) Pie charts versus treemaps. (a) Pie chart for the variable 'Margin' of the Mammographic dataset. (b) Pie chart of variable Day of the Forest Fires dataset. (c) Treemap of variable Margin of the Mammographic dataset. (d) Treemap of variable Day of the Forest Fires dataset.

Another example of the use of treemaps is presented in Figure 5.15 using the Gapminder dataset. It shows the treemap for those countries with a GDP greater than a predefined threshold, 5% in the case shown. Note that the treemap divides the countries by continent, with each continent represented in a different color. Within the countries' rectangles, we printed each country's GDP contribution to its continent. Even if you try to manually define the font sizes, the `treemap` function automatically adjusts them within the treemap based on the rectangle size, which is why some labels appear smaller than others. In this example, the United Arab Emirates and Hong Kong labels became very small and difficult to read.

Code 5.10 shows a script to generate the treemap of Figure 5.15 using the `treemap` function of the `plotly.express` library. It first loads the dataset, calculates the GDP by continent and each country's percentage contribution on the continent, then applies the minimum percentage contribution filter for including it in the treemap. The command

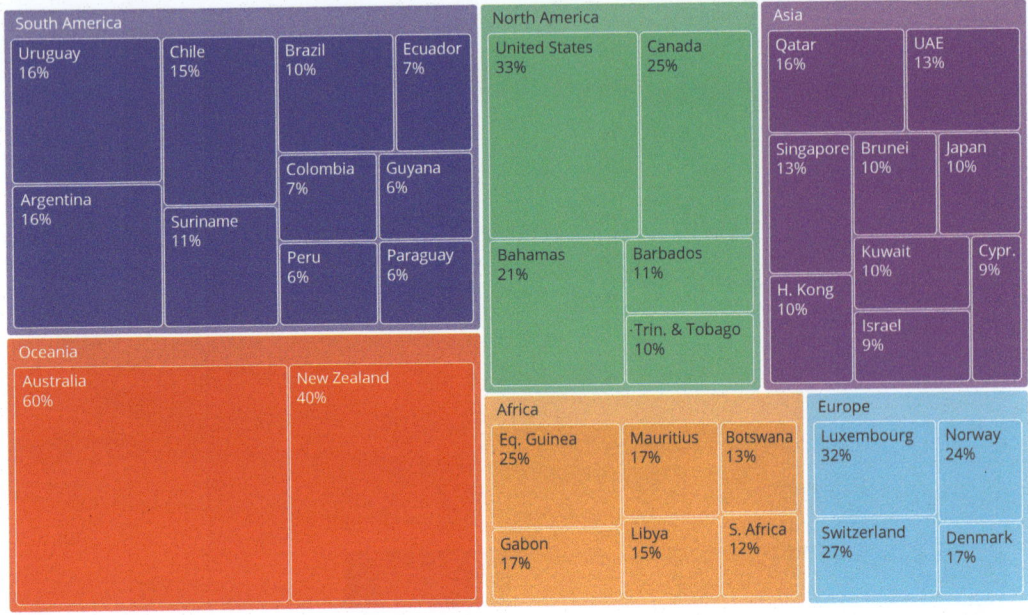

FIGURE 5.15   Treemap for the Gapminder dataset plotting the GDP only of those countries with a percentage GDP ≥ 5.0%.

`px.treemap` creates the treemap with the filtered data, using "continent" and "country" to build the treemap hierarchy and "gdp" as the value to plot.

CODE 5.10   Script to generate the treemap of Figure 5.15.

```python
# Generate the treemap for the Gapminder dataset having the countries as the
# rectangles, their GDP in the slice sizes, and the continents in the colors

import pandas as pd
import plotly.express as px
# Load the Gapminder dataset
dgapminder = pd.read_csv('gapminder.csv')

# Calculate total GDP per continent
gdp_per_continent = dgapminder.groupby('continent')['gdp'].sum()

# Calculate the percentage of GDP by country in each continent
gdp_perc_by_country = dgapminder.groupby(['continent','country'])['gdp'].sum()/
gdp_per_continent

# Set a minimum size for the rectangles
min_size = 0.05

# Filter out rectangles smaller than the minimum size
gdp_perc_by_country_filtered = gdp_perc_by_country[gdp_perc_by_country > min_size]

# Calculate the percentage of GDP by country in each continent
gdp_perc_by_country = dgapminder.groupby(['continent','country'])['gdp'].sum()/
gdp_per_continent

# Reset the index for Plotly Express
```

```
gdp_perc_by_country_filtered = gdp_perc_by_country_filtered.reset_index()

# Create the treemap using Plotly Express
fig = px.treemap(gdp_perc_by_country_filtered,
                 path=['continent', 'country'],
                 values='gdp',
                 title=f'GDP by Country and Continent: Values greater than
                 {min_size*100:.1f}%',
                 width=1150, height=700)

# Update layout and legend
fig.update_traces(textinfo='label+percent parent')
fig.update_layout(margin=dict(t=40, b=0, l=0, r=0), title_x=0.5, legend_title_
text='Continent', uniformtext=dict(minsize=12, mode='show'))
# Show the treemap
fig.show()

# Print the tree structure
print(gdp_perc_by_country)
```

5.5 EVOLUTION AND FLOW

There is a vast array of data that shows the change in variables with time. For example, a data set may contain information about the number of people in a city over time, the average income, the age, the number of children, and the list goes on. There is also data available for stocks, temperature, industrial production, etc. Data collected over time is certainly among the most common ones and plays a crucial role in understanding how a certain variable evolves. Differently from the evolution case, in which the variables change over time, in the flow case, the idea is to investigate the flow of data through different stages of a transition process. Examples include transitions from middle to high school, then college, master's, and Ph.D., or from operations to management, then to directorship and presidency. This section reviews the *line chart* as the main technique for studying the variation of data with time (evolution) and the *Sankey* and *Gantt charts* as tools for visualizing data flow.

5.5.1 Line Chart

Purpose (when to use): to show patterns, trends, changes, and anomalies in data over time or a strictly increasing variable (quantity).

Common type of data: continuous one-dimensional sequences.

Interpretation: to identify the trend, changes in direction or magnitude of the trend, looking for spikes or dips, identifying repeating patterns or cycles, etc.

Examples of applications: to visualize stock prices, weather data, population trends, disease spread, etc.

Line charts are useful for identifying patterns and trends in a one-dimensional sequence of univariate data, that is, continuous data over time with a single value per data item. They map the sequence data (e.g., time) to one dimension, typically the *x*-axis, and the data value to another dimension, typically the *y*-axis, forming a line; or to the color of a mark or region along the spatial axis, forming a bar. The data is adjusted in size to be within the limits of the display attribute.

For multivariate datasets, it is possible to either stack non-overlapping graphs or create a graph containing one line for each variable. In the latter scenario, we should use different line styles or colors to distinguish the variables (Ward et al., 2010).

Figure 5.16 shows some line charts plotted with the Gapminder dataset. Figure 5.16a shows the variation in time of life expectancy and CO_2 consumption over the years. Line charts can also be used to compare multiple trends or data series by plotting them on the same chart, as illustrated in Figure 5.16b, which groups the life expectancy and HDI variables by continent. As can be observed, the life expectancy and HDI index have almost monotonically increased over the years in all continents, while CO_2 consumption started decreasing after 2007.

Code 5.11 presents the scripts to plot the individual line graphs of life expectancy ("life-exp"), CO_2 consumption ("co2_consump"), and HDI index ("hdi_index") over the years for the Gapminder dataset, as well as the life expectancy and HDI index comparing the trends for each continent over the years. These scripts used the plot() method in Matplotlib and played with line colors and styles to differentiate the line trends. It also

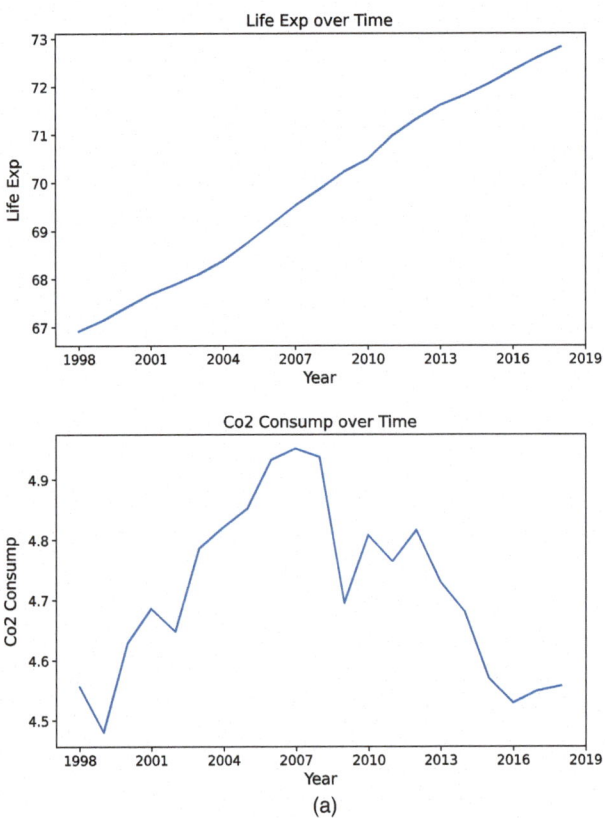

(a)

FIGURE 5.16   Line charts for the Gapminder dataset. (a) Line charts showing the variation of the life expectancy ('life_exp') and CO_2 consumption ('co2_consump') over time. (b) Life expectancy and HDI both grouped by continent.

(Continued)

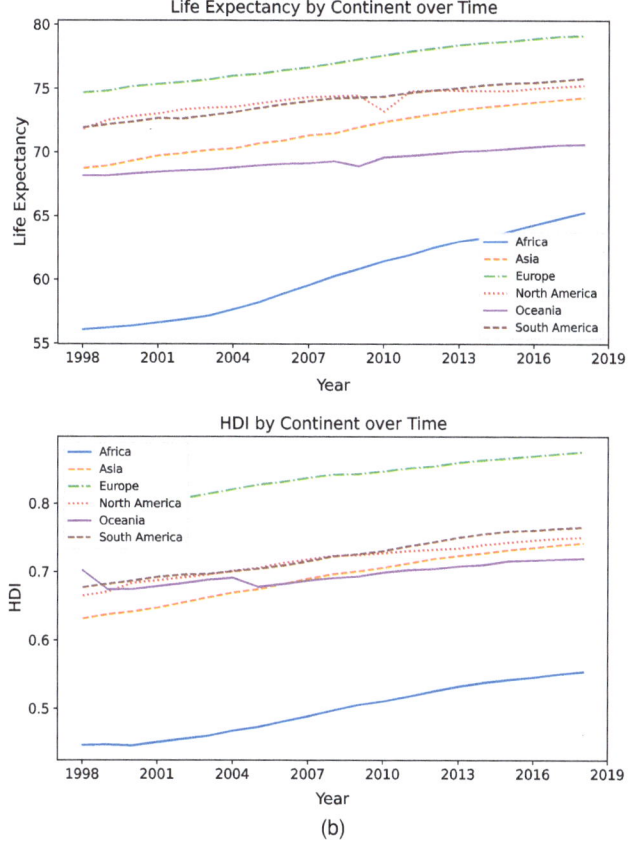

FIGURE 5.16 (Continued) Line charts for the Gapminder dataset. (a) Line charts showing the variation of the life expectancy ('life_exp') and CO_2 consumption ('co2_consump')over time. (b) Life expectancy and HDI both grouped by continent.

used the `groupby()` method in `Pandas` to group the data in a DataFrame based on the "year" and "continent". In such cases, we used the `mean` statistics for each group (year and continent).

CODE 5.11 Scripts to plot (a) the individual line graphs of life expectancy and CO_2 consumption, over the years for the Gapminder dataset, and (b) the life expectancy and HDI index comparing the trends for each continent over the years. HDI, Human Development Index.

```python
# (a) Create the line charts for Life Expectancy, CO2 Consumption, and
# HDI index vs the year for the Gapminder dataset

import pandas as pd
import matplotlib.pyplot as plt
# Load the dataset, select the target variables and group by year
# Load the Gapminder dataset
dgapminder = pd.read_csv('gapminder.csv')[['life_exp', 'co2_consump', 'hdi_index',
'year']]
dby = dgapminder.groupby('year').mean()   # dby: data by year

# Loop through a list of tuples and plot each variable in a separate subplot
```

```python
fig, axes = plt.subplots(ncols=3, figsize=(18,5))
for i, var in enumerate(['life_exp', 'co2_consump', 'hdi_index']):
    axes[i].plot(dby.index, dby[var])
    axes[i].set_title(var.replace('_', ' ').title() + ' over Time', fontsize=16)
    axes[i].set_xlabel('Year', fontsize=14)
    axes[i].set_ylabel(var.replace('_', ' ').title(), fontsize=14)
    axes[i].xaxis.set_major_locator(plt.MaxNLocator(integer=True))
    axes[i].tick_params(axis='both', which='major', labelsize=12)

# Adjust the layout to add space between subplots
plt.subplots_adjust(wspace=0.3)

# Save and display the pie charts
plt.savefig("Figure_5_16a_Line_Chart.svg", format="svg", dpi=1500,
bbox_inches='tight')
plt.show()

# (b) Create the line charts for Life Expectancy, CO2 Consumption, and
# HDI index vs the year for the Gapminder dataset

import pandas as pd
import matplotlib.pyplot as plt

# Load the dataset, select the target variables and group by 'continent' and 'year'
# Load the Gapminder dataset
dgapminder = pd.read_csv('gapminder.csv')[['life_exp', 'hdi_index', 'continent',
'year']]
dbc = dgapminder.groupby(['continent', 'year']).mean()  #dbc: data by continent

# Loop the unique continents and plot a line graph of 'life_exp' vs 'year' for
each continent
fig, axes = plt.subplots(ncols=2, figsize=(20,5))
ls = ['-', '--', '-.', ':', '-', '--']
for i, c in enumerate(dbc.index.get_level_values('continent').unique()):
    axes[0].plot(dbc.loc[c].index, dbc.loc[c]['life_exp'], label=c, linestyle = ls[i])
    axes[0].xaxis.set_major_locator(plt.MaxNLocator(integer=True))
    axes[1].plot(dbc.loc[c].index, dbc.loc[c]['hdi_index'], label=c, linestyle = ls[i])
    axes[1].xaxis.set_major_locator(plt.MaxNLocator(integer=True))

# Set the plot titles, legends, x-labels, and ylabels
axes[0].set_title('Life Expectancy by Continent over Time', fontsize=16); axes[0].
legend()
axes[0].set_xlabel('Year', fontsize=14)
axes[0].set_ylabel('Life Expectancy', fontsize=14)
axes[0].tick_params(axis='both', which='major', labelsize=12)

axes[1].set_title('HDI by Continent over Time', fontsize=16); axes[1].legend()
axes[1].set_xlabel('Year', fontsize=14)
axes[1].set_ylabel('HDI', fontsize=14)
axes[1].tick_params(axis='both', which='major', labelsize=12)

# Adjust the layout to add space between subplots
plt.subplots_adjust(wspace=0.3)

# Show plot
plt.show()
```

5.5.2 Sankey Chart

Purpose (when to use): to compare and visualize the flow of data through various stages or transitions of a process.

Common types of data: categorical and numerical (ordinal and continuous) data.

Interpretation: the Sankey chart involves nodes (usually represented by rectangles or text) and flows (usually represented by arrows or arcs) that correspond to the data and its amount being moved over the flow. Larger (wider) flows mean larger amounts, or the level of importance, of data being moved from one node to another. Therefore, the widths of the flows allow us to observe bottlenecks and paths of higher flows.

Examples of applications: the flow of energy in a power grid, the flow of people over airports or countries, the flow of goods and services in a supply chain, the flow of cars on a highway, the flow of students over the years, etc.

A *Sankey diagram*, also called *Sankey chart*, is a type of graph that allows the visualization of data flow, where the items are represented as nodes and their flows are represented by arcs of varying widths proportional to their importance or amount being transported.

In the example of Figure 5.17, the nodes correspond to the various progressions of an academic career, including an undergraduate course, M.Sc., Ph.D., Postdoc, and then a Faculty and/or Industry career. In this diagram, the width of the flows is related to the percentage of professionals who follow each possible path, with values empirically chosen for each path. It can be observed that from an undergraduate degree, the person has a 20% probability of going to an M.Sc. program, a 10% probability of going straight to a Ph.D., a 10% probability of becoming a faculty, and a 60% probability of going to industry. Also, it is observed that a faculty has an 80% probability of remaining a faculty and a 20% probability of moving to the industry. Although these values were chosen empirically, they illustrate the possible paths in an academic career that an individual can take and with what probabilities.

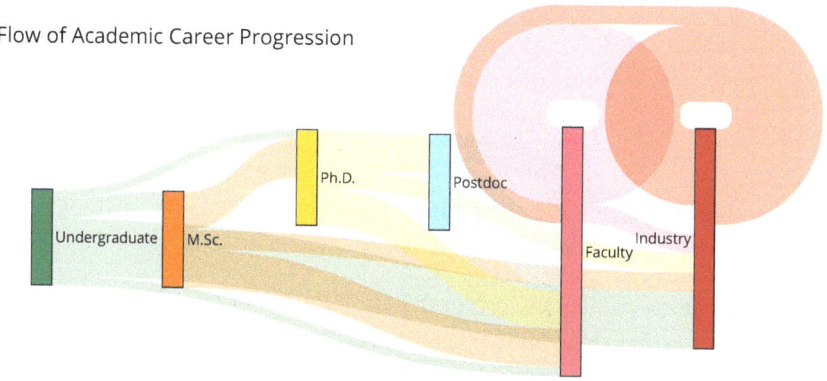

FIGURE 5.17   Sankey diagram illustrating the flow of academic career progression.

Code 5.12 shows the script used to generate the Sankey diagram of Figure 5.17. This code imports the `graph_objects` library in `Plotly` and defines as nodes the following steps in an academic career progression: "undergraduate" = 0, "M.Sc." = 1, "Ph.D." = 2, "Postdoc" = 3, "Faculty" = 4, and "Industry" = 5. It then defines the links between each of these steps (those that are possible) by assigning the `source` and `target` nodes of each link with a given probability `value`. Note that while almost all paths are possible, an individual cannot go from "undergraduate" to "Postdoc" without completing the "Ph.D.". This graph is also interactive, and moving the cursor over the figure allows us to check the source, target, and value of each path in the diagram.

CODE 5.12   Script to generate the Sankey diagram of Figure 5.17.

```python
# Sankey diagram with the flow of an academic career progression

import plotly.graph_objects as go

nodes = dict(
    type='sankey',
    node=dict(
        pad=200,
        thickness=20,
        line=dict(color='black', width=0.5),
        label=["Undergraduate", "M.Sc.", "Ph.D.", "Postdoc", "Faculty", "Industry"],
        color=["#3D9970", "#FF851B", "#FFDC00", "#7FDBFF", "#FF7F99", "#D62728"]),
    # Define the links between the nodes
    link=dict(source=[0, 0, 0, 0, 1, 1, 1, 2, 2, 2, 3, 3, 4, 4, 5, 5],
        target=[1, 2, 4, 5, 2, 4, 5, 3, 4, 5, 4, 5, 4, 5, 5, 4],
        value=[20,10,10,60,40,40,20,40,40,20,70,30,80,20,80,20]))

# Define the layout of the Sankey diagram
layout = dict(title="Flow of Academic Career Progression", font=dict(size=14),
margin=dict(t=150))

# Create the figure
fig = go.Figure(data=[nodes], layout=layout)

# Show the Sankey chart
fig.show()
```

5.5.3 Gantt Chart

Purpose (when to use): to visualize and explore the timeline of tasks, their durations, and dependencies over time.

Common type of data: the tasks are normally described by nominal variables, while start dates, end dates, and durations can be described in hours, days, months, years, or any other time-related numeric variable. Other qualitative variables can be added, such as dependencies, milestones, resources, etc.

Interpretation: horizontal bars represent the tasks, their lengths correspond to the duration of the tasks, their initial position is the initial time of the task, and their end position is the end time of the task. Connecting lines or arrows can be used to show dependencies among tasks, and aggregated bars represent subtasks.

Examples of applications: used mainly to visualize project schedules for project management purposes. It allows progress monitoring, the identification of bottlenecks and delays, resource allocation, and decision-making.

The *Gantt chart* was invented in 1910 by the mechanical engineer and management consultant Henry Gantt as a visualization tool to support the scheduling and management of projects (Kerzner, 2025).

Although there are many variations of a Gantt chart, its basic version involves plotting several horizontal bars corresponding to tasks labeled on the *y*-axis versus time on the *x*-axis. The length of each bar represents the duration of each task, and, thus, the proportionality of the bar lengths corresponds to the proportionality of the tasks' durations. To add subtasks to the Gantt chart, it is necessary to define parent tasks and aggregate the subtasks under each parent task.

Figure 5.18 shows the Gantt chart for the career stages described in the previous section on the Sankey diagram. Note that the horizontal bar lengths allow us to compare the duration of each stage, and their positions give an overview of when they are going to happen.

The script to generate this Gantt chart is presented in Code 5.13. It used the `plotly. express` library, and a dataframe was created to accommodate the tasks and their start and end dates. The `px.timeline()` function was used because it is easy to style, and it represents each data point as a horizontal bar with a start and end point specified by dates. This function sets the *x*-axis to be of type date by default, allowing it to be configured as a time-series chart.

CODE 5.13 Script to generate the Gantt chart of Figure 5.18.

```
# Gantt Chart to show the career evolution for the stages in the previous Sankey Chart
```

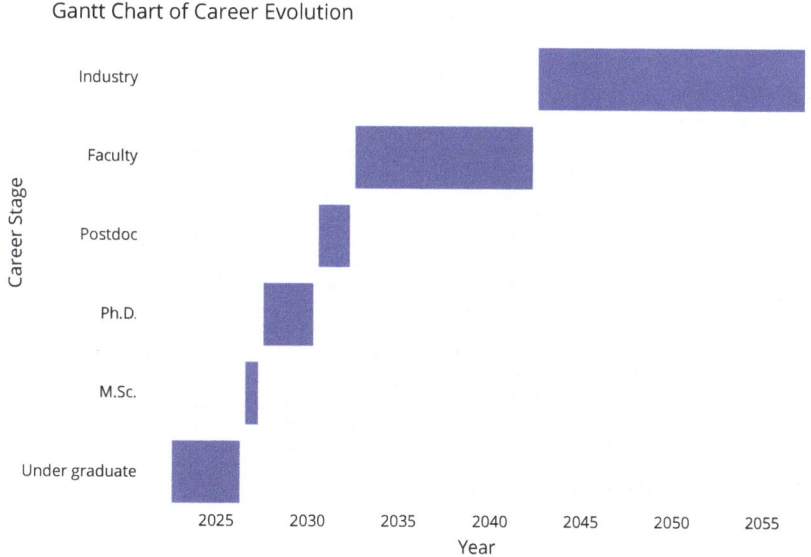

FIGURE 5.18 Gantt chart for the career stages presented in the Sankey diagram of Figure 5.17.

```
import plotly.express as px

# Define the tasks and their start/end dates
tasks = ["Undergraduate", "M.Sc.", "Ph.D.", "Postdoc", "Faculty", "Industry"]
start_dates = ["2022-08", "2026-08", "2027-08", "2030-08", "2032-08", "2042-08"]
end_dates = ["2026-05", "2027-05", "2030-05", "2032-05", "2042-05", "2057-05"]

# Create a DataFrame with the task data
data = {'Career Stage': tasks, 'Start': start_dates, 'Finish': end_dates}
df = pd.DataFrame(data)

# Create the Gantt chart
fig = px.timeline(df, x_start="Start", x_end="Finish", y="Career Stage")

# Customize the Gantt chart appearance
fig.update_layout(
    title="Gantt Chart of Career Evolution", title_font=dict(size=24),
    xaxis_title="Year", xaxis=dict(title_font=dict(size=20),tickfont=dict(size=16)),
    yaxis_title="Career Stage", yaxis=dict(title_font=dict(size=20),tickfont=dict(
    size=16))
)

# Show the Gantt chart
fig.show()
```

5.6 GEOSPATIAL

Geospatial data visualization methods are suitable for plotting variables related to locations in the physical world. For example, the Gapminder data set (Section 2.4.5) brings information about the life expectancy, HDI index, CO_2 consumption, and GDP of countries in many continents. This data can be visualized in a world map containing continents and countries. This section reviews the *Choropleth* and *Bubble maps* as important tools for geospatial data visualization.

5.6.1 Choropleth Map

Purpose (when to use): to explore and visualize spatial data in an area map.

Common type of data: spatial data, that is, data containing different values or categories associated with specific (geographic) regions.

Interpretation: the map involves coloring or shading the regions such that darker colors usually indicate higher values, while lighter colors usually indicate smaller values.

Examples of applications: to visualize spatial data, such as population density, disease spread, electricity consumption, weather data, political preferences, employment rates, economic indices (e.g., GDP and HDI), etc.

A *choropleth map* is a type of chart that uses color or shading over a map to represent different region values. For example, a variable containing the GDP or HDI of a population in each country could be used to generate a choropleth map, in which the color of each country would be associated with its GDP or HDI values, respectively. They can be classified into *classed choropleth maps*, in which the variable is discretized, and the map uses a finite set of colors to represent the variable's class intervals, or *unclassed choropleth maps*, which use a continuous color scale to represent the variable's values (Chen et al., 2008).

Figure 5.19a shows the unclassed choropleth map with the population by country available in the "naturalearth_lowres" dataset in `Geopandas`, while Figure 5.19b shows the classed choropleth map. Note that in the unclassed, or continuous, case it is more difficult to differentiate (estimate) the population size of most countries in the map because the population in Asia (India and China) is much larger than in the other countries. In the classed choropleth map of Figure 5.19b, the categorization of the countries in terms of population size makes it much easier to observe the differences. The legend shows the range in which each country fits, as follows (all values in millions of inhabitants): (0,20]; (20,50]; (50,100]; (100, 250]; (250, 1,000]; >1,000.

Code 5.14 shows the script used to generate the choropleth maps of Figure 5.19 using the "naturalearth_lowres" dataset in `Geopandas`, plus a simple world map in the beginning. The world map is plotted with the `plot()` method in `Matplotlib`, and the unclassed choropleth map is plotted with the `plot()` method of the `world` object, using "column"

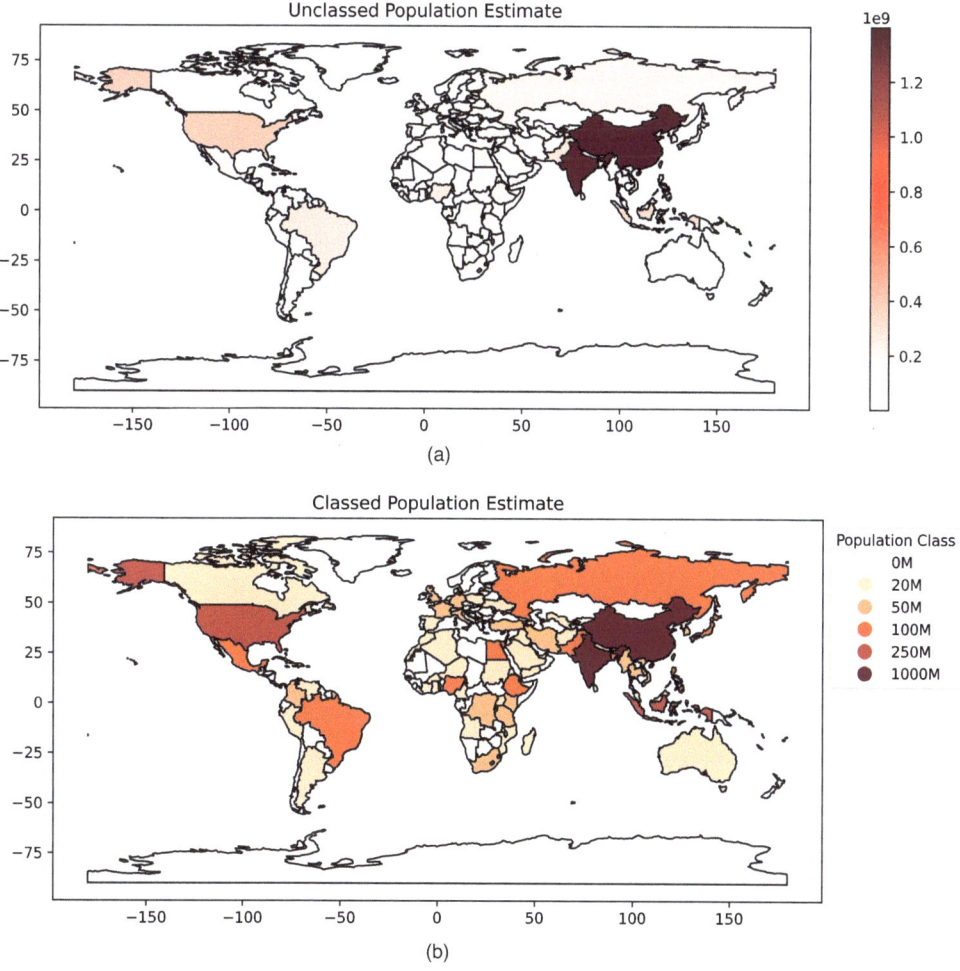

(a)

(b)

Choropleth maps with the population by country available in the 'naturalearth_lowres' dataset in `Geopandas`. (a) Unclassed choropleth map. (b) Classed choropleth map.

= "pop_est" to inform the data column that will be used to differentiate the colors in the map. A variable "breaks" is used to define the population size bins in the classed choropleth map, as explained previously.

CODE 5.14   Script to generate the choropleths of Figure 5.19.

```
# Choropleth map and its variations for Geopandas with naturalearth_lowres dataset

import geopandas as gpd
import matplotlib.pyplot as plt
import numpy as np  # Needed for infinity in breaks

# Load the dataset
world =
gpd.read_file('https://naciscdn.org/naturalearth/110m/cultural/ne_110m_admin_0_
countries.zip')

fig, (ax1, ax2) = plt.subplots(2, 1, figsize=(15, 10))

# Plot a choropleth map for population estimate
world.plot(column='POP_EST', cmap='Reds', legend=True, ax=ax1, edgecolor='black')
ax1.set_title("Unclassed Population Estimate")

# Define breaks for population estimate data
breaks = [0, 20000000, 50000000, 100000000, 250000000, 1000000000, np.inf]
# Extract labels from breaks (excluding infinity & Dividing by 1 million)
labels = [f"{int(b/1e6)}M" for b in breaks[:-1]]

# Assign each country to a class based on its population estimate
world['pop_class'] = pd.cut(world['POP_EST'], bins=breaks, labels=labels, include_
lowest=True, right=False)

# Plot a choropleth map with classed data
world.plot(column='pop_class', cmap='OrRd', legend=True, ax=ax2,
           edgecolor='black', legend_kwds= {'title': "Population Class", 'loc':
           'upper left', 'bbox_to_anchor': (1, 1)}
           )
ax2.set_title("Classed Population Estimate")

# Show plot
plt.show()
```

Another form of generating a choropleth map in Python is presented in Code 5.15 by using the chroplopleth() method in Plotly instead of the plot() in Matplotlib, as we did previously. The chroplopleth() method allows us to plot an interactive map with a dynamic variable. To illustrate, consider the maps plotted in Figure 5.20. This figure shows a world map designed with the Gapminder CO_2 consumption data merged with the world shapefile dataset. As the Gapminder dataset has the CO_2 consumption by country and year, and the shapefile data has the country boundaries, their merge produces a choropleth map showing the CO_2 consumption over time. This graph is interactive, and moving the cursor over the map allows us to see the information about the year, country, and CO_2 consumption (see Figure 5.20b).

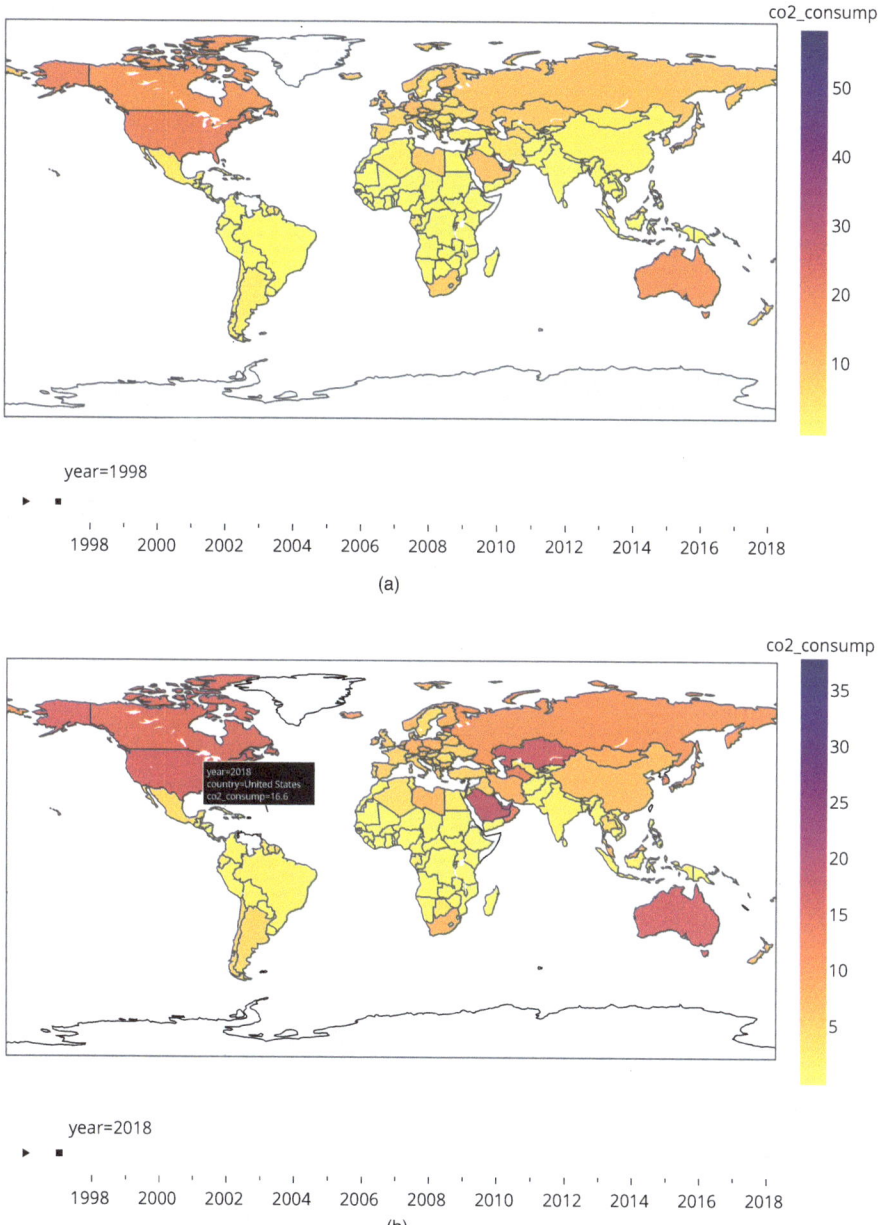

FIGURE 5.20   Choropleth maps of variable CO_2 consumption animated by year. (a) Map at year 1998. (b) Map at year 2018.

CODE 5.15   Script to generate an animated choropleth map combining the Gapminder data on the GDP and the 'naturalearth_lowres' world shapefile data.

```
# Animated Choropleth map for a merged dataset
# of Gapminder and naturalearth_lowres
```

```python
import pandas as pd
import geopandas as gpd
import plotly.express as px

# Load the Gapminder dataset
dgapminder = pd.read_csv('gapminder.csv')
dgapminder['gdp'] = dgapminder['gdp'].fillna(0)

# Load a world shapefile
dworld = gpd.read_file('https://naciscdn.org/naturalearth/110m/cultural/ne_110m_
admin_0_countries.zip')

# Merge the Gapminder dataset with the world shapefile
dmerged = dworld.merge(dgapminder, left_on='NAME', right_on='country',
how='outer')
# Drop rows where 'year' is NaN
dmerged = dmerged.dropna(subset=['year'])
# Convert the 'year' column to integers
dmerged['year'] = dmerged['year'].astype(int)
fig = px.choropleth(dmerged, locations='country', locationmode='country names',
                    color='co2_consump', animation_frame='year',
                    color_continuous_scale=px.colors.sequential.Plasma_r)
fig.update_layout(title={
        'text': 'Choropleth Map of CO2 Consumption Animated by Year',
        'font': {'size': 16}})

# Show plot
fig.show()
```

5.6.2 Bubble Map

Purpose (when to use): to explore and visualize spatial data represented by bubbles or circles of varying sizes in an area map.

Common type of data: spatial data, that is, data containing different values or categories associated with specific (geographic) regions.

Interpretation: the bubble map uses dots (bubbles) of varying sizes in the map to indicate the variable's value.

Examples of applications: to visualize spatial data, such as population density, disease spread, electricity consumption, weather data, employment rates, economic indices (e.g., GDP and HDI), etc.

The *bubble map* uses bubbles or circles of varying sizes to display a variable in a map. It requires a dataset containing the coordinates associated with each value of a variable or the region to which that value belongs to. This value is used to determine the bubbles' size in the map. Figure 5.21 shows the bubble map for the GDP by country and continent of the Gapminder dataset. The different colors represent the continents, and the bubble sizes correspond to the GDP value. Figure 5.21b shows the information that appears when the mouse cursor is placed on top of a bubble: continent, GDP, and country.

Code 5.16 shows the code to generate the bubble map presented in Figure 5.21 for the Gapminder dataset in `Geopandas`. The map plots the GDP value over each country with a size directly proportional to the GDP, and colors the map by continent. It uses the `scatter _ geo()` method in `Plotly`, defines Gapminder as the dataset, sets parameter `colors` as "continent", and the bubble `size` as "gdp". Similarly to the `choropleth()` method in `Plotly`, an important feature of this map is that it is interactive, in the sense that you can move the mouse over the map to check the information associated with each bubble, and it is also possible to scroll, zooming in or out of the map.

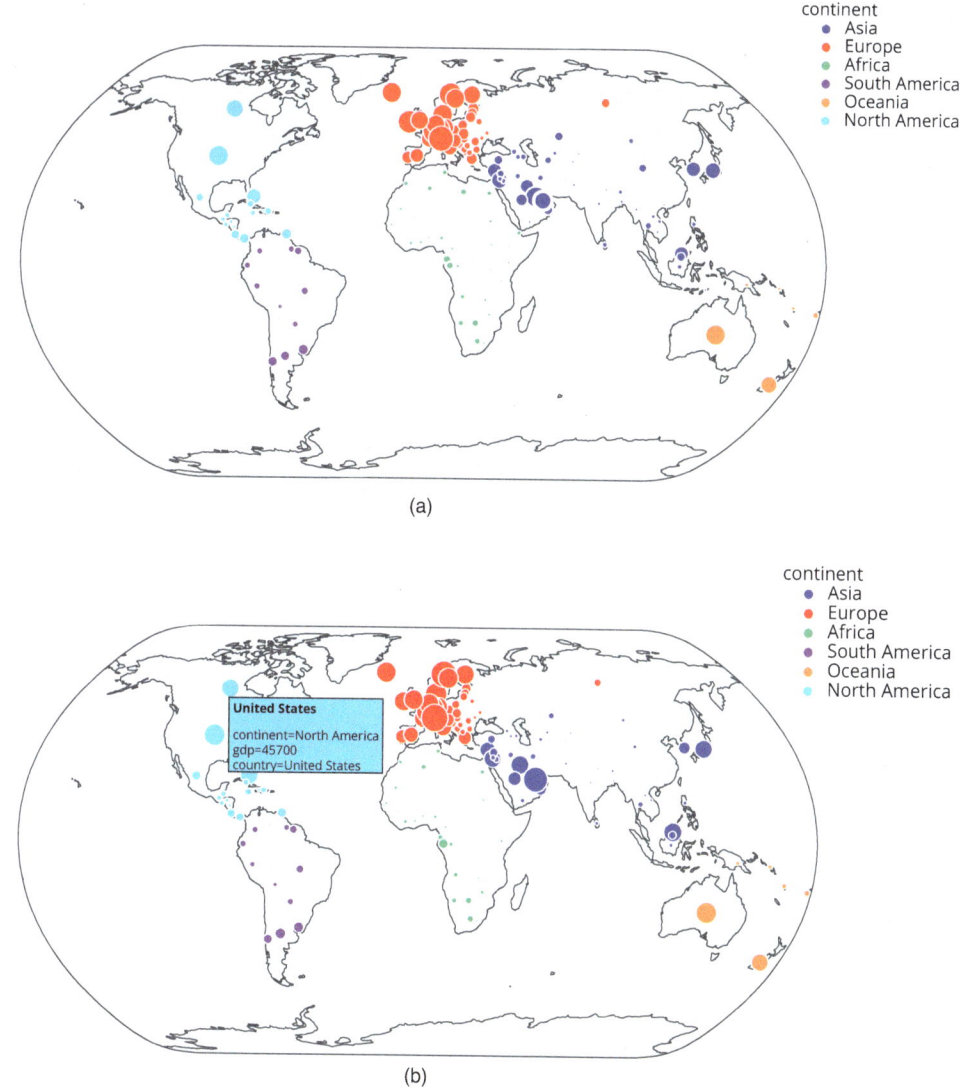

FIGURE 5.21 Bubble maps   (a) Bubble map of GDP by country and continent. (b) Tooltip when the cursor is on top of the country.

CODE 5.16   Script to generate the bubble map of Figure 5.21.

```python
# Bubble chart for the Gapminder dataset

import pandas as pd
import geopandas as gpd
import matplotlib.pyplot as plt
import plotly.express as px

# Load the Gapminder dataset
dgapminder = pd.read_csv('gapminder.csv')
dgapminder['gdp'] = dgapminder['gdp'].fillna(0)
# Filter dataset for year 1998
dgapminder = dgapminder[dgapminder['year'] == 1998]

# Plot a Bubble map
fig = px.scatter_geo(dgapminder, locations='country', locationmode='country names',
                     size='gdp', color='continent',
                     hover_name='country', projection='natural earth')
fig.update_layout(title={
    'text': 'Bubble Map of GDP by Country and Continent',
    'font': {'size': 16}})

# Show plot
fig.show()
```

5.7 EXERCISES

5.7.1 Research Topics and Questions

1. Explore the aspects of visualizing associations using scatter plots, bubble charts, scatterplot matrices, and heatmaps. How do these visualizations help us understand the relationships between variables?

2. Discuss the implications of visualizing amounts using bar charts and radar charts. How do these visualizations help us understand the magnitude of different categories or variables?

3. Explore the proportionality in pie charts. Discuss how the circular nature of pie charts may influence perceptions of proportion and consider questions about the effectiveness and accuracy of representing proportions in this visual format.

4. Explore the implications of representing data using histograms. Discuss how the choice of bin sizes and intervals may influence the perception of patterns, posing questions about the objectivity and subjectivity of data representation.

5.7.2 Quizzes

1. Which data visualization is used to represent the distribution of a single continuous variable?

   a. Boxplot.

   b. Scatter plot.

   c. Choropleth map.

   d. Treemap.

2. What is one of the primary purposes of data visualization?

   a. To make data look less appealing.

   b. To simplify complex data.

   c. To hide data inconsistencies.

   d. To replace data analysis.

3. What is the primary purpose of a choropleth map?

   a. Showing hierarchical data.

   b. Visualizing the distribution of a single variable.

   c. Representing geographical data with color gradients.

   d. Comparing parts of a whole.

4. What is the primary purpose of a radar chart?

   a. Comparing changes in data over time.

   b. Visualizing the relationship between two continuous variables.

   c. Comparing the performance of multiple categories across different attributes.

   d. Representing geographic data.

5. What type of data visualization is best suited for comparing multiple variables simultaneously by plotting them against each other in a grid?

   a. Bar chart.

   b. Scatterplot matrix.

   c. Line chart.

   d. Gantt chart.

6. Which visualization technique is commonly used to visualize the correlation between two continuous variables using color gradients?

   a. Scatter plot.

   b. Doughnut chart.

   c. Heatmap.

   d. Sankey chart.

7. What is the primary purpose of a treemap?

   a. To compare the distribution of a single continuous variable.

   b. To display relationships between two continuous variables.

   c. To show changes in data over time.

   d. To visualize hierarchical data.

8. Match the data visualization type with its primary use:

   a. Pie chart

   b. Choropleth map

   c. Sankey diagram

   (+)

   I. Showing the distribution of a single categorical variable.
   II. Visualizing geographic data with color gradients.
   III. Representing flow or process data.

   ----

   a. (A + I)/(B + II)/(C + III).

   b. (A + II)/(B + I)/(C + III).

   c. (A + I)/(B + III)/(C + II).

   d. (A + II)/(B + III)/(C + I).

9. What type of chart is used to represent data changes over time with a continuous line?

   a. Scatter plot.

   b. Bar chart.

   c. Line chart.

   d. Radar chart.

10. Which visualization method is commonly used to represent the flow of resources or information in a process?

   a. Bubble chart.

   b. Choropleth map.

   c. Sankey chart.

   d. Doughnut chart.

5.7.3 Computational Exercises

1. For the Forest Fires dataset, plot the frequency distribution using a log scale. What happens with the shape of the distribution?

2. For the Auto MPG dataset, create boxplots to compare the distribution (center, spread, outliers) of each continuous variable, explore using *notched boxplots* to compare medians more effectively, and investigate the presence of outliers and their potential impact.

3. For the Gapminder dataset, create violin plots to visualize the distribution and density of the life expectancy, HDI index, and CO_2 consumption across the continents. Compare violin plots to box plots and discuss the additional insights provided.

4. For the Daily Delhi Climate Train dataset, do:

   a. Visualize trends in various weather parameters (e.g., temperature, humidity, pressure) over time using line charts.

   b. Analyze daily, seasonal, or yearly patterns.

   c. Explore the distribution of temperature, humidity, and other variables using histograms or boxplots, and identify potential outliers or extreme weather events.

   d. Create scatter plots to investigate relationships between various weather parameters and see if there are correlations between temperature and humidity or wind speed.

5. For the Naturalearth_lowres dataset, do:

   a. Create choropleth maps to visualize various statistics across the world, such as population density, land area, or economic indicators for different countries.

   b. Use bubble maps to represent the population of major cities or the GDP of different countries while placing them on a world map.

   c. Explore combining choropleth maps with other visualizations (e.g., scatter plots) to show additional data points on top of the geographical map.

5.7.4 Case Studies

Chapter 3 presented three case studies focusing on descriptive analysis. For the same case studies, do:

1. Check for missing values and decide on an appropriate handling strategy (e.g., imputation, removal).

2. Analyze the data types of each variable and visualize their distributions using histograms, boxplots, or other techniques.

3. Examine the presence of outliers and decide whether to remove, transform, or keep them based on their impact on the analysis.

4. Use scatter plots, correlation matrices, or heatmaps to explore potential relationships between different features in the dataset.

5. Compare variables across different groups (e.g., disease presence vs. absence in cardiovascular data, product categories in superstore data, subscription types in Netflix data) using bar charts, boxplots, or violin plots.

6. Create informative visualizations tailored to the type of data and analysis goals. Use libraries like `Matplotlib`, `Seaborn`, or `Plotly` for interactive visualizations.

## CHAPTER 6

Special Types of Data

"Often the most effective way to describe, explore, and summarize a set of numbers - even a very large set - is to look at pictures of those numbers."

– Edward R. Tufte, The Visual Display of Quantitative Information, Graphics Press, *2001, p. 10*

Within data science, the exploration and analysis of diverse datasets drive insights and decision-making, allowing us to understand the unique characteristics of data. So far, we have focused on structured data in which single variables could be statistically described and visualized either in isolation or in pairs. There are some special types of data, however, that either carry specific characteristics or require specific types of analysis. Common examples are *time series data*, which bring a time component; *texts and documents*, which are either semi-structured or unstructured in nature; and *trees and networks*, characterized by pre-specified (weighted) connections among objects (nodes). This chapter focuses on these three special data types, each presenting its challenges and opportunities for exploration.

The opening section deals with time series data, where the temporal dimension adds layers of complexity and significance to the analysis. The specificities and characteristics inherent in time series datasets uncover the knowledge embedded in temporal patterns. Techniques like moving averages and seasonal decomposition are presented as tools for extracting meaningful insights, like trends and cycles, from temporal data, offering a better understanding of this type of data.

Then, the chapter presents the analysis of text and document data. With objectives driving the exploratory analysis of linguistic content, the following section presents the challenges and opportunities of unstructured or semi-structured textual data. Descriptive analysis techniques are introduced to characterize text, and data visualization methods are explored to communicate textual insights.

The final section of this chapter emphasizes trees and networks, introducing concepts from graph theory to lay the foundation for understanding these specialized data forms.

DOI: 10.1201/9781003570691-6

Descriptive analysis techniques for networks and graphs are presented to uncover patterns within these structures, offering insights into their inherent characteristics. Visualization methods for both trees and networks are explored, providing visual tools that go beyond traditional forms of data representation.

6.1 TIME SERIES

A series of data points or data observations measured over time is called a *time series* (TS). The time scale can be of any order of magnitude, such as milliseconds, seconds, hours, days, weeks, months, years, and even longer or different periods of time. The fact that time series are indexed by time is their distinguishing feature and makes them a special type of data, because it allows the analysis of the past and the prediction of the future of a given variable. To illustrate, it is possible to observe the increase in the life expectancy of a country in the past and estimate its value in the future. The concepts to be explored and illustrated in this section will use the Daily Delhi Climate Train Data presented in Section 2.4.7.

6.1.1 Types and Characteristics of Time Series

Time series are among the most common types of data available and have some representative categories, such as (Chatfield, 1995):

- **Economy**: the economy involves a wide range of data, including the inflation rate, employment and unemployment rates, stock prices and other stock market indices, the gross domestic product (GDP), interest rate, trade balance, and many others.

- **Physical**: physical data are those related to the physical sciences, like astronomy, physics, chemistry, and the Earth sciences (e.g., meteorology, climatology, hydrology, oceanography, paleontology, etc.).

- **Marketing**: most marketing data are related to specific marketing metrics and performance indicators, such as conversion rates, sales revenue and profit, click-through rates, number of likes, comments, and shares, churn rates, lifetime value, customer acquisition cost, the number of sales or consumption of a given product, etc.

- **Demography**: demographic data are those related to the characteristics of a population, such as age, gender, marital status, income, level of education, ethnicity, religion, life expectancy, Human Development Index, GDP, etc.

- **Process Control**: these data are related to the measurements of a given system or process over time, like the number of products produced in an industry plant, the amount of ethanol in a steel furnace, production quality measurements, etc.

Note that some types of data may belong to more than one of these categories, such as the GDP mentioned above, which is a demographic and an economic data. Table 6.1 summarizes the main time series characteristics (Chatfield, 1995; Cowpertwait &

TABLE 6.1 Some Characteristics That Can Be Observed in Time Series and Their Descriptions

Characteristic	Description
Time dependence	Time series data are ordered according to a given time scale.
Predictability	Time series can be either *deterministic*, in the sense that the series values can be predicted exactly, or *stochastic* (*random*), in the sense that future values are only partly determined by past values.
Seasonality	Seasonality is related with the patterns that can be repeated at fixed time intervals or within specific time periods.
Cyclicity	If the fluctuations in the time series behavior are not repeated at fixed time intervals or within specific periods, they are said to be cyclic. Thus, a seasonal behavior is a cyclic one that follows fixed time intervals.
Autocorrelation	Relationship of the data at different instants of time.
Stationarity	A time series may have some of its statistical properties constant over time.
Trend	A trend is a long-term pattern or direction presented by the time series, summarizing its behavior over longer periods of time. A trend can be *increasing* or *growing*, *decreasing*, or *stable*.

Metcalfe, 2009; Nielsen, 2019), which can be used as components for the analysis and prediction of TS data.

6.1.2 Objectives of Time Series Exploratory Data Analysis

There is a vast array of analyses that can be conducted on TS data, but most of the research in the field is *predictive*; that is, the goal is to use past data, and sometimes other information, to predict the future value of the series (Hamilton, 1994; Chatfield, 1995; Cowpertwait & Metcalfe, 2009; Nielsen, 2019). In the book by Chatfield (1995), the author categorizes time series analysis methods into four groups:

- **Description**: even the simple descriptive analyses presented here allow the analyst to have important insights into the series, such as the observation of trends, cycles, seasonality, and other patterns or features in the data.

- **Explanation**: aims at explaining the causes or factors that result in the observed patterns and the relationships between the variations in one variable and others.

- **Prediction**: is concerned with estimating or forecasting future values or patterns in the time series. It has a significant practical value because it allows us to avoid losses, increase gains, and make plan and decisions in general.

- **Control**: involves performing a specific action in the time series such that a desired outcome happens. In most cases, the design of time series control strategies will require the previous application of descriptive, explanatory, and predictive methods.

Here we will focus on the descriptive analysis of time series data with the methods presented in the previous chapters and will add two specific analysis techniques: *moving averages* and *series decomposition*. Both will serve the purpose of having an overview of the series' trends.

TABLE 6.2   Summary Measures for the Daily Delhi Climate Train Data (Section 2.4.7)

	meantemp	humidity	wind_speed	meanpressure
Mean	25.496	60.772	6.802	1,011.105
Std	7.348	16.770	4.562	180.232
min	6.000	13.429	0.000	−3.042
25%	18.857	50.375	3.475	1,001.580
50%	27.714	62.625	6.222	1,008.563
75%	31.306	72.219	9.238	1,014.945
max	38.714	100.000	42.220	7,679.333

6.1.3 Time Series Descriptive Analysis

To start the exploratory time series data analysis, let us first use the `describe()` method from `Pandas` to perform a summary analysis of the Daily Delhi Climate Train Data, as presented in Table 6.2. The minimum (min), maximum (max), average (mean), standard deviation (std), and quartiles are shown in the table for each of the four variables.

Some observations can be made from the summary data. For instance, it is noted that although the mean temperature varies in the range [6.0, 38.714], its mean value is 25.496°, much closer to its maximal value than to its minimal one, suggesting that most of the time, the weather is warm in Delhi. The "humidity" follows a similar trend, but the "wind_speed" and mean pressure averages are closer to their minimal values than to their maximal ones, suggesting that Delhi usually has drier weather with few wind blows. In terms of dispersion, "meantemp" and "humidity" have standard deviations around 30% of the mean, while "wind_speed" shows a standard deviation of approximately 70% of its mean, and "meanpressure" is approximately 18% of its mean. The negative value for the minimal mean pressure may be indicative of an anomaly or measurement error in the data. In terms of quartiles, the values presented by the mean pressure deserve attention, with most values clustered around its median. In this case, it is worth identifying and eliminating outliers and then calculating the summary measures again. First, let us perform a visual analysis to see if it confirms the presence of outliers.

6.1.4 Time Series Data Visualization

Section 2.4 presented two datasets that are particularly interesting for this time series data analysis section: the Gapminder dataset and the Daily Delhi Climate Train Data. From among the many visualization methods studied in Chapter 5, the *line chart* will be used for a general visualization of the time series shape, trend, seasonality, and cyclicity; the *boxplot* will be used to display the distribution of values across time periods; *scatterplot matrices* will be employed to investigate the frequency distribution and the associations among the series values; and *heatmaps* will be used to calculate and visualize correlations in the time series data.

6.1.4.1 Line Charts

Figure 6.1 shows the line charts for variables "meantemp", "humidity", "wind_speed", and "meanpressure" of the dataset. It can be observed that the mean temperature in Delhi has a cyclic and seasonal behavior over time, presenting maximal values around June and July and minimal values around December and January. The humidity follows a similar pattern, but with a reverse phase; that is, when the temperatures are higher, the humidity is lower, and vice versa. Note also that the seasonal pattern of humidity is not as evident as it is for the temperature. The wind speed shows a trend that seems to be in phase with that of the temperature, but the trend line is not as evident as it is for the previously analyzed variables. Also, there are some peaks in the chart that squeeze the trend line. When looking at the "meanpressure", an almost constant value is observed, with some huge outliers (peaks and valleys) that may be a reading or input error.

6.1.4.2 Boxplot

Figure 6.2a shows the boxplot of the four variables in their original scales. Note that the ranges of the first three variables are close to one another, but the range of the mean pressure is much wider and different from the others. Therefore, the direct comparison of the shape of the four boxplots becomes unfeasible in their original scales. To solve this problem, we applied a min-max normalization (Section 2.5.3) to the variables and obtained the boxplots of Figure 6.2b. This picture confirms the conclusion of the visual analysis of the line chart for the wind speed, which showed several outliers and the summary analysis of the mean pressure that suggested a very compact data distribution with a few outliers completely different from the trend, suggesting reading or typing errors.

6.1.4.3 Scatterplot Matrix

The scatterplot matrix of Figure 6.3 shows the frequency distribution of each of the four variables on the main diagonal, and the scatterplots of the pairs of variables plot at the upper and lower triangular matrices. The "meantemp" and "humidity" variables both have a distribution slightly negatively skewed, while the "wind_speed" is more positively skewed, and the "meanpressure" is practically constant with a few outliers. The correlation between the temperature and the humidity is highly negative. As we had observed and discussed while looking at the line charts of these variables, there is a slightly positive correlation between the wind speed and the mean temperature and a slightly negative correlation between the wind speed and the humidity.

6.1.4.4 Heatmap

The heatmap of Figure 6.4 quantifies the observations made previously with the analysis of the scatterplot matrix. In the case of the mean pressure, whose scatterplots could not reveal much due to its pattern, it can be observed that there is almost no correlation between its values and the other three variables.

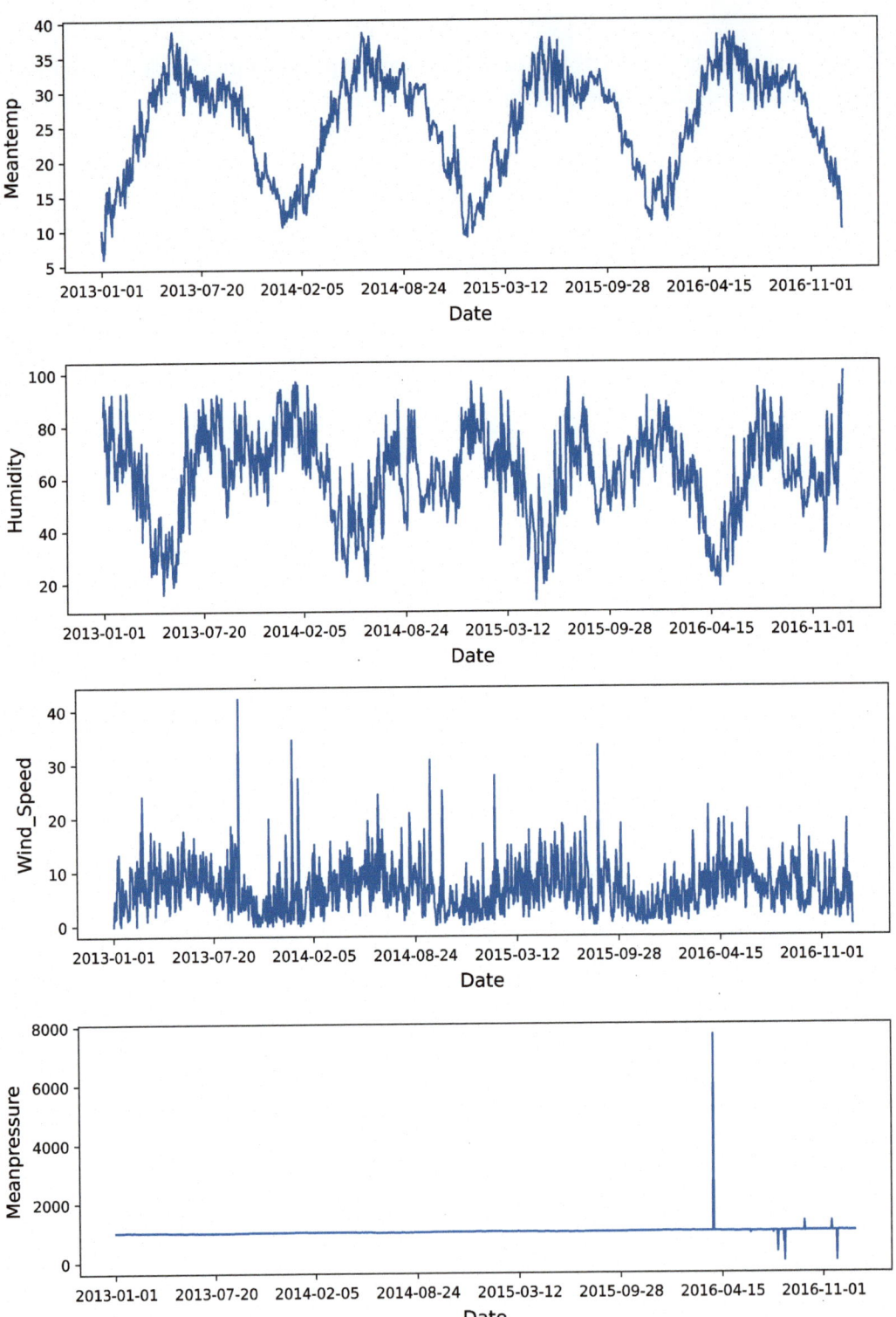

FIGURE 6.1   Line charts of the four variables of the Daily Delhi Climate Train Data.

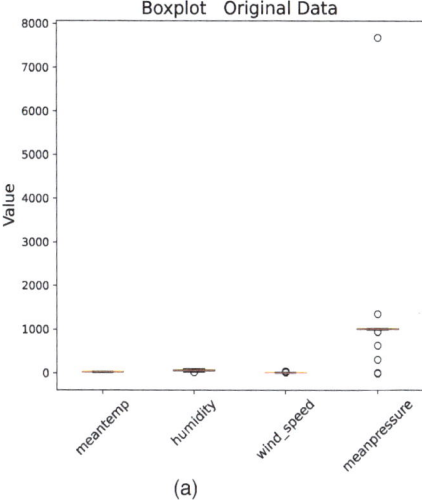
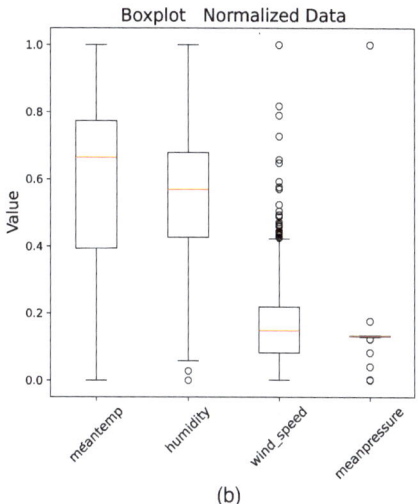

(a)   (b)

FIGURE 6.2   Boxplots comparing the four variables of the Daily Delhi Climate data. (a) Original data. (b) Data normalized in the [0, 1] range.

Code 6.1 shows the script used to plot the graphs presented in this section. The code starts by importing the libraries that will be used to plot the graphs (Pandas, Matplotlib. Pyplot, and Seaborn), loads the dataset, and then plots each of the graphs. It uses the plot() method to plot the line charts, the boxplot() from Matplotlib for the box-and-whisker plots, the pairplot() in Seaborn to plot the scatterplot matrix, and the heatmap() also in Seaborn for the heatmap.

CODE 6.1   Script to generate the line charts, boxplots, scatterplot matrices, and heatmaps of the Daily Delhi Climate Train Data.

```
# Code to generate the line charts, boxplots, scatterplot matrix and heatmap
# of the Daily Delhi Climate Train Data

import pandas as pd
import matplotlib.pyplot as plt
import seaborn as sns

# Line charts for the Daily Delhi Climate Train Data
df = pd.read_csv('DailyDelhiClimateTrain.csv')
variables = ['meantemp', 'humidity', 'wind_speed', 'meanpressure']
dDelhi = df[variables]

# Line charts
fig, axes = plt.subplots(nrows=len(variables), figsize=(10, 16))
for i, var in enumerate(variables):
    axes[i].plot(df['date'], dDelhi[var], linestyle='-')
    axes[i].xaxis.set_major_locator(plt.MaxNLocator(integer=True))
plt.show()

# Box plots
dDelhi_normalized = (dDelhi - dDelhi.min()) / (dDelhi.max() - dDelhi.min())
fig, axes = plt.subplots(1, 2, figsize=(14, 6))
for i, ax in enumerate(axes):
```

```
    ax.boxplot(dDelhi if i == 0 else dDelhi_normalized)
    ax.set_title('Boxplot - {}'.format('Original Data' if i == 0 else 'Normalized
Data'))
    ax.set_ylabel('Value')
    ax.set_xticklabels(variables)
plt.show()

# Scatterplot matrix and Heatmap for the Daily Delhi Climate Train Data
g = sns.pairplot(dDelhi)
plt.suptitle('Scatterplot Matrix', y=1.02)
plt.show()

# Heatmap
corr_matrix = dDelhi.corr()
plt.figure(figsize=(8, 6))
g = sns.heatmap(corr_matrix, annot=True, cmap='coolwarm')
plt.title('Heatmap - Correlation')
plt.show()
```

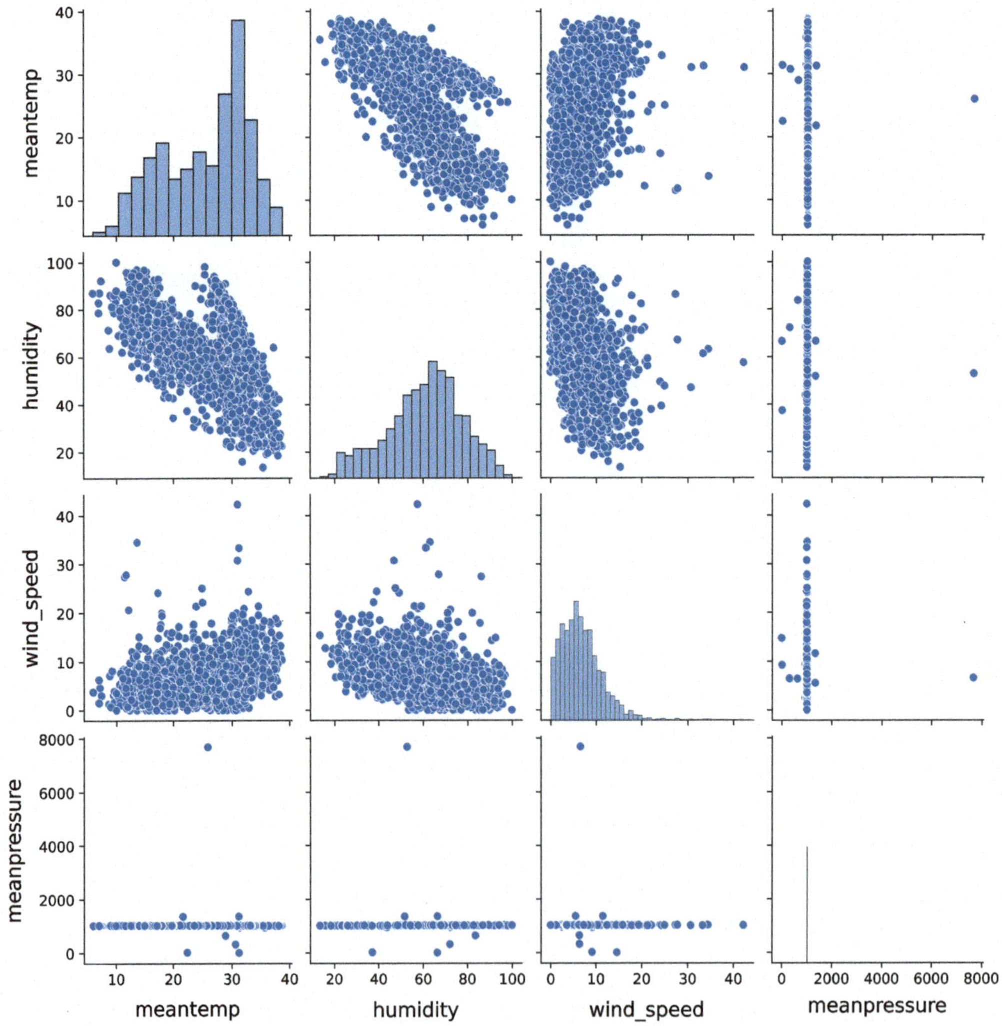

FIGURE 6.3   Scatterplot matrix of the four variables of the Daily Delhi Climate Train Data.

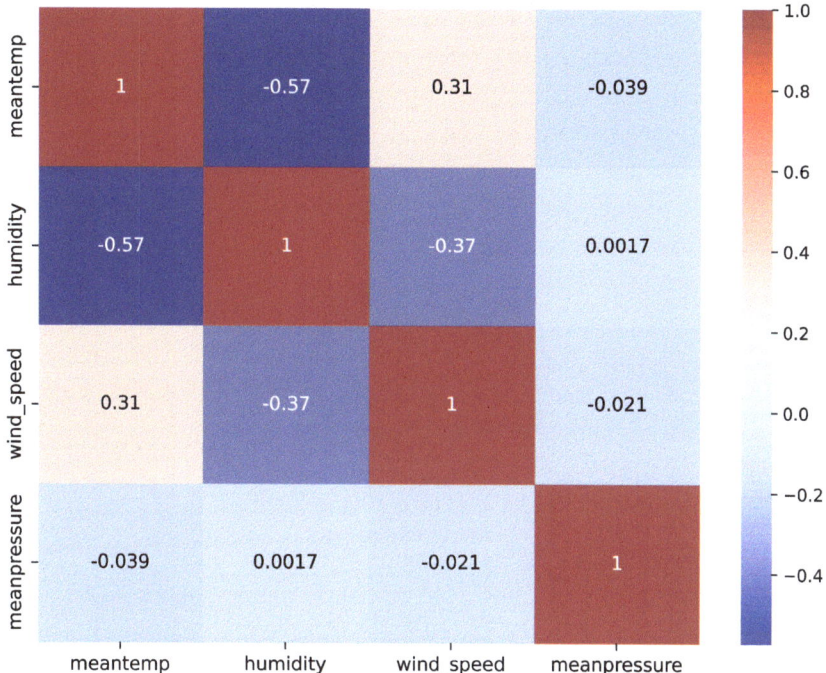

FIGURE 6.4 Heatmap of the four variables of the Daily Delhi Climate Train Data.

6.1.5 Moving Average and Seasonal Decomposition

In addition to the standard exploratory data analysis methods studied so far, there are two visualization methods to be explored in this section that are particularly useful for time series data analysis: *moving average* and *seasonal decomposition* (Cowpertwait & Metcalfe, 2009).

6.1.5.1 Moving Average

Section 3.1.1 presented a discussion on the shapes of distributions and introduced the concept of smooth curves as a method to describe the overall shape of a distribution. A similar approach could be performed for time series analysis, and there is one specific method called *moving averages*, or *rolling averages*, that is commonly used for smoothing out TS fluctuations and revealing the underlying pattern or trend in the data.

A moving average involves averaging a specified number of neighboring time series values for each data point. This technique effectively smooths out short-term fluctuations and helps capture the underlying trend. The length of the moving average is typically selected to minimize the impact of seasonal effects, which can be examined separately (Cowpertwait & Metcalfe, 2009).

The way the moving average method works is quite simple: calculate the average value of a series of data points within a window of predefined size, move the window one step further in time, and calculate the average value again; repeat this process until the end of the time series. The size of the window refers to the number of time steps within the window, regardless of the time scale used. Note that in this procedure, the window has a fixed size and moves over time, resulting in a *moving window*.

Figure 6.5 shows the application of the moving averages method to the time series data for two different moving window sizes. Figure 6.5a shows the moving average for a window of size 5, and Figure 6.5b shows it for a window of size 20. It is observed that larger values of the window result in a smoother curve and an easier visualization of the series trends.

The script used to generate Figure 6.5 is presented in Code 6.2. The `rolling()` function from `Pandas` was used to perform the moving (rolling) window calculation. In this function, the parameter `window` defines the window size, and the parameter `min _ periods` specifies the minimum number of data points within the window required to have a value. The script also plotted the original time series in light gray and the moving average as a dashed line.

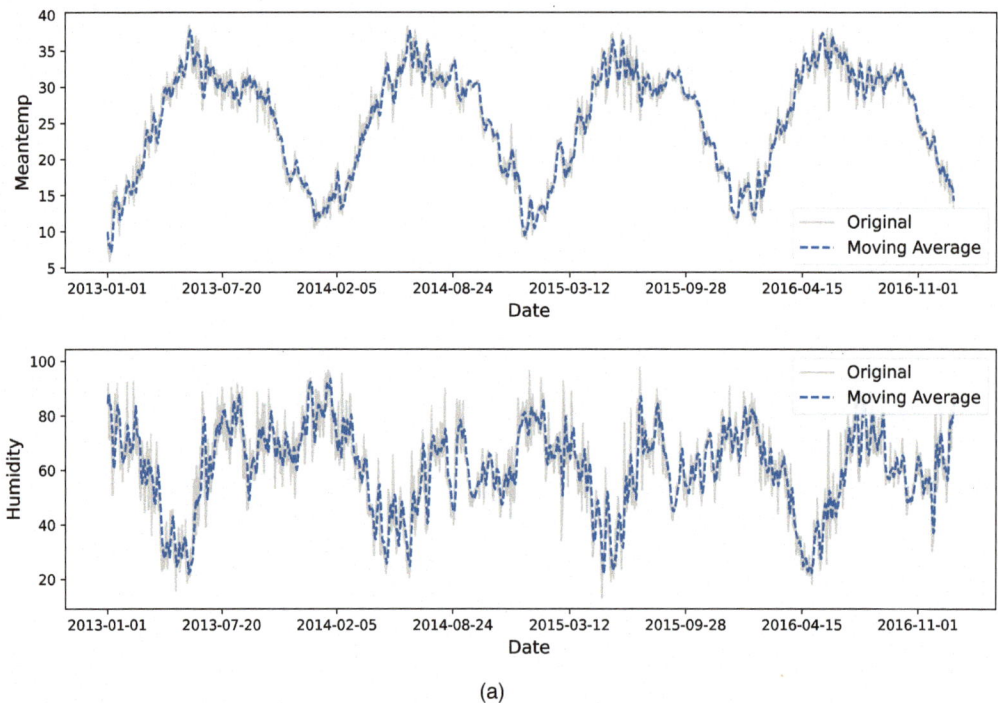

(a)

FIGURE 6.5 Moving averages applied over the "meantemp" and "humidity" variables of the Daily Delhi Climate Train data. (a) Window of size 5. (b) Window of size 20.

(Continued)

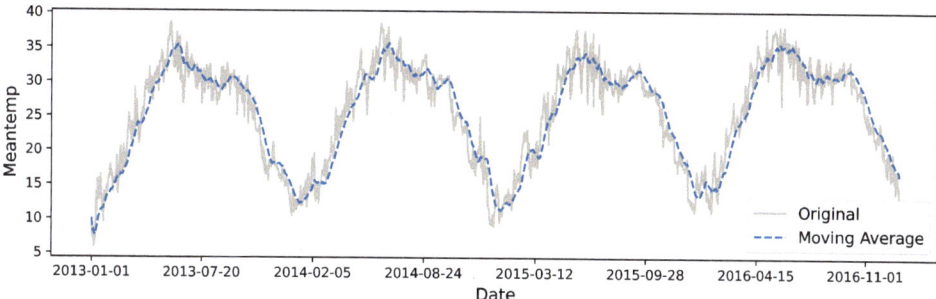

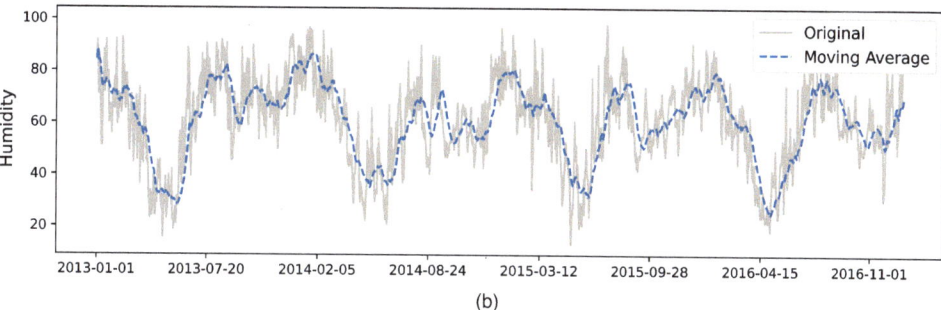

(b)

FIGURE 6.5 (*Continued*)   Moving averages applied over the "meantemp" and "humidity" variables of the Daily Delhi Climate Train data. (a) Window of size 5. (b) Window of size 20.

CODE 6.2   Script to generate the graphs with the moving averages for variables "meantemp" and "humidity" of the Delhi data.

```python
# Moving averages for variables 'meantemp' and 'humidity'
# of the Daily Delhi Climate Train Data

import pandas as pd
import matplotlib.pyplot as plt

# Load the dataset and extract the variables
df = pd.read_csv('DailyDelhiClimateTrain.csv')
dDelhi = df[['meantemp', 'humidity', 'date']]

# Create a single figure with subplots stacked vertically
fig, axes = plt.subplots(nrows=2, figsize=(12, 8))
vars_and_indices = [('meantemp', 0), ('humidity', 1)]
for var, i in vars_and_indices:
    axes[i].plot(dDelhi['date'], dDelhi[var], linestyle='-', color='gray',
alpha=.5, label='Original')
    axes[i].plot(dDelhi['date'], dDelhi[var].rolling(window=5, min_periods=1).
mean(),
                 linestyle='--', label='Moving Average')
    axes[i].set_xlabel('Date')
    axes[i].xaxis.set_major_locator(plt.MaxNLocator(integer=True))
    axes[i].legend(fontsize=12)

# Show plot
```

```
plt.show()

# Create a single figure with subplots stacked vertically
fig, axes = plt.subplots(nrows=2, figsize=(12, 8))
vars_and_indices = [('meantemp', 0), ('humidity', 1)]
for var, i in vars_and_indices:
    axes[i].plot(dDelhi['date'], dDelhi[var], linestyle='-', color='gray',
alpha=.5, label='Original')
    axes[i].plot(dDelhi['date'], dDelhi[var].rolling(window=20, min_periods=1).
mean(),
                 linestyle='--', label='Moving Average')
    axes[i].set_xlabel('Date')
    axes[i].xaxis.set_major_locator(plt.MaxNLocator(integer=True))
    axes[i].legend(fontsize=12)

# Show plot
plt.show()
```

6.1.5.2 Decomposition

In terms of components, a time series can be considered as composed of three main parts:

- **Trend**: the trend component corresponds to the long-term tendency or movement of the time series. It allows observation, for example, if the series is increasing, decreasing, remaining constant, or cycling with time.

- **Seasonal**: the seasonal component aims at identifying repetitive patterns or cycles within specific time intervals, such as days, weeks, months, or any other measure of time.

- **Residual**: the residual component, also called *noise*, *error*, or *random*, is the irregular component that remains after the others have been identified and removed.

Performing the time series decomposition corresponds to the application of an algorithm to identify and separate the components from the original time series data. There are basically two methods to decompose a time series: an *additive decomposition*, in which the TS components are added together to recompose the time series (TS = trend + seasonality + residual), and a *multiplicative method*, in which the components are multiplied to recompose the time series (TS = trend × seasonality × residual).

As discussed in the previous section, the moving average can be used to identify and, thus, remove the trend part of the series. If the additive method is used, one can apply the moving averages to calculate the trend component and then subtract it from the original time series. The remaining will be the seasonal and residual components. The resultant detrended series can then be further analyzed to identify and decompose the remaining two components.

Figure 6.6 shows a time series decomposition using a moving average with a window size of 50 for the trend component. Note that the TS trend is similar to a sinusoidal function, and the cycles presented in the seasonal component have a well-behaved period.

Code 6.3 presents a script to perform the time series decomposition of the Daily Delhi Climate Train data using the function `seasonal_decompose()` of the `Statsmodel.tsa.seasonal` library. The parameter `period` corresponds to the window size of the moving average algorithm, and the parameter `model` can be chosen as "additive" or "multiplicative". By running Code 6.3, one obtains the graphs of Figure 6.6.

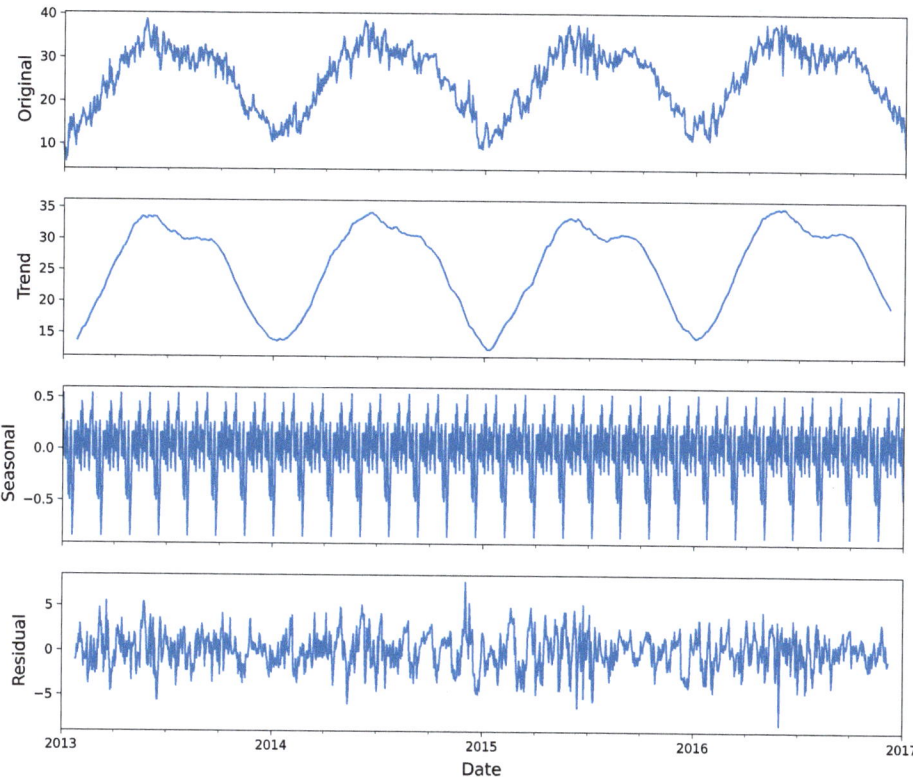

FIGURE 6.6   Time series decomposition of variable mintemp using a moving average algorithm with a window of size 50.

CODE 6.3   Script to perform the time series decomposition of the Daily Delhi Climate Train data using function `seasonal _ decompose()` of the `Statsmodel.tsa.seasonal` library.

```python
# Time series decomposition of the 'meantemp' variable
# of the Daily Delhi Climate Train data

import pandas as pd
import matplotlib.pyplot as plt
from statsmodels.tsa.seasonal import seasonal_decompose

# Load the dataset
dDelhi = pd.read_csv('DailyDelhiClimateTrain.csv')

# Extract the variable and set the date column as the index
variable = 'meantemp'
dDelhi['date'] = pd.to_datetime(dDelhi['date'])
dDelhi.set_index('date', inplace=True)
# Perform seasonal decomposition
decomposition = seasonal_decompose(dDelhi[variable], model='additive', period = 50)

# Plot the original, trend, seasonal, and residual components
fig, (ori, trnd, seas, resi) = plt.subplots(4, 1, figsize=(12, 10), sharex=True)
dDelhi[variable].plot(ax=ori)
ori.set_ylabel('Original', fontsize=14)
decomposition.trend.plot(ax=trnd)
trnd.set_ylabel('Trend', fontsize=14)
decomposition.seasonal.plot(ax=seas)
```

```
seas.set_ylabel('Seasonal', fontsize=14)
decomposition.resid.plot(ax=resi)
resi.set_ylabel('Residual', fontsize=14)

plt.xlabel('Date', fontsize=14)
plt.suptitle(f'Time Series Decomposition - {variable}', fontsize=16, y=0.92)
# Show plot
plt.show()
```

6.2 TEXT AND DOCUMENT DATA

The amount of text and document data generated and stored has increased enormously over the past years, mainly due to the sheer use of the internet, mobile devices, and digital transformation, particularly in the corporate world. Texts and documents are special types of data used to convey information related to natural language or a communicative process. Although there is no consistency over the meaning and use of the terms text and document, *text data* will be considered here plain text, that is, a sequence of characters or words like e-mails, product reviews, essays, tweets, etc., while *document data* add attributes or information to the text data, such as metadata, formatting, and media (Lund, 2010). Despite these differences, in parts of this section, we will use these terminologies interchangeably.

Text data is not organized around a data model or a specific data structure and, thus, is either unstructured or semi-structured, depending on the existence of additional information (e.g., metadata) to describe the objects. There are two main analytical areas around texts and documents: *text mining* and *natural language processing* (NLP).

Text mining is a multidisciplinary field of investigation that follows a similar process as data mining but aims at extracting regularities and patterns from natural language texts, usually with specific objectives (Silge & Robinson, 2017). Based on data mining, which seeks to discover patterns in structured datasets, text mining seeks to extract useful knowledge from unstructured or semi-structured text data. Thus, text mining prepares text and document data for processing, analysis, and mining.

NLP, by contrast, emerged from the intersection of AI and linguistics, focusing on language learning, understanding, and generation (Nadkarni et al., 2011). Its early applications targeted the development of machine translation, speech recognition, and speech synthesis. Research and applications in the field currently deal with the development of spoken dialogue systems, speech understanding, automatic translation, text summarization, chatbots, and virtual assistants, among others (Hirschberg & Manning, 2015; Chowdhary, 2020).

Exploratory analysis aims to quantitatively summarize and visualize data, but as texts and documents are qualitative data, specific methods and processes are required. The exploratory analysis of texts will use concepts and techniques from text mining and NLP, delivering numeric measures and visualization methods that can be used for an understanding of the text structure and its characteristics.

6.2.1 Objectives of Text and Document Exploratory Data Analysis

Quantitative measures like mean, mode, and variance must be placed in the context of a text to make sense from an analytical perspective. Measures like the average number of characters per word, number of (unique) words and paragraphs, vocabulary size, average word length, etc., may be useful for a proper text summarization. The descriptive analysis of texts includes these and other quantitative measures that will be presented in this chapter.

Different from the numeric data case, the visualization of text may allow us, among other things, to extract information about the *relevance* or *frequency of words, sentences, or texts*; the *detection* or *recognition of topics and entities*; and the *identification of relationships* among words, sentences, and texts. This section will cover methods for these three tasks using the IMDb movie reviews corpus available in the NLTK toolkit (Section 2.4.8).

6.2.2 Text Structuring

Structured data, such as the ones presented so far, can be organized in a table or database using a data model, even if they have nominal variables. When dealing with text and document data, their semi- or unstructured nature demands preprocessing to structure the data for their analysis and mining. Common forms of structuring text data for exploratory analysis are based on *lexical* or *syntactic* representations (Ward et al., 2010).

6.2.2.1 Lexical Representation

The *lexical representation* structures the data, emphasizing the words or terms in the text, transforming them into atomic entities called *tokens*. A text or a document represents one object in a dataset containing many texts/documents, and the tokens are the variables of these objects. Usually, each unique token corresponds to one variable, and the dimension of the object is equal to the number of unique tokens composing the set of texts/documents, known as the *corpus*. Note that this type of representation may result in a large dimensionality in space, because small texts may have a large number of unique words (tokens), in the order of hundreds or even thousands.

The text representation method described above is known as the *vector space model*, introduced as a mathematical model to represent text data for analytic processing (Salton et al., 1975). Each text or document is represented as a feature vector, where each feature (variable) corresponds to a unique term (token) in the set of terms. The value (*weight*) of a term in the feature vector corresponds to its relevance in the document or set of documents.

There are different ways of calculating the relevance of a term, but most of them use information about the term frequency in the document and/or set of documents. As this form of calculating relevance breaks the text down into tokens and does not take syntax or grammar into account, it is known as *lexical*.

The main steps to perform the lexical representation of documents are:

1. **Tokenization**: this first step in text structuring corresponds to the conversion of texts into sets of words (also known as *terms* or *tokens*), which will be used to build the feature vectors. Normally, the tokenizer uses dictionaries of tokens and sets of rules to break down the text into tokens.

   The separation of the document into terms occurs by choosing some term delimiters, such as a whole word (e.g., "semi-supervision"), part of the word (e.g., "semi"), and a blank space. Other common delimiters are punctuation marks (e.g., ";" (semicolon),

"," (comma), "." (dot)), special characters (e.g., "$", "%", "#"), and markup language tags (e.g., "<html>", "</xml>").

2. **Stop words removal**: *stopword* is the name given to words that are filtered before or after text processing because they are not relevant to the analysis.

   Stop words can be seen as a kind of noise in the information, making it difficult to quickly identify the relevance of the search result or the meaning and importance of words in a document. Filtering stop words makes the document clearer and more useful.

   The set of words classified as stop words is called a *stoplist* and usually depends on the language. Examples of stop words include articles, like "a" and "the"; pronouns, like "I", "you", and "they"; and conjunctions, such as "and", "nor", and "yet". The elimination of stop words is important, as it considerably reduces the number of words used in the representation of a document, thereby reducing the vector space dimension and making it possible to increase the precision in calculating the frequency of words in documents. The result is an improvement in the quality of word dictionary generation, since the most common and unnecessary words will not be included in the dictionary.

3. **Lemmatization and stemming**: once the document has been tokenized and stop words removed, the next step is to convert each of the remaining terms into a standard format, a process commonly referred to as *lemmatization* or *stemming*.

   While stemming is the process of reducing words by removing prefixes or suffixes to obtain a base or root form known as a *stem*, lemmatization reduces a word to its base or dictionary form, known as a *lemma*. Note that the result of stemming is a word that is not necessarily valid, while the result of lemmatization is always a dictionary word. To illustrate, the stem of "happily" would be "happi", but its lemma is "happy", and the stem of "leaves" would be "leav", but its lemma is "leaf".

   Both processes are said to *normalize* the documents, though they have significantly different computational costs. Stemming basically involves applying heuristics and pattern matching to words, while lemmatizing requires the use of a vocabulary or word lexicon to identify the lemmas. Also, stemming may result in words that are difficult to interpret without context, which is not the case with lemmatization. The choice of one or another will depend on the application, and usually, only one of them is applied in each case.

4. **Vector generation (vectorization)**: after the texts or documents have been tokenized, the stop words removed, and the terms stemmed or lemmatized, it is necessary to calculate the relevance or *weight* ($w_{ij}, \forall_{i,j}$) of each term in the matrix that represents the set of documents.

   The features of a document are the terms or tokens it contains. The entire set of words from all documents is called a *dictionary* or *vocabulary*, which forms the basis for creating a numeric dataset in which rows correspond to documents and columns to tokens (terms). The following table illustrates a set of N feature vectors, $\mathbf{d}_i$, $i = 1, \ldots, N$, each of dimension m, where each feature vector corresponds to one text or document, and each dimension t_j, $j = 1, \ldots, m$, represents a term (token) in the dictionary:

	t_1	t_2	$\cdots$	t_m
d_1	w_{11}	w_{12}	$\cdots$	w_{1m}
d_2	w_{21}	w_{22}	$\cdots$	w_{2m}
$\vdots$	$\vdots$	$\vdots$	$\ddots$	$\vdots$
d_N	w_{N1}	w_{N2}	$\cdots$	w_{Nm}

To describe the vector generation process, let **D** be the matrix containing all documents d_i, $i = 1, ..., N$, and let $w_{i,j}$ be the frequency with which term j appears in document i. Given this notation, the generation of feature vectors to numerically represent texts may consider several feature transformations, such as:

- **Binary:** inserts "0" or "1" in the matrix according to the presence or absence of a certain term in the document.

- **Absolute frequency:** inserts the frequency of occurrence of a given term (token) in the document:

$$w_{i,j} = \text{number of occurrences of term } j \text{ in document } i. \tag{6.1}$$

- **Relative or normalized frequency:** calculates the relative frequency of occurrence of a given term in the document (absolute frequency divided by the total frequency among the terms in the document), known as $TF_{i,j}$:

$$TF_{i,j} = \frac{w_{i,j}}{\sum_k w_{i,k}}, \tag{6.2}$$

where the sum is computed over the frequencies $w_{i,k}$ of all words k that appear in document i.

- **TF-IDF:** term frequency (*TF*) modified by a scale factor, called the *inverse document frequency* (*IDF*), which accounts for the importance of the term across all documents:

$$IDF_j = \log \frac{N}{\left|\{d_i \in \mathbf{d} : j \in d_i\}\right|}, \tag{6.3}$$

where $\left|\{d_i \in \mathbf{d} : j \in d_i\}\right|$ corresponds to the number of documents where token j appears.

$$TF\text{-}IDF = TF_{i,j} * IDF_j. \tag{6.4}$$

Note that, in this representation, terms that appear in multiple documents have a potentially lower weight than terms that appear in a few different documents, because the goal is to increase the relevance of discriminatory terms.

All the methods described above aim at defining a weight $w_{i,j}$ for each term j in document i that will be used in the construction of the attribute vector of the document. This weight $w_{i,j}$ can be any one of the values calculated by Eqs. (6.1)–(6.4).

To illustrate how these steps can be implemented in Python, consider the script presented in Code 6.4. This script was divided into two parts to facilitate reading and understanding.

The first part (Code 6.4a) contains the functions and files from `NLTK` and `Sklearn` that will be imported, the steps to download the necessary files, and the three initial phases of the lexical representation: tokenization, stop words removal, and stemming. The IMDb corpus is named `movie _ reviews`, and there is another item downloaded in this code: `stop words`, which is also a corpus with the stoplist. The function `word _ tokenize` is responsible for splitting the text into individual words, and `PorterStemmer` is an algorithm available in `nltk.stem` to reduce the words to their root form. The stemming algorithm developed by Porter is among the most widely used and well-known in the NLP literature. It employs heuristic rules to reduce the words to their stems. After running the first part of the code (Code 6.4a), the following stoplist is printed:

```
Stop words contained in the stop words file in NLTK:
{'most', 'own', 'll', 'being', "you're", 'into', 'won', 'ours', 'both', 'hadn',
'not', 'them', 'ma', 'before', 'no', 'once', 'with', 'then', 'shan', 'off',
"couldn't", 'didn', "weren't", 'who', "shouldn't", 'i', 'if', 'am', 'from', 'was',
"it's", 'should', 'as', 'more', "hasn't", 'himself', 'wasn', 'again', 'our', 'do',
'your', 'theirs', 'so', 'myself', 'those', 'during', 'ourselves', "won't", 'will',
'yourselves', 'between', "she's", 'm', 'doesn', "mightn't", 'against', 'through',
'same', 'you', 'can', "should've", "you'd", 'each', 'yourself', 'further', 'we',
'up', 'mustn', 'such', 'than', 're', 'only', 'were', 'him', "you've", 'she', 'any',
"hadn't", 'isn', 'some', 'does', 'it', 'by', 'did', 'd', 'couldn', 'over', 'and',
'here', 't', 'itself', 'doing', 'yours', 'me', 'of', 'after', 'aren', 'until',
'been', 'having', "doesn't", "isn't", "mustn't", 'her', 've', 'an', 'how', 'mightn',
'needn', "wasn't", 'other', 'themselves', 'at', 'nor', 'these', 'down', 'that',
"you'll", "didn't", 'hers', 'o', 'about', 'its', 'shouldn', 'had', 'just', 'herself',
'they', 'very', 'or', 'because', 'too', 'haven', 'under', 'few', 'where', 'whom',
'are', 'on', 'for', 'has', 'hasn', 'all', "needn't", 'wouldn', "aren't", "don't",
'to', 'my', 'have', 'there', "haven't", 'why', "shan't", 'he', 'be', 'the', 'is',
'a', 'when', 'in', 'above', 'don', 'what', 's', 'ain', 'y', 'but', 'weren', 'this',
"that'll", 'below', 'their', 'which', 'while', 'out', "wouldn't", 'now', 'his'}
```

The second part of the script, Code 6.4b, generates the feature vectors based on the four representation methods described previously: binary, absolute frequency, relative frequency, and TF-IDF. This code snippet prints the first 20 tokens (features) in each representation, and the first 20 columns of the first five reviews (texts) for each representation. The output of this part of the code is presented below:

```
Feature names (words) for the Data Matrix:
['aa' 'aaa' 'aaaaaaaaah' 'aaaaaaaahhhh' 'aaaaaah' 'aaaahhh' 'aah'
 'aaliyah' 'aalyah' 'aamir' 'aardman' 'aaron' 'aatish' 'ab' 'aback'
 'abandon' 'abat' 'abb' 'abba' 'abber']

Binary Data Matrix:
[[0 0 0 0 0 0 0 0 0 0 0 0 0 0 0 0 0 0 0 0]
 [0 0 0 0 0 0 0 0 0 0 0 0 0 0 0 0 0 0 0 0]
 [0 0 0 0 0 0 0 0 0 0 0 0 0 0 0 0 0 0 0 0]
 [0 0 0 0 0 0 0 0 0 0 0 0 0 0 0 0 0 0 0 0]
 [0 0 0 0 0 0 0 0 0 0 0 0 0 0 0 0 0 0 0 0]]

Absolute Frequency Data Matrix:
[[0 0 0 0 0 0 0 0 0 0 0 0 0 0 0 0 0 0 0 0]
 [0 0 0 0 0 0 0 0 0 0 0 0 0 0 0 0 0 0 0 0]
 [0 0 0 0 0 0 0 0 0 0 0 0 0 0 0 0 0 0 0 0]
 [0 0 0 0 0 0 0 0 0 0 0 0 0 0 0 0 0 0 0 0]
```

```
[0 0 0 0 0 0 0 0 0 0 0 0 0 0 0 0 0 0 0 0 0]]

Relative Frequency (Term-Frequency) Data Matrix:
[[0 0 0 0 0 0 0 0 0 0 0 0 0 0 0 0 0 0 0 0 0]
 [0 0 0 0 0 0 0 0 0 0 0 0 0 0 0 0 0 0 0 0 0]
 [0 0 0 0 0 0 0 0 0 0 0 0 0 0 0 0 0 0 0 0 0]
 [0 0 0 0 0 0 0 0 0 0 0 0 0 0 0 0 0 0 0 0 0]
 [0 0 0 0 0 0 0 0 0 0 0 0 0 0 0 0 0 0 0 0 0]]

TF-IDF Data Matrix:
[[0. 0. 0. 0. 0. 0. 0. 0. 0. 0. 0. 0. 0. 0. 0. 0. 0. 0. 0.]
 [0. 0. 0. 0. 0. 0. 0. 0. 0. 0. 0. 0. 0. 0. 0. 0. 0. 0. 0.]
 [0. 0. 0. 0. 0. 0. 0. 0. 0. 0. 0. 0. 0. 0. 0. 0. 0. 0. 0.]
 [0. 0. 0. 0. 0. 0. 0. 0. 0. 0. 0. 0. 0. 0. 0. 0. 0. 0. 0.]
 [0. 0. 0. 0. 0. 0. 0. 0. 0. 0. 0. 0. 0. 0. 0. 0. 0. 0. 0.]]
```

CODE 6.4 Script to generate a lexical representation of a text corpus. (a) Download the IMDb file, the stoplist, and the tokenization rules from the NLTK toolkit, and then tokenize, remove stop words, and stem the texts. (b) Generates the feature vectors of all texts in the corpus.

```python
# Code to structure texts using Lexical Representations

import nltk
from nltk.corpus import movie_reviews
from nltk.tokenize import word_tokenize
from nltk.corpus import stopwords
from nltk.stem import PorterStemmer
from sklearn.feature_extraction.text import CountVectorizer, TfidfVectorizer

# Download the IMDb corpus and the stoplist
nltk.download('movie_reviews')
nltk.download('stopwords')
nltk.download('punkt_tab')

# Load the movie reviews dataset
documents = [(list(movie_reviews.words(fileid)), category)
             for category in movie_reviews.categories()
             for fileid in movie_reviews.fileids(category)]

# Tokenization
tokenized_docs = [" ".join(words) for words, category in documents]

# Stopwords removal and printing
stop_words = set(stopwords.words('english'))
print("Stopwords contained in the stopwords file in NLTK:")
print(stop_words)
filtered_docs = [" ".join([word for word in word_tokenize(doc.lower())
                           if word.isalpha() and word not in stop_words])
                 for doc in tokenized_docs]

# Stemming
stemmer = PorterStemmer()
stemmed_docs = [" ".join([stemmer.stem(word) for word in word_tokenize(doc)])
                for doc in filtered_docs]

# Create the data matrix using different methods
# Binary

binary_vectorizer = CountVectorizer(binary=True)
```

```
data_matrix_binary = binary_vectorizer.fit_transform(stemmed_docs)

# Absolute Frequency
count_vectorizer = CountVectorizer()
data_matrix_abs_freq = count_vectorizer.fit_transform(stemmed_docs)

# Relative Frequency (Term-Frequency)
tf_vectorizer = CountVectorizer()
data_matrix_rel_freq = tf_vectorizer.fit_transform(stemmed_docs)

# TF-IDF
tfidf_vectorizer = TfidfVectorizer()
data_matrix_tfidf = tfidf_vectorizer.fit_transform(stemmed_docs)

# Printing the feature names (words)
print("\nFeature names (words) for the Data Matrix:")
print(binary_vectorizer.get_feature_names_out()[:20])

# Printing each data matrix
print("\nBinary Data Matrix:")
print(data_matrix_binary[:5, :20].toarray())
print("\nAbsolute Frequency Data Matrix:")
print(data_matrix_abs_freq[:5, :20].toarray())
print("\nRelative Frequency (Term-Frequency) Data Matrix:")
print(data_matrix_rel_freq[:5, :20].toarray())
print("\nTF-IDF Data Matrix:")
print(data_matrix_tfidf[:5, :20].toarray())
```

6.2.2.2 Interpreting the Results

Although simple, these results deserve some comments useful for text analysis in general. The first issue to be raised is the fact that removing stop words requires a predefined stoplist, and this approach has several limitations. For example, in the results presented, it was observed that the built-in stoplist in the NLTK library is restricted and generic, suggesting that it should be extended and tailored to each specific application. This stoplist contains only 179 words, but when we look at the first 20 words generated, we note that most of them are stop words, such as "aa", "aaa", "aaaaaaaaah", etc. Another issue that emerges in the results is the fact that the data matrices are highly sparse; that is, there is a large number of zeros in the matrices. This sparsity may result in approximation errors and distortions when comparing feature vectors among themselves. In such cases, it is important to use distance or similarity measures less prone to errors due to high dimensionality and sparsity, such as the cosine and correlation measures.

6.2.2.3 Syntactic Representation

The syntactic representation uses a pre-specified set of tags representing the categories of words, usually related to the grammatical structure or syntax of a text or document. Examples of categories used in syntactic representations include pronouns, articles, prepositions, anger words, anxiety words, and many others. In this case, the number of categories is finite and usually small, resulting in much lower-dimensional feature vectors representing the documents in the corpora.

Well-known methods to generate syntactic representations are the *Linguistic Inquiry and Word Count* (LIWC) and *Part-of-Speech* (PoS) Taggers (Tausczik & Pennebaker, 2010; Toutanova & Manning, 2000).

- **Linguistic inquiry and word count (LIWC)**: LIWC is a software designed to analyze the linguistic and psychological characteristics of a text by taking into account predefined word categories and linguistic dimensions. It works by parsing the texts in search of words that belong to the predefined categories and then tagging them according to these categories. It then counts the number of words in each category, providing an overview of the linguistic and psychological patterns of the text. In the original version of LIWC, Pennebaker et al. (2001) adopted 74 categories divided into five dimensions (standard linguistic dimensions, psychological processes, relativity, personal concerns, and experimental dimensions). Appendix C brings a list of the LIWC 2001 output categories.

- **PoS tagging**: PoS tagging also follows the principle of tagging the words in a document, but it works by assigning part-of-speech or grammatical categories to the words, indicating their syntactic functions and, thus, the grammatical structure of the text (Daelemans, 2011). There are various libraries for PoS tagging, including the Natural Language Toolkit (NLTK) and the spaCy libraries in Python. Examples of predefined categories (tags) in PoS Tagging include verbs, adjectives, adverbs, pronouns, prepositions, etc. Appendix C brings a list of tags for the Stanford PoS Tagger (Toutanova & Manning, 2000).

Despite the similarities, LIWC and PoS Tagging have different purposes and serve to analyze texts at different levels. While LIWC focuses on the psychological and emotional content of the text, PoS Tagging aims at determining the grammatical categories and function of the words in the text. Independent of their application, they can both be used to structure texts and documents for text mining and NLP applications.

6.2.3 Text and Document Descriptive Analysis

Chapter 3 introduced the main descriptive statistics measures, including central tendency, dispersion, and measures of form. When dealing with texts, other measures are relevant, such as the total number of words (*word count*), the number of distinct words used in the text (*unique word count*), the number of words composing the vocabulary (*vocabulary size*), the average number of characters in the words (*average word length*), the words that appear more frequently in the document (*most common words*), the frequency distribution of words (*word frequencies*), the number of sentences in the document (*sentence count*), the average number of words in each sentence (*average sentence length*), and the number of stop words found in the text (*stop word count*).

These concepts are easy to understand and implement using Python code and some specific libraries. Code 6.5 presents a script to calculate all the descriptive measures presented above for the IMDb corpus available at NLTK. The execution of Code 6.5 results in the following output:

```
Descriptive Statistics for the IMDb Dataset:
Word Count: 1,274,165
Unique Word Count: 38,107
Vocabulary Size: 38,107
Average Word Length: 4.540951917530304
Most Common Words: [('the', 76276), ('a', 37995), ('and', 35404), ('of', 33972),
('to', 31772), ('is', 26054), ('in', 21611), ('it', 16059), ('that', 15912),
('as', 11349)]
Sentence Count: 65,258
Average Sentence Length: 23.369119494927826
Number of Stop words: 595,438
```

Note that the absolute values presented, such as word count and vocabulary size, are for the whole text corpus. The word count exceeds one million, and the number of unique words, that is, tokens, is 38,107, meaning that the feature vectors lie in a space of 38,107 dimensions. Therefore, performing some analytic tasks with this data representation implies manipulating vectors in a space of 38,107 dimensions. It is also interesting to observe that the average word length generated is low, around 4.54, and the first ten common words found are stop words ("the", "a", "and", "of", "to", "is", "in", "it", "that", and "as"), which should be included in the stoplist for a more effective analysis of this text corpus.

CODE 6.5   Script to calculate the basic descriptive statistics for text data using lexical representation.

```python
# Code to generate simple descriptive statistics for text data

import nltk
from nltk.corpus import movie_reviews
from nltk.tokenize import word_tokenize, sent_tokenize
from nltk.corpus import stopwords
import string
from collections import Counter

# Download the IMDb dataset and stopwords corpus
nltk.download('movie_reviews'); nltk.download('stopwords')
# Load the movie reviews dataset
documents = [(movie_reviews.raw(fileid), category)
             for category in movie_reviews.categories()
             for fileid in movie_reviews.fileids(category)]

# Initialize variables for descriptive statistics
word_count = word_length_sum = sentence_count = sentence_length_sum = stopwords_
count = 0
unique_words = set()
word_frequencies = Counter()

for document, _ in documents:
    # Tokenization and lowercase
    tokens = word_tokenize(document.lower())
    # Remove punctuation and digits
    tokens = [token for token in tokens if token.isalpha()]
    # Update word count and unique words
    word_count += len(tokens)
    unique_words.update(tokens)
    # Update word length sum
    word_length_sum += sum(len(word) for word in tokens)
    # Update word frequencies
```

```
    word_frequencies.update(tokens)
    # Sentence tokenization
    sentences = sent_tokenize(document)
    # Update sentence count and sentence length sum
    sentence_count += len(sentences)
    sentence_length_sum += sum(len(word_tokenize(sentence)) for sentence in
sentences)
    # Count stopwords
    stopwords_count += sum(1 for token in tokens if token in stopwords.
words('english'))

# Calculate descriptive statistics and print the results
print("Descriptive Statistics for the IMDb Dataset:")
print("Word Count:", word_count)
print("Unique Word Count:", len(unique_words))
print("Vocabulary Size:", len(unique_words))

print("Average Word Length:", word_length_sum / word_count)
print("Most Common Words:", word_frequencies.most_common(10))
print("Sentence Count:", sentence_count)
print("Average Sentence Length:", sentence_length_sum / sentence_count)
print("Number of Stopwords:", stopwords_count)
print("Average Word Length:", word_length_sum / word_count)
print("Most Common Words:", word_frequencies.most_common(10))
print("Sentence Count:", sentence_count)
print("Average Sentence Length:", sentence_length_sum / sentence_count)
print("Number of Stopwords:", stopwords_count)
```

The descriptive statistics described previously are all based on counting characters, words, or sentences in the text corpus and deliver a knowledge that is simply related to these counts. There are specific text statistics that allow us to summarize the distribution of different parts of speech (categories), readability measures, and the co-occurrence of words, among others. In this sense, consider the other descriptive statistics for texts:

- **PoS tagging**: this is the process of tagging (marking) words in a corpus as belonging to a specific category, as discussed previously.

- **Readability measures**: readability measures aim to estimate the level of difficulty in reading a text and can be used as a reference to assess the US grade level necessary to understand it (McClure, 1987; Lee & Lee, 2023). They usually take into account the number of characters, syllables, words, and sentences in a corpus.

  Examples of such measures are the *Flesch-Kincaid Grade Level* (FKGL) readability score and the *Automated Readability Index* (ARI), calculated as follows:

$$FKGL = a.\frac{number\ of\ words}{number\ of\ sentences} + b.\frac{number\ of\ syllables}{number\ of\ words} + c, \tag{6.5}$$

$$ARI = d.\frac{number\ of\ characters}{number\ of\ words} + e.\frac{number\ of\ words}{number\ of\ sentences} + f, \tag{6.6}$$

where $a = 0.39$, $b = 11.8$, $c = -15.59$, $d = 4.71$, $e = 0.5$, and $f = -21.43$ are coefficients that weigh the influence of each term in the readability index.

Note that the higher the values of FKGL and ARI, the higher the grade level of a US student to be able to comprehend the text. Thus, higher values mean more complex texts.

- **Co-occurrence matrix**: the co-occurrence of words in a text is important for understanding associations between pairs of words, that is, the relationships between words and their semantic associations. It can be calculated from the *TF-IDF* lexical representation, and higher values in the matrix mean words with higher associations.

Code 6.6 contains a script to calculate the PoS Tagging distributions, the FKGL and ARI readability measures, and the co-occurrence matrix for the IMDb corpus available at the NLTK toolbox. In addition to the NLTK functions used to structure the texts, this code uses the textstat library and the functions CountVectorizer and TfidfTransformer. The Counter function from the Collections is used to calculate the PoS distribution, and the specific functions flesch _ kincaid _ grade and automated _ readability _ index from textstat calculate the FKGL and ARI scores, respectively. The execution of this script generates the following output:

```
Part-of-Speech Distribution:
Counter({'NN': 278642, 'IN': 155028, 'DT': 148777, 'JJ': 129582, 'RB': 82371, ',':
77717, '.': 71360, 'VBZ': 68920, 'NNS': 65134, 'VB': 50532, 'PRP': 50382, 'CC':
48199, 'TO': 31825, 'VBN': 27849, 'VBP': 27691, 'VBG': 27422, 'PRP$': 21769, 'VBD':
21158, '``': 18112, 'CD': 13958, 'MD': 13435, ')': 11782, '(': 11665, 'POS': 11514,
'WP': 9205, ':': 8370, 'WDT': 7612, 'WRB': 7195, 'RP': 6795, 'JJS': 4429, 'JJR':
4058, 'EX': 3316, 'RBR': 2448, 'RBS': 1319, 'PDT': 1272, 'NNP': 996, 'FW': 887,
"'": 861, 'UH': 530, 'WP$': 435, '$': 334, 'SYM': 72, '#': 55, 'NNPS': 8, 'LS': 1})

Flesch-Kincaid Grade Level: 8.7

Automated Readability Index: 11.2

Co-occurrence Matrix:
[[0. 0. 0. ... 0. 0. 0.]
 [0. 0. 0. ... 0. 0. 0.]
 [0. 0. 0. ... 0. 0. 0.]
 ...
 [0. 0. 0. ... 0. 0. 0.]
 [0. 0. 0. ... 0. 0. 0.]
 [0. 0. 0. ... 0. 0. 0.]]
```

The tags used in PoS Tagging (see Appendix C) are represented by abbreviations or symbols, such as "NN" for nouns, "IN" for prepositions, "DT" for determiners, "JJ" for adjectives, "RB" for adverbs, "VBZ" for third person-singular verbs, "NNS" for plural nouns, "VB" for verbs in the base form, "PRP" for personal pronouns, "CC" for coordinating conjunctions, "TO" for to as a preposition, etc. The number associated with each tag is its frequency of occurrence in the text and is printed next to the tag. The values obtained for the readability indices (FKGL = 8.7 and ARI = 11.2) indicate that the texts require a fairly high level of education for comprehension. Note that the co-occurrence matrix appears empty because all numbers presented are zero. However, this is not the case; the high sparsity of the matrix prevents the visualization of non-zero weights.

CODE 6.6 Script to generate the PoS distribution, calculate some readability measures, and the co-occurrence matrix of the IMDb corpus. *PoS*, Part-of-Speech.

```
# Code to generate specific descriptive statistics for text data

import nltk, string, textstat
from nltk.corpus import movie_reviews
from nltk.tokenize import word_tokenize, sent_tokenize
from nltk.corpus import stopwords
from collections import Counter
from sklearn.feature_extraction.text import CountVectorizer, TfidfTransformer

# Download popular paakages, including "averaged_perceptron_tagger", "movie_
reviews", and "stopwords"
nltk.download('popular')

# Load the movie reviews dataset
documents = [(movie_reviews.raw(fileid), category)
             for category in movie_reviews.categories()
             for fileid in movie_reviews.fileids(category)]

# Part-of-Speech (POS) Distribution
pos_tags = [tag for words, _ in documents for word, tag in nltk.
pos_tag(word_tokenize(words))]
pos_distribution = Counter(pos_tags)

# Flesch-Kincaid Grade Level and Automated Readability Index (ARI)
all_reviews_text = " ".join([text for text, _ in documents])
flesch_kincaid_grade = textstat.flesch_kincaid_grade(all_reviews_text)
automated_readability_index = textstat.
automated_readability_index(all_reviews_text)

# Co-occurrence Matrix
preprocessed_documents = [" ".join([word.lower() for word in word_tokenize
(words)])
                          for words, _ in documents]
count_vectorizer = CountVectorizer()
count_matrix = count_vectorizer.fit_transform(preprocessed_documents)
tfidf_transformer = TfidfTransformer()
tfidf_matrix = tfidf_transformer.fit_transform(count_matrix)

# Print the results
print("Part-of-Speech Distribution:")
print(pos_distribution)
print("\nFlesch-Kincaid Grade Level:", flesch_kincaid_grade)
print("\nAutomated Readability Index:", automated_readability_index)
print("\nCo-occurrence Matrix:")
print(tfidf_matrix.toarray())
```

6.2.4 Text and Document Visualization

The increase in the generation and storage of text and document data has also promoted an increase in the application and development of visualization techniques for this type of data. *Text visualization* is a terminology normally used for information visualization methods that focus on *raw textual data*, differently from those approaches used to visualize the result of text mining algorithms and NLP tasks (Kucher & Kerren, 2015).

The exploratory analysis of texts and documents not only has challenges in terms of summarization but also in terms of visualization, such as its unstructured nature, a usually high dimensionality depending on the representation approach used, irregularity, and uncertainty inherent in natural languages (Alharbi & Laramee, 2019). Therefore, specific techniques and data preprocessing can be used to visualize text data. Useful surveys on text and document visualization can be found in the works of Kucher and Kerren (2015), Alharbi and Laramee (2019), and Liu et al. (2019).

This section provides methods to visualize word frequency, category detection, and word/sentence connections. Word frequencies can be visualized using word clouds, bar charts, or histograms. The difference is that word clouds are qualitative, while the other graphs are quantitative and accurately show word frequencies. Category visualization can be made using a heatmap that contains the categories in one axis of the graph and the words in the other. Finally, the visualization of connections among words or sentences can be made using network visualization methods. At least one example of each of these will be presented in the sequence.

6.2.4.1 Word or Tag Clouds

Purpose (when to use): to explore and visualize text and document data.

Common types of data: texts and documents.

Interpretation: word clouds are used to visually represent text data, such that words are displayed in varying font sizes based on their relevance or frequency of occurrence in a given corpus. More frequent words appear larger in the cloud than less frequent ones. This representation allows a quick summarization of the main topics and subjects present in the corpus.

Examples of applications: to summarize, explore, and communicate text data, such as social media data, reports, reviews, news, web content, etc.

Word clouds, also known as *tag clouds*, are qualitative representations of text and document data that visually project words (tags) in a cloud of words with the size or color proportional to their relevance (e.g., frequency of occurrence) in the corpus. The cloud shape may be random or chosen to promote specific visual effects, such as the shape of an object or a brand.

As a qualitative graph, word clouds help in the identification of topics and even the context of a text corpus, but they do not allow us to have an accurate perspective of the relevance of the words in the corpus. If this is the goal of the analysis, then a bar chart may provide a good complement to the knowledge extracted from the word clouds. This is illustrated in Figure 6.7a with the word cloud generated from the IMDb corpus available in the NLTK toolkit, and the frequency distribution (Figure 6.7b) of the 25 most frequent words in the corpus. The cloud clearly identifies the context of film reviews.

Code 6.7 shows a script that generates the word cloud and the frequency distribution of the IMDb corpus available in the `NLTK` toolkit. This code downloads the `movie _ reviews` corpus, concatenates all reviews into a single text, calculates the lexical

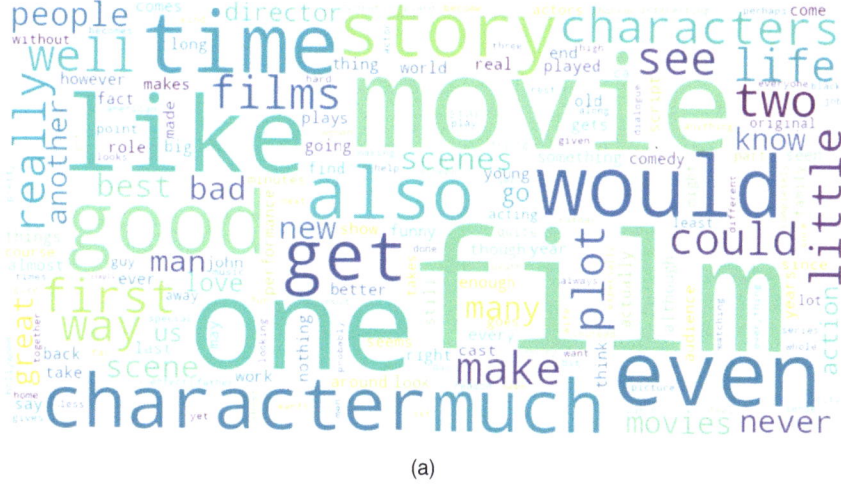

(a)

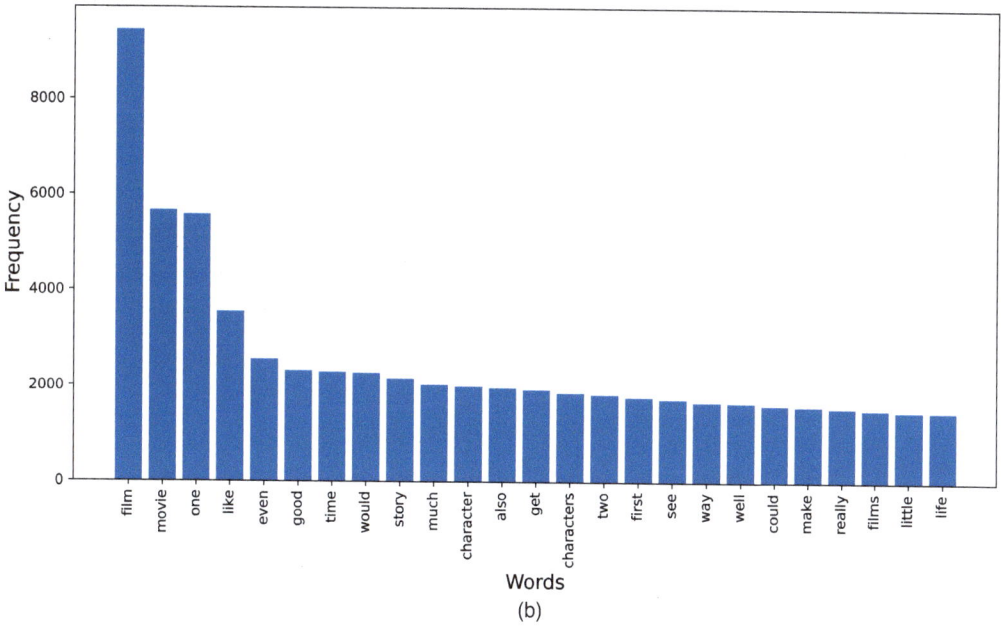

(b)

FIGURE 6.7 Visualizing the IMDb dataset in the NLTK toolkit. (a) Word cloud. (b) Bar chart with the frequency distribution of the most relevant (frequent) words.

representation, generates the tag cloud using the WordCloud library, and plots it with Matplotlib. The word _ frequency dictionary is sorted in descending order, and a bar chart is plotted with the top 25 most frequent words.

CODE 6.7   Script to generate the word cloud (a) and the frequency distribution (b) for the IMDb corpus available in NLTK.

```python
# Code to generate a Tag Cloud and a Frequency Distribution of the words in the
IMDb corpus

import nltk
from nltk.util import bigrams, trigrams
from nltk.corpus import movie_reviews
from nltk.probability import FreqDist
from nltk.tokenize import word_tokenize
from nltk.corpus import stopwords
from wordcloud import WordCloud
import matplotlib.pyplot as plt

print('working.....')
# Download the IMDb dataset and stopwords corpusz
nltk.download('movie_reviews')
nltk.download('stopwords')

# Load the movie reviews dataset
documents = [(movie_reviews.raw(fileid), category)
              for category in movie_reviews.categories()
              for fileid in movie_reviews.fileids(category)]

# Concatenate all the reviews into a single text
all_reviews_text = " ".join([text for text, _ in documents])

# Tokenization and Preprocessing
tokens = word_tokenize(all_reviews_text.lower())
tokens = [token for token in tokens if token.isalpha()]
filtered_tokens = [token for token in tokens if token not in stopwords.
words('english')]

# Calculate word frequency
word_frequency = FreqDist(filtered_tokens)

# Generate the tag cloud
wordcloud = WordCloud(width=800, height=400,
                      background_color='white').
generate_from_frequencies(word_frequency)

# Display the tag cloud
plt.figure(figsize=(10, 5))
plt.imshow(wordcloud, interpolation='bilinear')
plt.axis('off')
plt.title('Tag Cloud for IMDb Dataset', fontsize=16)
# Show plot
plt.show()
# Sort the word_frequency dictionary by frequency in descending order
sorted_word_frequency = dict(sorted(word_frequency.items(), key=lambda item:
item[1], reverse=True))

# Get the first words and their frequencies
top_25_words = list(sorted_word_frequency.keys())[:25]
top_25_frequencies = list(sorted_word_frequency.values())[:25]

# Plot the bar chart for the first 20 words
plt.figure(figsize=(12, 6))
```

```
plt.bar(top_25_words, top_25_frequencies)
plt.title('Top 25 Most Frequent Words in IMDb Dataset', fontsize=16)
plt.xlabel('Words', fontsize=14)
plt.ylabel('Frequency', fontsize=14)
plt.xticks(rotation=90)
# Show plot
plt.show()
```

6.2.4.2 Word Clouds of *n*-Grams

Although word clouds are useful for understanding the context of a text, single words may not capture the required information in the corpus. A contiguous sequence of *n* words forms the so-called *n-gram*. In this case, each *n*-gram is a feature of a vector space model, and its dimension is equal to the number of *n*-grams. A weight value is associated with each pair ⟨text, *n*-gram⟩, as was done with the 1-grams.

Figure 6.8a shows the bi-grams generated for the IMDb corpus, where the bi-grams can be found by observing the size and color of the words. For example, by looking at the tag cloud, it is possible to find "first movie", "ghosts mars", "big john", "john carpenter", "mortal kombat", and many other bi-grams. The same type of analysis can be made with the tri-grams of Figure 6.8b. It is also common to use the underline "_" between the words in the *n*-gram to show that they belong to the same sequence of words.

6.2.4.3 Categorical Heatmaps

The visualization methods described above all aim to show word frequencies. It is also possible to visualize word categories by using, for instance, a heatmap (Section 5.2.4). In this case, it is only necessary to use one axis of the heatmap to represent the words, and other to represent the tags (grammatical categories). This is illustrated in Figure 6.9, which shows the categorical heatmap of the 20 most frequent words of the IMDb corpus, in which the colors represent the absolute frequency of the words. The PoS tagging categories used can be found in Appendix C.

(a)

FIGURE 6.8   Tag clouds of the *n*-grams generated for the IMDb corpus. (a) Bi-grams. (b) Tri-grams.

(Continued)

(b)

FIGURE 6.8 *(Continued)* Tag clouds of the *n*-grams generated for the IMDb corpus. (a) Bi-grams. (b) Tri-grams.

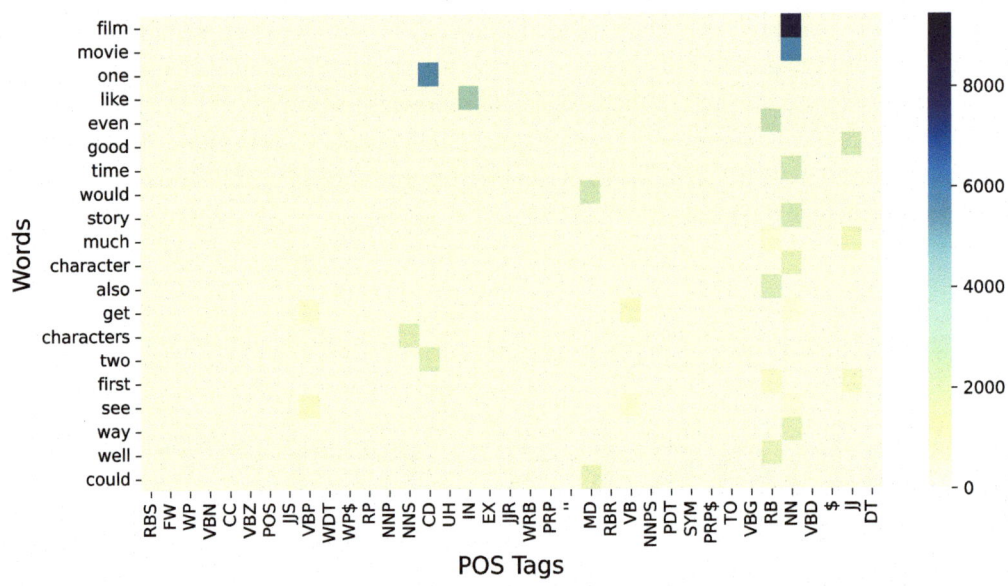

FIGURE 6.9 Categorical heatmap for the IMDb corpus in the NLTK toolkit.

6.2.4.4 Dependency Parse Trees

Purpose (when to use): to explore and hierarchically visualize the syntactic structure of a sentence, showing the syntactic relationship between the words.

Common types of data: texts and documents.

Interpretation: as the nodes represent the words, the directed edges correspond to the relationship between the words, and the arc labels are the types of such relationships, a dependency tree shows the syntactic relationships within sentences.

Examples of applications: to perform several analyses with text data, such as syntactic parsing, information extraction, named entity recognition, machine translation, text generation, etc.

Dependency parsing trees, or simply *dependency trees* or *dependency parses*, are graphical representations of the syntactic structure of a sentence, which allows the identification of semantic relationships between the words in a sentence. The dependency tree is composed of *nodes*, which represent the words in the sentence, directed *edges*, which represent the relationships between the words, and *dependency labels*, which are the edge labels that represent the grammatical relationship between the words.

To illustrate dependency trees, let us consider two sentences from the first review of the IMDb corpus in NLTK, as shown in Figure 6.10. In these trees, we can find the following syntactic relationships: nsubj (nominal subject), prep (prepositional modifier), punct (punctuation mark), det (determiner), dep (unspecified dependency), and attr (attribute). In Figure 6.10a we observe that "they get" (nsubj(get, they)), "get into" (prep(get, into)), "get accident" (punct(get,accident .)), "an accident" (det(accident ., an)), and "accident . " (dep(accident .,)). A similar analysis can be made with the sentence in Figure 6.10b.

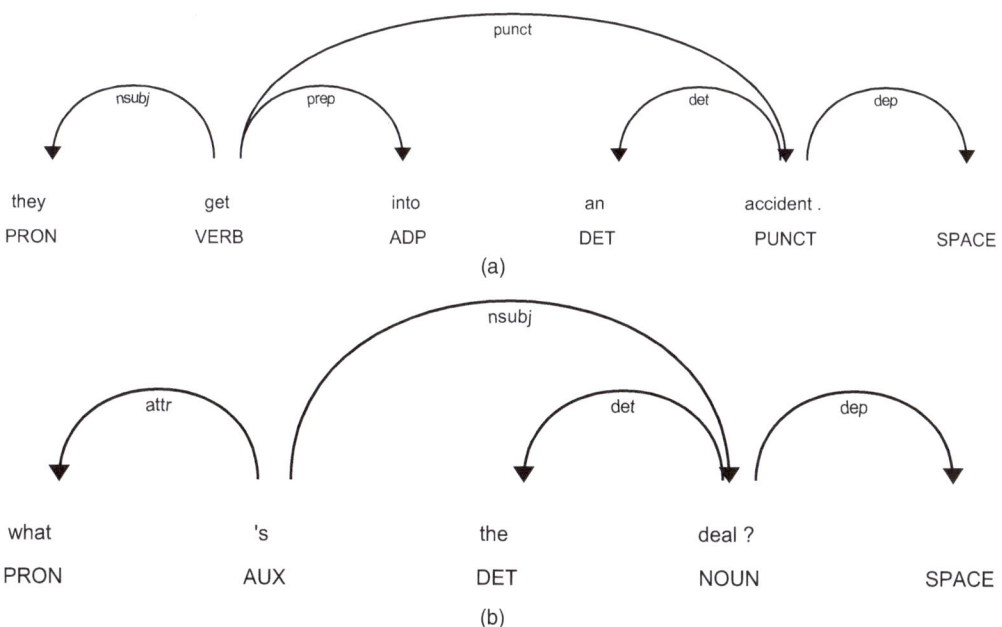

FIGURE 6.10 Dependency parse trees for the first review of the IMDb corpus. (a) Sentence: They get into an accident. (b) What's the deal?

Code 6.8 is a script to generate the dependency parse trees for the IMDB corpus in NLTK. This code uses the spaCy NLP library available in Python, which provides models for Named Entity Recognition, PoS Tagging, dependency parsing, and other analyses. The displacy function allows the visualization of the dependency parse tree for each sentence in a text. The code allows the selection of the desired document(s) to be analyzed, concatenates all reviews in a single document (nlp), loads the spaCy English model (spacy.load), obtains the individual sentences, and then prints each sentence and its corresponding dependency tree (displacy.render).

CODE 6.8   Script to generate the dependency parse trees for the IMDb corpus in NLTK.

```python
# Code to generate the Dependency Parse Tree for the IMDb dataset in NLTK

import nltk, spacy
from nltk.corpus import movie_reviews
from spacy import displacy
import en_core_web_sm
from pathlib import Path

# Download the IMDb dataset
nltk.download('movie_reviews')

# Load the movie reviews dataset
documents = [(movie_reviews.raw(fileid), category)
             for category in movie_reviews.categories()
             for fileid in movie_reviews.fileids(category)]

# Select the documents to be displayed
documents = documents[:1]

# Concatenate all the reviews into a single text
all_reviews_text = " ".join([text for text, _ in documents])

# Load the spaCy English model
nlp = en_core_web_sm.load()

# Process the text with spaCy
doc = nlp(all_reviews_text)

# Get individual sentences
sentences = list(doc.sents)

# Print each sentence and its dependency tree
for idx, sentence in enumerate(sentences):
    if idx == 1:
        print(f'Sentence: {sentence}')
        svg = displacy.render(sentence, style="dep", jupyter=False)
        file_name = 'Figure_6_10a_Dependency_Parse_Trees.svg'
        output_path = Path(file_name)
        output_path.open("w", encoding="utf-8").write(svg)
    elif idx == 3:
        print(f'Sentence: {sentence}')
        svg = displacy.render(sentence, style="dep", jupyter=False)
        file_name = 'Figure_6_10b_Dependency_Parse_Trees.svg'
        output_path = Path(file_name)
        output_path.open("w", encoding="utf-8").write(svg)
```

6.3 TREES AND NETWORKS

Until this part of the book, most of the methods presented and discussed have focused on analyzing isolated single variables or pairs of variables. However, vast amounts of *relational data* are generated that can lead to useful and insightful knowledge. By relational data here we mean data (objects) that are somehow connected to one another. Examples include groups of people connected by social networks, cities connected by roads, computers connected within a network, people connected through family trees, etc.

Graph theory provides a formal framework for studying the relationships between items, whether they be objects, individuals, or entities. With the formalism provided by graph theory, we can analyze various types of relationships, identify nodes (or vertices), and define edges (or links) between them. These relationships can have attributes such as strength and direction, leading to the analysis of complex relational data. *Trees*, by contrast, are a special case of graphs that play a crucial role in hierarchical structures. They possess defining properties, such as a single path between every pair of nodes and the absence of cycles. Finally, *networks* are more general structures that can exhibit various properties, such as directionality, cycles, and connectivity.

Trees and networks are fundamental concepts in various fields of study, ranging from computer science to social sciences. Understanding their structure, properties, and patterns of connectivity is essential for analyzing complex systems and data. This section focuses on the exploratory analysis of trees and networks, reviewing concepts from graph theory, descriptive analysis techniques, and visualization methods.

6.3.1 Concepts of Graph Theory

Graph theory is a well-established discipline that has applications in virtually any area, from social sciences to technology. It presents the formalism to the study of graphs and networks (Deo, 1974; Trudeau, 1993; Wilson, 1996). Although *graph* and *network* are terminologies used interchangeably, there are slight differences between them. On the one hand, a graph is a formalism used to represent and analyze the relationship between items, and on the other hand, a network is a term that refers to interconnected items, usually implying a context that is broader than the mathematical structure explored by graph theory (Menczer et al., 2000; Kolaczyk & Csárdi, 2014; Barabási & Pósfai, 2016).

To describe the types of relationships addressed by graphs, two main components must be defined. First, it is important to identify the objects, that is, the elements or items, that will be connected. These elements are called *nodes* or *vertices*. Second, it is necessary to identify who is connected with whom, and this connection is going to be represented as an *edge*, also called an *arc* or *link*. After these definitions, it is possible to specify several attributes associated with this type of relational data, such as the *strength* and *direction* of the connection.

Figure 6.11 illustrates the type of relational data that will be explored here. This is called a *graph* (G) and can be defined as $G = (V,E)$, where $V = \{v_1, v_2, ..., v_N\}$ is the set of N objects (nodes or vertices), and $E = \{e_1, e_2, ..., e_m\}$ is the set of m edges, where each edge corresponds

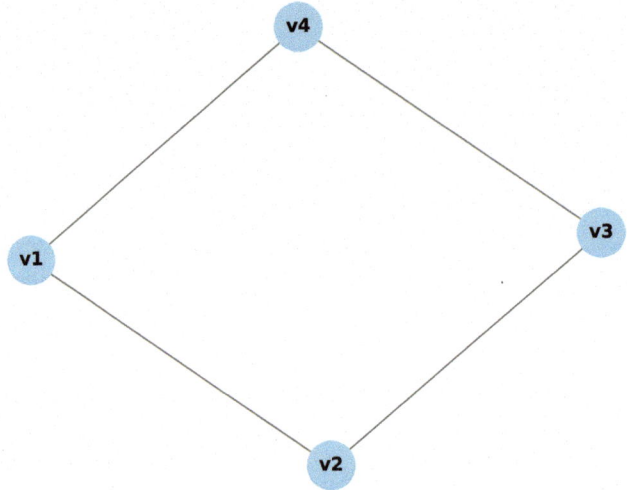

FIGURE 6.11   A simple graph with four nodes and four edges.

to a pair (v_i, v_j) of vertices. In this example, $V = \{v_1, v_2, v_3, v_4\}$ and $E = \{(v_1,v_2), (v_1,v_4), (v_2,v_3),$ $(v_3,v_4)\}$. Note that, in this example, $(v_1,v_4) = (v_4,v_1)$, and this holds true for all edges.

The number of edges that are incident to a vertex is called its *degree*, and by knowing that each edge connects two vertices the *degree of a vertex* can also be determined by the number of vertices adjacent to it. Two vertices are *adjacent* if and only if they are connected by the same edge. In the example of Figure 6.11, all vertices have degree 2, and the adjacent vertices are (v_1,v_2), (v_1,v_4), (v_2,v_3), and (v_3,v_4).

Figure 6.12 presents two new graphs that allow us to introduce further concepts. Figure 6.12a illustrates a small network with seven cities in the state of Florida, USA, and some of their distances. In this graph, the distances between the cities were added to the edges, serving as *weights* that allow us to calculate the cost (distance) of going from one city to another. This type of graph is known as a *weighted graph*. Other important properties of this graph are that all nodes are *connected* and the fact that it contains *cycles*, such as the one that goes from Tampa to Orlando to Miami to Fort Myers and then back to Tampa (Tampa → Orlando → Miami → Fort Myers → Tampa). If all the nodes of the graph are connected, then it is said to be a *connected graph*, otherwise it is a *disconnected graph*.

The graph presented in Figure 6.12b has some distinguishing characteristics when compared with the previous one: it has no cycles; there is a single path between each pair of nodes; and it is connected. This type of graph is called a *tree* and generalizes the concept of a hierarchical relation between the nodes. Trees are also *undirected graphs* in the sense that their edges have no specific direction, but it is assumed that the information flows from the root to the leaves. When a direction is added to the tree edges, it is known as a *polytree* (Dasgupta, 1999).

Figure 6.12c shows a weighted polytree, which is a particular case of a tree that is directed and weighted. In this example, the tree shows how a salary can be divided into

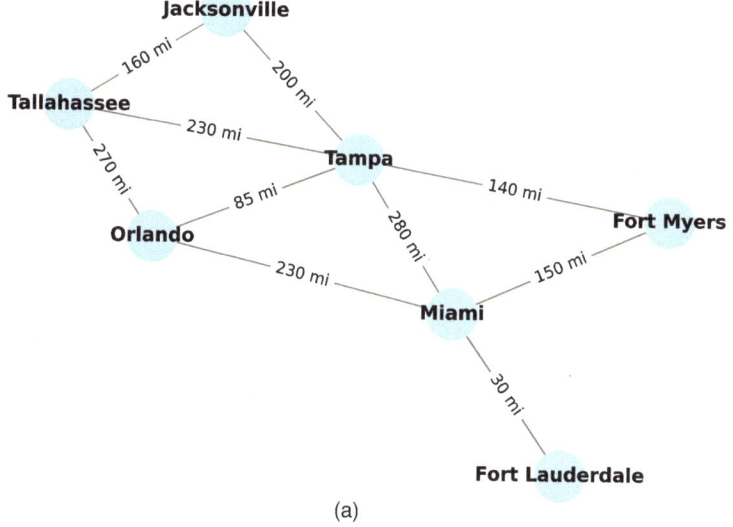

(a)

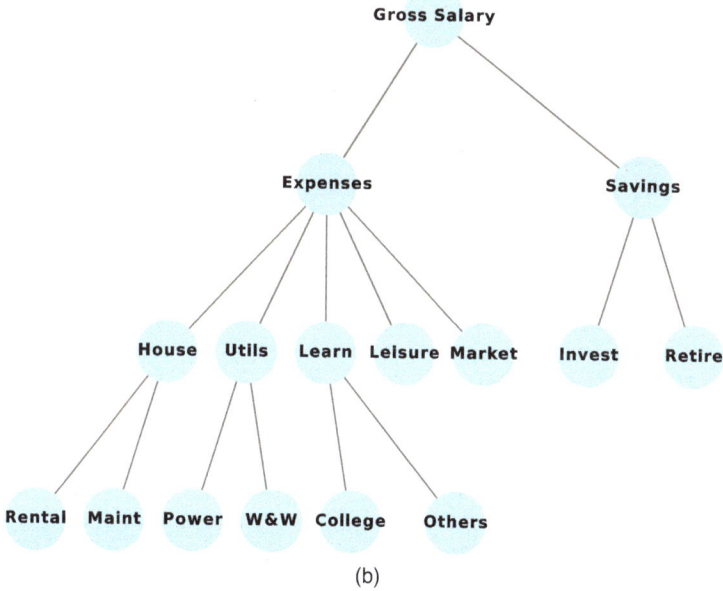

(b)

FIGURE 6.12 Graphs representing (a) the distance between some Florida cities, (b) the relationship between an income (gross salary), some expenses and savings, and (c) a weighted polytree. Utils: utilities; Maint: maintenance; W&W: water and waste.

(Continued)

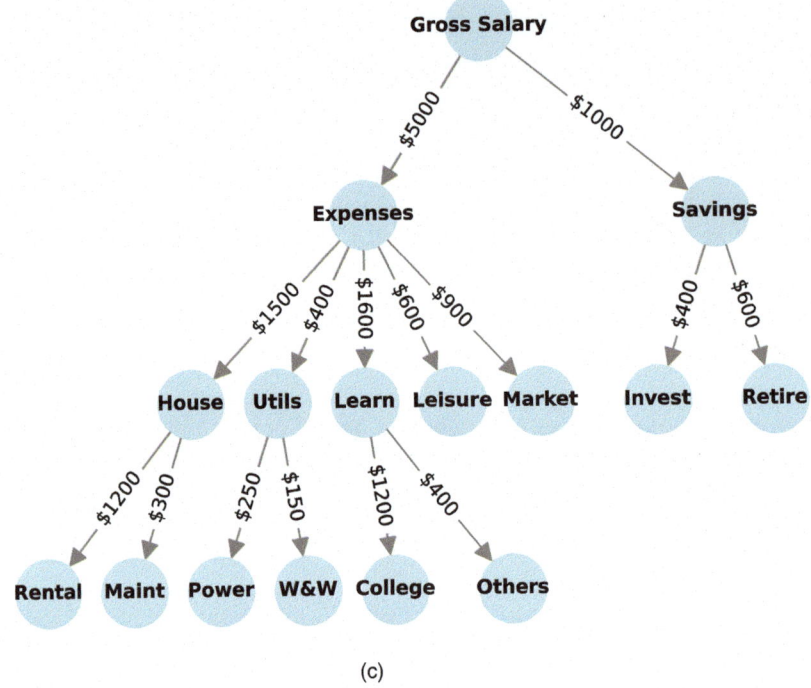

(c)

FIGURE 6.12 (*Continued*) Graphs representing (a) the distance between some Florida cities, (b) the relationship between an income (gross salary), some expenses and savings, and (c) a weighted polytree. Utils: utilities; Maint: maintenance; W&W: water and waste.

different "accounts" to facilitate managing your personal budget. It is important to stress that typically trees are unweighted graphs, that is, the edges in a tree are not weighted, and they only connect one node to another. The weights here were included only to represent the budget distribution.

A *walk* can be defined as a finite alternating sequence of nodes and edges. It starts and ends with nodes and maintains the property that every edge is connected to the nodes that come before and after it. An open walk where each node appears only once in the sequence is called a *path*. The number of edges (or the sum of the edges' weights) in a path is called its *length*. For example, in Figure 6.12a there is a path "FL 30 MI 280 TA 200 JA", where FL is Fort Lauderdale, MI is Miami, TA is Tampa, and JA is Jacksonville, and the numeric values are their distances. The length of this path is 3 if we consider only the number of edges, or 510 miles if we sum the edge weights. The use of one or another depends on the desired analysis.

6.3.2 Objectives of Trees and Network Exploratory Data Analysis

The exploratory analysis of trees is ideal for studying hierarchical data, where there is a clear parent-child relationship between elements, while network EDA is suited for exploring interconnected data, where elements can have multiple relationships with one another. In both cases, exploratory analysis helps to gain insights into the structure and relationships within data, to identify patterns, trends, and anomalies, to summarize key characteristics of the data, and to prepare the data for further analysis, such as modeling and machine learning.

In the case of trees, EDA will focus on presenting various summary measures that are specific to trees, such as height, degree of a node, branching factor, diameter, and level. In terms of visualization methods, both non-space-filling and space-filling methods will be presented (Ward et al., 2010). For networks, summary measures like the clustering coefficient, density, diameter, and assortativity coefficient will be reviewed, in addition to various centrality measures. For network visualization, some node-link diagrams with various layouts will be explored, together with the adjacency matrix heatmap.

6.3.3 Descriptive Analysis for Trees

Within graph theory, trees are certainly among the most important structures. They have defining properties, such as the existence of a single path between every pair of nodes and the absence of cycles. Some trees are *rooted*, in the sense that there is a *root node* from which the tree starts and branches, and *leaf nodes*, from which the tree ends. It is very common for the trees to be represented upside down, with the roots plotted at the top and the leaves at the bottom. The node from which another node descends is called its *parent node*, and the descendant is called a *child node*.

With these concepts in hand, it is possible to list some measures that can be used to make a descriptive analysis of (summarize) a tree, such as:

- **Number of nodes (*N*)**: total number of nodes that compose the tree.

- **Number of edges (*E*)**: total number of edges that compose the tree ($E = N - 1$).

- **Height**: length of the longest path from the root to a leaf node.

- **Degree of a node**: number of edges incident to a node. If the tree or graph is directed, the *in-degree* is the number of edges entering the node, and the *out-degree* is the number of edges going out of the node.

- **Branching factor**: average out-degree of nodes in the tree.

- **Diameter**: length of the longest path between any two nodes in the tree.

- **Level**: distance of a node from the root node (starting with 0).

Code 6.9 contains a script to generate the descriptive statistics of a tree, as described above, for the Budget Tree example of Figure 6.12b. This script uses the `NetworkX` library in Python to calculate the desired measures. In the creation of the directed graph, the code loads the nodes from a dictionary previously created and does the same with the edges (Code 6.9a). Code 6.9b then creates the directed graph "*G*" and calculates each of the measures presented in sequence. Note that most of these measures are built-in functions in the `NetworkX` library, and in those cases when we needed to do some calculations, some `NetworkX` functions were used, such as the calculus of the "branching factor" and the "diameter". Running this code for the Budget Tree leads to the following output:

```
Number of nodes: 16
Number of edges: 15
Height of the tree: 3

In-Degree of each node:
Gross Salary: 0
Expenses: 1
House: 1
Learn: 1
Leisure: 1
Grocery: 1
Utils: 1
College: 1
Others: 1
Power: 1
W&W: 1
Rental: 1
Maint: 1
Savings: 1
Invest: 1
Retire: 1

Out-Degree of each node:
Gross Salary: 2
Expenses: 5
House: 2
Learn: 2
Leisure: 0
Grocery: 0
Utils: 2
College: 0
Others: 0
Power: 0
W&W: 0
Rental: 0
Maint: 0
Savings: 2
Invest: 0
Retire: 0

Branching factor: 0.9375
Tree Diameter: 3

Level of each node:
Gross Salary: 0
Expenses: 1
House: 2
Learn: 2
Leisure: 2
Grocery: 2
Utils: 2
College: 3
Others: 3
Power: 3
W&W: 3
Rental: 3
Maint: 3
Savings: 1
Invest: 2
Retire: 2
```

6.3.3.1 *Interpreting the Results*

The height of the tree shows that the network has three layers of edges and four layers of nodes, including the root node. The results also show that the root node, as expected, has no edge but has two edges going out of it. The node with the largest number of edges out of it is "Expenses", with an out-degree of 5. The branching factor of 0.9375 indicates that, on average, each node has approximately one descendant. In this particular tree, the diameter is the same as the tree height, but it is important to acknowledge that these two measures are distinct, because the diameter measures the longest path between any two nodes, while the height measures the longest path from the root to a leaf node.

CODE 6.9   Script to calculate the descriptive statistics for the Budget Tree example. (a) Dictionaries for the tree nodes and edges. (b) Code to calculate the summary measures.

```
# (a) Nodes and edges that have to be loaded before running the next code

# Add nodes (expense categories)

nodes= ["Gross Salary", "Expenses","House","Learn","Leisure","Grocery","Utils",
    "College","Others","Power","W&W","Rental","Maint","Savings","Invest","Retire"]

# Add edges (expense relationships) with values
edges = [
    ("Gross Salary", "Expenses", {'value': 5000}),
    ("Gross Salary", "Savings", {'value': 1000}),
    ("Expenses", "House", {'value': 1500}),
    ("Expenses", "Learn", {'value': 1600}),
    ("Expenses", "Leisure", {'value': 600}),
    ("Expenses", "Grocery", {'value': 900}),
    ("Expenses", "Utils", {'value': 400}),
    ("Learn", "College", {'value': 1200}),
    ("Learn", "Others", {'value': 400}),
    ("Utils", "Power", {'value': 250}),
    ("Utils", "W&W", {'value': 150}),
    ("House", "Rental", {'value': 1200}),
    ("House", "Maint", {'value': 300}),
    ("Savings", "Invest", {'value': 400}),
    ("Savings", "Retire", {'value': 600}),
]

# (b) Code to perform the Descriptive Analysis of trees
# It requires that the nodes and edges are loaded previously

import networkx as nx

# Create a directed graph
G = nx.DiGraph()
G.add_nodes_from(nodes)
G.add_edges_from(edges)

# Calculate and print measures
print("Number of nodes:", G.number_of_nodes())
print("Number of edges:", G.number_of_edges())
# Calculate height of the tree (maximum depth from root)
height = nx.dag_longest_path_length(G)
```

```
print("Height of the tree:", height)

# Calculate degree of each node
in_degree_dict = dict(G.in_degree())
out_degree_dict = dict(G.out_degree())
print("\nIn-Degree of each node:")
for node in nodes:
    print(f"{node}: {in_degree_dict.get(node, 0)}")
print("\nOut-Degree of each node:")
for node in nodes:
    print(f"{node}: {out_degree_dict.get(node, 0)}")

# Calculate branching factor (average out-degree)
branching_factor = G.number_of_edges() / G.number_of_nodes()
print("\nBranching factor:", branching_factor)

# Calculate and print tree diameter
diameter = 0
for node in nodes:
    if G.out_degree(node) == 0:  # Only consider leaf nodes
        path_lengths = nx.single_source_shortest_path_length(G.reverse(),
source=node)
        max_path_length = max(path_lengths.values())
        diameter = max(diameter, max_path_length)
print("Tree Diameter:", diameter)

# Calculate level of each node (depth from the root)
root = "Gross Salary"
level_dict = {root: 0}
for node in nodes:
    if node != root:
        parent = list(G.predecessors(node))[0]  # Assuming single parent
        level_dict[node] = level_dict[parent] + 1
print("\nLevel of each node:")
for node in nodes:
    print(f"{node}: {level_dict[node]}")
```

6.3.4 Visualizing Trees

Trees are a special type of network that represents hierarchical structures. They can be visualized using *non-space-filling* algorithms or *space-filling* algorithms (Ward et al., 2010). The space-filling methods employ juxtapositioning to generate a representation of the hierarchical structure that maximizes the display area. To illustrate some visualization methods for trees, two simple datasets will be used. The first one is a partial genealogical tree of Queen Elizabeth II, and the second one is a synthetic dataset of the Budget Tree presented in Figure 6.12b.

6.3.4.1 Non-Space-Filling Methods

The non-space-filling methods are very common and well-known in different areas, from social science to computer science. Figure 6.13 provides two different representations of a hierarchical tree with some members of Queen Elizabeth II's family. The left figure has a representation type that was commonly used in the description of computer folders, and the tree on the right-hand side is commonly observed in the literature.

Code 6.10 contains a script to generate two different representations of a genealogical tree of part of Queen Elizabeth II's family. The relationships were defined using a dictionary,

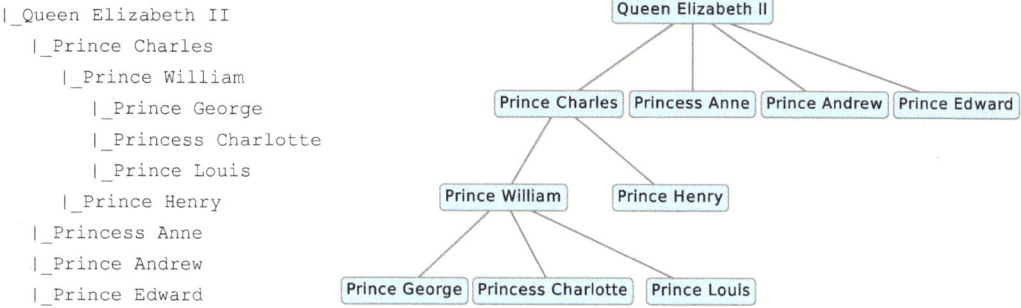

```
|_Queen Elizabeth II
   |_Prince Charles
      |_Prince William
         |_Prince George
         |_Princess Charlotte
         |_Prince Louis
      |_Prince Henry
   |_Princess Anne
   |_Prince Andrew
   |_Prince Edward
```

FIGURE 6.13   Two different representations of hierarchical trees.

where the keys represent the family members and their respective values are their children. Figure 6.13a uses a structured format to plot the tree, starting with Queen Elizabeth II as the root node and iterating the nodes in a depth-first indentation approach. Figure 6.13b shows a visual representation created with the Matplotlib library. In this case, each node (rectangle) represents a family member, and the connections link parents to children.

CODE 6.10   Script to generate the two hierarchical trees with part of Queen's Elizabeth II genealogic tree.

```python
# Code to generate partial genealogic trees of Queen Elizabeth II
import matplotlib.pyplot as plt

# Define the family members and relationships
family_tree = {
    "Queen Elizabeth II": ["Prince Charles", "Princess Anne", "Prince Andrew",
"Prince Edward"],
    "Prince Philip": ["Prince Charles", "Princess Anne", "Prince Andrew", "Prince
Edward"],
    "Prince Charles": ["Prince William", "Prince Henry"],
    "Princess Anne": [],
    "Prince Andrew": [],
    "Prince Edward": [],
    "Prince William": ["Prince George", "Princess Charlotte", "Prince Louis"]}

# Print genealogy tree
print("Genealogical Tree:")
node_stack = [("Queen Elizabeth II", 0)]
while node_stack:
    node, depth = node_stack.pop()
    print("   " * depth + "|_" + node)
    if node in family_tree:
        for child in family_tree[node]:
            node_stack.append((child, depth + 1))

# Plot using Matplotlib
fig, ax = plt.subplots(figsize=(8, 6))
ax.set_xlim(0, 10)
ax.set_ylim(0, 6)
node_queue = [("Queen Elizabeth II", 5, 5.5)]
while node_queue:
    node, x, y = node_queue.pop(0)
```

```
    ax.text(x, y, node, ha='center', va='center',
            bbox=dict(facecolor='lightblue', edgecolor='gray',
boxstyle='round,pad=0.3'))
    if node in family_tree:
        num_children = len(family_tree[node])
        child_spacing = 18 / (num_children + 6)
        for i, child in enumerate(family_tree[node]):
            child_x = x + (i - (num_children - 1) / 3) * child_spacing
            child_y = y - 1
            ax.plot([x, child_x], [y, child_y], color='gray')
            node_queue.append((child, child_x, child_y))

plt.title("Genealogical Tree Visualization")
plt.axis("off")

# Show plot
plt.show()
```

6.3.4.2 Space-Filling Methods

Section 5.4.3 introduced the treemap as a tool to visualize hierarchical data in nested and mutually exclusive rectangles of varying sizes, where each category is a fraction (slice) of the whole. Figure 6.14 illustrates a treemap generated with the simple Budget Tree synthetic data. The outer rectangle represents the "gross salary", which is divided into "expenses" and "savings", and each one of them is further subdivided into its subtrees, as presented in Figure 6.12b. The inner rectangles contain their absolute values and the percentage of each expense or savings in relation to the whole (gross salary).

Code 6.11 presents the script used to generate the treemap of Figure 6.14. A data dictionary containing the "labels", the hierarchical relationships of the network nodes ("parents"), and the edge "values" are the main `treemap` function parameters input. The parameter "branchvalues" was taken as "total" to determine that the items in values are taken as the sum of their descendants. Function `update _ traces` was used to include the label, the absolute value, and the percentage values in each rectangle.

CODE 6.11   Script to generate the treemap of the Budget Tree synthetic data.

```
# Treemap example with the Budget Tree synthetic data

import plotly.express as px
import orca
import plotly.io as pio

# Use kaleido as the image export engine
pio.kaleido.scope.default_format = "svg"

# Define data for the treemap
data = {
    'labels': ['Gross Salary','Expenses','Savings','House','Utils','Learn','Leisur
e','Market',
               'Invest','Retire','Rental','Maint','Power','W&W','College','Others'],
    'parents': ['', 'Gross Salary', 'Gross Salary', 'Expenses', 'Expenses',
'Expenses',
                'Expenses', 'Expenses', 'Savings', 'Savings', 'House', 'House',
```

Gross Salary

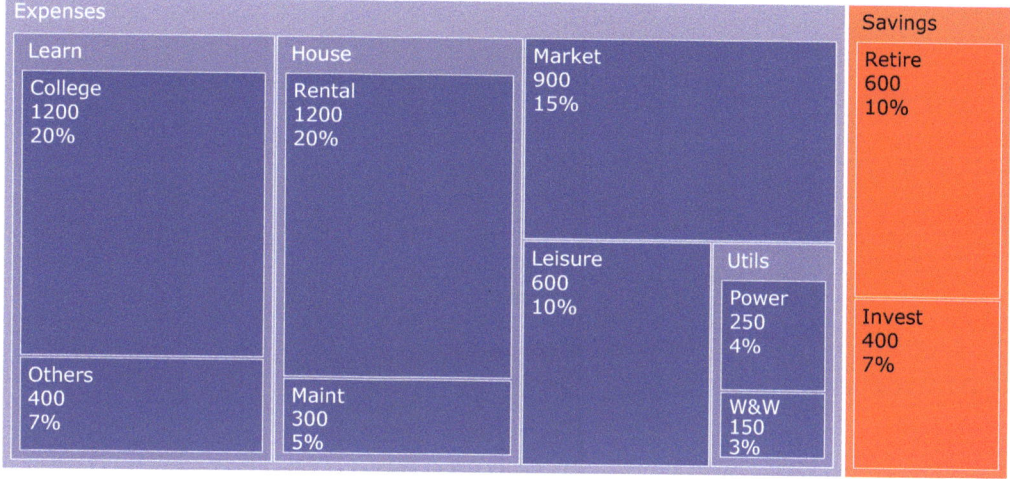

FIGURE 6.14   Treemap generated with the Budget Tree synthetic data.

```
                'Utils', 'Utils', 'Learn', 'Learn'],
    'values': [6000, 5000, 1000, 1500, 400, 1600, 600, 900, 400, 600, 1200, 300,
250,
                150, 1200, 400]
}

# Create a treemap
fig = px.treemap(data, names='labels', parents='parents', values='values',
branchvalues='total')

# Update font size of labels
fig.update_traces(textinfo='label+percent entry+value', textfont=dict(size=16,
family="Verdana, Bold"))
fig.update_layout(title_x=.5)

# Show plot
fig.show()
```

6.3.4.3 Sunburst Chart

Sunburst is a type of chart composed of concentric rings used to display hierarchical data. The innermost ring corresponds to the root node of the tree, and the outermost ring corresponds to the highest-level nodes or categories. The nested rings represent the hierarchy of layers, and each ring is sliced based on the number of nodes at that level, with the size of each slice being proportional to the category size.

Purpose (when to use): to explore and visualize hierarchical data in a circle or nested rings of varying sizes, where each category is a fraction (slice) of the whole.

Common type of data: data with a hierarchical structure and categories that can be divided into subcategories.

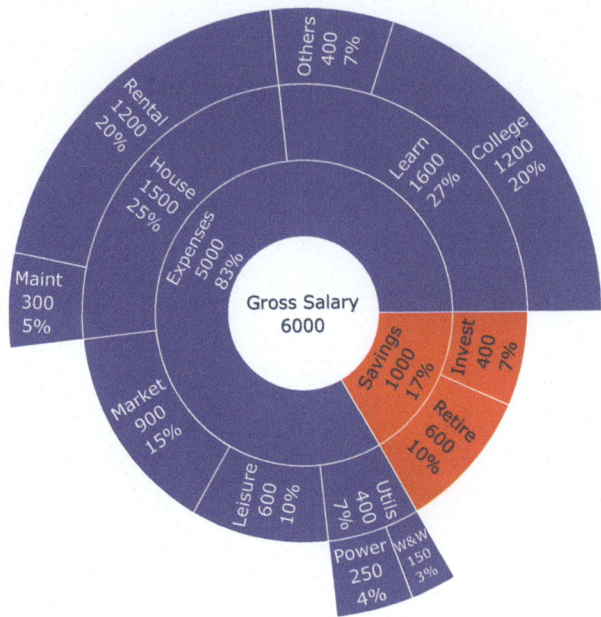

FIGURE 6.15   Sunburst chart generated with the Budget Tree synthetic data.

Interpretation: each ring represents a category within the whole, and the innermost circle is the top of the hierarchy. If there is no hierarchy in the data, the sunburst plot will look like a doughnut chart. Colors can be used to represent different levels (hierarchy) or branches (categories) in the tree.

Examples of applications: to visualize the proportion of hierarchical variables, such as continents, countries, and populations; month, day, and rain volume; etc.

Figure 6.15 shows the sunburst chart generated with the Budget Tree synthetic data. As can be observed, the "Gross Salary" appears in the center ring, and each hierarchical level is plotted concentrically in an outward direction. Also, one color is used for the "Savings", and another for the "Expenses". The absolute and relative values of the nodes were printed inside each ring slice.

Code 6.12 presents the script used to generate the sunburst chart of Figure 6.15. It uses the Sunburst function of the Plotly library and defines the "labels" (nodes), "parents" (hierarchy), and values of each edge in the tree. The Sunburst function receives the parameter "branchvalues" = "total" so that the parent value represents the sum of the width of its wedges. Parameter "textinfo" = "label+percent entry+value" prints the label, the percentage, and the absolute values within each wedge.

CODE 6.12   Script to generate the sunburst chart of the Budget Tree synthetic data.

```
# Sunburst example with the Budget Tree synthetic data

import plotly.graph_objects as go
```

```
# Define data for the sunburst chart
labels = ['Gross Salary','Expenses','Savings','House','Utils','Learn','Leisure','M
arket',
         'Invest','Retire','Rental','Maint','Power','W&W','College','Others']
parents = ['','Gross Salary','Gross Salary','Expenses','Expenses','Expenses','Expe
nses',
           'Expenses','Savings','Savings','House','House','Utils','Utils','Learn',
'Learn']
values = [6000, 5000, 1000, 1500, 400, 1600, 600, 900, 400, 600, 1200, 300, 250,
150, 1200, 400]

# Create a sunburst chart
fig = go.Figure(go.Sunburst(labels=labels,parents=parents,values=values,branchvalu
es="total"))

# Set the title
fig.update_traces(textinfo='label+percent entry+value', textfont=dict(size=16,
family="Verdana, Bold"))
fig.update_layout(title="Sunburst Chart Example", title_x=.5, title_y=.85)

# Show plot
fig.show()
```

6.3.5 Descriptive Analysis for Networks

The descriptive analysis of networks can range from the calculation of simple metrics that characterize their topological structure to more elaborate analyses that extract patterns from the network. Although networks are a generalization of trees, some of the measures used in the description of trees, such as height and level, have no meaning when discussing networks.

6.3.5.1 General Measures

To summarize networks, consider the following general measures:

- **Number of nodes (N):** total number of nodes that compose the network.

- **Number of edges (E):** total number of edges that compose the network.

- **Local clustering coefficient:** this measure captures the degree to which the neighbors of a given node link to each other; that is, the degree to which the network nodes tend to form *communities* or *clusters*. The local clustering coefficient measures the local connectivity of a given node i, reflecting the formation of clusters within the network. A low clustering coefficient means that a node tends to be little connected with its neighbors, and vice versa. For a node i of degree k_i, the local clustering coefficient C_i is defined by (Barabási & Pósfai, 2016):

$$C_i = \frac{2L_i}{k_i(k_i - 1)},$$

(6.7)

where L_i is the number of edges between the k_i neighbors of node i.

- **Average clustering coefficient:** the average clustering coefficient $\langle C \rangle$ is obtained by simply calculating the average of the local clustering coefficient of all nodes in the network, capturing the network degree of clustering (Barabási & Pósfai, 2016):

$$C_i = \frac{1}{N} \sum_{i=1}^{N} C_i,$$ (6.8)

where N is the number of nodes in the network.

- **Shortest path length:** it corresponds to the smallest number of edges in the network necessary to go from one node to another. For weighted networks, it corresponds to the path with the smallest sum of weights between two nodes.

- **Connected components:** a connected component of a network is a maximally connected subgraph; that is, a subset of nodes within a network in which each node is connected to every other node in the same subset (Kolaczyk, 2009).

- **Network density:** the maximum number of edges, E_{max}, in a network is bounded by the possible number of connections between the nodes and is, thus, given by the number of pairs of nodes. The network density is the ratio between the number of edges in the network and E_{max} (Menczer et al., 2020):

$$d = E / E_{max},$$ (6.9)

where E is the number of nodes.

- **Network diameter:** the value of the longest distance in the network.

- **Degree of a node:** number of edges incident to a node. If the network is directed, the *in-degree* is the number of edges entering the node, and the *out-degree* is the number of edges going out of the node.

- **Assortativity coefficient:** in the social network literature, *assortative mixing* is the terminology used to refer to the selective connection among nodes based on specific characteristics. Measures designed to quantify the degree of assortative mixing within a particular network are commonly known as *assortative coefficients*, and most of them are variations of correlation coefficients (Kolaczyk, 2009). A positive assortative coefficient suggests that nodes with similar characteristics (attributes) tend to be connected, while a negative assortative coefficient indicates that nodes with dissimilar characteristics tend to be connected.

6.3.5.2 Centrality Measures

In addition to the measures described above, there is a set of measures used to quantify the importance or relevance of a node in a network. For example, in a road network, it is important to know which crossing receives the most traffic; in a social network, the person with the largest number of connections is relevant; and in a flight network, the hub airports play an important role in the movement of people and cargo.

These importance measures are known as *centrality measures*, each capturing different aspects of node relevance and thus deserving particular attention in network analysis.

Although there is a large variety of centrality measures, the four most typical ones are (Kolaczyk, 2009; Kolaczyk & Csárdi, 2014):

- **Degree centrality:** this is the same as the degree of a node, that is, the number of edges connected to it.

  A high degree of centrality means that a node is well connected and has a great potential to spread information.

- **Betweenness centrality:** summarizes the extent to which a node is located "between" other pairs of nodes, which is measured by taking into account the number of paths that pass through the node. A commonly used betweenness centrality measure is:

$$C_B(e) = \sum_{s \neq t \neq e \in E} \frac{\sigma(s,t|e)}{\sigma(s,t)}, \tag{6.10}$$

  where $\sigma(s,t|e)$ is the total number of shortest paths between s and t that pass by e, and $\sigma(s,t)$ is the total number of shortest paths between s and t.

  A high betweenness centrality node works as a bridge, facilitating the transmission of information between different parts of the network.

- **Closeness centrality:** assumes that the notion of centrality is a measure of a node's "closeness" to many other nodes:

$$C_{cl}(e) = \frac{1}{\sum_{u \in E} d(e,u)}, \tag{6.11}$$

  where $d(e,u)$ is the number of edges of the shortest path between nodes $e, u \in E$, known as *geodesic distance*. This measure is usually normalized over the interval [0,1] to allow for relative comparisons.

  A high closeness centrality node has a strategic position to communicate with other nodes and spread information.

- **Eigenvector centrality:** this centrality measure computes the centrality of a node based on the centrality of its neighbors:

$$C_{Gi}(e) = \alpha \sum_{\{u,e\} \in G} C_{Gi}(u), \tag{6.12}$$

  where C_{Gi} is the solution to a linear problem that solves for the eigenvectors.

  A high eigenvector centrality node is connected with other influential nodes, contributing to the overall network influence.

Code 6.13 presents a script to calculate the descriptive statistics measures for the Zachary's Karate Club Social Network using the `NetworkX` library (Hagberg et al., 2008). It starts by loading the dataset from the library itself and then uses the function `is _ tree()` to check if the network is a tree or not. Note that each of the measures presented is an internal method of `NetworkX`. Also, as the centrality measures are related to each node, there is a loop to calculate and print their values for each node. Running this code leads to the following output:

```
Is the graph a tree? False
Number of nodes: 34
Number of edges: 78
Is the graph directed? False
Is the graph connected? True
Average clustering coefficient: 0.5706384782076823
Average shortest path length: 2.408199643493761
Number of connected components: 1
Density: 0.13903743315508021
Maximum degree: 17
Minimum degree: 1
Average degree: 4.588235294117647
Assortativity coefficient: -0.47561309768461413
```

```
Degree centrality:          Betweenness centrality:

Node 0: 0.4848              Node 0: 0.4376
Node 1: 0.2727              Node 1: 0.0539
Node 2: 0.3030              Node 2: 0.1437
Node 3: 0.1818              Node 3: 0.0119
Node 4: 0.0909              Node 4: 0.0006
Node 5: 0.1212              Node 5: 0.0300
Node 6: 0.1212              Node 6: 0.0300
Node 7: 0.1212              Node 7: 0.0000
Node 8: 0.1515              Node 8: 0.0559
Node 9: 0.0606              Node 9: 0.0008
Node 10: 0.0909             Node 10: 0.0006
Node 11: 0.0303            Node 11: 0.0000
Node 12: 0.0606            Node 12: 0.0000
Node 13: 0.1515            Node 13: 0.0459
Node 14: 0.0606            Node 14: 0.0000
Node 15: 0.0606            Node 15: 0.0000
Node 16: 0.0606            Node 16: 0.0000
Node 17: 0.0606            Node 17: 0.0000
Node 18: 0.0606            Node 18: 0.0000
Node 19: 0.0909            Node 19: 0.0325
Node 20: 0.0606            Node 20: 0.0000
Node 21: 0.0606            Node 21: 0.0000
Node 22: 0.0606            Node 22: 0.0000
Node 23: 0.1515            Node 23: 0.0176
Node 24: 0.0909            Node 24: 0.0022
Node 25: 0.0909            Node 25: 0.0038
Node 26: 0.0606            Node 26: 0.0000
Node 27: 0.1212            Node 27: 0.0223
Node 28: 0.0909            Node 28: 0.0018
Node 29: 0.1212            Node 29: 0.0029
Node 30: 0.1212            Node 30: 0.0144
```

```
Node 31: 0.1818        Node 31: 0.1383
Node 32: 0.3636        Node 32: 0.1452
Node 33: 0.5152        Node 33: 0.3041

Closeness cen-         Eigenvector cen-
trality:               trality:

Node 0: 0.5690         Node 0: 0.3555
Node 1: 0.4853         Node 1: 0.2660
Node 2: 0.5593         Node 2: 0.3172
Node 3: 0.4648         Node 3: 0.2112
Node 4: 0.3793         Node 4: 0.0760
Node 5: 0.3837         Node 5: 0.0795
Node 6: 0.3837         Node 6: 0.0795
Node 7: 0.4400         Node 7: 0.1710
Node 8: 0.5156         Node 8: 0.2274
Node 9: 0.4342         Node 9: 0.1027
Node 10: 0.3793        Node 10: 0.0760
Node 11: 0.3667        Node 11: 0.0529
Node 12: 0.3708        Node 12: 0.0843
Node 13: 0.5156        Node 13: 0.2265
Node 14: 0.3708        Node 14: 0.1014
Node 15: 0.3708        Node 15: 0.1014
Node 16: 0.2845        Node 16: 0.0236
Node 17: 0.3750        Node 17: 0.0924
Node 18: 0.3708        Node 18: 0.1014
Node 19: 0.5000        Node 19: 0.1479
Node 20: 0.3708        Node 20: 0.1014
Node 21: 0.3750        Node 21: 0.0924
Node 22: 0.3708        Node 22: 0.1014
Node 23: 0.3929        Node 23: 0.1501
Node 24: 0.3750        Node 24: 0.0571
Node 25: 0.3750        Node 25: 0.0592
Node 26: 0.3626        Node 26: 0.0756
Node 27: 0.4583        Node 27: 0.1335
Node 28: 0.4521        Node 28: 0.1311
Node 29: 0.3837        Node 29: 0.1350
Node 30: 0.4583        Node 30: 0.1748
Node 31: 0.5410        Node 31: 0.1910
Node 32: 0.5156        Node 32: 0.3087
Node 33: 0.5500        Node 33: 0.3734
```

6.3.5.3 Interpreting the Results

The first steps in the code perform simple and direct checks on the network structure, including the number of nodes and edges, directedness, and connectedness.

The clustering coefficient offers some insights into the presence of local clustering or the formation of small communities in the graph. An average value of 0.57 suggests that, on average, the nodes in the graph have a relatively high tendency to form clusters. In Zachary's dataset case, this suggests that the interactions and friendships within the network are not random; that is, the network members tend to cluster with each other based on some type of affinity. This is also observed when looking at the graph, because there are two main clusters formed around the club administrator and the instructor, respectively.

The average shortest path length measures the average number of edges that need to be crossed to go from one node to another in the network. Therefore, a value of 2.41 for the average shortest path length in the Zachary's data indicates that it takes around 2.41

edges to go from one member in the social network to another. This is a relatively small number, showing that the network and club members are closely connected. In social networks, this leads to a structure known as a *small world*, where individuals are only a few steps away from each other, indicating a high level of social cohesion (Watts & Strogatz, 1998).

A number of connected components equal to 1 means that the Zachary's network is a single unit, with no subnetworks. A maximum degree of 17 indicates that the node with most edges is connected with 17 other nodes, while a minimum degree of 1 indicates that the least connected node is linked to only one node.

The network density indicates the proportion of connected nodes in relation to the total number of possible connections. A value of 0.139 indicates that approximately 13.9% of Zachary's social network members' potential connections are present in the network. An average degree of 4.588 indicates that each club member has approximately 4.588 connections (e.g., friendships) with the other members.

The assortative coefficient brings another interesting insight into Zachary's social network. Its negative value of −0.476 indicates that the highly connected nodes are connected with nodes of low degrees. This also suggests that some members act as group influencers, transmitting their information to several members, but without mixing the groups.

CODE 6.13   Script to calculate the descriptive statistics of Zachary's Karate Club Social Network.

```python
# Code to calculate Descriptive Statistics of the
# Zachary's Karate Club Social Network

import networkx as nx

# Load the Zachary's Karate Club dataset
G = nx.karate_club_graph()

# Network Data Statistics
print("Is the graph a tree?", nx.is_tree(G))
print("Number of nodes:", G.number_of_nodes())
print("Number of edges:", G.number_of_edges())
print("Is the graph directed?", G.is_directed())
print("Is the graph connected?", nx.is_connected(G))
print("Average clustering coefficient:", nx.average_clustering(G))
print("Average shortest path length:", nx.average_shortest_path_length(G))
print("Number of connected components:", nx.number_connected_components(G))
print("Density:", nx.density(G))
print("Maximum degree:", max(dict(G.degree()).values()))
print("Minimum degree:", min(dict(G.degree()).values()))
print("Average degree:", sum(dict(G.degree()).values()) / G.number_of_nodes())
print("Assortativity coefficient:", nx.assortativity.
degree_assortativity_coefficient(G))
print("Degree centrality:")
for node, centrality in nx.degree_centrality(G).items():
    print(f"Node {node}: {centrality:.4f}")
print("Betweenness centrality:")
for node, centrality in nx.betweenness_centrality(G).items():
    print(f"Node {node}: {centrality:.4f}")
print("Closeness centrality:")
```

```
for node, centrality in nx.closeness_centrality(G).items():
    print(f"Node {node}: {centrality:.4f}")
print("Eigenvector centrality:")
for node, centrality in nx.eigenvector_centrality(G).items():
    print(f"Node {node}: {centrality:.4f}")
```

6.3.6 Visualizing Networks

Differently from trees that are connected, acyclic, and unweighted graphs, networks can be weighted, directed, cyclic, disconnected, etc. There is a large combination of possibilities for networks, and plotting them in a way that allows us to identify patterns and perform specific visual analyses can be a tricky task. To keep the description brief, we will present a standard *node-link diagram* with some different visualization layouts and one *matrix display* that will allow us to visualize the network connectivity. Those readers interested in knowing more about networks and their visualization are invited to have a look at the works of Menczer et al. (2000), Newman (2003), Kolaczyk and Csárdi (2014), and Barabási and Pósfai (2016).

Figure 6.16 shows four different visualization layouts for the Zachary's Karate Club social network data. These plots were generated with Code 6.14, which uses the NetworkX library. The *spring layout* positions nodes by simulating a force-directed representation of the network, aiming to optimize the distribution of nodes in the space for better visualization. The *circular layout* plots the network in a circular format, and the *shell layout* positions the nodes in concentric circles as specified in the layout code. It is also possible to fix the positions of nodes in the graph to highlight some desired characteristics. In this example, some of the highest degree nodes were spread apart from the network to emphasize their high degrees.

CODE 6.14 Script to plot different layout visualizations of Zachary's Karate Club data.

```
# Code to Visualize the Zachary's Karate Club Social Network in different layouts
import networkx as nx
import matplotlib.pyplot as plt

# Load the Zachary's Karate Club dataset
G = nx.karate_club_graph()

# Plot using spring layout
pos_spring = nx.spring_layout(G, seed=4)
figA, (sprg, circ) = plt.subplots(nrows=2, ncols=1, figsize=(10, 12.5))

nx.draw_networkx(G, pos_spring, node_color='lightblue', font_size=8, edge_
color='gray', ax=sprg)
sprg.set_title("Spring Layout", fontsize=16)
# Plot using circular layout
pos_circular = nx.circular_layout(G)
nx.draw_networkx(G, pos_circular, node_color='lightblue', font_size=8, edge_
color='gray', ax=circ)
circ.set_title("Circular Layout", fontsize=16)
# Save and display the networks

plt.savefig("Figure_6_16a_Network_Layouts.svg", format="svg", dpi=1500,
bbox_inches='tight')
```

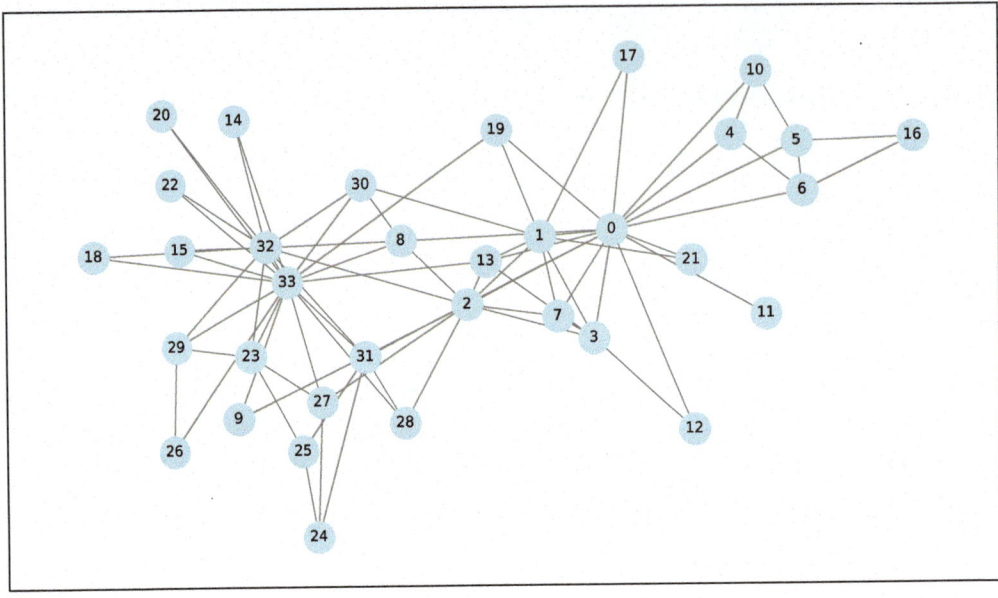

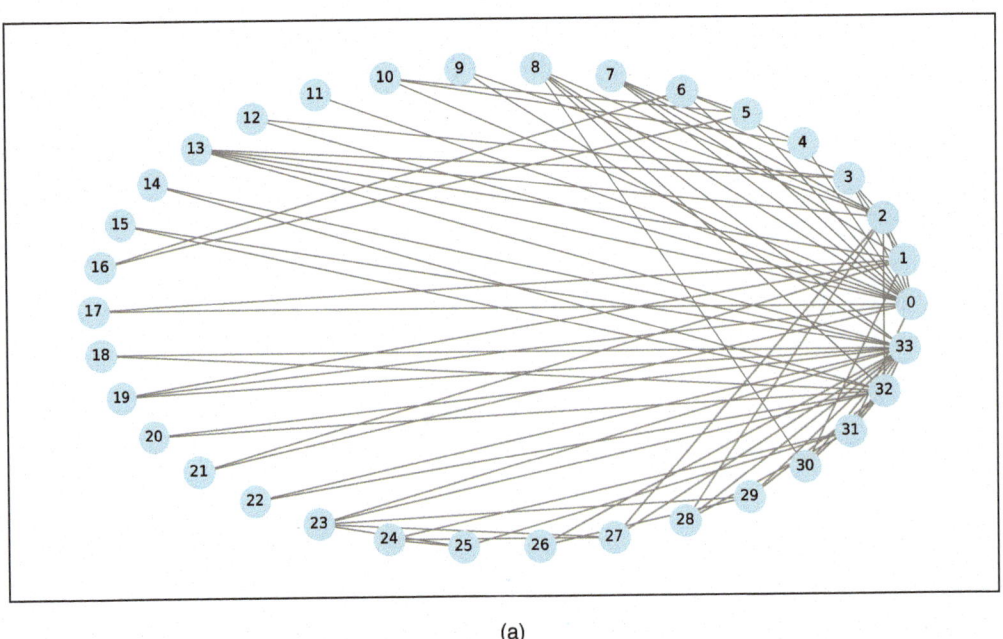

(a)

FIGURE 6.16 Different visualization layouts for Zachary's Karate Club social network data. (a) Spring and circular layouts. (b) Shell and custom spring layouts.

(*Continued*)

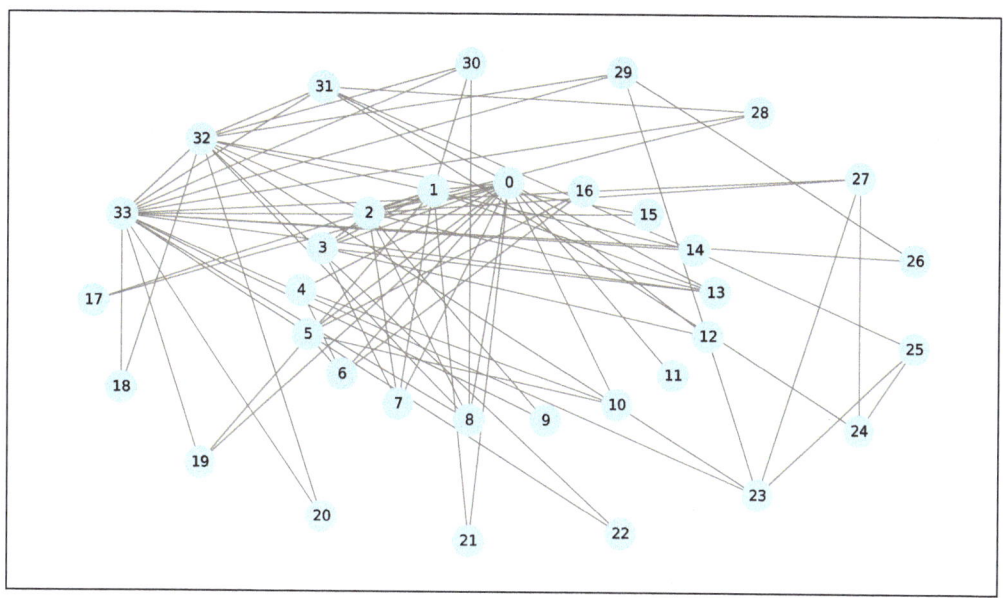

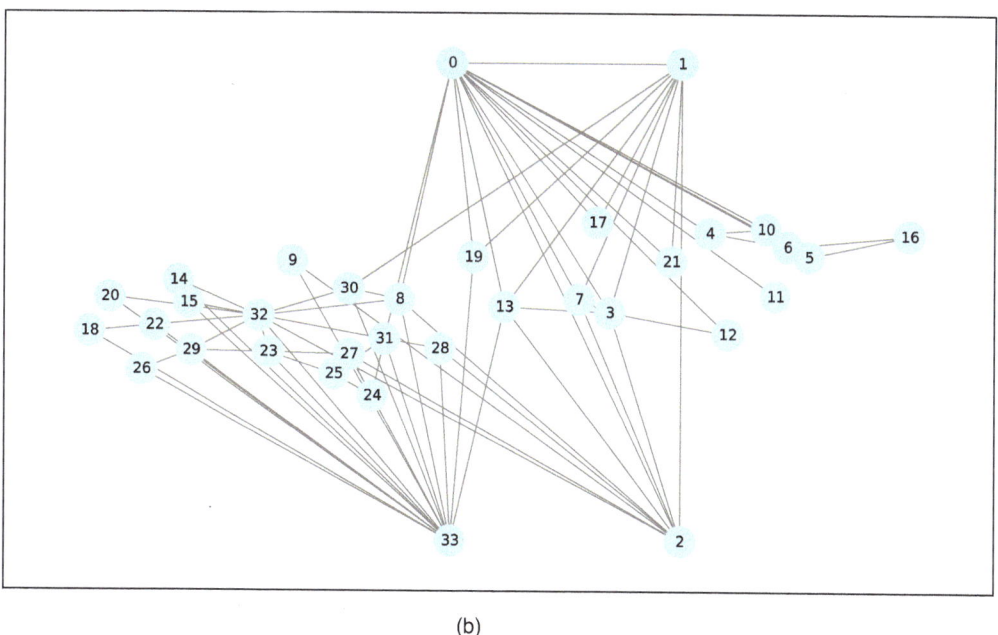

(b)

FIGURE 6.16 (Continued) Different visualization layouts for Zachary's Karate Club social network data. (a) Spring and circular layouts. (b) Shell and custom spring layouts.

```
plt.show()

figB, (shll, cstm) = plt.subplots(nrows=2, ncols=1, figsize=(10, 12.5))
# Plot using shell Layout

shell_layout = [list(range(0, 17)), list(range(17, 34))]
pos_shell = nx.shell_layout(G, nlist=shell_layout)
nx.draw_networkx(G, pos_shell, node_color='lightblue', font_size=8, edge_
color='gray', ax=shll)
shll.set_title("Shell Layout", fontsize=16)

# Plot using spring layout with custom positions
pos_custom = nx.spring_layout(G, seed=4, iterations=200)
custom_positions = {0: (0.0, 1.5), 1: (.5, 1.5), 2: (0.5, -1.5), 33: (0.0, -1.5)}
pos_custom.update(custom_positions)
nx.draw_networkx(G, pos_custom, node_color='lightblue', font_size=8, edge_
color='gray', ax=cstm)
cstm.set_title("Custom Spring Layout", fontsize=16)

# Show plot
plt.show()
```

As another form of visualizing a network, let us consider the adjacency matrix for the Zachary's data. Figure 6.17a shows Zachary's Karate Club graph with the edge weights between each pair of nodes. The Karate Club graph uses weighted edges to represent the strength or frequency of interactions between individuals. Higher values in the matrix indicate stronger connections or more frequent interactions. Figure 6.17b shows the heatmap of the adjacency matrix of the data. It displays structural information of the network by showing the relationships between pairs of nodes. The colors are used to stress the strength of the connections, with darker colors representing stronger connections, and lighter colors representing weaker connections or the absence of connections. By observing the heatmap in Figure 6.17b, it is possible to identify two clusters of connections, one around the first nodes and another around the last nodes.

6.4 EXERCISES

6.4.1 Research Topics and Questions

1. How does the process of text structuring influence the outcomes of text and document exploratory data analysis?

2. What are the challenges in conducting descriptive analysis for graphs and networks, and how can they be addressed?

3. Discuss the ethical considerations surrounding the representation of various data types, including the potential biases introduced in visualizations and descriptive analyses, and the impact on decision-making.

4. Discuss the philosophical implications of predicting future events based on historical time series data, questioning the concept of causality and the ethical dilemmas associated with using past information to foresee the future.

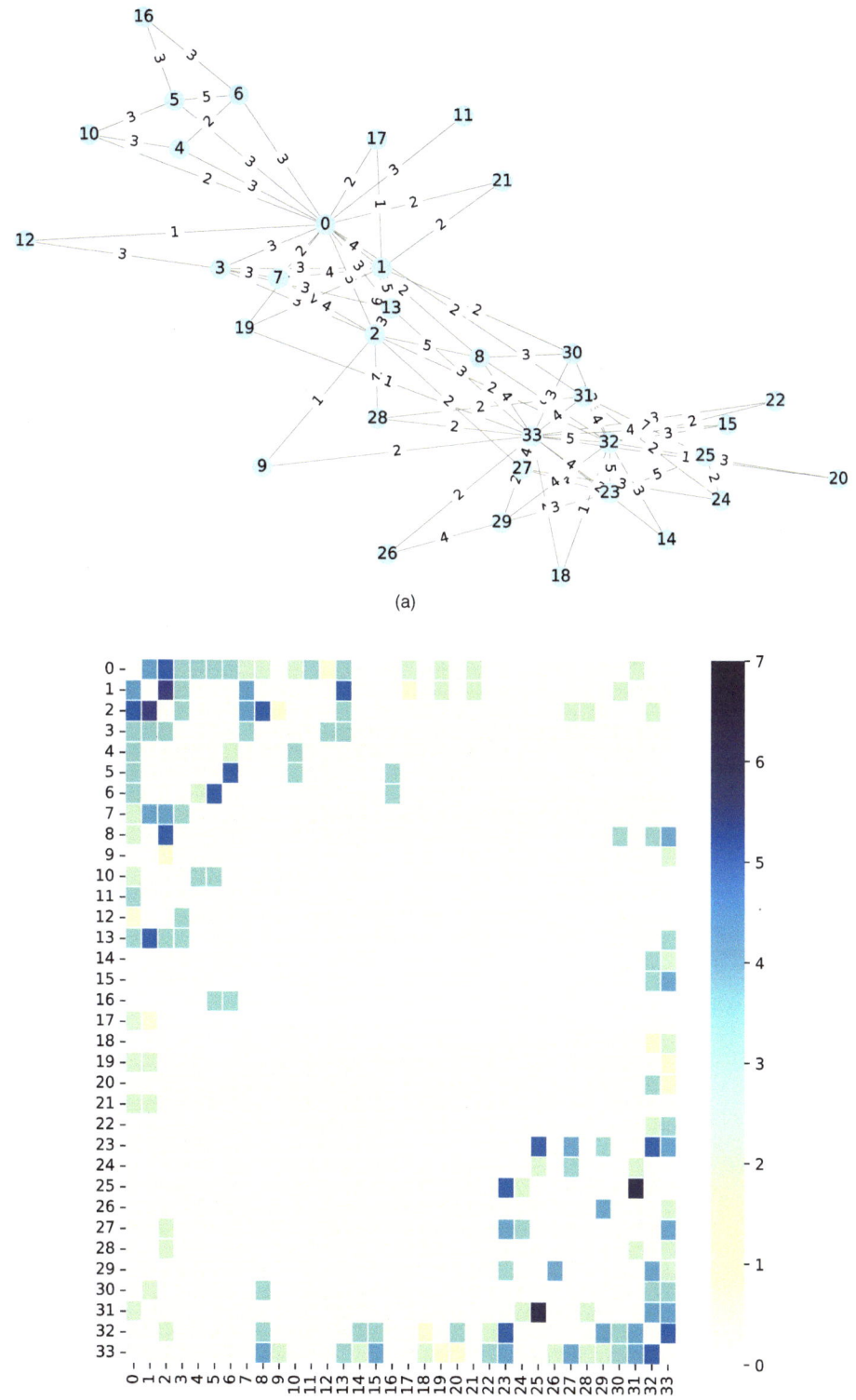

FIGURE 6.17 Zachary's Karate Club social network visualization. (a) Karate club graph with edge weights. (b) Adjacency matrix heatmap.

6.4.2 Quizzes

1. What is a primary objective of time series data analysis?

   a. Finding the mean and median.

   b. Identifying patterns and trends over time.

   c. Creating bar charts.

   d. Counting missing values.

2. Which visualization technique is commonly used to visualize time series data?

   a. Scatter plots.

   b. Histograms.

   c. Line plots.

   d. Pie charts.

3. When dealing with seasonal time series data, what is deseasonalization?

   a. Removing the seasonality component from the data.

   b. Measuring the seasonality component from the data.

   c. Adding a seasonal trend to the data.

   d. Scaling the data to fit a specific season.

4. What is the term for transforming text data into a numerical format suitable for analysis?

   a. Tokenization.

   b. Normalization.

   c. Vectorization.

   d. Aggregation.

5. What is a word cloud visualization primarily used for in text analysis?

   a. Sentiment analysis.

   b. Identifying outliers.

   c. Showing the distribution of word lengths.

   d. Visualizing word frequency.

6. What is TF-IDF (Term Frequency-Inverse Document Frequency) used for in text analysis?

   a. To measure the frequency of a term within a document.

   b. To measure the importance of a term in a collection of documents.

   c. To count the total number of words in a document.

   d. To count the total number of documents in a corpus.

7. In natural language processing, what is stemming?

   a. The process of removing stop words from a text.

   b. The process of reducing words to their base or root form.

   c. The process of translating text from one language to another.

   d. The process of determining the relevance of a word in a document.

8. In a network graph, what do nodes and edges typically represent?

   a. Nodes represent attributes, and edges represent relationships between attributes.

   b. Nodes represent data points, and edges represent clustering.

   c. Nodes represent objects, and edges represent connections or relationships between objects.

   d. Nodes represent feature importance, and edges represent decision boundaries.

9. What is centrality in network analysis?

   a. A measure of the size of a network.

   b. A measure of the strength of edges in a network.

   c. A measure of the importance or influence of a node in a network.

   d. A measure of the density of a network.

10. What does the "degree" of a node represent in a network graph?

    a. The importance of the node within the network.

    b. The color of the node.

    c. The size of the node.

    d. The temperature of the node.

6.4.3 Computational Exercises

1. For the IMDb Movie Reviews Dataset, explore techniques like word clouds or frequency analysis to visualize the most common words or phrases used in positive vs. negative movie reviews. Create scatter plots or bar charts to explore relationships between movie ratings and review sentiment or word length.

2. For the Zachary's Karate Club Dataset use network graphs to visualize the social connections between members of the karate club, highlighting different communities based on the eventual club split. Apply algorithms to identify communities within the network and analyze their characteristics. Explore properties like community size or the number of edges within and between communities. Investigate potential reasons for the club split based on the network structure.

3. The Facebook Social Circles Network data[1] consists of circles from Facebook collected through surveys. The data is anonymized and includes node features (profiles), circles, and ego networks. For this dataset, do:

   a. Analyze the network structure, including the number of nodes and edges, degree distribution, and clustering coefficient.

   b. Identify communities and influential nodes using community detection algorithms and centrality measures.

NOTE

1 https://snap.stanford.edu/data/ego-Facebook.html and https://www.kaggle.com/code/morecoding/facebook-network

## CHAPTER 7

Data Storytelling and Dashboard Design

"There is a story in your data. But your tools don't know what that story is. That's where it takes you—the analyst or communicator of the information—to bring that story visually and contextually to life."

– Cole N. Knaflic, Storytelling with Data: A Data Visualization Guide for Business Professionals, Wiley, *2015, p. 3*

The previous chapters covered, in a comprehensive manner, the most relevant concepts in business intelligence and data analysis, including descriptive statistics, visualization techniques for structured data, and the visualization of special types of data, such as time series, texts, and networks. All these concepts and techniques are usually part of a greater context involving *data storytelling* and *dashboard design*. These two concepts, while distinct, are closely intertwined and serve the common purpose of making data more accessible, understandable, and actionable.

Data storytelling is the practice of building a narrative around data and its accompanying analysis and visualizations (Knaflic, 2015; Duarte, 2019; Dykes, 2020). Unlike a standard presentation of numbers and graphs, a data story provides context, highlights key points, and guides the audience toward a certain understanding or action. It is not just about presenting data, but about telling a story that engages the audience and leads to insight and action. Data storytelling is important because it helps to bridge the gap between data, insights, and human understanding. It makes data more relatable and easier to understand, helping to reveal trends and insights that might otherwise go unnoticed. Whether influencing strategic decisions, communicating business performance, or fostering a data-driven culture, data storytelling allows the power of data to be harnessed.

While data storytelling is the narrative, *dashboard design* is the process by which the result of the exploratory data analysis is built and presented in an intuitive and aesthetically pleasing manner. *Dashboards* serve as the visual interface that transforms the data

DOI: 10.1201/9781003570691-7

analysis process into dynamic and intuitive displays. They act as a control center, providing a snapshot of key metrics, trends, and performance indicators. The art of dashboard design lies in presenting complex information in a visually appealing format, enabling users to explore data, gain insights, and make informed decisions quickly and interactively. Through thoughtful design, dashboards facilitate seamless data exploration, allowing users to drill down into specific details, analyze trends, and uncover hidden knowledge effortlessly. Moreover, dashboards empower collaboration by providing a centralized platform for teams to align their understanding of critical information and collectively contribute to organizational goals.

Data storytelling and dashboard design are not standalone concepts; rather, they are connected in the data analysis journey. While data storytelling gives data context and relevance, dashboard design provides the canvas on which this narrative unfolds. The synergy between these two elements empowers data analysts to communicate insights effectively, fostering a culture where data becomes a shared language for business analysis. This is the so-called *data culture*.

This chapter explores the principles of data storytelling and dashboard design, providing guidelines for these two important and usually final steps in the data analysis workflow. Whether you are a data analyst, a business intelligence professional, or anyone who works with data, this chapter will provide you with the remaining tools and understanding you need to effectively communicate with data. After introducing the general concepts and process flow, two case studies will be presented to illustrate their application.

7.1 DATA STORYTELLING

Data storytelling is a powerful approach to communicating data and analytics because it makes the whole process understandable, helps to capture and maintain the audience's attention, highlights insights, drives actions, facilitates memory, and even evokes emotions. While descriptive analysis and data visualization offer the analytical and visual aspects of data exploration, data storytelling moves one step forward by integrating these elements into a compelling narrative that resonates with the audience, fostering better comprehension, decision-making, and action.

Data storytelling involves an effective combination of *data*, *narrative*, and *visuals* (Dykes, 2020). Data is the core of any data story, the raw information that you want to convey. Every data story should originate from data; that is, the insights and messages being communicated must be derived from, supported by, and guided by the data. A narrative is the storyline or sequence of events that gives the data meaning, helping to inform and engage the audience through the data, highlight key points, and provide context. Finally, visuals are the charts, graphs, tables, and other visual elements used to represent and illustrate the data and its relationships, making complex data more understandable and highlighting trends or patterns. Figure 7.1 summarizes the relationship among data, narrative, and visuals for the creation of a story around the available data and its context.

Effective data storytelling can make complex data more understandable and memorable. In the approach to be presented in this book, data storytelling will serve as a guideline and framework for the design of a dashboard. This means that our storytelling process will

FIGURE 7.1   Relationship among data, narrative, and visuals for the storytelling design process.

not be closed, but will allow us to build a dashboard that, when explored, will lead the user to his/her insights, conclusions, decision-making, and actions. From this perspective, the following steps will be used to build an effective story around data:

1. Define your audience and purpose;

2. Identify the key message and depth;

3. Perform the exploratory data analysis; and

4. Prepare a compelling narrative.

This process is illustrated in Figure 7.2, and each of these steps will be detailed in the following sections.

7.1.1 Define the Audience and Purpose

Defining your audience and purpose is a fundamental step in creating an effective data story. This involves identifying the specific group or individuals you intend to communicate with and clarifying the objectives you aim to accomplish through your data narrative. To define your audience, consider factors such as demographics, interests, and knowledge level. Understanding these aspects helps tailor your data story to resonate with the audience, making it more engaging and relevant to their needs. Moreover, recognizing the purpose behind your data story is essential; it could be to inform, persuade, educate, or inspire action. Clearly outlining your objectives enables you to structure the narrative in a way that aligns with your goals. In essence, this initial step sets the foundation for crafting a data story that not only communicates effectively but also connects with the intended audience on a meaningful level.

FIGURE 7.2   Data storytelling design process flow.

7.1.2 Identify the Key Message and Depth

The next step in effective communication through data is to identify the key message and determine the depth of information and insights to be presented. The key message serves as the central theme or insight that you aim to communicate to your audience. It is the primary takeaway that you want your audience to grasp from the data presented. This message should be clear, concise, and relevant to the purpose of your communication. To enhance the impact of your data story, it is essential to understand the depth of information needed to support and reinforce the key message. This involves evaluating the level of detail, context, and supporting data required to provide a comprehensive understanding of the main message. By defining the key message and understanding the depth of information, you set the foundation for crafting a compelling and focused data narrative that effectively communicates your intended insights to your audience.

7.1.3 Perform the Exploratory Data Analysis

The exploratory data analysis phase involves several key steps aimed at extracting meaningful insights from data. Initially, the emphasis is on gathering and analyzing relevant data, ensuring its accuracy, currency, and quality. This foundational step is crucial as the subsequent analysis heavily relies on the integrity of the collected information and insights.

Once the data are in hand, the next step is to determine the overall goal of the data analysis. This involves defining the specific objectives or outcomes the analysis aims to achieve. A set of guiding questions is proposed to guide and refine the analysis:

1. What questions do you want to answer with the data?

2. What kind of relationships exists in the data?

3. What are the best techniques for displaying the variables and their relationships?

These questions are designed to elucidate the purpose, audience, and nature of the data. They prompt the analyst to clarify the specific questions he/she seeks to answer through the data and to identify any existing relationships within the dataset. The choice of visualization techniques is emphasized, with a focus on selecting tables, charts, graphs, or other visualizations that effectively convey the intended message. Factors such as the type of data, audience preferences, and the narrative to be constructed all play a role in this decision.

7.1.4 Prepare a Compelling Narrative

In the process of crafting a persuasive and impactful presentation or report, it is essential to focus on two key aspects: preparing a compelling narrative and contextualizing the data. This involves constructing a narrative structure that guides the audience through the insights and information. This structure typically comprises an introduction to set the stage, a well-defined storyline to present the data coherently, and a conclusion that ties together the key insights. The narrative should follow a logical flow, capturing the audience's attention and maintaining its engagement.

TABLE 7.1   Matrix with the Four Storytelling Design Principles

Audience and Purpose	Exploratory Analysis
• Specific group or individuals: demographics, interests, and knowledge level. • Clarify the objectives through the narrative.	• What questions do you want to answer with the data? • What kind of relationships exist in the data? • What are the best techniques for displaying the variables and their relationships?
Key Message and Depth	**Compelling Narrative**
• Central theme or insight: clear, concise, and relevant. • Depth: level of detail, context, and supporting data.	• Persuasive and impactful presentation. • Guide the audience through the insights and information.

Contextualizing the data involves providing background information and context to help the audience understand the significance of the presented data and analysis. It is crucial to explain any industry-specific terms or concepts, ensuring that the audience, regardless of its familiarity with the subject matter, can comprehend the information.

Real-life stories and concrete examples serve to illustrate the practical implications of the data, making it more relatable and accessible to the audience. By integrating storytelling elements, the presenter can humanize the data, creating a connection between the information and the experiences of the audience. This approach not only adds a compelling dimension to the presentation but also facilitates a deeper understanding and retention of the data by making it more tangible and memorable.

Remember that effective data storytelling not only communicates data-driven insights but also engages the audience, making the information memorable and actionable. Tailoring the approach to the audience and purpose is key to successful data storytelling.

Table 7.1 summarizes the four storytelling design principles: define the audience and purpose; identify the key message and depth; perform the exploratory data analysis; and prepare a compelling narrative. With these aspects ready, one can move on to plan and design the dashboard.

7.2 DASHBOARD DESIGN

A dashboard is a visual representation of critical information required to accomplish one or more goals, presented in a consolidated and organized format on a single screen for easy and quick monitoring (Few, 2006). It is designed to provide an objective overview of the status or performance of a system, process, or business.

Dashboards can be used in various contexts, including business intelligence, project management, monitoring systems, and data analysis. They typically use charts, graphs, tables, and other visual elements to present data in a user-friendly and comprehensible format. The goal is to enable users to make informed decisions and take actions by quickly grasping the essential information and trends.

Dashboards can be *static* or *interactive*, and they are often customizable to meet the specific needs of users. Common features include the ability to navigate through detailed information, find insights, set filters, and receive real-time updates. Many businesses and

FIGURE 7.3   Dashboard design process flow.

organizations use dashboards to monitor and analyze performance metrics, track goals, and gain insights into their operations.

Defining the audience and purpose of your dashboard, identifying the key message and its depth, performing the exploratory data analysis, and crafting a compelling narrative are the data storytelling steps that serve as the preliminary steps to design an effective dashboard for data visualization. Assuming you have already completed all these steps, the next steps involve selecting appropriate visualizations, designing the dashboard layout or wireframe, choosing a color scheme, applying interactivity, defining security and access control, testing, and deploying. These steps are summarized in Figure 7.3 and detailed in the following sections.

7.2.1 Selecting Appropriate Visualizations

This book explored a vast array of data visualization techniques, emphasizing structured data while also including special cases such as text and document data, as well as trees and networks. The visualization methods were organized based on their ability to display distributions, associations of variables, amounts, proportions, evolution and flow, and geospatial data.

The choice of visualizations to be incorporated in the dashboard will depend on the data available and the story to be told, that is, the key message to be conveyed and the narrative to be used. When selecting visualizations, consider the nature of data, because different types of data (categorical, numerical, time series, text, networks) require different visualizations. It is also important to take into account the level of familiarity your audience has with certain types of visualizations and select visualizations that best highlight and emphasize the key points to be conveyed. Keep visualizations simple and easy to interpret, avoiding clutter and choosing a format that minimizes confusion.

As a simple empirical rule for the choice of suitable visuals, consider the three exploratory analysis guiding questions presented above: what questions you want to answer with the data; what are the relationships to be observed; and what are the best methods to display the variables and their relationships.

7.2.2 Designing the Dashboard Layout

Designing the layout of a dashboard is a critical step in ensuring that the story is presented in a clear, effective, and user-friendly manner. A visually appealing dashboard is not only pleasant to look at but also makes it easier for users to understand and interpret the data and insights. This can involve the use of consistent and pleasing color schemes, appropriate fonts, and spacing. The aesthetics of a dashboard can greatly influence a user's experience and his/her ability to quickly grasp the information presented.

The layout should be organized in a way that follows a logical flow of information. This could be from left to right, top to bottom, or in any other pattern that suits the data and the story you are trying to tell. The arrangement should guide the user's eye through the dashboard in a meaningful sequence.

The placement of charts and widgets on the dashboard should be carefully considered. Important information should be placed in prominent positions. Similar or related data should be grouped. The size of each chart or widget should reflect its importance, the complexity of the data it represents, or the general aesthetics of the dashboards.

It is also important to mention that a cluttered dashboard can be overwhelming and make it difficult for users to find the information they need. Strive for simplicity and clarity. Use space effectively to separate different sections or elements and avoid unnecessary decorations or elements that do not contribute to the understanding of the data, insights, and story.

7.2.3 Choosing a Color Scheme

Section 7.4.2 presented some design principles for data visualization and started a discussion about the use of colors in visuals. Let us now add some comments and guidelines to this process.

Choosing a color scheme is an important aspect of designing any visual representation, especially when it comes to data visualization and dashboard design. The goal is to create a visually appealing and easily understandable dashboard that enhances data readability and storytelling. When selecting a color scheme for data visualization, it is important to account for:

1. **Contrast and readability**: Give preference to colors with sufficient contrast to ensure readability. Contrast has been discussed in the Gestalt principle of figure-ground (Section 4.1.3), and when suitably used between text and background plays an important role in legibility. For data points or categories, choose colors that stand out from one another to make distinctions clear.

2. **Color harmony**: A harmonious color palette uses colors that complement one another, enhancing the overall aesthetic and helping users focus on the data without being distracted by clashing colors.

3. **Consistency**: Use colors consistently throughout the visualization to represent specific visuals. Consistency aids in building a clear and intuitive association between colors and the information they convey. For instance, if green represents a certain category, it should consistently do so across all charts or graphs in the dashboard.

4. **Accessibility**: It is important to acknowledge that some people are colorblind or have any type of color deficiency. Therefore, consider accessibility guidelines, ensuring that the color scheme is accessible to individuals with color vision deficiencies. Use a combination of color, labels, and patterns to convey information, allowing for inclusivity in your audience.

5. **Limited palette**: Avoid using too many colors, as it can lead to visual clutter and confusion. A limited color palette simplifies the visualization and makes it easier for viewers to interpret the information. Maintain a manageable number of colors that represent distinct categories or data points.

6. **Meaningful color choices**: Select colors that have inherent meanings or associations, for example, green for allowed actions or positive values and red for forbidden actions or negative values.

By thoughtfully selecting and implementing a color scheme based on these principles, you create a dashboard that is both aesthetically pleasing and effectively communicates information to your audience.

7.2.4 Applying Interactivity

The idea of applying interactivity in a dashboard is to enhance the user experience and provide control over the data exploration process. There are many forms of adding interactivity to dashboards, such as:

1. **Filters**: Filters are tools that allow users to limit the data that is displayed in a visual, acting as a set of criteria that the data must meet to be included in the dashboard. There are various types of filters that can be applied, such as categorical (e.g., filtering by product type or region), numerical (e.g., filtering by sales amount or quantity), or temporal (e.g., filtering by date or time). Filters are usually presented in the form of dropdown menus, checkboxes, or sliders that allow users to select the data they want to see.

2. **Drill-through**: Allows users to click on a data point in a chart or table and "drill through" to a more detailed report based on that data point. For example, you might click on a data point representing sales for a particular product and be taken to a different report showing detailed sales data for that product. The key aspect of drill-through is that it takes you to a different report or dashboard for more specific information.

3. **Drill-down**: This feature, however, allows users to start with a high-level overview of data and then explore the data at a more granular level. For example, you might start by looking at sales data for an entire country, then drill down to see sales data for individual states, counties, cities, and so on. The key aspect of drill-down is that you stay within the same report or dashboard, but the level of detail changes.

4. **Tooltips**: Tooltips are small information boxes that appear when you hover over an item on a dashboard, providing additional details about the item, such as exact values, labels, or explanations. This feature is particularly useful for presenting concise details without cluttering the main visualization.

The overall aim of interactivity is to make the dashboard user-friendly and intuitive. Users should be able to interact with the data effortlessly, gaining insights through exploration rather than being limited to static views. This promotes a more engaging and dynamic experience, encouraging users to actively participate in the analysis process.

7.2.5 Security and Access Control

Security and access control are critical components of any information system or network, aiming to safeguard sensitive data and ensure that only authorized people have access to specific resources. Implementing proper security measures involves a combination of technical, procedural, and organizational measures to protect against unauthorized access, data breaches, and other potential security threats. This may involve data protection, access control, permissions and authorization, authentication mechanisms, monitoring and auditing, and incident response. All these are out of the scope of this book and course but must be accounted for if proper security and access control are to be added to the dashboard.

7.2.6 Test and Iterate

Testing and iterating a dashboard are critical processes that involve evaluating, continually refining, and improving its design, functionality, and usability. Through testing, designers and developers gather valuable feedback from users, allowing them to identify and address issues, usability concerns, and areas for improvement. This iterative approach ensures that the final dashboard aligns closely with user needs and objectives, resulting in a more intuitive, user-friendly, and effective tool. By incorporating user feedback into the design process, the dashboard becomes more tailored to the specific requirements of its intended audience, ultimately enhancing user satisfaction and the overall success of the dashboard in delivering meaningful insights and supporting decision-making processes.

Testing and iteration must include:

- Test each visual in terms of functionality and accuracy;

- Test the dashboard and all its visuals with potential users and adjust based on feedback;

- Ensure responsiveness across different devices and screen sizes;

- Optimize performance for quick loading times, especially with large datasets;

- Provide documentation and training for users;

- Regularly update the dashboard to reflect changes in data, technology, and user needs.

7.3 CASE STUDY 1: GAPMINDER DATASET

Table 2.9 presents the Gapminder dataset, which contains an overview of global development trends, focusing on social, economic, and health indicators across different countries over time. Throughout this book, we used the Gapminder dataset to present and discuss various concepts and visuals, including bubble charts, tree maps, line charts, and choropleth maps.

The goal of this initial case study is to provide a simple analysis of global development based on the Gapminder dataset. The dashboard will offer insights about the relationship between the human development index (HDI), life expectancy, and CO_2 consumption in each continent. The users will be able to choose the continent and country they want to investigate, and there will also be insights into the countries with the highest GDP in each continent.

7.3.1 Data Storytelling

1. **Audience and purpose**: This dashboard will be designed for policymakers, researchers, educators, and anyone interested in understanding global development trends. The purpose is to provide a simple interactive tool that allows users to explore socioeconomic and environmental trends across countries and regions over time, helping them understand the complex relationships between variables such as the HDI, life expectancy, GDP, CO_2 emissions, and more.

2. **Key message and depth**: The key message of this dashboard is that global development is multidimensional, encompassing health, economic, and environmental factors. By visualizing these variables over time and across regions, users can uncover important relationships and trends that show how development affects different areas of life. The dashboard provides both a broad overview of global trends and specific insights into individual countries, making it accessible to users at different levels of data literacy.

3. **Exploratory analysis**:

   1. *What questions do you want to answer with the data?*

      – How do HDI and life expectancy vary across continents and countries?

      – How does development look across different continents? Are there clear regional disparities?

      – Are there observable patterns in life expectancy and HDI over time?

      – How has CO_2 consumption evolved globally and regionally over time?

      – Which countries have the highest GDP?

   2. *What kind of relationships exists in the data?*
      Positive correlations:

      – **HDI and life expectancy**: Higher HDI is generally associated with longer life expectancy, reflecting better health conditions and access to resources.

      – **GDP and CO_2 emissions**: Countries with higher GDP often have higher CO_2 emissions due to industrial activities and higher energy consumption.

Negative correlations:

- **Economic growth vs. environmental impact**: Some countries show rapid economic growth accompanied by environmental degradation, highlighting sustainability challenges.

- **Regional disparities in HDI and life expectancy**: Different regions may exhibit varying levels of development due to historical, economic, or geographical factors.

3. *What are the best techniques for displaying the variables and their relationships?*

- An HDI vs. Life Expectancy bubble chart with CO_2 emissions as bubble size and color by continent visually emphasizes the relationship between development, health, and environmental impact.

- A GDP treemap shows the economic weight of countries within each continent, revealing disparities in economic power.

- Time series line charts for life expectancy and HDI allow users to track changes over time in each variable, providing insights into historical trends.

- An animated map of CO_2 consumption over time offers a geographic perspective on emissions, making it easy to see how CO_2 consumption has evolved globally.

- A bubble map allows users to see the global distribution of GDP, highlighting regional economic powerhouses and providing a quick comparison of economic influence by country.

4. **Compelling narrative**: "The world is developing rapidly, but the impacts of this growth are not uniformly distributed. The Gapminder dataset allows us to explore how economic growth, human development, and environmental impacts interrelate across continents and countries. Let us begin with a broader view: globally, regions with higher HDI tend to enjoy longer life expectancies. This picture changes when we add CO_2 consumption as a layer. Here, we see that high development and life expectancy often come with significant environmental impacts, as reflected in the size of each country's CO_2 consumption bubble.

By looking at the GDP, it can be noted that the economic contributions of countries reveal vast disparities. The treemap shows that while some regions contribute significantly to global GDP, others remain economically marginalized, often resulting in lower HDI and life expectancy.

Finally, we can track the global journey of development through the individual line charts of HDI and life expectancy over time. Each line tells a story of progress, challenges, and the trade-offs countries face on the road to development. The question we are left with is how we can foster sustainable growth without compromising our planet's future.

This dashboard invites you to explore these questions and uncover the complex, interdependent relationships between development, health, economy, and the environment."

7.3.2 Dashboard Design

1. **Selecting appropriate visualizations**: As a response to question (3) of the exploratory analysis above, we have already described the visuals that are going to be used in this dashboard: bubble charts, tree maps, line charts, animated choropleth maps, and bubble maps.

2. **Designing the dashboard layout**: The wireframe presented in Figure 7.4 describes the layout to be used to build the dashboard.

3. **Choosing a color scheme**: The dashboard for this case study will be developed in Python using a library called `Dash`, specially designed for building analytical web applications and useful for creating interactive dashboards and data visualization interfaces. In this example, we will not apply any color scheme, and we will use the standard color schemes of each graph chosen. This will allow us to compare a dashboard with random colors with a dashboard when a specific color scheme is applied, as will be performed in the second case study.

4. **Applying interactivity**: Interactive features enhance user experience by enabling data exploration through various tools. Filters for continents and countries will allow users to select specific regions or nations, making it easy to view data relevant to their interests. Hover tooltips will provide additional details in all graphs, offering insights on demand. Additionally, zoom and pan functionalities in the bubble map and animated map allow users to focus on specific areas for more in-depth regional analysis, creating an immersive, user-driven experience.

5. **Security and access control**: In terms of security and access control, the dashboard implementation focuses on safeguarding sensitive data and ensuring that only authorized individuals have access to specific resources. While detailed technical measures such as data protection, access control, authentication mechanisms, and incident response fall outside the scope of this book and course, we acknowledge their importance in maintaining the security of the dashboard.

6. **Test and iterate**: Testing and iterating are integral to ensuring the dashboard's functionality, usability, and effectiveness. We conduct thorough testing of each visual component to ensure functionality, connection, and accuracy.

Figure 7.5 shows the final dashboard built using the library Dash in Python. From top to bottom, the following components were used: combo boxes for selecting the continent and country; a bubble chart for the life expectancy vs HDI, with different colors for the continents and bubble sizes for the CO_2 consumption; a tree map with the GDP by country and continent; two line charts, one for the life expectancy and another for the HDI, both

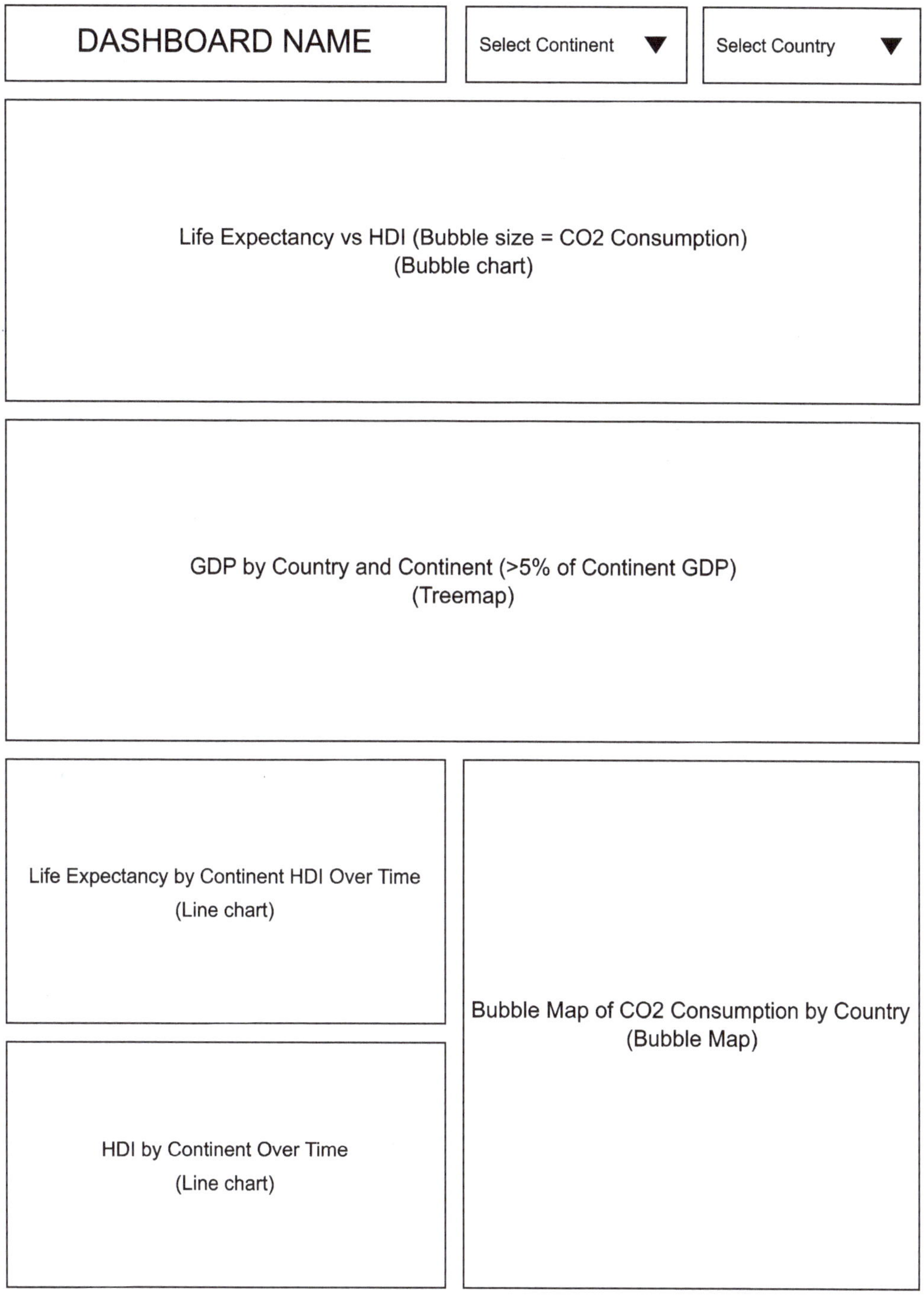

| DASHBOARD NAME | Select Continent ▼ | Select Country ▼ |

Life Expectancy vs HDI (Bubble size = CO2 Consumption)
(Bubble chart)

GDP by Country and Continent (>5% of Continent GDP)
(Treemap)

Life Expectancy by Continent HDI Over Time
(Line chart)

Bubble Map of CO2 Consumption by Country
(Bubble Map)

HDI by Continent Over Time
(Line chart)

FIGURE 7.4   Wireframe with the dashboard layout.

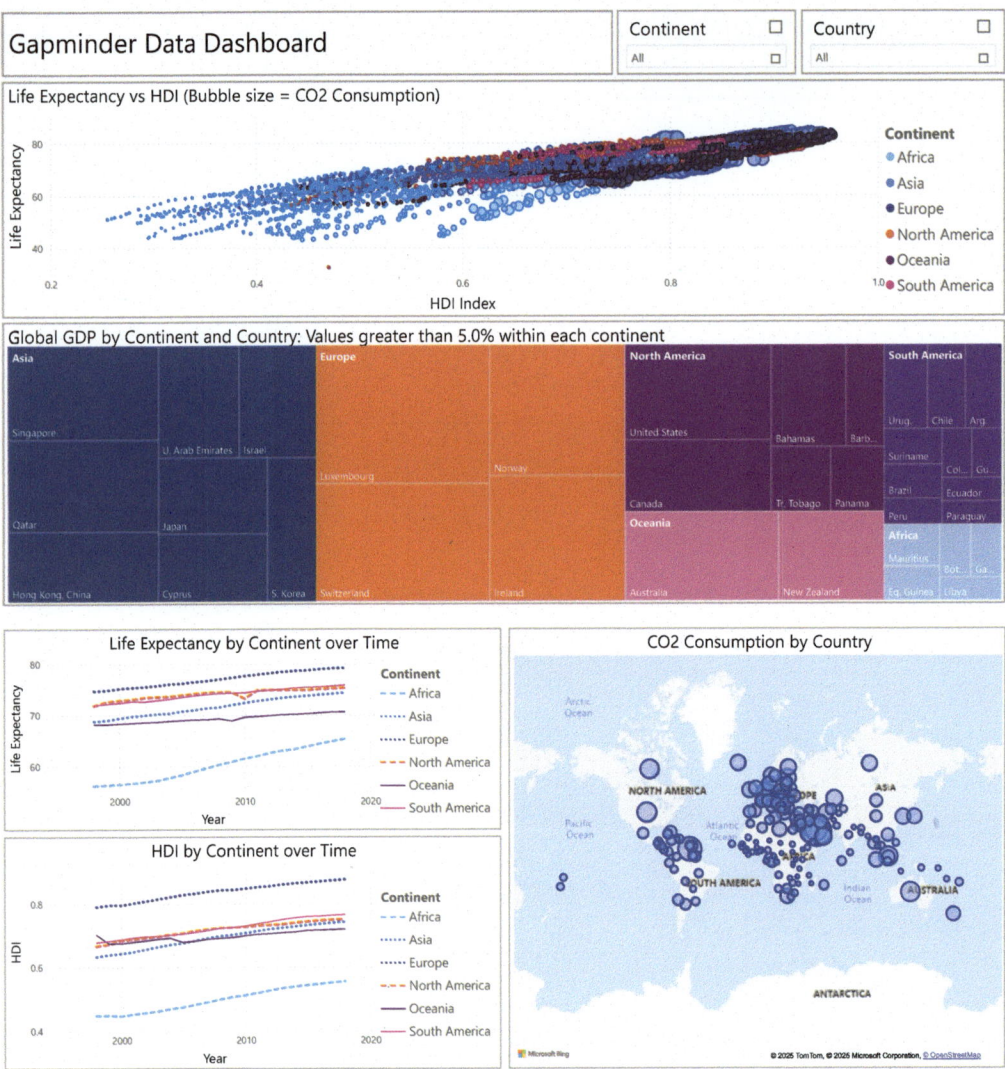

FIGURE 7.5 Dashboard built in Power BI for the Gapminder dataset. The names of the countries in the Global GDP by Continent graph were suppressed to avoid a cluttered figure.

taken by continent over time; an animated choropleth map with the CO_2 consumption geolocated; and a bubble map with the GDP per region.

7.4 CASE STUDY 2: SUPERSTORE SALES DATASET

The Superstore Sales Dataset consists of a retail data of a global superstore for 4 years.[1] The dataset contains 18 attributes, including the row ID, order ID, order data, shipment date and mode, segment, country, city, etc., as described in the data dictionary presented in Table 7.2.

The goal of this case study is to provide a comprehensive analysis of sales performance for a global superstore over a period of time. The dashboard will aim to uncover insights into customer behavior, sales trends, and geographical distribution of orders.

Through interactive visualizations, the dashboard will allow users to explore key metrics such as total sales value, number of sales, category-wise performance, and segment-wise analysis. By providing a user-friendly interface with customizable filters, the dashboard will enable users to tailor their analysis to specific time periods, shipping preferences, and customer segments. Ultimately, the goal is to empower decision-makers with actionable insights that can drive strategic business decisions, optimize operations, and enhance customer satisfaction.

TABLE 7.2 Data Dictionary for the Superstore Sales Dataset

Variable Name	Definition (Meaning)	Variable Type	Range or Domain
Row ID	ID number of each row	Numerical (integer)	Integer value (code)
Order ID	ID number of each order	String (alphanumeric)	{CA, US}-Year-integer value (code)
Order date	Date product was ordered by the customer	Numerical (integer)	Date
Ship date	Date product was shipped to the customer	Numerical (integer)	Date
Ship mode	Class chosen for shipping	Categorical	{Same day, First Class, Second Class, Standard Class}
Customer ID	ID number for each customer	String (alphanumeric)	First and last initials of customer name}-integer value (code)
Customer name	First and last name of customers	Categorical (nominal)	{First and last name}
Segment	Category of customers	Categorical (nominal)	{Consumer, Home office, Corporate}
Country	Customers' country of residence	Categorical (nominal)	{United States}
City	Customers' city of residence	Categorical (nominal)	City in the United States
State	Customers' state of residence	Categorical (nominal)	State in the United States
Postal code	Customers' postal code	Categorical (integer)	Postal code in the United States
Region	Customers' region of residence in the United States	Categorical (nominal)	{Central, South, West, East}
Product ID	ID number of each product	String (alphanumeric)	Category-Sub-category-integer code
Category	Products' category	Categorical (nominal)	{Office Supplies, Furniture, Technology}
Subcategory	Type of products in each category	Categorical (nominal)	{Accessories, Appliances, Art, Binders, Bookcases, Chairs, Copiers, Envelopes, Fasteners, Furnishings, Labels, Machines, Paper, Phones, Storage, Supplies, Tables}
Product name	Names of products in each category	Categorical (nominal)	Any product names
Sales	Total US$ by order	Numerical (continuous)	[0.444, 22,638.48]

7.4.1 Data Storytelling

1. **Audience and purpose**: The dashboard will be designed for individuals or groups who are involved in the decision-making process of a retail business, such as business analysts, sales managers, or executives. These individuals are expected to have a good understanding of sales metrics and retail business operations. They are interested in monitoring sales performance, identifying trends, and making data-driven decisions to improve business outcomes. The purpose of the dashboard is to inform and educate, providing a comprehensive view of sales performance over time, across different categories, and in different geographical locations.

2. **Key message and depth**: The key message of the dashboard is "understanding sales performance and trends to drive strategic decision-making in retail business". This message aligns with the purpose of the dashboard, which is to provide insights into sales data for decision-making. To support this key message, the depth of information presented in the dashboard should be comprehensive yet focused:

    1. **Sales trends over time:** The line charts of total sales value and number of sales by month provide a detailed view of sales trends over time. This can help the user to understand seasonal patterns and identify periods of high or low sales.

    2. **Sales by category:** The bar chart showing total sales values by category and subcategory provides insights into which products are performing well. This helps the user to identify profitable categories and focus on improving sales in underperforming ones.

    3. **Geographical distribution of orders:** The map showing the number of orders by state can help the users understand the geographical distribution of sales. This can be useful for market analysis and strategic planning.

    4. **Overall sales performance:** The KPI for total sales value gives a snapshot of the overall sales performance. This helps the user to quickly assess the business's financial health.

    5. **Customizable views:** The slicers for year and segment, and the slider for shipment mode, allow users to customize the view according to their specific needs. This can help the users to further explore the data and generate more specific insights.

3. **Exploratory analysis**: The EDA is expected to provide specific answers to the guiding questions.

    1. *What questions do you want to answer with the data?*

        - How have sales values and the number of sales changed over time?

        - Which categories and subcategories have the highest sales values?

        - How are orders distributed across different states?

        - What is the total value of sales?

- How do sales values and the number of sales vary by year, shipment mode, and segment?

2. *What kind of relationships exists in the data?*

   - There might be a relationship between the time (month/year) and the total value or number of sales, indicating seasonal trends.

   - There could be a relationship between the category/subcategory of products and the total sales values, suggesting some products are more popular or profitable than others.

   - The number of orders might vary by state, indicating geographical trends in sales.

   - The total value of sales could be influenced by factors such as the year, shipment mode, and segment.

3. *What are the best techniques for displaying the variables and their relationships?*

   - Line charts for displaying trends in total sales value and the number of sales over time.

   - A bar chart for showing the total sales values by category and subcategory.

   - A map for visualizing the number of orders by state.

   - A KPI for presenting the total value of sales.

   - Slicers for filtering the data by year, shipment mode, and segment, allowing the audience to explore the data in more depth.

4. **Compelling narrative**: "Welcome to the Superstore Sales Dashboard, where we explore the world of retail sales data to uncover valuable insights and trends. This dashboard has a collection of visualizations that provide a comprehensive overview of the sales performance of the global superstore over the years. Through interactive charts and maps, we explore the dynamics of sales, understand customer behavior, and identify opportunities for growth and optimization.

   In today's competitive retail landscape, understanding customer preferences and market trends is crucial to keeping a competitive differential. The dashboard presents a snapshot of the sales data, allowing us to analyze key metrics and gain actionable insights. By examining factors such as sales by month, category-wise performance, geographical distribution of orders, and segment-wise analysis, we can uncover patterns and make data-driven decisions. Let us now describe our storyline."

Sales trends over time: The line charts reveal the total value and number of sales over the period. By tracking sales trends month by month, we can identify seasonal fluctuations and periods of high or low sales activity. Understanding these patterns helps in optimizing inventory management and marketing strategies.

Category and subcategory performance: The bar chart provides insights into the performance of different product categories and subcategories. By analyzing which categories contribute the most to the sales revenue, we can focus efforts on high-performing areas and explore opportunities for cross-selling and upselling.

Geographical distribution of orders: The map visualization focuses on the number of orders by state, offering a geographical perspective on the sales distribution. Understanding regional preferences and market dynamics allows us to tailor product offerings and marketing campaigns to specific regions.

Key performance indicators (KPIs): The KPI displays the total value of sales, providing a quick overview of the overall performance. This metric serves as a benchmark for evaluating success and setting future targets.

Interactive filters: The slicers for the year, shipment mode, and segment allow users to customize their analysis to focus on specific time periods, shipping preferences, and customer segments. This interactivity enhances the user experience and allows for deeper insights.

7.4.2 Dashboard Design

1. **Selecting appropriate visualizations**: The line charts of total sales value and number of sales by month can help track sales trends and seasonality. The bar chart will provide insights into which categories and subcategories are performing well. The map will visualize the distribution of orders across different states, which can be useful for market analysis. The KPI will give a quick snapshot of the total sales value. The slicers will allow the users to filter the data based on year, shipment mode, and segment, enabling them to customize the view according to their specific needs.

2. **Designing the dashboard layout**: The wireframe presented in Figure 7.6 describes the layout to be used to build the dashboard. The proposed layout follows a logical and user-friendly design that emphasizes clarity, simplicity, and visual appeal. The top banner provides consistency throughout the dashboard, creating a cohesive look and feel. Placing the total value of sales KPI in the top left corner ensures that users immediately see the most important metric upon accessing the dashboard. The line charts for total sales value and number of sales by month are positioned at the top, allowing users to quickly view the overall sales trends over time. The bar chart showing total sales by category and subcategory is placed at the bottom, providing insights into the performance of different product categories. This arrangement allows users to understand the composition of sales in more detail. The map displaying the number of orders by state is positioned in the bottom right, enabling users to visualize geographical distribution and identify regions with high order volumes. On the left side of the dashboard, the slicers allow users to filter data as desired. The use of space effectively separates different sections and avoids clutter, ensuring that users can easily navigate the dashboard and find the information they need.

3. **Choosing a color scheme**: We chose different shades of green for the dashboard because it aligns well with several key principles of color selection for data visualization. Firstly, green is a color associated with positivity, growth, and harmony,

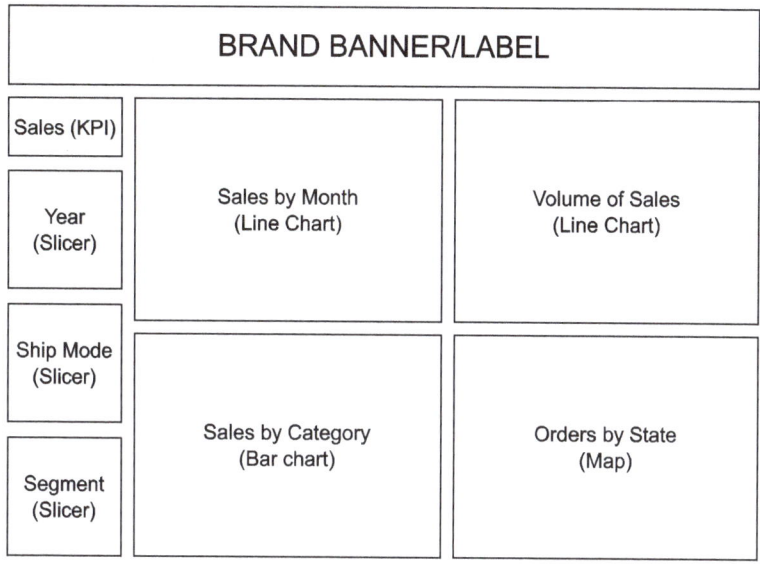

FIGURE 7.6   Wireframe with the dashboard layout.

making it suitable for conveying positive aspects of the data, such as sales growth or profitability. Additionally, green is recognized as a color representing "go" or "allowed", making it intuitive for indicating positive values or actions, which is often the case in sales dashboards. Moreover, green provides excellent contrast against a white or light background, enhancing readability and ensuring that data points stand out effectively. This choice supports the principle of contrast and readability, allowing users to easily distinguish between different categories or data points. Note that we can set rules in the dashboard such that some visuals become orange or red if some target performance is not met. Finally, but not less important, green is generally accessible to individuals with color vision deficiencies, especially when combined with other visual cues like labels or patterns, ensuring inclusivity in the audience.

4. **Applying interactivity**: The dashboard incorporates several interactive features to enhance the user experience and provide control over the data exploration process. Firstly, the slicers allow users to filter data based on specific time periods, shipment modes, and customer segments. Additionally, the dashboard includes tooltips in all four visuals, which appear when hovering over data points, providing users with additional details such as exact values or labels without cluttering the main visualization. These tooltips help users gain insights without overwhelming them with excessive information. Overall, these interactive features promote a user-friendly and intuitive experience, empowering users to explore the data effortlessly and gain valuable insights through active participation in the analysis process.

5. **Security and access control**: See discussion in the previous case study.

6. **Test and iterate**: See discussion in the previous case study.

Figure 7.7 shows the final dashboard built using Power BI by Microsoft. Figure 7.7a shows the dashboard with all slicer options chosen, and Figure 7.7b shows some filters applied and their impact on the generated graphs. Figure 7.7c shows a drill-down when the subcategory binders from the office supply is chosen, and also highlights the tooltip that pops up when the cursor is over the binders bar in the bar chart.

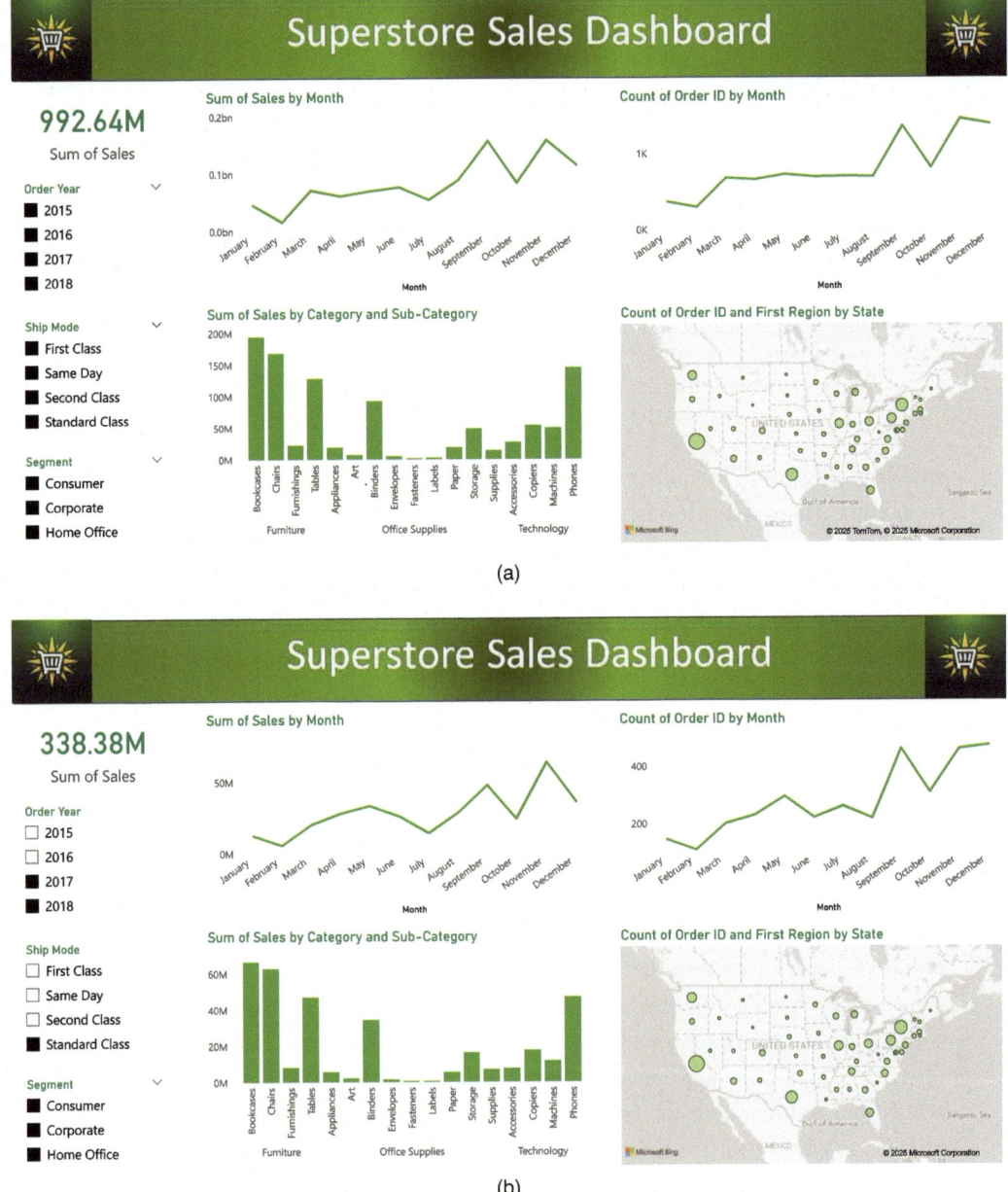

FIGURE 7.7 Dashboard built in Power BI for the Superstore Sales dataset. (a) Dashboard with all options of the slicers chosen. (b) Application of some filters and their impact on the graphs displayed. (c) Drill-down when the subcategory binders from the office supply is chosen, and the tooltip that pops up when the cursor is over the binders bar in the bar chart.

(Continued)

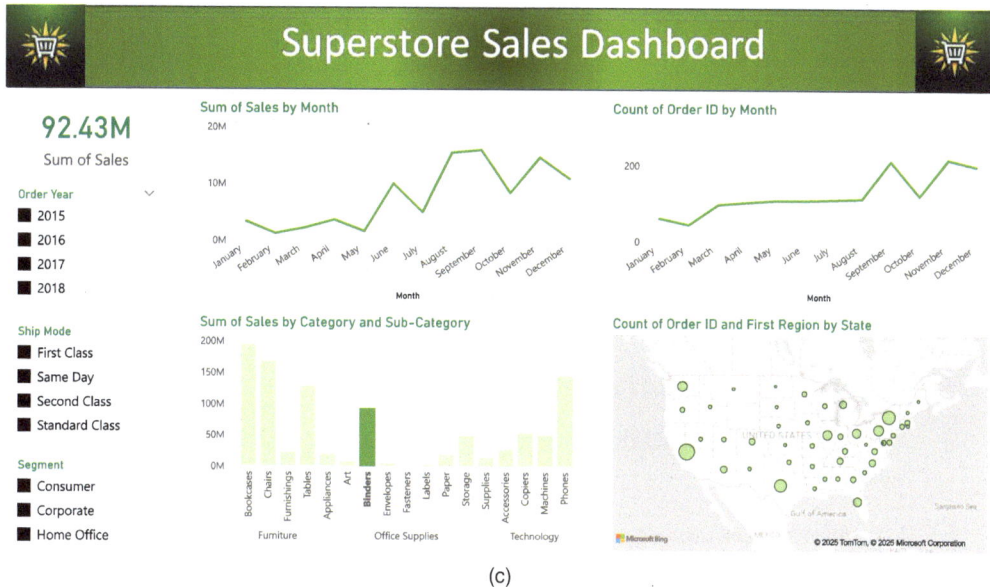

(c)

FIGURE 7.7 (*Continued*)   Dashboard built in Power BI for the Superstore Sales dataset. (a) Dashboard with all options of the slicers chosen. (b) Application of some filters and their impact on the graphs displayed. (c) Drill-down when the subcategory binders from the office supply is chosen, and the tooltip that pops up when the cursor is over the binders bar in the bar chart.

7.5 EXERCISES

7.5.1 Questions and Topics for Discussion

1. How can data storytelling be manipulated to mislead audiences? What ethical considerations should be taken into account when telling a story with data?

2. Are KPIs truly objective measures of performance, or can they be influenced by subjective factors? How can we ensure fairness and accuracy in KPI selection and interpretation?

3. Do dashboards democratize data, making it accessible to non-experts, or do they oversimplify complex data sets, potentially leading to misinterpretation?

4. How do we strike a balance between aesthetic appeal and functional utility in dashboard design? Can a well-designed dashboard be both beautiful and useful, or do these goals conflict?

5. Debate the level of responsibility data professionals hold in the decision-making process. Discuss the ethical implications of presenting data and insights to decision-makers and how these professionals can contribute to ethical and informed decision-making.

7.5.2 Quizzes

1. What is the main purpose of data storytelling?

    a. To present data in a complex way.

    b. To make data understandable and engaging.

    c. To illuminate the audience.

    d. None of the above.

2. What is a Key Performance Indicator (KPI)?

    a. A measurable value that demonstrates how effectively a company is achieving key business objectives.

    b. A qualitative assessment of a company's performance.

    c. A measure of how many keys a company has.

    d. None of the above.

3. What is the main purpose of a dashboard in data analysis?

    a. To display one specific measure.

    b. To provide a detailed report of a company's financial status.

    c. To visually display the most important information needed to achieve one or more objectives.

    d. None of the above.

4. Which of the following is not typically a step in the process of dashboard design?

    a. Understanding the needs of the end-users.

    b. Selecting the right charts and graphs to display the data.

    c. Ignoring the feedback from the end-users.

    d. Iteratively refining the dashboard based on feedback.

5. Why is data storytelling important in analytics?

    a. It adds complexity to the analysis.

    b. It enhances communication and understanding.

    c. It makes data less accessible.

    d. It focuses solely on raw numbers.

6. How can KPIs contribute to decision-making in an organization?

   a. By making data more complex.

   b. By providing irrelevant information.

   c. By measuring performance against goals.

   d. By focusing on data storytelling.

7. Why is the planning phase crucial in the dashboard design process?

   a. It adds unnecessary complexity.

   b. It ensures alignment with user needs and business goals.

   c. It focuses solely on data storytelling.

   d. It ignores the relevance of key metrics.

8. Why should KPIs be aligned with strategic goals?

   a. They should not be aligned with strategic goals.

   b. To ensure they are measuring what matters to the organization.

   c. To make them more complex.

   d. To make them less useful.

9. Why should a dashboard be interactive?

   a. To make it more confusing.

   b. To engage the user and allow exploration of the data.

   c. To make it look fancy.

   d. Interaction is not important in a dashboard.

10. Why is context important in data storytelling?

    a. It makes the story longer.

    b. It provides background that helps interpret the data.

    c. It is not important.

    d. It makes the story more confusing.

7.5.3 Final Project

The final course project is designed to comprehensively put into practice the knowledge and skills you have acquired throughout this course on EDA. In this project, you will have the opportunity to select a dataset of your choice and create an interactive and informative dashboard to visualize and analyze the data. The goal is to apply the principles of descriptive analysis, data visualization, and dashboard design to effectively communicate insights and patterns hidden within the data. Furthermore, this project will challenge you to think entrepreneurially and/or impactfully, aiming not only to create an insightful dashboard but also to develop a concept for a data-driven solution based on the dataset and insights you uncover.

Project Requirements

1 Business or Impact Concept Development

- Begin by identifying a real-world problem or opportunity that can be addressed or leveraged using data.

- Create a business or impact concept that outlines the value proposition, target audience, and the potential impact (social, environmental, financial, etc.) of your data-driven solution.

- Clearly articulate how your project could lead to a viable business opportunity or impact.

2. Dataset Selection

   Choose a dataset that interests you and aligns with your academic or professional goals. It can be related to any domain, such as finance, healthcare, social sciences, games, environment, etc.

3. Data Cleaning and Preparation

- Clean and preprocess the dataset to handle missing values, outliers, and any data quality issues.

- Document the data cleaning steps and create a data dictionary to explain the dataset's variables and their meanings.

4. Descriptive Analysis

   Conduct a thorough descriptive data analysis to gain an understanding and characterize the dataset. Include frequency distributions, measures of central tendency, measures of variability, measures of form, and association measures.

5. Data Visualization

- Apply the principles of data visualization to create visual representations of the data.

- Design and implement various types of visualizations to present different aspects of the dataset, such as histograms, scatter plots, bar charts, line charts, etc.

- Choose appropriate visualization techniques for different data types and research questions.

6. Data Storytelling

- Define the audience and purpose.
- Define the key message and depth.
- Perform the exploratory analysis (Step 4 above).
- Prepare a compelling narrative.

7. Dashboard Design and Prototype

- Select Appropriate Visualizations
- Design the Dashboard Layout
- Choose a Color Scheme
- Apply Interactivity
- Security and Access Control
- Test and Iterate

8. Presentation

Prepare a presentation to showcase your project. Your presentation should include a live demonstration of your dashboard and a walkthrough of the whole data analysis process.

NOTE

1 https://www.kaggle.com/datasets/rohitsahoo/sales-forecasting

Appendix A
Python: A Quick Reference Guide

A.1 PYTHON BASICS

Python was released by Guido van Rossum in 1991 as a successor to the ABC programming language. It is an open-source, interpreted, high-level, multiplatform, and multiparadigm programming language.[1] By multiparadigm, we mean that Python supports imperative, functional, procedural, and object-oriented programming paradigms, and by multiplatform, we mean that it runs on Windows, Mac, Linux, etc. Its syntax is clear and concise, with several resources available in its standard library and many modules and framework contributions developed by the community. Its features and capabilities make it attractive to work with structured and unstructured data in all types of data-related applications, including exploratory data analysis.

This appendix provides a quick reference guide for beginners in Python and is aimed at presenting its syntax, data types, control structures, and how to create functions. This is the basic knowledge necessary for understanding the code snippets used in the book, and those interested in finding further information are welcome to visit many online resources and the books by Matthes (2023) and Lutz (2013). All explanations presented here are summarized as a reference, but in all cases, much more can be performed. As prerequisites for this appendix and the book, it is important to have some background knowledge of programming and object-oriented programming (OOP), because Python is a heavily OOP language.

A.1.1 Python Libraries

The book provides several Python scripts that perform the analyses and visualizations explained. The following libraries are used:

- `Statistics`: Built-in library with functions to calculate basic statistical properties of data, such as mean, median, mode, variance, standard deviation, and correlation.

- `Pandas`: Library for data manipulation and analysis, which provides data structures for efficiently handling large datasets, such as Series and DataFrames, and functions for cleaning, filtering, merging, and reshaping data.

- NumPy: Library for scientific computing that provides support for working with large, multi-dimensional arrays and matrices, as well as functions for linear algebra, Fourier analysis, and random number generation.

- Seaborn: Library for the creation of data visualizations that provides a high-level interface for creating various types of plots, such as scatter plots, line plots, bar plots, and heatmaps, and includes built-in functions for customization.

- Matplotlib: It is also a library that allows the creation of static, interactive, and animated visualizations in Python. It provides a low-level interface for creating a wide range of plots, from simple line and scatter plots to more complex 3D visualizations.

- Pyplot: Sub library of Matplotlib that provides a simplified interface for creating basic plots, such as line plots, scatter plots, and histograms, commonly used for quick exploratory data analysis and prototyping.

- SciPy: Library for scientific and technical computing, which provides functions for optimization, integration, interpolation, signal processing, linear algebra, and more. It also includes sub-libraries for special functions and statistical distributions.

- GeoPandas: Open-source library that extends the Pandas data types to more easily deal with spatial operations on geospatial data.

- Statsmodels: Library that contains classes and functions to estimate and interpret statistical models, conduct statistical tests, and perform statistical data analysis.

- ResearchPy: Python library that combines packages such as Pandas, Scipy. stats, NumPy, and others to perform statistical analysis and tests with data. As such, it is useful for researchers and professionals in the many branches of data science, particularly in data analysis.

- NLTK: This is the most comprehensive library to work with Natural Language in Python. NLTK has interfaces with many corpora and resources, such as WordNet, public data sets, dictionaries, lexicons, etc. It can be used to perform text structuring, named entity recognition, sentiment analysis, etc.

- SpaCy: Python library that performs advanced Natural Language Processing. It contains pre-trained models known for their high performance and ease of use.

- Textstat: This is a library designed to calculate statistics and metrics from texts, such as readability, complexity, and grade level indices.

- Wordcloud: Library specially created to plot visually appealing word clouds from text and document data.

- NetworkX: Python library for the creation, manipulation, and analysis of complex networks

- Squarify: Python library used to plot treemaps and visualize hierarchical data using nested rectangles.

A.1.2 Basic Syntax in Python

A.1.2.1 Identifiers and Variables

An *identifier* is a name given to a *variable*, a *function*, a *module*, a *class*, or any other object so that the program can identify it specifically during its execution. *Variable* is the name (identifier) given to a memory location that stores a value; thus, when we change the value of a variable, we are changing the content of that memory location.

In Python, neither the variables nor their types need to be declared, but they cannot start with a number, have special characters, or have blank spaces; they can only start with a letter or an underline character. Also, the name of a variable in Python is *case-sensitive*.

Python is an object-oriented language in which virtually all data items are objects of a specific class or type. This can be observed by using the built-in `type()` function, as illustrated in Code A.1.

CODE A.1   Declaring and initializing variables.

```python
# Declaring and initializing variables
v1 = 1974
v2 = 12.34
v3 = "I am a data analyst"
# Printing (displaying) variables
print('Type(v1)',type(v1))
print('Type(v2)',type(v2))
print('Type(v3)',type(v3))

Output
Type(v1) <class 'int'>
Type(v2) <class 'float'>
Type(v3) <class 'str'>
```

Although it is not necessary to pre-specify the type of a Python variable, it is possible to do so with a process called *casting*. Note that you can assign a new value to a variable, and it will automatically change its type accordingly. It is also possible to make *chained assignments*, that is, to assign the same value to more than one variable at a time, or to assign many values to many variables at once. Finally, Python does not distinguish between single and double quotes for strings (see Code A.2).

CODE A.2   Casting, chaining assignments, and multiple assignments.

```python
# Casting and changing double for single quotes
v1 = float(1974)
v2 = int(12.34)
v3 = str('I am a data analyst')  # Single quotes
# Printing (displaying) variables
print('**Casting:')
print('Float v1: ',v1)
print('Int v2: ',v2)
# Chained assignments
v1 = v2 = v3 = 1974
print('**Chained assignments:')
print(v1, v2, v3)
v1, v2, v3 = 10, 20, 30
print('**Multiple assignments simultaneously:')
print(v1,v2,v3)
```

```
Output
**Casting:
Float v1:  1974.0
Int v2:  12
**Chained assignments:
1974 1974 1974
**Multiple assignments simultaneously:
10 20 30
```

A.1.2.2 Reserved Words

There are many *reserved words*, also called *keywords*, which cannot be used as variable names in Python. To see this list just, type help('keywords') or import the library keywords.py and test the desired variable to check if it is a keyword or not, as exemplified in Code A.3. The meaning and purpose of most of these keywords will be presented throughout this chapter.

CODE A.3   Printing the current keyword list in Python and testing variables as keywords.

```
# Keyword generation and testing
help('keywords')
import keyword # Import the keyword.py library
print('false is a keyword?',keyword.iskeyword('false'))
print('False is a keyword?',keyword.iskeyword('False'))
print('elif is a keyword?',keyword.iskeyword('elif'))
```

```
Output
Here is a list of the Python keywords.  Enter any keyword to get more help.

False               class               from                or
None                continue            global              pass
True                def                 if                  raise
and                 del                 import              return
as                  elif                in                  try
assert              else                is                  while
async               except              lambda              with
await               finally             nonlocal            yield
break               for                 not

false is a keyword? False
False is a keyword? True
elif is a keyword? True
```

A.1.2.3 Comparisons

Performing comparisons is an integral part of programming, and Python allows all the main types of comparisons available in programming languages (Code A.4).

CODE A.4   Examples of using comparisons in Python.

```
# Comparisons
v1 = 1974
v2 = 12.34
print('Is', v1, '<', v2,'?',v1 < v2) # Strictly less than
print('Is', v1, '<=', v2,'?',v1 <= v2) # Less than or equal to
print('Is', v1, '>', v2,'?',v1 > v2) # Strictly greater than
print('Is', v1, '>=', v2,'?',v1 >= v2) # Greater than or equal to
```

```
print('Is', v1, '==', v2,'?',v1 == v2) # Equal to
print('Is', v1, '!=', v2,'?',v1 != v2) # Different from
print('Is', v1, 'a float number?',v1 is float) # Identity
print('Is', v1, 'not a float number?',v1 is not float) # Identity negation
```

```
Output
Is 1974 < 12.34 ? False
Is 1974 <= 12.34 ? False
Is 1974 > 12.34 ? True
Is 1974 >= 12.34 ? True
Is 1974 == 12.34 ? False
Is 1974 != 12.34 ? True
Is 1974 a float number? False
Is 1974 not a float number? True
```

A.1.2.4 Data Input and Output

Data can be *input* into a program in different manners, for instance, by prompting an input from a user, by loading a specific file, or by coding the data into the program. Let us explore each of these methods in the following.

Prompting data from a user can be performed by simply using the function input(). Note that, by default, Python reads all input from the user as a *string,* and it may be explicitly converted by the user if another type is required, as illustrated in Code A.5. In this example, if you input 49.5 as your age and try to convert it for the *int* type, an error will occur because this string converts into a *float* instead of an *int*.

CODE A.5   Data input from the user.

```
# Data input from a user
age = input('What is your age? ')
print('Default type: ',type(age))
age = float(age) # Converting the string into a float type
print('Converted type: ',type(age))
```

```
Output
What is your age?   51
Default type:   <class 'str'>
Converted type:   <class 'float'>
```

Datasets used for data analysis are normally stored in one or more files and it will be necessary to *open* such files and load the data for analysis. Most structured data are stored in .txt or .csv files. The command used in Python to open files is:

```
open(): open(filename, mode, encoding=None).
```

The first argument (filename) is a string with the file name, the second one (mode) is optional and corresponds to a string that describes the file use ("r" for reading, "w" for writing, "a" for appending, "r+" for reading and writing), and the last argument (encoding) is also optional, specifying the type of file encoding.

After doing the desired processing with a file, it is necessary to *close* it to free memory space. There are basically two forms of closing a file in Python: one is by using the try-finally block (Code A.6a), and another is to use the with statement (Code A.6b).

Method read() returns the file content, and method readline() returns one line from the file (if called many times in sequence, each call will return one line in the sequence). Note that it is also possible to open a file, perform all the necessary processing in the following lines of code snippets, and then simply use the method close() to close the file.

CODE A.6 Opening, processing, and closing a file. (a) Try-finally block. Only the first 13 lines of the output of the read() method are presented. (b) With statement.

```
# Opening and closing files using the try-finally block
dinsect = open('insect.csv')
try:
    # File processing is included here
    print(dinsect.read()) # Read and print the whole content of the file
finally:
    dinsect.close()

Output
"count","spray"
10,"A"
7,"A"
20,"A"
14,"A"
14,"A"
12,"A"
10,"A"
23,"A"
17,"A"
20,"A"
14,"A"
13,"A"


# Opening and closing files using the with statement
# This code reads the first three lines of the file
with open('insect.csv') as dinsect:
    # File processing is included here
    print(dinsect.readline())
    print(dinsect.readline())
    print(dinsect.readline())

Output
"count","spray"
10,"A"
7,"A"
```

It is also possible to open a dataset using methods from specific libraries, such as Pandas. Pandas is an open-source Python data analysis and manipulation library built on top of the NumPy library. It provides effective ways of manipulating and analyzing data, easy handling of missing data, and many other functionalities. When loading a dataset with Pandas, a *DataFrame* will be created, as shown in Code A.7. *DataFrames* are bi-dimensional tabular data structures with labeled axes (rows and columns) suitable for manipulating and analyzing data. The method shape() shows the dimensions of the DataFrame, and the method head() shows the first and last five rows.

CODE A.7   Opening a dataset with the Pandas library.

```python
# Opening a dataset using a specific library (Pandas)
import pandas as pd  # Pandas is a data manipulation and analysis library

# Loading the UCI 'Mammo' dataset
# https://archive.ics.uci.edu/ml/datasets/Mammographic+Mass
dmammo = pd.read_csv('mammographic_masses_nominal.csv')
print(dmammo.shape)
print(dmammo.head)
print(type(dmammo))
```

```
Output
(961, 6)
<bound method NDFrame.head of      BI-RADS Age       Shape          Margin Density
Severity
0         5  67      Lobular     Spiculated   Low   Malignant
1         4  43        Round  Circumscribed     ?   Malignant
2         5  58    Irregular     Spiculated   Low   Malignant
3         4  28        Round  Circumscribed   Low      Benign
4         5  74        Round     Spiculated     ?   Malignant
..      ...  ..          ...            ...   ...         ...
956       4  47         Oval  Circumscribed   Low      Benign
957       4  56    Irregular     Spiculated   Low   Malignant
958       4  64    Irregular     Spiculated   Low      Benign
959       5  66    Irregular     Spiculated   Low   Malignant
960       4  62      Lobular       Obscured   Low      Benign
[961 rows x 6 columns]>
<class 'pandas.core.frame.DataFrame'>
```

The output of a program can be printed in a readable way or written to a file, and there are different forms of doing it. Let us focus on the print() function, as illustrated in Code A.8. This function may be a starting point in your Python journey and can be used to display formatted messages on the screen and even to help debug your code. The syntax of the print() function is: print(object(s), sep=separator, end=end, file=file, flush=flush), where object(s) are the objects to be printed, sep is the optional separator, end is the optional item to be printed at the end, file is the optional object with a write method, and flush is an optional Boolean that specifies if the output is flushed or buffered (default is False).

CODE A.8   Print() function. (a) Printing data on the screen. (b) Printing (writing) data in a file.

```python
# (a) Illustrating some common uses of function print()
print('Hello, world!')
import os  # Provides functions to interact with the operating system
print() # Print a blanck line
print('Hi, '+ os.getlogin() +', welcome to Python for dummies!')
# Using a specific separator
print('Hi', os.getlogin(), 'welcome to Python for dummies!', sep=", ")
```

```
Output
Hello, world!
Hi, lnune, welcome to Python for dummies!
Hi, lnune, welcome to Python for dummies!
```

```
# (b) Using the print() function to write directly within a file
with open('emptyfile.txt', mode='r+') as femptyfile:
    print(femptyfile.read()) # Print the content of the file before writing
    print('Writing in the empty file', file=femptyfile)
```

```
Output
Writing in the empty file
Writing in the empty file
```

It is also possible to write in a file using the `write()` method, as depicted in Code A.9.

CODE A.9   Writing in a file using the `write()` function.

```
# Using the write() method to write within a file
with open('emptyfile.txt', mode='r+') as femptyfile:
    print(femptyfile.read()) # Print the content of the file before writing
    femptyfile.write('Writing with the write() method\n')
```

```
Output
Writing in the empty file
Writing in the empty file
```

The `format()` method can be used to create a string containing fields between curly brackets that will be replaced by the arguments of `format()`, and this can be used in conjunction with the `print()` function, as shown in Code A.10. Note that it is possible to define a specific identifier for the arguments of `format()`, e.g., {v1}, {v2}, and {v3}, or you may just use the standard identifiers {0}, {1}, etc.

CODE A.10   Using the `format()` method with the print function.

```
# Using the print function with the format() method
str = 'My name is {0}, I am {1} years old, and I am {2}.'
print(str.format('Leo', 50, "married"))  # Format() with object str
myname = 'Leo'
age = 50
mstatus = "married"

# Printing (displaying) variables
print('\n**Using format() within the print function')
print('My name is {v1}, I am {v2} years old, and I am {v3}.'
      .format(v1=myname,v2=age,v3=mstatus))
```

```
Output
My name is Leo, I am 50 years old, and I am married.

**Using format() within the print function
My name is Leo, I am 50 years old, and I am married.
```

A.1.2.5 Indentation in Python

Indentation refers to a set of spaces (usually four) on the left-hand side of a line of code. Some programming languages, like C, use {} to specify a block of code, but Python uses indentation. In the example shown in Code A.11, the last `print()` function will always print its message because it appears out of the `if-else` indented block, but the other `print()` functions will only print if their conditions are met.

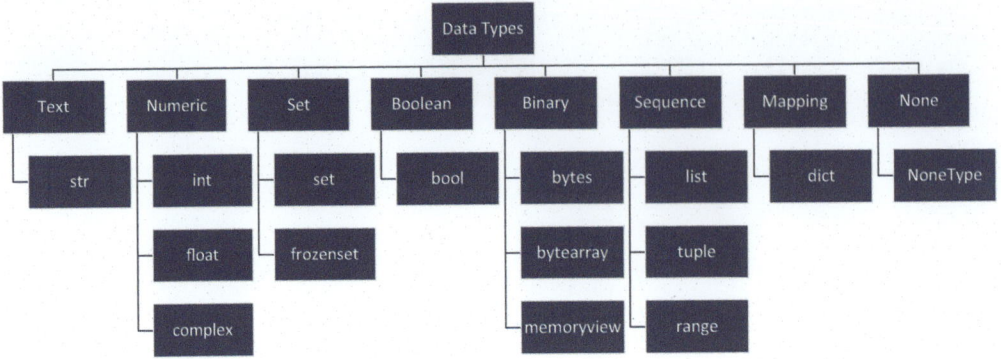

FIGURE A.1   Built-in data types in Python 3.0.

CODE A.11   Use of indentation in Python.

```python
# Indentation in Python
var1 = int(input('Enter an integer value from 1 to 10: '))
if var1 > 5:
    print('The value is greater than 5')
    print('*If* tested')
else:
    print('The value is smaller than 5')
    print('*Else* tested')
print('Program finished (always printed)')
```

```
Output
Enter an integer value from 1 to 10:   4
The value is smaller than 5
*Else* tested
Program finished (always printed)
```

A.1.3 Data Types in Python

A *data type* is a classification or categorization of a collection or set of data items, which represents the type of value and specifies the possible operations on each value type. In Python, data types are *classes*, and variables are *objects* instantiated from these classes. Figure A.1 and Code A.12 summarize the standard built-in data types in Python 3.0. An online help on Python's data types can be found at https://docs.python.org/3/library/datatypes.html.

CODE A.12   Main built-in data types in Python. Note that all variables are instances of an object.

```python
var = 'Exploratory Data Analysis'; print(type(var),'Example: ',var)
var = 10; print(type(var),'Example: ',var)
var = 10.35; print(type(var),'Example: ',var)
var = complex(1,2); print(type(var),'Example: ',var)
var = ['one','two', 'three']; print(type(var),'Example: ',var)
var = ('one','two', 'three'); print(type(var),'Example: ',var)
var = range(10); print(type(var),'Example: ',var)
var = {'one','two', 'three'}; print(type(var),'Example: ',var)
var = {'Temperature' : '70', 'Scale' : 'Farenheit'}; print(type(var),
                                                'Example: ',var)
var = frozenset({'one','two', 'three'}); print(type(var),'Example: ',var)
var = False; print(type(var),'Example: ',var)
```

```
var = b'one'; print(type(var),'Example: ',var)
var = bytearray(10); print(type(var),'Example: ',var)
var = memoryview(bytes(10)); print(type(var),'Example: ',var)
var = None; print(type(var),'Example: ',var)

Output
<class 'str'> Example:  Exploratory Data Analysis
<class 'int'> Example:  10
<class 'float'> Example:  10.35
<class 'complex'> Example:  (1+2j)
<class 'list'> Example:  ['one', 'two', 'three']
<class 'tuple'> Example:  ('one', 'two', 'three')
<class 'range'> Example:  range(0, 10)
<class 'set'> Example:  {'two', 'three', 'one'}
<class 'dict'> Example:  {'Temperature': '70', 'Scale': 'Farenheit'}
<class 'frozenset'> Example:  frozenset({'two', 'three', 'one'})
<class 'bool'> Example:  False
<class 'bytes'> Example:  b'one'
<class 'bytearray'> Example:  bytearray(b'\x00\x00\x00\x00\x00\x00\x00\x00\x00\x00')
<class 'memoryview'> Example:  <memory at 0x00000270085F2A40>
<class 'NoneType'> Example:  None
```

A.1.3.1 Numeric

Numeric data types are the most common and used ones in exploratory data analysis. Operating with them is a standard process in Python, as shown in Code A.13 with the basic arithmetic operations.

CODE A.13   Manipulating numeric data types.

```
# Numeric data types
n1 = 10
n2 = 5.5
n3 = 1 + 2j
print(type(n1),type(n2),type(n3))
print(float(n1)) # Convert only to print
print(int(n2)) # Convert only to print
# Main arithmetic operations
print('n1+n2 =',n1+n2)
print('n1-n2 =',n1-n2)
print('n1/n2 =',n1/n2)
print('Floored: n1//n2 =',n1//n2) # Floored quotient
print('Remainder: n1%n2 =',n1%n2) # Remainder
print('n1*n2 =',n1*n2)
print('n1^2 =',n1**2)
print('pow(n1,2) =',pow(n1,2))

Output
<class 'int'> <class 'float'> <class 'complex'>
10.0
5
n1+n2 = 15.5
n1-n2 = 4.5
n1/n2 = 1.8181818181818181
Floored: n1//n2 = 1.0
Remainder: n1%n2 = 4.5
n1*n2 = 55.0
n1^2 = 100
pow(n1,2) = 100
```

A.1.3.2 Strings

A *string* is a data type that represents a sequence of characters, often implemented as an *array* data structure. In Python, it is a collection of characters placed within *single*, *double*, or *triple* quotes. Strings are indexed structures that can be accessed by specifying their indices in a *forward* (from 0 to $N-1$, where N is the string length) or *backward* manner (from $-N$ to -1, where N is the string length). Several operations can be performed with strings, such as *comparison*, *concatenation*, *replacement*, and many others. Code A.14 illustrates some forms of manipulating strings. Note that the method `replace(old,new,count)` accepts as input the substring to be replaced `(old)`, the new substring that will substitute the old one `(new)`, and the number of times the replacements has to be performed `(count)`.

CODE A.14   Manipulating strings.

```
# Strings: accessing, concatenating, replacing
p1 = 'My name is'
p2 = 'Leandro de Castro'
print(p1[0:2]) # Accessing the first two characters
print(p1[:2]) # Accessing the first two characters (alternative)
print(p1[3:7]) # Accessing the substring 'name' (chars 4 to 7)
print(p2[-6:]) # Backward accessing the substring 'Castro'
p3 = p1+' '+p2 # Concatenating strings
print(p3)
ind = p3.find('name') # Find the index of a string within p3
print(ind)
p4 = p2.replace('de Castro','Silva')
print('My new name is',p4) # Replace a substring

Output
My
My
name
Castro
My name is Leandro de Castro
3
My new name is Leandro Silva
```

A.1.3.3 Lists

A *list* is an ordered collection of data used to store multiple items in a single variable. Items can be of different types, must be separated by commas and the whole list must be within square brackets. Each item in a list has an index starting with [0], then [1], and the list goes on. A number of operations can be performed on lists by using specific methods, such as `append()`, `remove()`, `pop()`, `insert()`, `count()`, `sort()`, `reverse()`, `copy()`, and others. Code A.15 illustrates how to manipulate lists and use specific list methods.

CODE A.15   Manipulating lists.

```
# Lists: declaring, reading, and operating
mylist = ['There','are',50,'states','in','USA']
print(type(mylist)) # Print the data type
print(mylist) # Print the whole list
print(mylist[0],mylist[2],mylist[5]) # Print items in a list
print(len(mylist)) # List length
```

```
mylist.append(30.2) # Append an item to the end of the list
print(mylist)
mylist.remove(30.2) # Remove an item from the list
print(mylist)
mylist.pop(2) # Remove item at position 3
print(mylist)
mylist.insert(2,50) # Insert item '50' at index 3
print(mylist)
print(mylist.count('states')) # Number of times the word 'states' appear
mylist.reverse(); print(mylist) # Reversing the list
```

```
Output
<class 'list'>
['There', 'are', 50, 'states', 'in', 'USA']
There 50 USA
6
['There', 'are', 50, 'states', 'in', 'USA', 30.2]
['There', 'are', 50, 'states', 'in', 'USA']
['There', 'are', 'states', 'in', 'USA']
['There', 'are', 50, 'states', 'in', 'USA']
1
['USA', 'in', 'states', 50, 'are', 'There']
```

A.1.3.4 Tuples

A *tuple* is similar to a list in the sense that it represents an ordered collection of objects separated by commas but within parentheses instead of brackets. The difference between a tuple and a list is that tuples are immutable; that is, they cannot be modified after creation. Code A.16 illustrates how to create and manipulate tuples, and shows that if you try to assign a new value to an item in a tuple, it will generate an error message.

CODE A.16   Manipulating tuples.

```
# Tuples: declaring, reading, and operating
mytuple = ('There','are',50,'states','in','USA')
print(type(mytuple)) # Print the data type
print(mytuple) # Print the whole tuple
print(mytuple[0],mytuple[2],mytuple[5]) # Print items in a tuple
print(len(mytuple)) # Tuple length
newtuple = ('and',67,'counties','in','Florida.')
fulltuple = mytuple + newtuple # Concatenate tuples
print(fulltuple)
nestedtuple = (mytuple,newtuple)
print(nestedtuple) # Nested tuple
newtuple[1] = 50 # Tuples do not support item assignment
```

```
Output
<class 'tuple'>
('There', 'are', 50, 'states', 'in', 'USA')
There 50 USA
6
('There', 'are', 50, 'states', 'in', 'USA', 'and', 67, 'counties', 'in',
'Florida.')
(('There', 'are', 50, 'states', 'in', 'USA'), ('and', 67, 'counties', 'in',
'Florida.'))
---------------------------------------------------------------------------
TypeError                                         Traceback (most recent call last)
```

```
Cell In[145], line 13
    11 nestedtuple = (mytuple,newtuple)
    12 print(nestedtuple) # Nested tuple
---> 13 newtuple[1] = 50

TypeError: 'tuple' object does not support item assignment
```

A.1.3.5 Range

Range(start,stop,step) is a function that generates an immutable sequence of numbers starting in start, up to stop, with increments of step. It is a very useful function in *loop* operations, such as the while and for structures. Its arguments must be integers, and the default values for start and step are 0 and 1, respectively. The only necessary argument is stop, indicating the sequence's final number. The contents of a range rg can be calculated by: rg[i] = start + step*i. Code A.17 illustrates some uses of the range() function.

CODE A.17   Manipulating the range function.

```
rg = range(10) # Create the sequence
print(type(rg)) # Print the type
print(list(rg)) # Transform in a list
print(tuple(rg)) # Transform in a tuple
rg = range(0,10,2) # Steps of 2
print(list(rg))
rg = range(0,-10,-1) # Steps of -1
print(list(rg))
print(rg[2]) # Accessing an item by its index

Output
<class 'range'>
[0, 1, 2, 3, 4, 5, 6, 7, 8, 9]
(0, 1, 2, 3, 4, 5, 6, 7, 8, 9)
[0, 2, 4, 6, 8]
[0, -1, -2, -3, -4, -5, -6, -7, -8, -9]
-2
```

A.1.3.6 Mapping Type: Dict

A *mapping* is a mutable object that uses a *key-value model* to store, access, and manipulate an ordered collection of items. In Python, *dictionaries*, dict(), are enclosed by curly brackets, and their items can be accessed using square brackets. *Keys* are the unique identifiers associated with each *value* in the key-value pair. Dictionaries are of great relevance for data analysis because they allow the assignment of values to a given object or variable within a data structure. Code A.18 shows several actions that can be performed with dictionaries, including reading, writing, adding key-value pairs, ordering, and reducing.

CODE A.18   Manipulating dictionaries.

```
# Dictionaries (dict)
dic_ages = {'Anna':27, 'Maria':33,'Peter':42,'Robert':35}
print('Original dictionary:',dic_ages)
dic_ages['Allyson'] = 29 # Adding a person to the dict
print('Increased dictionary:',dic_ages)
```

```
keys = dic_ages.keys()
print('Keys:',keys) # Print all keys
print('Values:',dic_ages.values()) # Print all values
# Print value for key = Maria
print('Maria is {v1}-years old.'.format(v1=dic_ages['Maria']))
dic_ages['Allyson'] = 20 # Updating Allyson's age
print('Updated Allyson age:',dic_ages)
dic_ages = dict(sorted(dic_ages.items())) # Sorting the keys
print('Ordered dictionary:',dic_ages)
del dic_ages['Allyson'] # Removing Allyson from the dictionary
print('Reduced dictionary:',dic_ages)

Output
Original dictionary: {'Anna': 27, 'Maria': 33, 'Peter': 42, 'Robert': 35}
Increased dictionary: {'Anna': 27, 'Maria': 33, 'Peter': 42, 'Robert': 35,
'Allyson': 29}
Keys: dict_keys(['Anna', 'Maria', 'Peter', 'Robert', 'Allyson'])
Values: dict_values([27, 33, 42, 35, 29])
Maria is 33-years old.
Updated Allyson age: {'Anna': 27, 'Maria': 33, 'Peter': 42, 'Robert': 35, 'Allyson': 20}
Ordered dictionary: {'Allyson': 20, 'Anna': 27, 'Maria': 33, 'Peter': 42, 'Robert': 35}
Reduced dictionary: {'Anna': 27, 'Maria': 33, 'Peter': 42, 'Robert': 35}
```

A.1.3.7 Boolean

The *boolean* data type, `bool()`, allows a variable to assume either a `True` or a `False` value, and is normally used as the *truth value* of an expression. Code A.19 shows how the basics of the Boolean data type work.

CODE A.19   The Boolean data type.

```
# Boolean data type
v1 = 5
v2 = 10
comp = v1==v2
print(type(comp))
print('Is v1 equals to v2?',comp)
print('Is v1 different from v2?',v1!=v2)
print('Is v1 equals to v2?',bool(v1==v2))

Output
<class 'bool'>
Is v1 equals to v2? False
Is v1 different from v2? True
Is v1 equals to v2? False
```

A.1.3.8 Set and Frozenset

A *set* is an unordered, mutable, and iterable collection of items with no duplicates. In Python, a set can be created using the built-in `set()` function and a sequence or an iterable object separated by commas and placed within curly brackets (Code A.20a). The `set()` function allows different types of data and is normally used to test membership or eliminate duplicate entries. Sets allow a number of logical and mathematical operations, such as *union*, *intersection*, *difference*, and *symmetric difference* (Code A.20b). *Frozenset* is an immutable set type whose contents cannot be changed after created and, thus, can be used as a dictionary key or part of another set.

CODE A.20   Sets and their operations.

```
# Creating sets
# Directly creating set s1
print('**Creating sets')
s1 = {'soccer','basketball','baseball','football','soccer'}
print('Creating s1 directly:',s1)
# Creating set s1 using function set()
s1 = set(['soccer','basketball','baseball','football','soccer'])
print('Using function set():',s1)
s2 = {'volleyball','baseball','table_tennis','tennis'}
print('\n**Available sets \nS1:',s1)
print('S2:',s2)
```

```
Output
**Creating sets
Creating s1 directly: {'basketball', 'football', 'soccer', 'baseball'}
Using function set(): {'basketball', 'football', 'soccer', 'baseball'}

**Available sets
S1: {'basketball', 'football', 'soccer', 'baseball'}
S2: {'tennis', 'table_tennis', 'volleyball', 'baseball'}
```

```
# Set operations
print('\n**Set operations')
print('Union:',s1|s2) # Union
print('Intersection:',s1&s2) # Intersection
print('Difference (s1-s2):',s1-s2) # Difference (In s1 but not in s2)
print('Symmetric Difference:',s1^s2) # Symmetric difference
a = 'table_tennis'
# Membership
print('\n**Membership')
print('Is', a, 'in', s1,'?', a in s1)
print('Is', a, 'in', s2,'?', a in s2)
```

```
Output
**Set operations
Union: {'basketball', 'tennis', 'table_tennis', 'football', 'soccer',
'volleyball', 'baseball'}
Intersection: {'baseball'}
Difference (s1-s2): {'basketball', 'football', 'soccer'}
Symmetric Difference: {'basketball', 'soccer', 'tennis', 'table_tennis',
'football', 'volleyball'}

**Membership
Is table_tennis in {'basketball', 'football', 'soccer', 'baseball'} ? False
Is table_tennis in {'tennis', 'table_tennis', 'volleyball', 'baseball'} ? True
```

A.1.3.9 Binary: Bytes, Bytearray, Memoryview

Binary data may be very common in data science applications. Python has two main data types to manipulate binary data: *bytes* and *bytearray* (Code A.21), both supported by *memoryview*. As can be observed in Code A.21a, *bytes* are immutable sequences of bytes whose syntax uses a prefix b. As *bytes* are immutable, *bytearray* can be used as a mutable alternative (Code A.21b). *Memoryview* is an object that accesses the internal data of an object that supports the buffer (internal data) protocol without copying. It allows direct reading and writing access to the data of an object without the need to copy it in advance, promoting a gain in performance.

CODE A.21   Using bytes and bytearray.

```
# Bytes
bstr = bytes(b'String of bytes')
print(type(bstr))
print(bstr)
print('Bytes string length:',len(bstr))
print('Print a substrings of bytes:',bstr[7:9])
bstr[7:9] = b'in' # Bytes are immutable

Output
<class 'bytes'>
b'String of bytes'
Bytes string length: 15
Print a substrings of bytes: b'of'
------------------------------------------------------------------------
TypeError                               Traceback (most recent call last)
Cell In[159], line 8
      6 print('Bytes string length:',len(bstr))
      7 print('Print a substrings of bytes:',bstr[7:9])
----> 8 bstr[7:9] = b'in'

TypeError: 'bytes' object does not support item assignment

# Bytearray
bastr = bytearray(b'String of bytes')
print(type(bastr))
print('Print the original bytearray:',bastr)
print('Bytearray string length:',len(bastr))
print('Print a substrings of bytearray:',bastr[7:9])
bastr[7:9] = b'in' # Bytearrays are mutable
print('Print the mutated bytearray:',bastr)
print('Print the original bytearray:',bastr.replace(b' in',b' of'))

Output
<class 'bytearray'>
Print the original bytearray: bytearray(b'String of bytes')
Bytearray string length: 15
Print a substrings of bytearray: bytearray(b'of')
Print the mutated bytearray: bytearray(b'String in bytes')
Print the original bytearray: bytearray(b'String of bytes')
```

A.1.3.10 NoneType

The None keyword represents the absence of a value and is the single object that can be instantiated from the class *NoneType* (Code A.22). None is a data type in itself and shall not be confused with an empty string, null, 0, or False.

CODE A.22   NoneType data type.

```
# None
v1 = None
print(v1)
print(type(v1))

Output
None
<class 'NoneType'>
```

A.1.4 Control Structures

Control structures are code blocks responsible for analyzing conditions (e.g., variables) and deciding a path to follow, a repetition, or a bypass to make based on specific parameters. This is because a program may not follow a linear sequence of steps during execution.

The three basic control structures are *sequence control structures*, *decision control structures*, and *repetition control structures*. Sequence control structures correspond to the line-by-line, sequential execution of a program in the order they appear in the code. Decision control structures define the path of execution based on some conditional statements, and repetition control structures allow the execution of a code block multiple times until a specific condition is met. As sequence control structures have been studied previously, only decision and repetition control structures will be reviewed here.

A.1.4.1 Decision Control Structures

Conditional statements, also called *decision-making statements* or *decision control structures*, are used in programming to control the flow of program execution, that is, they evaluate specific information (conditions) and, based on the results, take specific decisions. Basically, if the condition is True, then a certain code block will be executed; otherwise, another code block will be executed. There are basically five types of conditional statements in Python:

- `if` statement (Code A.23a).

- `if-else` statement (Code A.23b).

- `if-elif` statement (Code A.23c).

- Nested-`if` statement (Code A.23d).

- `if-elif-else` ladder (Code A.23e).

Remember that Python uses indentation (instead of brackets) to separate code blocks and does not require commas or semicolons at the end of lines; thus, the syntax for each of the three types of statements becomes very simple.

CODE A.23   Conditional statements. (a) If. (b) If-else. (c) If-elif. (d) Nested if. (e) If-elif-else.

```
# If statement
dic_ages = {'Anna':27, 'Maria':33,'Peter':42,'Robert':35}
if dic_ages['Anna'] > 18:
    print('Anna is of legal age')
print('End of code')

Output
Anna is of legal age
End of code

# If-else statement
# Condition 1
dic_ages = {'Anna':27, 'Maria':33,'Peter':42,'Robert':35}
```

```python
print('*Anna is',dic_ages['Anna'],'years old*')
if dic_ages['Anna'] > 18:
    print('Anna is of legal age')
else:
    print('Anna is underage')
print('End of code') # New code block

# Condition 2
dic_ages = {'Anna':17, 'Maria':33,'Peter':42,'Robert':35}
print('\n*Anna is',dic_ages['Anna'],'years old*')
if dic_ages['Anna'] > 18:
    print('Anna is of legal age')
else:
    print('Anna is underage')
print('End of code') # New code block
```

Output
```
*Anna is 27 years old*
Anna is of legal age
End of code

*Anna is 17 years old*
Anna is underage
End of code
```

```python
# If-elif statement
# Condition 1
dic_ages = {'Anna':27, 'Maria':73,'Peter':42,'Robert':35}
print('*Anna is',dic_ages['Anna'],'years old*')
print('*Maria is',dic_ages['Maria'],'years old*')
if dic_ages['Anna'] < 18:
    print('Anna is underage')
elif dic_ages['Maria'] >= 65:
    print('Maria is an older adult and Anna is an adult')
print('End of code') # New code block

# Condition 2
dic_ages = {'Anna':27, 'Maria':63,'Peter':42,'Robert':35}
print('\n*Anna is',dic_ages['Anna'],'years old*')
print('*Maria is',dic_ages['Maria'],'years old*')
if dic_ages['Anna'] < 18:
    print('Anna is underage')
elif dic_ages['Maria'] >= 65:
    print('Maria is an older adult')
print('End of code') # New code block
```

Output
```
*Anna is 27 years old*
*Maria is 73 years old*
Maria is an older adult and Anna is an adult
End of code

*Anna is 27 years old*
*Maria is 63 years old*
End of code
```

```python
# Nested if statements
dic_ages = {'Anna':27, 'Maria':73,'Peter':42,'Robert':35}
```

```
print('*Maria is',dic_ages['Maria'],'years old*')
if dic_ages['Maria'] >= 18:
    print('Maria is an adult')
    if dic_ages['Maria'] >= 65:
        print('Maria is an older adult')
print('End of code') # New code block
```

```
Output
*Maria is 73 years old*
Maria is an adult
Maria is an older adult
End of code
```

```
# If-elif-else statement
# Condition 1
dic_ages = {'Anna':27, 'Maria':73,'Peter':42,'Robert':35}
print('*Anna is',dic_ages['Anna'],'years old*')
print('*Maria is',dic_ages['Maria'],'years old*')
if dic_ages['Anna'] < 18:
    print('Anna is underage')
elif dic_ages['Maria'] >= 65:
    print('Maria is an older adult and Anna is an adult')
else:
    print('Maria is an adult')
print('End of code') # New code block
```

```
# Condition 2
dic_ages = {'Anna':27, 'Maria':63,'Peter':42,'Robert':35}
print('\n*Anna is',dic_ages['Anna'],'years old*')
print('*Maria is',dic_ages['Maria'],'years old*')
if dic_ages['Anna'] < 18:
    print('Anna is underage')
elif dic_ages['Maria'] >= 65:
    print('Maria is an older adult')
else:
    print('Maria and Anna are adults')
print('End of code') # New code block
```

```
Output
*Anna is 27 years old*
*Maria is 73 years old*
Maria is an older adult and Anna is an adult
End of code

*Anna is 27 years old*
*Maria is 63 years old*
Maria and Anna are adults
End of code
```

A.1.4.2 Repetition Control Structures

Repetition control structures, also called *loop statements* or *loop instructions*, allow the repetition of one or more steps in a block of code until a specific condition is met. This has given a lot of power to computers, because it has allowed the repetition of steps as much as required. There are basically two types of looping structures: *while loops* and *for loops*.

A.1.4.2.1 While

In Python, the *while loop* is implemented similarly to the if statement, that is,

```
while condition:
    statement(s)
```

In this syntax, all the statement(s) will be executed until the condition turns `False,` and then the line immediately after the loop will be executed. Again, for the statement(s) to be executed, all of them must be within the same code block (i.e., with the same indentation). Code A.24 shows how to use the while loop to append items to a list and to iterate over a list.

CODE A.24   While loop.

```
# While statement (creating a list)
stop = 5; it = 0; v = []
while it < stop:
    it = it + 1
    v.append(it)
    print(it) # Print every iteration
print('The list is:',v) # Print after the while loop

Output
1
2
3
4
5
The list is: [1, 2, 3, 4, 5]

# While statement (counting and conditional statement)
s1 = ['soccer', 'basketball', 'tennis', 'table_tennis', 'football',
      'baseball', 'volleyball']
it = 0; soma = 0
print('List s1:',s1)
while it < len(s1)-1:
    if s1[it] != 'table_tennis':
        soma = soma + 1
    it = it + 1
print('The number of items different from table_tennis is:', it)

Output
List s1: ['soccer', 'basketball', 'tennis', 'table_tennis', 'football',
'baseball', 'volleyball']
The number of items different from table_tennis is: 6
```

A.1.4.2.2 For

The *loop statement* is different from the *while statement* in the sense that the loop is used for a sequential traversal, that is, it iterates (repeats) once for each item in a sequence. Thus, at each iteration in the loop, it is possible to access the current item of the sequence. In Python, the loop statement is particularly useful to deal with strings, sequences, mapping, and set data types, because it allows the program to iterate over the characters or items in a simple way, as illustrated in Code A.25.

CODE A.25   **For loop.**

```
# For statement (creating a list)
stop = 5; it = 0; v = []
for it in range(stop):
    it = it + 1
    v.append(it)
    print(it) # Print every iteration
print('The list is:',v) # Print after the while loop
```

```
Output
1
2
3
4
5
The list is: [1, 2, 3, 4, 5]
```

```
# For statement (iterating over a string)
p1 = 'My name is'
print('String p1:',p1)
for i in p1:
    print(i)
```

```
Output
String p1: My name is
M
y

n
a
m
e

i
s
```

```
# For statement (iterating over a list)
s1 = ['soccer', 'basketball', 'tennis', 'table_tennis', 'football',
      'baseball', 'volleyball']
print('List s1:',s1)
for i in s1:
    print(i)
print(type(i))
```

```
Output
List s1: ['soccer', 'basketball', 'tennis', 'table_tennis', 'football',
'baseball', 'volleyball']
soccer
basketball
tennis
table_tennis
football
baseball
volleyball
<class 'str'>
```

```
# For statement (iterating over a tuple)
mytuple = ('There','are',50,'states','in','USA')
```

```
print('Tuple mytuple:',mytuple)
for i in mytuple:
    print(i)
print(type(i))
```

```
Output
Tuple mytuple: ('There', 'are', 50, 'states', 'in', 'USA')
There
are
50
states
in
USA
<class 'str'>
```

```
# For statement (iterating over a dictionary)
dic_ages = {'Anna':27, 'Maria':33,'Peter':42,'Robert':35}
print('Dictionary dic_ages:',dic_ages)
for i in dic_ages:
    print('%s %d' % (i,dic_ages[i]))
print(type(i),type(dic_ages[i]))
```

```
Output
Dictionary dic_ages: {'Anna': 27, 'Maria': 33, 'Peter': 42, 'Robert': 35}
Anna 27
Maria 33
Peter 42
Robert 35
<class 'str'> <class 'int'>
```

```
# For statement (iterating over a set)
s1 = {'soccer','basketball','baseball','football','soccer'}
print('Set s1:',s1)
for i in s1:
    print(i)
print(type(i))
```

```
Output
Set s1: {'basketball', 'football', 'soccer', 'baseball'}
basketball
football
soccer
baseball
<class 'str'>
```

A.1.5 Functions

A *function* is a reusable block of code written to perform a specific task. In addition to several built-in functions in Python (Table A.1), it is also possible to create your own. The default syntax of a function in Python is:

```
def function_name(parameters):
    statement(s)
    return output(s)
```

The keyword def is necessary to identify the definition of a function; the function *arguments* are optional and entered as parameters within parentheses after the

TABLE A.1   Built-in Functions in Python

abs()	aiter()	all()	any()
anext()	ascii()	bin()	bool()
breakpoint()	bytearray()	bytes()	callable()
chr()	classmethod()	compile()	complex()
delattr()	dict()	dir()	divmod()
enumerate()	eval()	exec()	filter()
float()	format()	frozenset()	getattr()
globals()	hasattr()	hash()	help()
hex()	id()	input()	int()
isinstance()	issubclass()	iter()	len()
list()	locals()	map()	max()
memoryview()	min()	next()	object()
oct()	open()	ord()	pow()
print()	property()	range()	repr()
reversed()	round()	set()	setattr()
slice()	sorted()	staticmethod()	str()
sum()	super()	tuple()	type()
vars()	zip()	__import__()	

function _ name. The `return` statement, which is also optional, outputs the result of the function. Code A.26 illustrates how to create simple functions, how to define the type of parameters and use the return statement, and how to manipulate dictionaries in Python.

CODE A.26   Creating functions in Python.

```python
# Function example 1
def my_first_function():
    print("I am a data analyst")
my_first_function() # Call to function my_first_function

Output
I am a data analyst
# Function example 2
def my_func():
    name = input('Enter your name: ')
    print('Your name is',name)
my_func()

Output
Enter your name:  Leandro de Castro
Your name is Leandro de Castro

# Function calculates the area of a square
def fsq_area(sq_side:float):
    sq_area = sq_side*sq_side
    print('The area of the square is',sq_area,'sqmt')
    return(sq_area)

print('*Function calculates the area of a square*')
sq_side = float(input('Size of the square side:'))
fsq_area(sq_side)
```

Output
Function calculates the area of a square
Size of the square side: 100
The area of the square is 10000.0 sqmt
[197]:
10000.0

```python
# Function determines if a number is even or odd
def feven_odd(val:int):
    if (val % 2 == 0):
        print('Answer: number',val,'is even')
    else:
        print('Answer: number',val,'is odd')


print('*Function determines if a number is even or odd*')
num = int(input('Input the number:'))
feven_odd(num)
```

Output
Function determines if a number is even or odd
Input the number: 33
Answer: number 33 is odd

```python
# Function using keyword arguments allows the user to enter the
# corresponding argument for each keyword independently of the order
def fpd(name:str,age:int):
    dic_ages = {}
    dic_ages[name] = age
    print(dic_ages)


fpd(age=50, name='Pietra')
```

Output
{'Pietra': 50}

```python
# Function fills in a dataset with personal data
def fpd(num): # Function personal data (fpd)
    dic_ages = {}
    for i in range(num):
        name = input('Name of user:')
        age = int(input('Age of user:'))
        dic_ages[name] = age
    print('Saved dataset (dict):',dic_ages)

print('*Function fills in a dataset with personal data*')
num = int(input('Number of users to save the data:'))
fpd(num)
```

Output
Function fills in a dataset with personal data
Number of users to save the data: 2
Name of user: Robert Shultz
Age of user: 44
Name of user: Marina Becks
Age of user: 29
Saved dataset (dict): {'Robert Shultz': 44, 'Marina Becks': 29}

A.1.6 Exercises

1. Write a function to convert degree Celsius (°C) into degree Fahrenheit (°F) and vice versa. Prompt the user which conversion will be performed, and then prompt the user for the temperature to be converted.

2. Write a function to convert square feet (ft²) into square meters (m²) and vice versa. Prompt the user which conversion will be performed, and then prompt the user for the area to be converted.

3. Use a repetition structure to write a function that draws a pyramid using '*' in the screen. The pyramid height must be an input parameter.

4. Write a function that determines if a word or sentence is a palindrome. A palindrome is a word or sentence that reads the same forward and backward.

5. Download the Mammographic dataset available at the UCI repository (link below) and extract the following information for the dataframe loaded: https://archive.ics. uci.edu/ml/datasets/Mammographic+Mass

   • Determine the number of missing values in variable Density (missing values are represented by "?" in this dataset).

   • Determine the number of objects in each of the classes (variable Severity).

   • Determine the maximal, minimal, and average age of the patients.
     Write a program that solves a specific problem by exploring at least two data types and two different control structures in Python.

NOTE

1 https://www.python.org/

Appendix B

Code Snippets for the Gestalt Principles of Chapter 4

CODE B.1:   Continuity Gestalt Principle.

```python
# 1. CONTINUITY GESTALT PRINCIPLE
# Code to illustrate the three cases of the Continuity Gestalt principle

from matplotlib.sankey import Sankey

# 1. Line chart connecting datapoints showing a continuous trend over time
x = np.linspace(0, 10, 100)
y = np.sin(x)
fig, axs = plt.subplots(1, 3, figsize=(12, 4))
axs[0].plot(x, y, 'o-', color='blue', linewidth=2)
axs[0].set_xlabel('X')
axs[0].set_ylabel('Y')
axs[0].set_xticks([]); axs[0].set_yticks([])
axs[0].set_title('Line Chart')

# 2. Sankey diagram (flow chart) using a series of arrows to show the flow of data

df = pd.DataFrame({'source': ['A', 'A', 'B', 'B', 'C', 'C'],
                   'target': ['B', 'C', 'D', 'E', 'F', 'G'],
                   'value': [1, 2, 3, 4, 5, 6]})
sankey = Sankey(ax=axs[1], scale=0.1, unit=None)
sankey.add(flows=df['value'], labels=df['source'], orientations=[0, 1, -1, 1, -1, 1])
sankey.finish()
axs[1].set_xticks([]); axs[1].set_yticks([])
axs[1].set_title('Sankey Diagram')

# 3. Scatterplot with a trend line, indicating a connection or trend
np.random.seed(123)
x = np.random.randn(100)
y = 2*x + np.random.randn(100)
axs[2].scatter(x, y, color='red', alpha=0.5)
coefficients = np.polyfit(x, y, 1)
trendline_x = np.linspace(np.min(x), np.max(x), 100)
trendline_y = coefficients[0]*trendline_x + coefficients[1]
```

```
axs[2].plot(trendline_x, trendline_y, color='blue', linewidth=2)
axs[2].set_xlabel('X')
axs[2].set_ylabel('Y')
axs[2].set_xticks([]); axs[2].set_yticks([])
axs[2].set_title('Scatterplot with Trend Line')

plt.tight_layout()
plt.show()
```

CODE B.2:   Closure Gestalt Principle.

```
# 2. CLOSURE GESTALT PRINCIPLE
# Code to illustrate the three cases of the Closure Gestalt principle

from wordcloud import WordCloud
import squarify
from PIL import Image
import matplotlib.pyplot as plt

# 1. Pie chart showing the closure of the pie
labels = ['Apples', 'Oranges', 'Bananas', 'Pears']
sizes = [25, 30, 20, 25]
pie_colors = ['skyblue', 'royalblue', 'deepskyblue', 'steelblue']  # Different
shades of blue
fig, axs = plt.subplots(1, 3, figsize=(12, 4))
axs[0].pie(sizes, labels=labels, colors=pie_colors, startangle=90,
autopct='%1.1f%%')
axs[0].set_title('Pie Chart')

# 2. Word cloud showing the cloud closed shape
text = 'The goal of EDA is to understand the distribution and structure of data, \
to summarize data characteristics, to extract insights and indicators from data, \
to identify relevance and/or select variables, to visualize potential
relationships \
between variables, to identify anomalies, to allow the application and/or
selection \
of learning-based methods'
mask = np.array(Image.open('comment.png'))
wordcloud = WordCloud(background_color=None, mode='RGBA', mask=mask,
colormap='Blues').generate(text)
axs[1].imshow(wordcloud, interpolation='bilinear')
axs[1].imshow(mask, alpha=0.3, cmap='gray', interpolation='bilinear')
axs[1].set_xticks([]); axs[1].set_yticks([])
axs[1].set_title('Word Cloud')

# 3. Treemap
values = [10, 20, 30, 15, 25]
labels = ['Apples', 'Oranges', 'Bananas', 'Pears', 'Grapes']
treemap_colors = ['lightblue', 'dodgerblue', 'cornflowerblue', 'mediumblue',
'navy']
squarify.plot(sizes=values, label=labels, color=treemap_colors, alpha=0.7,
ax=axs[2])
axs[2].set_xticks([]); axs[2].set_yticks([])
axs[2].set_title('Treemap')

# Adjust the layout and display the plot
fig.tight_layout()
plt.show()
```

CODE B.3: Proximity Gestalt Principle.

```python
# 3. PROXIMITY GESTALT PRINCIPLE
# Code to illustrate three cases of the Proximity Gestalt principle with the
Forest Fires data

import pandas as pd
import matplotlib.pyplot as plt
import seaborn as sns

# Load dataset
data = pd.read_csv('https://archive.ics.uci.edu/ml/machine-learning-databases/
forest-fires/\
forestfires.csv')

# 1. Heatmap showing neighboring regions with similar correlations in the map
fig, axs = plt.subplots(1, 3, figsize=(12,4))
sns.heatmap(data.corr(), cmap='coolwarm', ax=axs[0])
axs[0].set_title('Correlation Heatmap')

# 2. Scatter plot showing neighboring regions with similar burned area levels
axs[1].scatter(data['temp'], data['RH'], s=data['area'], alpha=0.5)
axs[1].set_xlabel('Temperature')
axs[1].set_ylabel('Relative Humidity')
axs[1].set_title('Temperature vs. Relative Humidity')

# 3. Bar chart showing sets of months with burned areas
month_groups = data.groupby('month').mean()['area']

# Sort the months based on the average burned area
month_groups_sorted = month_groups.sort_values()
axs[2].bar(month_groups_sorted.index, month_groups_sorted)
axs[2].set_xlabel('Month')
axs[2].set_ylabel('Average Burned Area')
axs[2].set_title('Average Burned Area by Month')
plt.xticks(rotation=90)  # Rotate the x-axis labels vertically

# Adjust the layout and display the plot
fig.tight_layout()
plt.show()
```

CODE B.4: Similarity Gestalt Principle.

```python
# 4. SIMILARITY GESTALT PRINCIPLE
# Code to illustrate three cases of the Similarity Gestalt principle with the Iris
data

import pandas as pd
import numpy as np
from sklearn.datasets import load_iris
import matplotlib.pyplot as plt
import seaborn as sns
from sklearn.datasets import load_iris

diris = load_iris()  # Load the Iris dataset from Scikitlearn

# 1. Line chart with lines representing different species having the same style
dfiris = pd.DataFrame(data= np.c_[diris['data'], diris['target']],
                      columns= diris['feature_names'] + ['target'])
```

```python
dfiris['species'] = pd.Categorical.from_codes(diris.target, diris.target_names)
fig, axs = plt.subplots(1, 3, figsize=(12,4))
sns.lineplot(data=dfiris, x='sepal length (cm)', y='petal length (cm)',
hue='species',
               style='species', ax=axs[0])
axs[0].set_title('Line Chart')


# 2. Bar chart with bars having the same color for each species
sns.countplot(data=dfiris, x='species', color='royalblue', ax=axs[1])
axs[1].set_title('Bar Chart')


# 3. Scatterplot with different markers representing different species
sns.scatterplot(data=dfiris, x='sepal length (cm)', y='petal length (cm)',
hue='species',
               style='species', ax=axs[2])
axs[2].set_title('Scatterplot')


# Adjust the layout and display the plots
plt.tight_layout()
plt.show()
```

CODE B.5: Symmetry Gestalt Principle.

```python
# 5. SYMMETRY GESTALT PRINCIPLE
# Code to illustrate three cases of the Symmetry Gestalt principle
# Iris dataset of Fischer available at the Scikitlearn library

import numpy as np
import matplotlib.pyplot as plt
from sklearn.datasets import load_iris

diris = load_iris()  # Load the Iris dataset from Scikitlearn

# 1. Boxplot with symmetrically placed boxes around the median line
fig, axs = plt.subplots(figsize=(6, 4))
axs.boxplot([diris.data[diris.target == i, 0] for i in range(3)],

               sym='', widths=0.6, patch_artist=True,
               boxprops=dict(facecolor='royalblue', edgecolor='black'),
               whiskerprops=dict(color='black', linestyle='-'),
               medianprops=dict(color='black'),
               capprops=dict(color='black', linestyle='-'))

axs.set_xticklabels(diris.target_names)
axs.set_ylabel('Sepal Length (cm)')
axs.set_title('Boxplot')


# 2. Mirrored bar chart with symmetrically arranged bars around the vertical axis
fig, axs = plt.subplots(figsize=(6, 4))
y_pos = np.arange(len(diris.target_names))
axs.barh(y_pos, [diris.data[diris.target==0, 1].mean(), diris.data[diris.
target==1, 1].mean(),
               diris.data[diris.target==2, 1].mean()], align='center',
       color=['royalblue', 'royalblue', 'royalblue'])
axs.barh(y_pos, [-1*diris.data[diris.target==0, 1].mean(),
               -1*diris.data[diris.target==1, 1].mean(),
               -1*diris.data[diris.target==2, 1].mean()], align='center',
       color=['royalblue', 'royalblue', 'royalblue'])
axs.set_yticks(y_pos)
axs.set_yticklabels(diris.target_names)
```

```
axs.set_title('Mirrored Bar Chart (Petal Width)')

# 3. Radar chart with symmetrically arranged data points around the center point
fig = plt.figure(figsize=(15, 5))
axs = fig.add_subplot(polar=True)
angles = np.linspace(0, 2*np.pi, len(diris.feature_names), endpoint=False)
angles = np.concatenate((angles,[angles[0]]))
line = ['-','--','-.']
for i in range(3):
    values = diris.data[diris.target==i].mean(axis=0)
    values = np.concatenate((values,[values[0]]))
    axs.plot(angles, values, label=diris.target_names[i], ls=line[i])
plt.xticks(angles[:-1], diris.feature_names)
plt.yticks([2, 4, 6, 8], ["2", "4", "6", "8"], color="grey", size=12)
axs.legend()
axs.set_title('Radar Chart')

# Display the plot
plt.show()
```

CODE B.6:   Figure-Ground Gestalt Principle.

```
# 6. FIGURE-GROUND GESTALT PRINCIPLE
# Code to illustrate three cases of the Figure-ground Gestalt principle
# Car dataset available at UCI and in mwaskom Github

import geopandas as gpd
import plotly.express as px

# Load the auto-mpg dataset
# https://archive.ics.uci.edu/ml/machine-learning-databases/auto-mpg/
# Also available at: https://raw.githubusercontent.com/mwaskom/seaborn-data/
master/mpg.csv
cars = pd.read_csv('mpg.csv')

# 1. Scatterplot with colored background
fig, ax = plt.subplots(figsize=(7, 4))
ax.scatter(cars['weight'], cars['mpg'], c='blue', alpha=0.8)
ax.set_facecolor('#FFA500')  # '#F2F3F4'
ax.set_xlabel('Weight')
ax.set_ylabel('Miles per gallon')
ax.set_title('Scatterplot: MPG by Weight')
plt.show()

# 2. Bubble chart
# Load the Gapminder dataset
data_url = 'https://raw.githubusercontent.com/plotly/datasets/master/
gapminderDataFiveYear.csv'
dgapminder = pd.read_csv(data_url)
year = 2007  # Filter the data for a specific year
df_year = dgapminder[dgapminder['year'] == year]
fig = px.scatter(df_year, x='gdpPercap', y='lifeExp', size='pop',
color='continent',
                 log_x=True, hover_name='country', labels={'gdpPercap': 'GDP per
capita (USD)',
                                                           'lifeExp': 'Life
expectancy (years)'},
                 width=650, height=380)
fig.update_layout(plot_bgcolor='rgba(240,240,240,0.7)')
fig.show()
```

```
# 3. Choropleth map
world = gpd.read_file(gpd.datasets.get_path('naturalearth_lowres'))
world.plot(column='pop_est', legend=True, figsize=(10, 6))
plt.title('Choropleth map: World Population')
plt.show()
```

CODE B.7:   Common Fate Gestalt Principle.

```
# 7. COMMON FATE GESTALT PRINCIPLE
# Code to illustrate three cases of the Common Fate Gestalt principle
# Gapminder dataset available at UCI and the Karate Club data in Networkx

import pandas as pd
import numpy as np
import plotly.express as px  # Include Plotly Express
import matplotlib.pyplot as plt
import networkx as nx  # Include NetworkX

# 1. Motion chart using the Gapminder dataset
dgapminder = px.data.gapminder()
fig = px.scatter(dgapminder, x="gdpPercap", y="lifeExp", animation_frame="year",
                 size="pop", color="continent", hover_name="country", width=550,
                 height=380, log_x=True, range_x=[100,100000], range_y=[20,90],
                 labels=dict(gdpPercap="GDP per capita", lifeExp="Life
expectancy"))
fig.show()

# 2. Streamgraph with randomly generated data
dates = pd.date_range('20220101', periods=50)  # Create sample data
values = np.random.randint(1, 10, size=(50, 4))
df = pd.DataFrame(values, index=dates, columns=['A', 'B', 'C', 'D'])
fig, ax = plt.subplots(figsize=(8, 4))
ax.stackplot(df.index, df.values.T, baseline='wiggle', labels=df.columns)
plt.xticks(rotation=45)  # Adjust the angle as needed
plt.title('Sample Streamgraph')
plt.show()
# 3. Force-directed graph using the Karate Club Graph data
G = nx.karate_club_graph()
pos = nx.spring_layout(G)
# Calculate communities using Louvain method
from networkx.algorithms.community import greedy_modularity_communities
communities = list(greedy_modularity_communities(G))
# Assign colors based on community membership
node_colors = []
for node in G.nodes():
    for i, community in enumerate(communities):
        if node in community:
            node_colors.append(i)
            break
# Draw the graph
plt.figure(figsize=(10, 6))
nx.draw(G, pos, with_labels=True, node_color=node_colors, cmap=plt.cm.tab10,
node_size=300)
plt.title('Force-Directed Graph with Common Fate Illustration')
plt.show()
```

Appendix C
LIWC and Stanford PoS Tagger Categories

C.1 LIWC 2001 OUTPUT VARIABLE INFORMATION[1]

Dimension	Abbreviation	Examples
I. Standard Linguistic Dimensions		
Word Count	WC	
Words per sentence	WPS	
Sentences ending with?	Qmarks	
Unique words (type/token ratio)	Unique	
% words captured, dictionary words	Dic	
% words longer than six letters	Sixltr	
Total pronouns	Pronoun	I, our, they, you're
First person singular	I	I, my, me
First person plural	We	We, our, us
Total first person	Self	I, we, me
Total second person	You	You, you'll
Total third person	Other	She, their, them
Negations	Negate	No, never, not
Assents	Assent	Yes, OK, mmhmm
Articles	Article	A, an, the
Prepositions	Preps	On, to, from
Numbers	Number	One, thirty, million

(Continued)

Dimension	Abbreviation	Examples
II. Psychological Processes		
Affective or emotional processes	Affect	Happy, ugly, bitter
Positive emotions	Posemo	Happy, pretty, good
Positive feelings	Posfeel	Happy, joy, love
Optimism and energy	Optim	Certainty, pride, win
Negative emotions	Negemo	Hate, worthless, enemy
Anxiety or fear	Anx	Nervous, afraid, tense
Anger	Anger	Hate, kill, pissed
Sadness or depression	Sad	Grief, cry, sad
Cognitive processes	Cogmech	
Causation	Cause	Because, effect, hence
Insight	Insight	Think, know, consider
Discrepancy	Discrep	Should, would, could
Inhibition	Inhib	Block, constrain
Tentative	Tentat	Maybe, perhaps, guess
Certainty	Certain	Always, never
Sensory and perceptual processes	Senses see, touch, listen	
Seeing	See	View, saw, look
Hearing	Hear	Heard, listen, sound
Feeling	Feel	Touch, hold, felt
Social processes	Social	Talk, us, friend
Communication	Comm	Talk, share, converse
Other references to people	Othref	1st pl, 2nd, 3rd per prns
Friends	Friends	Pal, buddy, coworker
Family	Family	Mom, brother, cousin
Humans	Humans	Boy, woman, group
III. Relativity		
Time	Time	Hour, day, o'clock
Past tense verb	Past	Walked, were, had
Present tense verb	Present	Walk, is, be
Future tense verb	Future	Will, might, shall
Space	Space	Around, over, up
Up	Up	Up, above, over
Down	Down	Down, below, under
Inclusive	Incl	With, and, include
Exclusive	Excl	But, except, without
Motion	Motion	Walk, move, go
IV. Personal Concerns		
Occupation	Occup	Work, class, boss
School	School	Class, student, college
Job or work	Job	Employ, boss, career
Achievement	Achieve	Try, goal, win
Leisure activity	Leisure	House, TV, music
Home	Home	House, kitchen, lawn

(Continued)

Dimension	Abbreviation	Examples
Sports	Sports	Football, game, play
Television and movies	TV	TV, sitcom, cinema
Music	Music	Tunes, song, cd
Money and financial issues	Money	Cash, taxes, income
Metaphysical issues	Metaph	God, heaven, coffin
Religion	Relig	God, church, rabbi
Death and dying	Death	Dead, burial, coffin
Physical states and functions	Physcal	Ache, breast, sleep
Body states, symptoms	Body	Ache, heart, cough
Sex and sexuality	Sexual	Lust, penis, fuck
Eating, drinking, dieting	Eating	Eat, swallow, taste
Sleeping, dreaming	Sleep	Asleep, bed, dreams
Grooming	Groom	Wash, bath, clean
Appendix: Experimental Dimensions		
Swear words	Swear	Damn, fuck, piss
Nonfluencies	Nonfl	Uh, rr*
Fillers	Fillers	Youknow, Imean

C.2 POS TAGGING CATEGORIES[2]

Tag	Description
CC	Coordinating conjunction
CD	Cardinal number
DT	Determiner
EX	Existential *there*
FW	Foreign word
IN	Preposition or subordinating conjunction
JJ	Adjective
JJR	Adjective, comparative
JJS	Adjective, superlative
LS	List item marker
MD	Modal
NN	Noun, singular or mass
NNS	Noun, plural
NNP	Proper noun, singular
NNPS	Proper noun, plural
PDT	Predeterminer
POS	Possessive ending
PRP	Personal pronoun
PRP$	Possessive pronoun
RB	Adverb
RBR	Adverb, comparative

(Continued)

Tag	Description
RBS	Adverb, superlative
RP	Particle
SYM	Symbol
TO	*to*
UH	Interjection
VB	Verb, base form
VBD	Verb, past tense
VBG	Verb, gerund or present participle
VBN	Verb, past participle
VBP	Verb, non-3rd person singular present
VBZ	Verb, 3rd person singular present
WDT	Wh-determiner
WP	Wh-pronoun
WP$	Possessive wh-pronoun
WRB	Wh-adverb

NOTES

1. https://www.liwc.app/
2. https://www.ling.upenn.edu/courses/Fall_2003/ling001/penn_treebank_pos.html

References

Aggarwal, C. C. (2007). *Data Streams: Models and Algorithms*. Springer, New York.

Albustin, A.; Bacheitner, S.; Djerdjizi, A.; Hollerit, B. (2010). Pre-attentive processing. In: Bruce Goldstein, E. (ed), *Encyclopedia of Perception*. Sage Publications, Thousand Oaks, CA, pp. 797–799.

Alharbi, M.; Laramee, R. S. (2019). SoS TextVis: An extended survey of surveys on text visualization. *Computers*, 8(1), 17. https://doi.org/10.3390/computers8010017.

Anscombe, F. J. (1973). Graphs in statistical analysis. *American Statistician*, 27(1), 17–21. https://doi.org/10.2307/2682899.JSTOR 2682899.

Asimov, I. (1950). *Runaround. I, Robot (The Isaac Asimov Collection Edition)*. Doubleday, New York City, p. 40. ISBN 978-0-385-42304-5.

Barabási, A.-L.; Pósfai, M. (2016). *Network Science*. Cambridge University Press, Cambridge.

Brown, J. D. (2001). Point-biserial correlation coefficients. *Shiken: JLT Testing & Evolution SIG Newsletter*, 5(3), 13–17. Available at: https://hosted.jalt.org/test/PDF/Brown12.pdf.

Cairo, A. (2016). Download the Datasaurus: Never trust summary statistics alone; always visualize your data. *The Functional Art*. Retrieved January 5, 2024, from https://thefunctionalart.blogspot.com/2016/08/download-datasaurus-never-trust-summary.html.

Cao, L. (2017). Data science: A comprehensive overview. *ACM Computing Surveys*, 50, 3, Article 43, 42 pages. https://doi.org/10.1145/3076253.

Chatfield, C. (1995). *The Analysis of Time Series: An Introduction*, 5th Edition. Chapman & Hall/CRC, Boca Raton, FL.

Chen, C.-H.; Härdle, W.; Unwin, A. (2008). *Handbook of Data Visualization*. Springer, Berlin.

Chen, H. M. (2017). Chapter 2. Information visualization principles, techniques, and software. *Library Technology Reports*, 53(2), 8–16.

Chong, D.; Shi, H. (2015). Big data analytics: A literature review. *Journal of Management Analytics*, 2(3), 175–201. https://doi.org/10.1080/23270012.2015.1082449.

Chowdhary, K. R. (2020). Natural language processing. In: Chowdhary, K.R. (ed), *Fundamentals of Artificial Intelligence*. Springer, New Delhi. https://doi.org/10.1007/978-81-322-3972-7_19.

Cowpertwait, P. S. P.; Metcalfe, A. V. (2009). *Introductory Time Series with R*. Springer, New York.

Daelemans, W. (2011). POS tagging. In: Sammut, C., Webb, G.I. (eds), *Encyclopedia of Machine Learning*. Springer, Boston, MA. https://doi.org/10.1007/978-0-387-30164-8_643.

Dasgupta, S. (1999). Learning polytrees. In *Proceedings of 15th Conference on Uncertainty in Artificial Intelligence (UAI 1999)*, Stockholm, Sweden, pp. 134–141.

de Castro, L. N.; Ferrari, D. G. (2016), *Introduction to Data Mining: Basic Concepts, Algorithms, and Applications*, In Portuguese, Saraiva.

Deng, J.; Dong, W.; Socher, R. et al. (2009). ImageNet: A large-scale hierarchical image database. In *2009 IEEE Conference on Computer Vision and Pattern Recognition*, Miami, FL, pp. 248–255. https://doi.org/10.1109/CVPR.2009.5206848.

Deo, N. (1974). *Graph Theory with Applications to Engineering and Computer Science*. Dover Books on Mathematics, New York.

Duarte, N. (2019). *Data Story: Explain Data and Inspire Action through Story*. Idea Press Publishing, Oakton, VA.

Dykes, B. (2020). *Effective Data Storytelling: How to Drive Change with Data, Narrative, and Visuals*. Wiley, Hoboken, NJ.

Ebert, D. S. (2005). Extending visualization to perceptualization: The importance of perception in effective communication of information. In: Johnson, C.R., Hansen, C.D. (eds), *The Visualization Handbook*. Elsevier, Burlington, MA, pp. 771–780.

Elgendy, N.; Elragal, A. (2014). Big data analytics: A literature review paper. In: Perner, P. (ed), *Advances in Data Mining. Applications and Theoretical Aspects. ICDM 2014. Lecture Notes in Computer Science*, vol. 8557. Springer, Cham. https://doi.org/10.1007/978-3-319-08976-8_16.

Erl, T.; Khattak, W. (2016). *Big Data Fundamentals: Concepts, Drivers & Techniques*. Pearson, Sydney. Part of: The Pearson Service Technology Series from Thomas Erl.

Esling, P.; Agon, C. (2012). Time-series data mining. *ACM Computing Surveys*, 45(1), Article 12, 34 pages. https://doi.org/10.1145/2379776.2379788.

Few, S. (2006). *Dashboard Design: The Effective Visual Communication of Data*. O'Reilly, Beijing.

Few, S. (2012). *Show Me the Numbers: Designing Tables and Graphs to Enlighten*, 2nd Edition. Analytics Press, El Dorado Hills, CA.

Fiori, A. M.; Zenga, M. (2009). Karl Pearson and the origin of kurtosis. *International Statistical Review/Revue Internationale de Statistique*, 77(1), 40–50. Available at: https://www.jstor.org/stable/27919689.

Fisher, R. A. (1936). The use of multiple measurements in taxonomic problems. *Annual Eugenics*, 7(Part II), 179–188. Dataset available at: https://archive.ics.uci.edu/ml/datasets/iris.

Glorot, X.; Bordes, A.; Bengio, Y. (2011). Deep sparse rectifier neural networks. In *Proceedings of the Fourteenth International Conference on Artificial Intelligence and Statistics, Fort Lauderdale, FL, in Proceedings of Machine Learning Research*, 15, 315–323. Available at: https://proceedings.mlr.press/v15/glorot11a.html.

Goodfellow, I.; Pouget-Abadie, J.; Mirza, M. et al. (2014). Generative adversarial nets. In: Advances in Neural Information Processing Systems 27 (NIPS 2014: Proceedings of the 28th International Conference on Neural Information Processing Systems) Edited by: Z. Ghahramani and M. Welling and C. Cortes and N. Lawrence and K.Q. Weinberger, MIT Press, Montreal, Canada, pp. 2672-2680.

Hagberg, A. A.; Schult, D. A.; Swart, P. J. (2008). Exploring network structure, dynamics, and function using NetworkX. In: *Proceedings of the 7th Python in Science Conference (SciPy2008)*, Pasadena, CA, pp. 11–15.

Hamilton, J. D. (1994). *Time Series Analysis*. Princeton University Press, Princeton, NJ.

Han, J.; Kamber, M.; Pei, J. (2011). *Data Mining: Concepts and Techniques*, 3rd Edition. Morgan Kaufmann Publishers Inc., San Francisco, CA.

Healey, C. G.; Booth, K. S.; Enns, J. T. (1995). High-speed visual estimation using preattentive processing. *ACM Transactions on Computer-Human Interaction*, 3(2), 107–135.

Hebb, D. O. (1949). *The Organization of Behavior: A Neuropsychological Theory*. Wiley, New York.

Hinton, G.; Simon, O.; Teh, Y.-W. (2006). A fast learning algorithm for deep belief nets. *Neural Computation*, 18, 1527–1554. https://doi.org/10.1162/neco.2006.18.7.1527.

Hirschberg, J.; Manning, C. D. (2015). Advances in natural language processing. *Science*, 349, 261–266. https://doi.org/10.1126/science.aaa8685.

Hochreiter, S.; Schmidhuber, J. (1997). Long short-term memory. *Neural Computing*, 9(8), 1735–1780. https://doi.org/10.1162/neco.1997.9.8.1735.

Holtz, Y.; Healy, C. (2018). From data to viz. Available at: https://www.data-to-viz.com.

Johnson, B.; Shneiderman, B. (1991). Tree-maps: A space-filling approach to the visualization of hierarchical information structures. In *Proceedings of the 2nd Conference on Visualization '91 (VIS '91)*, San Diego, CA. IEEE Computer Society Press, Washington, DC, pp. 284–291.

Kelleher, J. D.; Tierney, B. (2018). *Data Science*, Illustrated Edition. The MIT Press, Cambridge, Massachusetts.

Kerzner, H. (2025). *Project Management: A Systems Approach to Planning, Scheduling, and Controlling*, 14th Edition. Wiley, Hoboken, NJ.

Knaflic, C. N. (2015). *Storytelling with Data: A Data Visualization Guide for Business Professionals*. Wiley, Hoboken, NJ.

Kolaczyk, E. D. (2009). *Statistical Analysis of Network Data*. Springer, Cham.

Kolaczyk, E. D.; Csárdi, G. (2014). *Statistical Analysis of Network Data with R*. Springer, Cham.

Komorowski, M.; Marshall, D. C.; Salciccioli, J. D.; Crutain, Y. (2016). Exploratory data analysis. In: *Secondary Analysis of Electronic Health Records*. Springer, Cham, pp. 185–203. https://doi.org/10.1007/978-3-319-43742-2_15.

Kucher, K.; Kerren, A. (2015), Text visualization techniques: Taxonomy, visual survey, and community insights. In *IEEE Pacific Visualization Symposium 2015*, IEEE, Hangzhou, China, pp. 117–121.

Lane, D. M.; Scott, D.; Hebl, M. et al. (2003). *Introduction to Statistics*. Rice University, Open Textbook Library. Available at: https://open.umn.edu/opentextbooks/textbooks/459.

Lee, B. W.; Lee, J. H.-J. (2023). Traditional readability formulas compared for English. https://doi.org/10.48550/arXiv.2301.02975.

Liu, S.; Wang, X.; Collins, C. et al. (2019). Bridging text visualization and mining: A task-driven survey. *IEEE Transaction on Visualization and Computer Graphics*, 25(7), 2482–2504.

Lund, N. W. (2010). Document, text and medium: Concepts, theories and disciplines. *Journal of Documentation*, 66(5), 734–749. https://doi.org/10.1108/00220411011066817.

Lutz, M. (2013). *Learning Python: Powerful Object-Oriented Programming*, 5th Edition. O'Reilly Media, Sebastopol, CA.

Matejka, J.; Fitzmaurice, G. (2017). Same stats, different graphs: Generating datasets with varied appearance and identical statistics through simulated annealing. In *ACM SIGCHI Conference on Human Factors in Computing Systems*, 105. https://doi.org/10.1145/3025453.3025912. Available at: https://www.autodesk.com/research/publications/same-stats-different-graphs.

McCarthy, J. (1960). Recursive functions of symbolic expressions and their computation by machine. *Communications of the ACM*, 3(4), 184–195.

McClelland, J. L.; Rumelhart, D.; the PDP Research Group. (1987). *Parallel Distributed Processing: Explorations in the Microstructure of Cognition. Foundations*, vol. 1. *Psychological and Biological Models*, vol. 2. MIT Press, Cambridge, MA.

McClure, G. M. (1987). Readability formulas: Useful or useless? *IEEE Transactions on Professional Communication*, PC-30, 12–15.

McCulloch, W. S.; Pitts, W. (1943). A logical calculus of the ideas immanent in nervous activity. *Bulletin of Mathematical Biophysics,* 5, 115–133. https://doi.org/10.1007/BF02478259.

Menczer, F.; Fortunato, S.; Davis, C. A. (2000). *A First Course in Network Science*. Cambridge University Press, Cambridge.

Mennan, Z. (2009). From simple to complex configuration: Sustainability of gestalt principles of visual perception within the complexity paradigm. *METU Journal of the Faculty of Architecture*, 26(2), 309–323. https://doi.org/10.4305/METU.JFA.2009.2.15.

Mikalef, P.; Pappas, I. O.; Krogstie, J. et al. (2018). Big data analytics capabilities: A systematic literature review and research agenda. *Information Systems and e-Business Management*, 16, 547–578. https://doi.org/10.1007/s10257-017-0362-y.

Minsky, M.; Papert, S. (1969). *Perceptrons: An Introduction to Computational Geometry*. MIT Press, Cambridge, MA.

Nadkarni, P. M.; Ohno-Machado, L.; Chapman, W. W. (2011). Natural language processing: An introduction. *Journal of the American Medical Informatics Association*, 18(5), 544–551. https://doi.org/10.1136/amiajnl-2011-000464.

Newman, M. E. J. (2003). The structure and function of complex networks. *SIAM Review*, 45, 167–256.

Nielsen, A. (2019). *Practical Time Series Analysis: Prediction with Statistics and Machine Learning*. O'Reilly, Sebastopol, CA.

OpenStax College.org. (2013). *Introductory Statistics*, Vol. 1. Textbookequity.org.

Peck, R.; Olsen, C.; Devore, J. (2008). *Introduction to Statistics and Data Analysis*, 3rd Edition. Thomson Brooks/Cole.

Pennebaker, J. W.; Francis, M. E.; Booth, R. J. (2001). *Linguistic Inquiry and Word Count: LIWC2001 – Operator's Manual*. LIWC.net, Austin, TX. Available at: https://www.liwc.app/.

Prematunga, R. K. (2012). Correlational analysis. *Australian Critical Care*, 25(3), 195–199. https://doi.org/10.1016/j.aucc.2012.02.003.

Provost, F.; Fawcett, T. (2013). *Data Science for Business: What You Need to Know about Data Mining and Data-Analytic Thinking*, 1st Edition. O'Reilly Media, Inc., Sebastopol, CA.

Quinlan, R. (1993). Combining instance-based and model-based learning. In *Proceedings on the Tenth International Conference of Machine Learning*, San Francisco, CA, pp. 236–243. Dataset available at: https://archive.ics.uci.edu/ml/datasets/auto+mpg.

Rayward-Smith, V. J. (2007). Statistics to measure correlation for data mining applications. *Computational Statistics & Data Analysis*, 51(8), 3968–3982. https://doi.org/10.1016/j.csda.2006.05.025.

Salton, G.; Wong, A.; Yang, C. S. (1975). A vector space model for automatic indexing. *Communications of the ACM*, 18(11), 613–620.

Samuel, A. L. (1959). Some studies in machine learning using the game of checkers. *IBM Journal of Research and Development*, 44, 206–226. CiteSeerX 10.1.1.368.2254. https://doi.org/10.1147/rd.441.0206.

Schwabish, J. (2021). *Better Data Visualizations: A Guide for Scholars, Researchers, and Wonks*. Columbia University Press, New York.

Shannon, C. E. (1959). Programming a computer playing chess. In *Philosophical Magazine*, Ser.7, 41.

Silge, J.; Robinson, D. (2017). *Text Mining with R: A Tidy Approach*. O'Reilly, Sebastopol, CA.

Silva, J. A.; Faria, E. R.; Barros, R. C. et al. (2013). Data stream clustering: A survey. *ACM Computing Surveys*, 46(1), Article 13, 31 pages. https://doi.org/10.1145/2522968.2522981.

Sommerville, I. (2015). *Software Engineering*, 10th Edition. Pearson.

Song, I.-Y.; Zhu, Y. (2016). Big data and data science: What should we teach? *Expert Systems: The Journal of Knowledge Engineering*, 33(4), 364–373. https://doi.org/10.1111/exsy.12130.

Sosulski, K. (2019). *Data Visualization Made Simple: Insights into Becoming Visual*. Routledge, New York.

Tausczik, Y. R.; Pennebaker, J. W. (2010). The psychological meaning of words: Liwc and computerized text analysis methods. *Journal of Language and Social Psychology*, 29, 24–54.

Thrun, S.; Montemerlo, M.; Dahlkamp, H. et al. (2007). Stanley: The robot that won the DARPA grand challenge. In: Buehler, M., Iagnemma, K., Singh, S. (eds), *The 2005 DARPA Grand Challenge*. Springer *Tracts in Advanced Robotics*, vol. 36. Springer, Berlin, p. 1. https://doi.org/10.1007/978-3-540-73429-1_1.

Toutanova, K.; Manning, C. D. (2000). Enriching the knowledge sources used in a maximum entropy part-of-speech tagger. In *Proceedings of the 2000 Joint SIGDAT Conference on Empirical Methods in Natural Language Processing and Very Large Corpora: Held in Conjunction with the 38th Annual Meeting of the Association for Computational Linguistics* – Vol. 13, pp. 63–70. Association for Computational Linguistics, Hong Kong, Stroudsburg, PA.

Treisman, A. (1985). Preattentive processing in vision. *Computer Vision, Graphics, and Image Processing*, 31(2). 156–177.

Triola, M. (2017). *Elementary Statistics*, 13th Edition. Pearson.

Trudeau, R. J. (1993). *Introduction to Graph Theory*. Dover Publications, New York.

Tsai, C. W.; Lai, C. F.; Chao, H. C. et al. (2015). *Big data analytics:* A survey. *Journal of Big Data*, 2, Article 21. https://doi.org/10.1186/s40537-015-0030-3.

Tufte, E. R. (2001). *The Visual Display of Quantitative Information*, 2nd Edition. Graphics Press, Cheshire, CT.

Turing, A. M. (1936). On computable numbers, with an application to the entscheidungsproblem. *Proceedings of the London Mathematical Society Series 2*, 24, 230–265.

Turing, A. M. (1950). Computing machinery and intelligence. *Mind*, 59(236), 433–460.

Wagemans, J.; Elder, J. H.; Kubovy, M. et al. (2012). A century of Gestalt psychology in visual perception: I. Perceptual grouping and figure–ground organization. *Psychological Bulletin*, 138(6), 1172–1217. https://doi.org/10.1037/a0029333.

Ward, M.; Grinstein, G.; Keim, D. (2010). *Interactive Data Visualization*. CRC Press, New York.

Wares, S.; Isaacs, J.; Elyan, E. (2019). Data stream mining: Methods and challenges for handling concept drift. *SN Applied Science*, 1, 1412. https://doi.org/10.1007/s42452-019-1433-0.

Watkins, J. C. (2016). *An Introduction to the Science of Statistics: From Theory to Implementation*, Preliminary Edition. Available at: https://www.academia.edu/31963995/An_Introduction_to_the_Science_of_Statistics_From_Theory_to_Implementation.

Watts, D. J.; Strogatz, S. H. (1998). Collective dynamics of 'small-world' networks. *Nature*, 393(6684), 440–442.

Wiener, N. (1950). *The Human Use of Human Beings: Cybernetics and Society*. Houghton Mifflin, Boston, MA.

Wilke, C. O. (2019). *Fundamentals of Data Visualization: A Primer on Making Informative and Compelling Figures*. O'Reilly, Sebastopol, CA.

Wilkinson, L. (2005). *The Grammar of Graphics*, 2nd Edition. Springer, New York.

Wilson, R. J. (1996). *Introduction to Graph Theory*, 4th Edition. Prentice Hall, London.

Witten, I. H.; Frank, E.; Hall, M. A.; Pal, C. J. (2016). *Data Mining: Practical Machine Learning Tools and Techniques, Morgan Kaufmann Series in Data Management Systems*, 4th Edition. Morgan Kaufmann, Burlington.

Wong, D. M. (2010). *The Wall Street Journal Guide to Information Graphics: The Dos and Don'ts of Presenting Data, Facts, and Figures*. W. W. Norton & Company, New York.

Zachary, W. W. (1977). An information flow model for conflict and fission in small groups. *Journal of Anthropological Research*, 33(4), 452–473. https://doi.org/10.1086/jar.33.4.3629752.

Zwillinger, D.; Kokoska, S. (2000). *CRC Standard Probability and Statistics Tables and Formulae*. Chapman & Hall, New York.

Index

Note: **Bold** page numbers refer to tables and *italic* page numbers refer to figures.